IRAQ'S ROAD
TO WAR

IRAQ'S ROAD TO WAR

Edited by
Amatzia Baram and Barry Rubin

St. Martin's Press
New York

In cooperation with the Gustav Heinemann
Center for Middle East Studies
University of Haifa

IRAQ'S ROAD TO WAR
Copyright © Amatzia Baram and Barry Rubin 1993.
All rights reserved. Printed in the United States of America. No part of this book
may be used or reproduced in any manner whatsoever without written permission
except in the case of brief quotations embodied in critical articles or reviews. For
information, address St. Martin's Press, 175 Fifth Avenue, New York, N.Y. 10010.

ISBN 0-312-16446-7 (paperback)

Library of Congress Cataloging-in-Publication Data

Iraq's road to war / edited by Amatzia Baram and Barry Rubin.
    p. cm.
Includes index.
ISBN 0-312-10171-6—ISBN 0-312-16446-7 (pbk.)
    1. Iraq—Politics and government—1979- 2. Iraq—Foreign
relations—1979- 3. Persian Gulf War, 1991—Causes. I. Baram,
Amatzia, 1938- . II. Rubin, Barry M.
DS79.7.I73 1993
327.567—dc20   93-24709
                                                  CIP

Design by ACME Art Inc.

First published in hardcover in the United States of America in 1993
First paperback edition: October 1996
· 10 9 8 7 6 5 4 3 2 1

To Professor Avner Yaniv

CONTENTS

Introduction

Amatzia Baram and Barry Rubin

Iraq, once considered a peripheral, second-rank power, moved to the center of Middle East—and often world—affairs since the late 1970s. Iraq's lesser importance in earlier times was largely due to the long struggle needed to mobilize its great resources and divided society. When Iraq did burst onto the scene as a major force, a combination of great pressures at home and soaring ambitions on the part of the Ba'th regime, together with mutual miscomprehension among the Iraqi leaders, Arab and Muslim neighbors, and Western countries would cost all of them dearly.

This book tries to provide a comprehensive picture of Iraq's politics, economics, and foreign relations in the critical years leading to the 1990-1991 Kuwait crisis. This conflict and the earlier 1980 to 1988 Iran-Iraq war—among the most important events in the post-1945 world—were both mainly initiated by Baghdad. The analytical articles and case studies contained in this book cover Iraq's domestic developments, political decision-making, and interactions with other countries during this turbulent period.

The Iraqi nation-state created by victorious Britain after World War I suffered from a combination of domestic and foreign impediments making it an unstable political community while giving it a perennial urge to change the regional status quo. Iraq's domestic conflicts arose largely from divisions in a population consisting of around 55% Shi'a Arabs, 20% Sunni Arabs, and 18 to 20% Kurds. The predominantly Sunni Arab ruling elite that monopolized political power suspected the Kurds wanted to secede and the Shi'a might give their allegiance to neighboring Shi'a Iran, either in order to undermine the Sunni-controlled state or to take over. The facts that the Shi'a and the Kurds have been unable to coordinate their struggle and that they were, internally, split along tribal lines enabled the far better organized Sunni Arabs to keep them underfoot. Due to their limited numbers and reluctance to open the political system, the Sunni Arab ruling elites have been unable to use fully the potential of the state and integrate the two other communities.

Thus, by the early 1990s Iraqi nationalism was still in its infancy. Most Kurds wanted to secede, and to the Shi'a opposition movements (and, apparently, to the majority of the Shi'a population) the Iraqi nation-state was acceptable only on the condition that they be given equal opportunity.

Aside from this perceived internal challenge, Iraq had geostrategic predicaments creating both insecurity and ambitions in its regional relations. In the first place, it had long, partly disputed borders with two far more powerful nations, Turkey and Iran. To achieve a strategic balance with these two strong neighbors and to dilute the Shi'a/Kurdish majority in a Sunni Arab ocean, Iraqi politicians sought to create an Arab union of the Fertile Crescent—including Syria, Lebanon, Jordan, and Palestine—that would assure its own regional hegemony.

Other considerations also pushed Iraq's leaders toward trying to unite the Fertile Crescent under their leadership, chiefly the need for access to the sea. Except for the long, exposed route from Basra through the Shatt al-Arab River to the Persian Gulf, Iraq had only a tiny harbor on the Gulf at Umm Qasr. In this context, Iraqi politicians and strategists since the 1930s expressed a desire to annex Kuwait, which they considered an integral part of Iraq torn away by British imperialism.

The quest for Iraqi regional hegemony stretching from the Mediterranean to Kuwait (or even beyond) also served a domestic political purpose. A volatile, often violent domestic scene served as an incentive for the regime's foreign ambitions. By promising their Shi'a majority the prospect of Arab leadership, the Sunni Arab elite hoped to convince this reluctant group to support it.

Iraq's involvement in the Arab-Israeli conflict—though it had no border with Palestine before 1948 and Israel thereafter—also stemmed from the same combination of an unstable political community and a drive to become the region's dominant power. Trying to legitimize its rule, the Sunni elite put a heavy stress on the Arab character of Iraqis arguing that this—rather than sect or religion—should be the basis for national identification. This notion, however, alienated the non-Arab Kurds. Once Iraqi nationalism was defined largely in terms of Arab identity, every important political development in the Arab world became a major domestic issue for Iraq.

The Palestine issue is a good example of this phenomenon. The first mass anti-Zionist demonstration anywhere in the Arab world occurred in Baghdad in February 1928. Iraq's ruling elite since the 1930s has considered the Palestine issue a sword that cuts both ways: It could drive home the notion of Iraq's seniority in the Arab family, and it could serve as a Sunni-Shi'a ideological common denominator. Finally, Palestine was an important component in the vision of an Iraqi-led Fertile Crescent.

In short, Iraq's foreign policy and relations—whether relating to the Arab-Israeli conflict, regional Arab politics, or the Kuwait issue—have always been closely intertwined with the consolidation of an Iraqi nation-state and the continued rule of the Sunni Arab elite.

To an already volatile domestic and regional situation, the Ba'th regime that has ruled Iraq since 1968 added several attributes that brought the Iraqi cauldron to a boiling point. Its leaders had a poor educational background and low understanding of countries outside Iraq. Ultimate power was concentrated in the hands of one man, Saddam Husayn, who had a constant need to portray himself as a hero of historic proportions. The Ba'th always put the interests of leader and regime over those of nation and country. Finally, the Ba'th regime could not tolerate any independent societal cell, be it a Shi'a mosque or another political party. The efforts it made to penetrate or destroy these bodies created acute resentment. The result of these factors has been an atmosphere of violence and dread at home that easily flowed over Iraq's borders in foreign adventures that the regime hoped would limit domestic unrest.

Between the Ba'th party's seizure of power in 1968 and Iraq's 1980 invasion of Iran, Saddam Husayn (since 1970 the regime's strong man) was largely preoccupied with the domestic front. First, he destroyed the Ba'th party's competitors and personal rivals. Second, he subordinated all the nation's institutions, including the army and economy, to the regime, using them to repress enemies and to distribute benefits to loyalists. Iraq's growing petroleum income was skillfully handled to win popular support and strengthen the state.

Third, he embarked on a serious program of what he considered to be nation-building at home. Shi'a Muslims and Kurds supporting the regime were rewarded and incorporated into some positions of power. Saddam promoted an ideology of Iraqi-centered imperial Pan-Arab nationalism to tie them together, replacing the radical egalitarian Pan-Arabism that the Ba'th had earlier espoused and to which it continued to give lip service. Communal dissent was ruthlessly suppressed. As long as the balance between repression and compensation could be maintained, the regime's rule was ensured.

Paralleling this approach, Iraq's foreign policy strategy shifted from ideological to pragmatic radicalism. Baghdad used extremist rhetoric to cover over its relative disinterest in foreign adventures during the 1970s, even though it never departed from its long-term revolutionary vision. Fearing severe military and political repercussions, the regime did not want to become too entangled in the Arab-Israeli conflict or to be seen as promoting revolution in the conservative Arab states. Diplomatic decisions were taken on the basis of Iraq's state and regime interests. Baghdad allied with the Soviet Union while being careful to block any chance that Moscow might gain internal influence.

By 1980, the Gulf, one of the world's wealthiest, most strategically vital regions, became also an extremely volatile one. At that point, four factors coincided: The Ba'th regime felt threatened domestically by Khomeini's [Shi'a] Islamic Revolution; Iraq was ready to play a wide regional role; it had an ambitious, aggressive leader at the head of an ambitious, aggressive, and tight-knit regime; and there appeared to be a great opportunity for the long-delayed foray to fulfill the country's and Saddam's goals. There were, of course, a variety of factors including a long historic rivalry and border disputes. But the key issues can be defined as a coming together of defensive and offensive motives.

The international context seemed promising for the war Iraq would launch in September 1980. Instead of Gulf Arab monarchies looking to the Shah's Iran to defend them from radical Iraq, they now looked at a more pragmatic, and seemingly more mellow Arab Iraq to protect them from the Iran of the ayatollahs. Instead of a strong U.S.-Iran alliance, the two former partners were deeply divided. Iran had lost its superpower protector without, however, securing the protection of the other superpower. Thus, Iraq launched a war that was, to an extent, an act of preemptive defense, but more so: one of aggressive imperialism.

On the defensive side, Iraq perceived Iran to be a strong ideological and subversive threat. Iraq feared that a militant Iran would export its influence into the Iraqi Shi'a community under the guise of an Islamic revolution. Indeed, the Tehran regime openly proclaimed its goal of spreading such a revolution in the Gulf and the Middle East. Pro-Iran Shi'a fundamentalists in Iraq were increasingly active and violent.

The government of the ayatollahs thus posed a clear and present danger to Baghdad. Before September 1980, however, the regime managed to break the back of the Shi'a opposition by deporting 40,000 people, the mass arrests of some 10,000 suspects, and the execution of a few hundred revolutionaries, including the most important leader, Ayatollah Muhammad Baqir al-Sadr. As a result, public demonstrations died out, and the opposition shifted to small-scale guerrilla operations that could not endanger the regime.

On the offensive side, Iran's revolution seemed an opportunity for Iraq to put forward its own claims to leadership in the Gulf and among the Arabs. Iraq saw an Iran shaken by revolution and international isolation as an easy victim whose defeat would make Baghdad the dominant power in the Gulf and leader of the Arab world. Iran appeared to be weak in conventional military terms, and torn by internal dissent. Gulf Arab rulers, who had previously looked to Iran's Shah to defend them from radical Iraq, now saw Baghdad as their shield against an alien Persian, Shi'a, and fundamentalist onslaught. The United States, Iran's former superpower ally, was now in heated conflict with the Khomeini regime over the hostages, and would shed no tears over an Iraqi invasion.

During the Iran-Iraq war, Iraq's Shi'a masses supported the regime because of Saddam's combination of *al-tarhib wal-targhib* (terrorizing and enticement) as well as their own reluctance, being Arabs and religiously more moderate, to come under Iranian extreme fundamentalist rule.

When the battle ended eight years later, Iraq had achieved a pyrrhic victory in the truest sense. Rather than enhance Iraq's position, the fighting wasted much of the resources accumulated over the previous decade. Having emerged as the putative victor in 1988, Saddam Husayn expected benefits but reaped only problems. He appeared to have triumphed over a military prostrate Iran, but what had he won? The costs were high yet no significant economic or strategic assets had been gained. Iran regained almost all its territory and continued to block the Shatt al-Arab. Iraq was thus landlocked, save the tiny port of Umm Qasr. Iran, too, lost temporarily the large ports of Khorramshahr and Abadan, but unlike Iraq it had other ports to rely upon. Due to the closure of its Basra harbor, the war losses, and a severe cash flow problem, Baghdad faced a serious economic crisis. With the Iranian danger no longer uniting the country, the regime feared social unrest. At the same time, believing that for the second time in just over a decade it had a historical opportunity to become a regional superpower, Iraq struck again.

The book's first section focuses on Iraq's domestic politics and decision-making. In Chapter 1 Amatzia Baram analyzes the full range of causes that led to Iraq's invasion of Kuwait and the stages of the regime's decision-making. In Chapter 2 Mark A. Heller looks at the history of Iraq's military, demonstrating its importance in internal politics and repression. While Saddam successfully demilitarized domestic politics, Heller suggests he also undercut the soldiers' ability to fight wars because he promoted officers on the basis of loyalty and imposed excessive centralization.

In Chapter 3 Ofra Bengio writes about the most consistent internal threat to a largely Sunni-dominated Ba'thist regime: the Shi'a Arab majority and Kurdish minority. Periodic Shi'a fundamentalist and Kurdish nationalist revolts have bedeviled the Baghdad government in the past. Iraq's defeat in the Kuwait war gave rise to major uprisings in the immediate aftermath of the international fighting.

On the economic level, the instability of Baghdad's petroleum income—compared to rising spending at home—helped push Iraq into aggression. Efforts to beg, borrow, and steal more resources did not meet the regime's needs and the population's demands. But, as Patrick Clawson shows in Chapter 4, the problems of Iraq's economy had more to do with the Baghdad regime's state-controlled economy and managerial incompetence than with foreign factors.

Despite the importance of Iraq and Kuwait for the world oil market, Robert J. Lieber shows in Chapter 5, the potential shock arising from the Kuwait crisis was handled successfully by that system. There was a serious vulnerability since two-thirds of the world's petroleum is located in the Gulf area. The potential petroleum shortage was avoided in large part due to Saudi Arabia's willingness to expand production.

The second section of the book considers Iraq's relations with foreign states and groups. In the Arab world, this section incorporates Chapter 6 by Joseph Kostiner on Kuwait; Chapter 7 by Jacob Goldberg on Saudi Arabia; Chapter 8 by Joseph Nevo on Jordan; Chapter 9 by Barry Rubin on the Palestine Liberation Organization; Chapter 10 by Ilan Pappe on Israeli Arabs; Chapter 11 by Michael Apel on Syria; and Chapter 12 on Egypt by Yoram Meital. Iraq's relations with the non-Arab powers of the region are covered in Chapter 13 by David Kushner on Turkey; Chapter 14 by Shaul Bakhash on Iran; and Chapter 15 by Avner Yaniv on Israel.

Finally, we survey Iraq's links with the main outside great powers: In Chapter 16 Barry Rubin discusses the United States and in Chapter 17 Helmut Hubel deals with Western Europe. In both cases, their support for Iraq during the Iran-Iraq war and appeasement thereafter encouraged Iraqi ambitions.

P. J. Vatikiotis, in Chapter 18, points to how the Kuwait crisis showed the weakness of Arab institutions, unity, and state legitimacy. On a global level, it began defining an era after the end of the Cold War and Communism, in which the United States is the sole superpower and Europe moves toward integration. On a conceptual level, it raised questions about modernization, links between dictatorship and aggression, and the content and potential for any Middle East or world "new order."

The chapters included in this book are revised and updated from papers presented at a May 1991 conference entitled "Iraq Under the Ba'th and the Gulf Crisis," sponsored by the University of Haifa's Jewish-Arab Center and Gustave Heinemann Center for Middle East Studies.

We wish to thank these institutions and their directors, Professors Stanley Waterman and Joseph Ginat. Ms. Sarah Tamir deserves special thanks for organizing the sessions and preparing the material for this book. Bonnie Belkin and Riuka Feder gave indispensable administrative support. We also wish to thank the participants, including particularly Gabriel Ben-Dor, Asher Arian, Shlomo Gazit, David Menashri, Yehoshua Porath, Yair Hirschfeld, and Gad Gilbar. Lastly, we wish to thank Navit Ilani for preparing the index.

We dedicate this book to Professor Avner Yaniv, a beloved friend and esteemed colleague for many years. He led the way in initiating this project. His untimely death is a great personal loss for us and a serious intellectual misfortune for the field of Middle East studies. Professor Yaniv's kindness, charm, creativity, and wisdom will be greatly missed and impossible to replace.

PART I

IRAQ'S POLITICS, ECONOMICS, AND SOCIETY

Why Iraq Invaded Kuwait
and Lost the Gulf War

1

The Iraqi Invasion of Kuwait: Decision-making in Baghdad

Amatzia Baram

From the first years of its existence as a nation-state in the wake of World War I, Iraq wanted to gain part or all of Kuwait. But only with Saddam Husayn's decision to invade his neighbor in 1990 did Baghdad make an all-out effort to implement that goal. Saddam's course toward this decision involved Iraq's history and interests as well as his own political environment, ambitions, and thinking.

Iraq's claim for Kuwait has been based chiefly on the argument that it had been a district governed from Basra during the Ottoman Empire. In fact, since 1758, long before the British created the Iraqi state from ex-Ottoman provinces, Kuwait was already an autonomous region under the Sabah family's rule. But Iraq's urge to annex Kuwait was also connected with a need to strengthen its ruling regimes' legitimacy and stability. Iraq's Sunni Arab ruling minority (some 20% of the population) had to keep a Shi'a majority (around 55% of the population) and a Kurdish minority (18 to 20% of the population) under control. A promise to expand Iraq's borders and power was designed to build the masses' enthusiasm and a sense of Iraqi patriotism.[1]

Equally, despite accepting the border with Kuwait in 1923 under British pressure and again in 1932 as a precondition for joining the League of Nations,

Baghdad never acquiesced to this situation. Iraq especially objected because the border, following a 1913 Anglo-Ottoman agreement, left it a very short coastline on the Gulf while giving Kuwait two islands, Warba and Bubyan, that controlled the entrance to Umm Qasr, Iraq's only Gulf port.

As early as 1933, official Iraqi government publications began demanding Kuwait's annexation. King Ghazy (1933-1939) broadcast appeals to Kuwaitis to overthrow their rulers and join Iraq. But as long as Britain was both states' patron, Iraq could not go beyond rhetoric.

When Kuwait became independent and the British protectorate ended in 1961, Iraq's anti-British dictator, 'Abd al-Karim Qasim, prepared an invasion that was averted only due to a rapid deployment of British forces.[2] These were soon replaced by Arab League troops. In 1963 Iraq's Ba'thist government accepted the border and recognized Kuwait's sovereignty. But the precise demarcation of the boundary was disputed, and, in 1973 and 1974, Iraqi troops briefly crossed into Kuwait before retreating under U.S.-Iran pressure.

Kuwait consistently refused to cede the two islands. It began asserting sovereignty over them in the early 1970s by establishing border posts and agricultural settlements there; in the late 1980s it planned the town of Sabiya across from Bubyan and connected it by bridge to the barren island. Kuwait's media reiterated more often than before the islands' status as integral parts of Kuwait.[3]

Aside from being deterred by Western protection for Kuwait, Iraq knew that its Soviet patron would not support a confrontation—and possible superpower confrontation—on the issue.[4] In the second half of the 1970s Iraq started to improve its relations with the Gulf Arab states, including Kuwait. Iran's 1978-1979 Islamic Revolution and the Iran-Iraq war tightened cooperation among these Arab regimes. During the war Kuwait gave Iraq at least $10 billion in aid and allowed it to receive supplies through Kuwaiti ports. But once the war ended, most of the aid was stopped, and Saddam's attitude toward his Kuwaiti benefactors began to change sharply.

THE IRAQI PREDICAMENT: INCENTIVES FOR WAR

Paradoxically, the post-Iraq-Iran war period was more dangerous for the regime than the war itself. The eight-year-long war sapped the country's resources and made Iraq dependent on financial and strategic support from Kuwait, Saudi Arabia, and other Arab states. Iraqi sources estimated the economic loss from lower oil revenue and higher arms purchases (excluding war-related destruction) at $208 billion. At least 200,000 died, about 400,000 were wounded, and 70,000 were taken prisoner.[5] This was a heavy price for a nation of 17 million people.

Iraqi authorities described the ceasefire as a great victory. Expectations for economic reconstruction, better living standards, and the quick return of prisoners were, however, quickly dispelled as the situation seemed to worsen rather than improve. Iraq's war debt to the Gulf Arab countries was nearly $40 billion which, although creditors did not expect repayment, damaged Iraq's credit rating as long as it was on the books. More pressing was another $40 billion in debts to the non-Arab world, both East and West.[6] Servicing this debt cost nearly $8 billion a year, and—given Iraqi inflexibility—Western banks were averse to make new loans.[7]

Reluctant to use hidden currency reserves, Iraq had to depend on its declining oil income.[8] The severe cash flow problem brought a deep recession that the regime tried to hide through expensive, ostentatious, and economically unproductive reconstruction projects in Basra, Faw, and Mosul.[9] It also tried to distract Iraqis from economic hardship by permitting citizens to go abroad, relaxing some foreign currency regulations, and promising more democracy.[10] But few could afford to travel and no real political changes were made.

Economic stagnation also meant that few soldiers could be demobilized. From August 1988 to August 1990 only 250,000 to 350,000 were released, with over a million still in uniform.[11] The regime preferred to pay soldiers rather than leave them unemployed to create social unrest, especially since the majority of those due to be released were Shi'a whose discontent might trigger a communal revolt. Keeping such a huge standing army, however, required an explanation. Hence Saddam's alarmist speeches beginning in February 1990, blaming two old hate objects—Zionism and Anglo-American imperialism—for preparing to attack Iraq.[12]

Iraq also continued spending huge sums on its military industry.[13] Since 1972 Saddam has been bent on the development of nuclear weapons. Following the June 1981 Israeli raid on his Tammuz reactor, these efforts entered a new, hectic phase that involved also medium-range missiles. Foreign Minister Tariq 'Aziz declared that Iraq needed advanced missiles because it "is still threatened by Iran."[14] Most important, owning these and other nonconventional weapons was a big step toward becoming the Gulf's hegemonic power. These arms could be described as Iraq's contribution to the Arab military effort against Israel, thus turning Iraq into the Arabs' "protector," as its 1981 National Anthem boasts. (For more recent and explicit such promises see below.) By brandishing such weapons Iraq could try to induce the rich Gulf Arabs to offer it much-needed financial aid, indeed, even to impose on them oil quotas and prices that would suit Iraq's interests. This, in turn, promised to make Iraq the most powerful Arab country, economically as well as militarily, and thus to enable Saddam to achieve the Arab hegemony that evaded Gamal 'Abd al-Nasir.[15] But developing these arms put a crushing burden on the crumbling economy.

One of the first casualties of the cash shortage were food subsidies. By the war's end, Iraq's annual imports of foodstuffs cost $2 to 3 billion. Given the regime's reluctance to continue wartime subsidies, food prices rose rapidly. Inflation reached between 25 to 40% annually, but salaries hardly went up.[16] Since Iraq's rulers would not commit more resources to subsidies, living standards deteriorated and, as a safety valve, the press was allowed to publish complaints. For example, a columnist in the party daily complained a few months before the invasion of Kuwait that basic foodstuffs could not be found at government shops at less than twice the official prices, that even these shops were often empty, and that private-market profiteers charged four to five times the official price.[17] The situation created a crisis of expectations.

At the same time, the war's strategic gains seemed to be disappearing as well. The Shatt al-Arab, Iraq's main outlet to the Gulf, remained blocked and Iran refused to allow its reopening. This damaged Iraq's strategic and economic security while undermining Baghdad's claims of victory.

Having never served in the armed forces, Saddam always distrusted the army and its officers' corps. When his party seized power in 1968, Saddam was put in charge of purging the army of disloyal elements. After the Iraq-Iran war ended, he dismissed some of Iraq's most illustrious officers, such as Generals Mahir 'Abd al-Rashid and Hisham Fakhri. Worse still, in January 1989 he arrested and executed scores of army and air force officers for allegedly preparing a coup.[18] Unconfirmed rumors reported another wave of purges and executions in late 1989 and early 1990.

Another development causing the regime great concern were the democratic revolutions in Eastern Europe starting in late 1989: After all, Iraq's system was modeled on these totalitarian regimes.[19] Comments in the Western media equating Arab dictators with Romania's Ceaucescu and predicting Saddam's downfall further alarmed the regime, especially a February 1990 Voice of America (VOA) broadcast which suggested that Middle East dictators, including Saddam, might also be overthrown.[20]

On a strategic level, (some silver lining notwithstanding, see below) the decline of the Soviet Union—the radical Arabs' traditional supporter—was a disaster. To make matters worse, the new regimes in Eastern Europe and the Soviet Union improved relations with Israel, and Moscow allowed a steep rise in Jewish immigration to Israel. Most Arabs saw this as an historic turning point for the worse.[21] Not only had the Arabs lost their main international ally, but it had, in fact, defected to the other camp.

Another Iraqi setback was a failure to evict Syria's army from Lebanon, despite aid to anti-Damascus Christian forces. There are indications that this inspired Iraq to do to Kuwait what Syria had done—with Arab blessing and

U.S. acquiescence—to Lebanon. Ten days after invading Kuwait, Iraq urged the problem be dealt with on the same footing as the Lebanese issue.[22] In his January 9, 1991, meeting with Secretary of State James Baker in Geneva, Tariq 'Aziz demanded "an Arab solution" for the Kuwaiti problem similar to the Ta'if agreement that left Syria as hegemonic power in Lebanon.[23] These events all pushed Iraq toward adventurism.

The Territorial Dispute with Kuwait Rediscovered

Between the Iraq-Iran war's end in August 1988 and its invasion of Kuwait two years later, Iraq brought up a series of issues that together created the crisis. These were: the Iraqi-Kuwaiti border dispute; the Israeli-Palestinian issue; the U.S. presence in the Gulf area and the Soviet Union's decline in the Middle East; disputes over oil prices and production quotas; and Iraqi demands for debt forgiveness and financial aid from the Gulf Arabs. The fusing of these questions in Iraqi thinking and propaganda was a step-by-step process. And while there are indications that the Iraqi leadership had been toying with the idea of invading Kuwait at least since 1988, only gradually did Baghdad come to see such an invasion as the solution for all its problems.

In May 1988 Iraq asked Kuwait during the Algiers Arab Summit to let it lease or annex the two Kuwaiti islands astride the Gulf entrance to Umm Qasr.[24] As long as the Faw Peninsula was in Iran's hands, Umm Qasr could not be used anyway, but after Iraq recaptured it in April, the issue reemerged.

Kuwait did not respond to Iraq's overture, apparently fearing Iran's wrath and even more Iraqi demands. In the fall of 1988 an Iraqi brigade occupied Bubyan without publicity, only to leave after a quiet Kuwaiti protest.[25] Iraq's nearby Republican Guard Advanced Command Post, attached during the war to the Seventh Corps Command at Faw, was kept intact after the ceasefire, and Saddam occasionally visited it with great publicity. Another early indication of Iraq's attitude was its request in 1988 for satellite photographs, with military applications, of Kuwait and Saudi Arabia from the French company Spot Image.[26]

In February 1989 Iraq again tried to extricate territorial concessions from Kuwait during the visit of Kuwait's heir apparent and Prime Minister Shaykh Sa'd al-'Abd Allah al-Sabah. Since Iraq's victory over Iran was a service to the whole Arab nation, he was told, it deserved to be rewarded.[27] The impasse was starker given an Iraqi-Saudi nonaggression agreement signed that same month. Saddam later claimed that he offered the same to Kuwait (apparently in return for a satisfactory border deal), but that Kuwait turned it down, "probably under the advice of a foreign power, possibly Britain." Iraq, he asserted, would have never invaded Kuwait had such a bargain been made. "Thank God, Kuwait did not sign that agreement with us!" he exclaimed.[28]

The Kuwaitis, for their part, were frustrated and angry. Just as Iraq felt that it deserved to be compensated by the Gulf Arabs because it saved them from Iran, the Kuwaitis felt that they had supported Iraq strategically and financially, risking Tehran's vengeance.[29]

But both countries retained an outward semblance of normal, even cordial relations. Only an occasional vicious glints in the Iraqi eye revealed that Baghdad was dreaming of revenge.[30]

TURNING AGAINST THE UNITED STATES AND BRITAIN

The next phase in Iraq's increasingly radical turn occurred during the February 1990 meeting of the heads of state of the Arab Cooperation Council. In a speech that took his pro-Western partners, Egypt and Jordan, by complete surprise, Saddam criticized the U.S. Navy's presence in the Gulf, since no Soviet or Iranian threat remained, and came close to demanding its removal. In fact, by then only about 5 of the about 50 ships the U.S. Navy stationed there during the war still remained. This initiative was clearly a bid for unchallenged Iraqi supremacy in the Gulf.

But Iraq's leader went further. Referring to the Soviet Union's decline and the U.S. role as sole superpower, Saddam warned that for the next five years there was a grave danger of U.S. and Zionist machinations and urged Arabs to unite against America. This was the first time since 1980 that Iraqi policy fused together designs for supremacy in the Gulf, vicious anti-Americanism, and vitriolic anti-Israeli propaganda. Saddam also suggested that, with Europe's help, the Arabs could eventually defeat America. While the situation was very dangerous, he implied, the Arabs could reverse matters if they accepted Iraq's leadership.[31] This way Iraq, for the first time, offered itself as a replacement for the Soviet Union in its capacity as the Arabs' protector.

At the time, U.S. officials tended to see this speech as a mere expression of Iraqi anger at the VOA broadcast.[32] Another reason for Saddam's anti-Western mood may have been Turkey's closure of the Euphrates River on January 12, 1990, for 30 days to fill a new dam. This caused hardship to Iraq's farmers in the lower Euphrates basin and produced official protests.[33] The combination of an increasing Iraqi sense of vulnerability and its soaring ambition in the Gulf and Arab world created a very volatile mood in Baghdad. On March 15, Iraq affronted Britain by executing Farzad Bazoft, an Iranian-born, London-based journalist traveling on British papers, on a charge of espionage for Israel.[34] In the past, foreign citizens found guilty of spying were spared in order not to damage Iraq's foreign relations. But now Saddam was willing to risk a $400 million British trade credit promised for 1990. It is quite possible, though, that since the British government had been ignoring its own regulations by selling him dual-purpose machine tools, Saddam felt this was a small danger.[35]

The reason behind the anti-American diatribe and execution seems twofold. Iraq's government wanted to show its citizens that a regime ready to confront great powers would not hesitate to repress its own citizens. Second, by showing America and Britain—Kuwait's protectors—that Iraq was not afraid to antagonize them, Saddam hoped to dissuade them from helping Kuwait when a showdown came and to terrorize Kuwait itself into submission. Relations with Britain and the United States deteriorated further following exposure at the end of March of Iraqi smuggling of such arms' technology as nuclear triggers and a "super-gun" artillery piece.[36]

A few days later Saddam made another quantum jump in his anti-Western rhetoric. On April 19, in a meeting with 'Arafat, Saddam warned that military aggression against him would be met by a counterattack to "sweep away U.S. influence in the region." Saddam even threatened to destroy British and American warships in the Gulf and to use terrorism against U.S. targets.[37]

As a U.S. military attack on Iraq under existing circumstances was unlikely given the Bush administration's great efforts to improve relations, it seems that Saddam was thinking in terms of a very different scenario: an Iraqi assault on a U.S. ally in which he wanted to deter U.S. help for his victim. This possibility is enhanced by a U.S. intelligence report that some Iraqi forces began moving to the Kuwaiti border in the spring of 1990.[38]

THE ISRAELI ANGLE

The need to divert the public's attention from economic difficulties, the impasse with Iran, events in Eastern Europe, and Iraq's failure to pry Syria out of Lebanon pushed Saddam to make his third important move in 1990. In December 1989 Iraq's leaders began to promise the early liberation of Palestine, something they had not done since 1980. On April 2, 1990, in a speech to military personnel, Saddam disclosed that Iraq had ultra-modern binary chemical weapons "that only the U.S. and the Soviet Union have." Then he warned: "I swear to God that we shall burn half of Israel if it tries to wage anything against Iraq."[39]

That Saddam's speech was designed for a domestic audience is reflected in its language, almost entirely in the Iraqi dialect and full of local images and metaphors, including a variation on the colloquial expression common among Baghdad bullies "I shall burn half your house" (*ukhruk nus beitak*). It related only secondarily to any Iraqi duty to help other Arab countries defend themselves and was carefully calibrated so as to commit Iraq only to defend its own territory.

The threat against Israel should also be understood in the context that Iraq feared a new Israeli raid against its nuclear industry. Since early 1989 Iraqi spokesmen repeatedly warned Israel against trying to repeat the 1981 raid on Iraq's nuclear reactor by raiding its missile and unconventional arms industry. As disclosed by Iraq's air force commander, at the end of the Iraq-Iran war Iraq's leaders felt that Israel, not Iran, posed the main danger to Iraq's security.[40]

Iraq implied that once it defeated Iran, the West no longer needed its help and thus encouraged Israel to attack. Statements by Israeli politicians and officers that they worried about Iraq's development of an unconventional arsenal, and concern over Iraq's arms industry in the U.S. media, were noted in Baghdad.

Iraq suggested that it could strike anywhere with its missiles (though until April 1990 only conventional warheads were implied) if Israel attacked, while both countries exchanged warnings through covert U.S., Egyptian, and other channels. At least one senior Israeli official met with Foreign Minister 'Aziz, Deputy Prime Minister Sa'dun Hammadi, chief of Iraq's delegation to the United Nations in Geneva (and ex-intelligence chief) Barzan Ibrahim al-Tikriti, Saddam's half brother. The two sides probed each other's positions on a wide range of issues, including the development of unconventional arms, but no binding assurances were made.[41]

In February 1990 Iraq secretly inaugurated its first uranium enrichment site at Tarmiyah. When fully operational, it could produce 33 pounds of weapons-grade, 93%-enriched uranium a year.[42] The proximity in time between this event and the threat on Israel suggests that Iraq worried lest Israel's intelligence had learned what was happening. These fears were heightened when, in March 1990, the United States and Britain exposed an Iraqi plot to smuggle nuclear triggers from the United States via London. Tariq 'Aziz stated that from this time Iraq's leaders feared an Israeli raid due to increased talk in the Western press of an impending war.[43]

In reality, there was no talk of war in the Western press, but there was much criticism of Iraq's unconventional arms industry, which Baghdad may have seen as a campaign to prepare Western public opinion for an Israeli raid. On April 5, Saddam asked Prince Bandar, the Saudi ambassador to Washington, who rushed to Baghdad on Iraq's request, to get him U.S. assurance that Israel was not going to attack. For his part, Saddam promised not to initiate war. According to his own version, in threatening Israel he was motivated partly by his fear of an Israeli raid and partly by the need to distract Iraq's people from daily hardships. Saddam told the prince, "I must whip them into a sort of frenzy or emotional mobilization, so they will be ready for whatever may happen."[44]

Israeli reactions were cautious, designed to deter Iraq while avoiding a military escalation. On one hand, Israeli leaders assured Iraq publicly, and through U.S. channels privately, that Israel had no intention of attacking. On the other, they warned that Israel would retaliate massively against Iraqi aggression, thus implying a readiness to use atomic weapons in response to a chemical attack.

The U.S. and Western European governments made clear their concern while Egyptian officials quietly expressed alarm and promised to "whisper into Iraq's ear: 'cool it.'"[45] It took Iraqi foreign minister Tariq 'Aziz one day to "clarify" that Iraq would use chemical weapons only in retaliation for an Israeli atomic attack on Iraq, a position repeated by Saddam.[46]

Typically, though, the Arab response to Iraq's threats and the international community's alarm was very different from what Egyptians said in private conversations. Part of the Arab world was fascinated and elated; the rest was frightened into submission. King Husayn of Jordan backed his Iraqi patron, saying Western criticism of Iraq "expresses an old enmity towards our Arab nation and a hostile desire to stop it from progressing and building its strength. . . . There are aggressive intentions behind this campaign." 'Arafat's adviser, Basam Abu Sharif, said that criticism of Iraq was part of a "complicated plot to curtail the development of this country as the nucleus [sic] of power for the whole Arab nation." Iraq's challenge to the West and Israel, he argued, shifted the power balance in favor of the Arabs and the Palestinian cause.[47]

Even Syria was sympathetic, while even President Mubarak of Egypt, having rushed to Baghdad to tell Saddam to "cool it," declared in a joint press conference with Iraq's ruler that Iraq was acting defensively. Mubarak stressed, "Iraq is not a state that wants war or calls for war."[48] In the Arab world, there was an upsurge of public admiration for Saddam and Iraq. For the first time since Gamal 'Abd al-Nasir, an Arab leader stood up to Israel and fearlessly threatened it with annihilation.[49]

Arab admiration was not lost on Iraq's leader, so desperate to find a way out of his multiple predicaments. This new prestige motivated him to make the next step. On April 22 Saddam's air force commander, Major General Muzahim Sa'b Hasan, announced that Iraq would use "all its might" against Israel in case of an attack on any Arab country, not just against Iraq alone.[50] Such declarations continually escalated. For example, speaking to an Islamic conference in

Baghdad in June, Saddam announced: "Yes, we will strike at [Israel] with all the arms in our possession if they attack Iraq or the Arabs. . . . If Iraq remains silent, it will lose the respect of those close to it. . . . Whoever strikes at the Arabs we will strike back from Iraq."[51]

In his April 19 talk with 'Arafat, Saddam also urged the Palestinians to take a hard line and promised to liberate them:

> Brother president ['Arafat], from now on we will not need any concessions or political efforts because you and I know that they are useless. In fact, they increase the enemy's arrogance and indifference to us . . . from now on, we need to strengthen our position and determination . . . no peace, no recognition and no negotiations [with Israel]. . . . We must support the heroism of the brave intifada. You should support it with strong stands and qualitative operations, and we should support it with what we have of qualified air and missile forces to deal a blow to and defeat the enemy, even without land fighting or confrontations. . . . We have in no way reduced our military force; we continue to strengthen it."[52]

In Israel, Iraq's warnings were read as relating to Jordan. (On February 19 Iraq and Jordan had announced the establishment of a joint "Pan-Arab" air squadron, and Israel reacted by sending a severe warning to Amman.[53]) But there was a danger that Saddam would be sucked into a war by his own rhetoric. Whatever the case, this was a clear departure from Saddam's long-standing policy of putting Iraq's domestic problems before entanglements in the Pan-Arab arena. Now he reversed priorities: Iraq would solve its own problems by foreign adventurism.

AN OVERTURE TO IRAN

An additional indication that the actual decision to use force against Kuwait (as different from contingency plans that may have existed for a long time) was taken during April 1990 is provided by the Iraqi initiative to improve relations with Iran late that month. It started with a letter that Saddam sent to Iran's 'Ali Akbar Hashemi Rafsanjani suggesting direct talks conducted on the basis of the 1975 Iran-Iraq agreement—which Saddam himself had declared null and void on September 17, 1980. This implied Iraqi concessions on the Shatt al-Arab leading to what Iraqi spokesmen called a "comprehensive and durable peace between Iraq and Iran."[54] Although serious differences between the two countries remained, bilateral meetings between mid-level officials began in June, and more sessions were planned for late August 1990.[55]

Iraq knew that Iran opposed its annexation of the Kuwaiti islands of Warba and Bubyan because any improvement of Iraq's strategic position on the Gulf would seem to be an Iranian loss.[56] According to the Iraqi version of Saddam's July 1990 conversation with Ambassador April Glaspie, Saddam warned—and Glaspie never denied—that if his demands on Kuwait were not met, Iraq would be ready to give up sovereignty over the eastern part of the Shatt al-Arab in exchange for Iran's acquiescence to an Iraqi armed operation against Kuwait.[57] To give his initiative an ideological cutting edge, Saddam also wrote Rafsanjani calling on Iran to create "an Arab-Islamic front against the increasing Zionist dangers."[58]

THE BAGHDAD ARAB SUMMIT, MAY 1990: THE GULF ARABS UNDER FIRE

By late April Iraq's turnabout was nearly complete. Iraq had turned against its wartime allies, the United States and Britain, while trying to befriend its old anti-Western enemy, Iran. And it assumed leadership of the radical Arab camp against Israel, something it had not done since the days of the Camp David Israeli-Egyptian peace agreement. The only missing piece—an aggressive posture vis-à-vis its Arab wartime allies, and Kuwait in particular—was put in place during the Arab summit in Baghdad.

The fact that the Arab summit meeting in Baghdad was neither postponed nor moved was a tremendous victory for Iraq, a de facto endorsement of its aggressive policies and an admission of weakness by moderate Arab states. Iraq and its supporters—chiefly Libya, the Palestine Liberation Organization (PLO), and Jordan—launched an offensive against Israel, Soviet Jewish immigration, the United States, and, by implication, the Arab moderates. The concluding resolutions supported Iraq's "right to take all measures that will guarantee the protection of its national security and . . . the possession of highly developed scientific and technological means" necessary for its defense.[59]

The resolutions added that this must be done in the framework of international law. Yet the "severe denunciation" of "the scientific and technological embargo" imposed on Iraq by the United States and Britain and of the Western media campaign "against [its] sovereignty and national security" meant that the Arabs were collectively denouncing any attempt to stop Saddam's nuclear, chemical, bacteriological, and missile efforts, even defining them as a positive contribution to "pan-Arab security."[60]

Even Mubarak enthusiastically applauded "the right of the Arab peoples to acquire and use modern technology." In context, such a declaration meant support for Iraq obtaining nuclear weapons.[61] Instead of distancing themselves from Iraq's chemical threats against Israel, leaders such as the Arab League's secretary-general praised Iraq as "a pan-Arab defensive shield."[62]

But Iraq did not reciprocate this praise. During the closed sessions, Saddam's real thrust was exposed when he accused some "Arab Brothers" of flooding the world oil market and bringing prices as low as $7 a barrel. Saddam called this an all-out war that gravely damaged Iraq. He added darkly: "We have reached a point when we can no longer withstand pressure."[63]

It seems that this was the moment when Saddam decided to turn the Iraqi masses' frustration from a liability to an asset, blaming their suffering on the rich Arabs and demanding compensation. According to some sources,[64] Saddam also demanded that the Arab summit compel the Gulf Arab states to forgive Iraq its war debt and give it $30 billion in economic aid. He accused Kuwait of stealing oil from an oilfield along the border and demanded that Kuwait give the two islands to Iraq. The summit never discussed the issue, but no one protested and the impression left was that of Arab sympathy for Saddam's demands or, at least, reluctance to confront him. Iraq's leadership interpreted it as further evidence of Iraq's new Arab status, even immunity, and ability to apply brutal pressure on the Gulf Arab states.[65]

PRELUDE TO WAR: OPEN CONFRONTATION WITH KUWAIT

Between mid-May and late June Iraq-Kuwait relations showed growing strain. The immediate reason was a decline in oil prices, a blow to Iraq's economy and Saddam's prestige. Saddam told the Saudi oil minister privately after the summit: "I will never agree to let Iraqis starve, and Iraqi women go naked because of need."[66]

But Saddam did not forget the islands, either. Elated by his great success as the summit's host and pacesetter, Saddam asked Kuwait's emir for the use of the islands while driving him back to Baghdad airport. The latter replied, "Even the Emir of Kuwait himself does not have the right to give away a part of his country's lands." Saddam then asked to be allowed to build two pipelines from the Shatt al-Arab to Kuwait City, one for oil, the other for water.[67]

When the emir agreed, Saddam immediately followed up by asking to "build cities, schools and airports along the pipelines." When the emir expressed concern,

Saddam suggested that in return Kuwait could use Iraqi territory. "There is no difference between the two countries. Do not worry about the borders," he told the emir.[68] The next quantum leap came in mid-July. Following the summit, the Iraqis scored a limited gain when, on July 10, an Iraqi-Saudi-Kuwaiti-United Arab Emirates (UAE) oil ministers' meeting agreed to abide by the Organization of Petroleum-Exporting Countries (OPEC) quotas. One day later, however, Kuwait announced that in the fall it would review, and possibly revoke, its promise. This way, the Iraqi side felt, Kuwait "killed the agreement."[69]

The Kuwaiti announcement enabled Iraq to present its next move as a defensive one. On July 16, analyzing satellite photographs, the U.S. Defense Intelligence Agency spotted, for the first time, a Republican Guard division, the Hammurabi, being deployed on the Kuwaiti border. The next morning (noon Baghdad time) the whole division was already there and a second one, al-Madina al-Munawwara, was showing up.[70]

In his July 17 Revolution Day speech, Saddam attacked unnamed Gulf Arab countries for plotting against Iraq with "imperialist and Zionist forces." This unholy coalition, he said, used economic means for their evil designs "more dangerous than those produced by the old direct methods." Having delegitimized the Gulf Arabs as the agents of imperialism and Zionism, Saddam then threatened to use force against them if they did not change their policy.[71]

A day later a third Republican Guard Division, Tawakkalna 'Ala allah, was monitored moving to the border. That same day Iraq's press published a July 15 letter from Iraq's foreign minister to the Arab League's secretary-general accusing Kuwait of harming Iraq "deliberately and continuously" after the Iran-Iraq war ended. Even during the war Kuwait was said to have exploited Iraq's preoccupation to encroach on its territory. Kuwait was allegedly dumping on world markets oil stolen "from the Iraqi Rumayla oil field" said to be worth $2.4 billion as "part of the imperialist-Zionist plan against Iraq and the Arab nation."[72]

By mid-July, then, Iraq was already past the turning point in its incremental decision to invade Kuwait. It is not clear whether there was anything Kuwait could have done to prevent an invasion at that stage, short of an urgent request to the United States to land troops. But even if the decision to use force could still be reversed provided Kuwait made concessions, as Iraqi spokesmen claimed, only complete surrender could have stopped the Iraqi army in its tracks.

Saddam never embarked on an important adventure without preparing his public. Before attacking Iran in 1980 he laid the groundwork in Iraq's media for five months. This time, preparations were brief and more ambiguous. Even the Revolution Day speech fell short of a sweeping delegitimization of Kuwait's regime, and Iraq's press accused only Kuwait's foreign minister (not the emir) of being "an American agent" plotting against Iraq.[73] The sense of being wronged by ungrateful Gulf Arabs was brought to a crescendo, but there were no claims that Kuwait was an integral part of Iraq. Thus, the occupation of the whole of Kuwait came as a surprise even to senior army—if not Republican Guard—officers.[74] At the end of the war Saddam fired his minister of information, the Shi'a Latif Nusayyif Jasim, for failure to mobilize public opinion behind the war, but this was, clearly, Saddam's own responsibility. Apparently happy that the West did not adhere his warning, he was reluctant to alert it further and thus force it to take preventive action.

Saddam also prepared the home front for war, starting in June 1990, by using Islamic rhetoric, clearly designed to secure mass support. This newly discovered Islam could, indeed, serve as a common platform for an anti-American front with Iran.[75] But Saddam himself undermined this campaign by not introducing Islamic law in Iraq and, trying to distance the Iraqi Shi'a from Iranian-Shi'a influence, by a chauvinistically Arab, anti-Iranian credo emphasizing the Arabs' leading role in Islam.[76]

To safeguard Arab support for an Iraqi invasion without, however, fully alerting them to his designs, Saddam, according to Iraqi sources, tried to convince Mubarak that the Arab wealth should be redistributed and that the "hungry people of Egypt" should be compensated at the expense of the "Kuwaiti Croesus."[77] To give Mubarak a taste of what he could expect after the "Croesuses" were removed, in late July Saddam gave Egypt $25 million "to buy wheat," and promised to deliver $25 million more soon, apparently after the invasion.[78]

But the Kuwaitis did not cave in. Responding to the Arab League's secretary-general, Kuwait expressed "indignation" at the Iraqi "distortion and falsification" of facts. "Iraq has a long record of encroachment on Kuwaiti lands" and always refused to settle the border issue through an impartial Arab arbitration committee. Kuwait never drilled wells in Iraqi territory, rather, Iraq drilled wells that impinged on Kuwait's oilfields.[79] Kuwait also protested to the UN secretary-general, thus internationalizing an Arab conflict, a step Arab countries normally try to avoid.[80] Iraq's foreign minister 'Aziz warned Kuwait "that foreigners will not protect those who conspire against the Arab nation."[81]

The end of July saw a flurry of activity. As reports mounted on July 24, denied by Baghdad, of an Iraqi troop buildup on the border, the Arab League secretary-general and Mubarak arrived in Baghdad. Saddam, Mubarak said, promised him, "There is no intention to attack Kuwait."[82] According to Saddam's own version, he said merely, "I will not use military force until the meeting agreed on is held in Jidda."[83] But Saddam also told Glaspie that he would also await a visit of Kuwait's crown prince to Baghdad "for serious negotiations."[84]

Meanwhile at the OPEC oil ministers' meeting in Geneva, Iraq used its troop buildup on the Kuwaiti border to impose a higher minimum price, contrary to the Gulf Arabs' interests, of $21 per barrel. Iraq's News Agency ascribed the decision by implication to Saddam's threat to use force.[85] Other OPEC ministers were not pleased. "We ought, all of us, to feel ashamed that we live in a world in which a man like Saddam Husayn is accepted by the international community," one minister is quoted as saying. Another noted: "the Saudis will regret this forever." A third delegate said despondently, "I sincerely hope that we can keep OPEC going [in the future] without gunboat quotas."[86]

With this victory, Iraq shifted its main emphasis back to territorial demands.[87] A government newspaper announced Iraq "is claiming its territory that has been infiltrated," the Kuwaiti-held part of the Rumayla oilfield being only part of the land.[88] In short, a few days before the Jidda meeting Iraq already made it clear that it would get its way on all counts or use force.

PROBING THE U.S. POSITION

Before invading Kuwait, however, Saddam had to probe the U.S. reaction. After Saddam's Revolution Day Speech President Bush himself expressed concern and his administration spoke of reviewing its policy toward Iraq.[89] On July 18 the State Department announced U.S. determination to ensure the free flow of oil through the straits of Hormuz; defend freedom of navigation; and support "the individual and collective self defense of our friends in the Gulf, with whom we have deep and long-standing ties."[90]

On July 24 Glaspie was instructed to convey again to Iraq the U.S. concern over its threats against Kuwait and the UAE. "The implications of having oil production and pricing policy in the Gulf determined and enforced by Iraqi guns [are] disturbing." She was also to reiterate the State Department formula of commitment to individual and collective self-defense, the free flow of oil, and freedom of navigation in the Gulf. The ambassador delivered this message by phone to Iraq's deputy foreign minister, Nizar Hamdoun.[91] On July 24 the United States also announced joint naval maneuvers with the UAE in response to Iraqi troop concentrations.

Saddam, thus, had to find out what all this meant. In the first place, he decided to try to induce the United States to force Kuwait, Munich style, to make all the concessions Iraq demanded. Failing that, he needed to know whether, in case of an invasion, Washington would take military action and how this could be deterred by his own threats or proposals.

At 10 A.M. on July 25 Glaspie met Nizar Hamdoun and gave him the same message, this time in person. At noon she was summoned for another meeting at the Foreign Ministry, only to find herself facing Saddam. The transcript of their conversation, published by the Iraqi embassy in Washington in September 1990, was challenged by Glaspie as "a fabrication" and "disinformation." State Department officials acknowledged that it contained omissions but described it as "essentially accurate."[92] Her own report, parts of which were published in American newspapers corroborates much—though not all—of the Iraqi version.[93] Even those parts not in dispute are disturbing. The situation called for an immediate, severe warning to Iraq and an alert in Washington. But due to Saddam's personal cordiality and because he intentionally blurred his threats somewhat, Glaspie completely misread the situation, sent Washington an all-clear signal, and gave Saddam a mixed message.

According to both versions, Saddam opened by promising the ambassador that Iraq fully sympathized with the U.S. wish for an undisturbed flow of oil but demanded U.S. neutrality in the Iraqi-Kuwaiti dispute. He accused America of using Kuwait to spearhead its anti-Iraqi policy and insisted ominously that Kuwait was threatening Iraq's very livelihood by engaging in "economic warfare," a situation Iraq could not accept.

Instead of responding with equal pressure, Glaspie tried to allay Saddam's fears of U.S. conspiracies against him, insisting that Bush had instructed her to seek better relations with Iraq. The ambassador reported that Saddam then demanded that the thankless rich Kuwaitis keep to their oil quota and "open their purses" to the Iraqis, who spilled for them "rivers of blood."

Saddam told Glaspie that verbal threats and a military buildup was the only way to show Kuwait how much Iraqis were suffering. When Saddam mentioned his promise to Mubarak not to use force if Kuwait met Iraq's demands in the scheduled Iraqi-Kuwaiti meetings, the ambassador regarded this as good news. Saddam also implied skepticism about U.S. resolve to defend its allies, asserting "American society is unable to sustain 10,000 fatalities in one battle," while Iraq did just that during eight years of war.

According to both versions, Saddam also raised the border issue, implying he would like U.S. pressure on Kuwait. The ambassador replied that U.S. policy took no position on such inter-Arab affairs. This assertion was in line with the State Department position. It was designed to avoid diplomatic complications as a result of American involvement in such disputes. But in the context of six Republican Guard armored and mechanized divisions on the Kuwaiti border and two more on the way, this certainly was not a strong warning to Iraq to stick to diplomatic means lest the United States, too, resort to force.

The ambassador never sought any authorization to take a tougher line. This was particularly necessary in view of Saddam's thinly veiled threat that, if Kuwait did not succumb to his demands, he would make concessions to Iran to bring its acquiescence, then he would attack Kuwait. All the ambassador did was to warn that the United States "cannot forgive" the use of force.

In summing up, the ambassador defined Saddam's attitude during the interview as "cordial, reasonable and even warm." She contended that Saddam was "worried" because he suspected that the joint U.S.-UAE maneuvers meant a U.S. decision "to take sides." Finally, she observed, "His emphasis that he wants peaceful settlement is surely sincere: Iraqis are sick of war. But the terms are difficult to achieve. Saddam seems to want pledges now on oil prices and production to cover the next several months."

It seems that the ambassador forgot altogether about Iraq's territorial demands. But her main purpose was not to warn Iraq but to save, even improve, bilateral relations. Thus, she went out of her way to convince Saddam that the United States was not conspiring against him with Kuwait and others. Her criticisms were expressed in apologetic terms, and she sounded much more convincing when expressing sympathy and promising to work to improve relations. Glaspie not only ignored Saddam's threats but even recommended that public criticism of Iraq would be "eased off" for a while.

The State Department and White House, having concluded that Iraqi troops were not ready for a full-scale invasion, thought Saddam was bluffing[94] and were unwilling to provoke him. Saddam had warned the ambassador that, if offended, he would be compelled to react strongly—even irrationally. The strongest warning they delivered was Bush's verbal message to Saddam sent on July 28 through Glaspie: "We believe that differences are best resolved by peaceful means and not by threats involving military force." The president also put America's friendship with Iraq on the same level as that with "our other friends in the region."[95]

On July 24, 1990, State Department spokeswomen Margaret Tutwiler had asserted, "We do not have any . . . special defense or security commitments to Kuwait." On the day of the Glaspie-Saddam meeting, Ambassador-Designate to Kuwait Edward Gnehm told the Senate Foreign Relations Committee that Iraq was "merely trying to intimidate a small country."[96]

Two days before the invasion, Assistant Secretary of State for Near Eastern and South Asian Affairs John Kelly reaffirmed that the United States had no defense treaty with any Gulf state and considered the Kuwait-Iraq border dispute to be their private affair. After the invasion a senior administration official told the *New York Times* that the government expected an Iraqi invasion to seize a limited border area. "We were reluctant to draw a line in the sand. . . . I can't see the American public supporting the deployment of troops over a dispute over twenty miles of desert territory, and it is not clear that the local countries would have supported that kind of commitment. The basic principle is not to make threats that you can't deliver on." Whatever the truth, the United States behaved as if this was its approach. This caution was enhanced by Mubarak and King Fahd of Saudi Arabia, who assured Washington that Saddam would not invade, arguing that "the best way to resolve an inter-Arab squabble was for the United States to avoid inflammatory words and actions."[97]

U.S. inertia was reflected in a surrealistic meeting between Saddam and U.S. chargé d'affaires Joseph Wilson four days after the invasion. Saddam claimed that because Kuwait "was a state without borders . . . the entry of the Iraqi forces cannot be measured within the framework of the relationship between [normal] states in the Arab world." He later added, "By the way, say hello to President Bush and tell him to consider [Shaykh] Jabir [al-Sabah] finished and history."

Saddam strongly warned the United States "against further meddling in the relations between Iraq and Saudi Arabia" and threatened that if the United States harmed Iraq, Iraq would hurt U.S. interests, again warning America against taking "any bold steps that they can not retreat from." But Saddam also had a proposition: he offered to serve as America's chief ally and—by implication—policeman of the Gulf. In exchange, he promised that there would be a free flow of oil at $25 per barrel.

Wilson merely promised to pass along the message. Not authorized to threaten that unless he withdrew from Kuwait the U.S. would forcefully evict him, Wilson declared: "during these difficult days, it appears to me that it is important that we keep a dialogue between us to avoid making mistakes. This is the only way in which we are going to be able to remove tension and cool emotions."[98]

At the same time it was probing the U.S. position, Iraq also gauged the Soviet stand. According to a Soviet source, some senior Soviet officials promised Iraq that, in case of an attack on Kuwait, the Soviet Union would not support the United States and Britain.[99]

SADDAM GOES TO WAR

The Jidda meeting was held on July 31, 1990, and lasted only two hours. If the previous Iraqi demands are any guide, Iraq gave Kuwait an unacceptable ultimatum: to cede or lease to Iraq the two islands and the southern tip of the Rumayla oilfield, to write off Iraq's war debt, and to pay Iraq for claimed financial losses. Iraq was represented at Jidda by a senior delegation led by Revolutionary Command Council (RCC) Vice Chairman 'Izzat Ibrahim al-Duri (whose daughter was married to Saddam's elder son, 'Uday) and including

Deputy Prime Minister Sa'dun Hammadi and 'Ali Hasan al-Majid, minister of local government and member of the Ba'th party Regional Leadership (but, most important, Saddam's cousin and one of the chiefs of Iraq's internal security). Sending such a delegation indicated Iraq's seriousness, and Iraq's media warned that Iraq would reject any attempt to "bury Iraqi rights under the rubble of postponements and delays."[100] The fact that the invasion had been fully prepared before the meeting was even convened, however, indicates that Saddam suspected that Kuwait would not accept his demands.

Kuwait's behavior was strange. On the one hand it was ready to stand up to Iraq, refusing to yield territory and offering minimal financial concessions. On the other hand, it put itself at Iraq's mercy, telling foreigners to keep out of this internal Arab affair. "Solving disputes between brothers is not difficult," it argued, and echoed Saddam's view that all Arabs need to cooperate in the post-Cold War world.[101] More dangerously, Kuwait publicly committed itself not to invite foreign troops to defend itself, lulled by U.S., Egyptian, and Saudi promises and, most of all, by their own hope that, if not offended, Saddam would stop short of violence.[102] Very possibly, what the Kuwaitis had in mind was a Bedouin-style lengthy process of negotiations and bargaining that would end with a compromise: some Kuwaiti and Saudi financial contribution to Saddam's coffers.

There are two versions of the Jidda meeting. According to one, the Iraqi delegation was under orders to obtain Kuwait's full surrender or to walk out.[103] Saddam claimed that his delegation requested a $10 billion "loan." Kuwait agreed to $9 billion and the Saudis offered to contribute the rest, but at the farewell party the Kuwaitis demanded a border agreement as precondition for the loan. Iraq then saw no point in continuing the talks, and they were suspended.[104] The delegations left Jidda and the Iraq-Kuwait border was closed.[105] Early the next day, August 2, 1990, Iraq invaded Kuwait.

WHY THE WHOLE OF KUWAIT? WHY NOT SAUDI ARABIA?

In hindsight, Foreign Minister Tariq 'Aziz disclosed that Iraq originally planned to occupy only the islands and the disputed oilfield. He described taking Kuwait City as Saddam's "last-moment" decision just before the invasion. Saddam's argument was that "it would make no difference [to the United States]" how much of Kuwait was conquered.[106] Although, clearly, the Republican Guard was ready for both options, this account sounds credible, if only because it put the blame for the war on Saddam, and thus it placed 'Aziz in jeopardy. ('Aziz never repeated this disclosure.)

The mystery is: What drove Saddam to the strange conclusion that "it would make no difference"? By publishing their version of Saddam's meeting with the American ambassador the Iraqis implied that, due to her vagueness, she at least shared with them the responsibility for their invasion. Saddam's own version was given in an astonishing interview in which he explained his interpretation of Ambassador Glaspie's message:

> "I . . . asked her to persuade [President Bush] to pressure Kuwait if necessary. She replied . . . 'the U.S. does not want to be involved in inter Arab disputes.' I then said: 'we do not want you to be involved either' . . . They said they would not interfere. In so saying they washed their hands. What response should I have waited for? We entered Kuwait four days later. Regardless [however], Bush rallied the world . . . and attacked Iraq. What was the problem? They had said that they would not intervene!"[107]

This sounds like feigned naïveté. Judging by the Iraqi transcript, even the overoptimistic Saddam should not have interpreted Glaspie's remark on the border dispute as permission to occupy all Kuwait.[108] Furthermore, by claiming that he did only what he thought the United States allowed him to do Saddam contradicted his own theme, repeated many times between July 17 and August 2, that Kuwaiti behavior was determined by a U.S. plot. Was it logical to expect the United States to plot with Kuwait against Iraq, only to give Iraq green light to invade Kuwait? Alternatively, if, indeed, the Americans were so hostile to Iraq, as Saddam claimed in his pre-invasion speeches, how could he possibly take anything they told him at face value? Why did he not suspect a trap?

Tariq 'Aziz himself explained in his interview with the journalist Milton Viorst that, as he understood it, the reference to U.S. reluctance to get involved did not mean permission to invade: "Those who say that we regarded what the ambassador said as a green light indicating that the U.S. would not react against Iraq if it launched a military intervention against Kuwait are wrong."[109]

It seems that even those in Baghdad who believed in a U.S. plot against Iraq (and many at least half believed in it) did not think this meant war. Except for Saddam's conversation with Arafat in April, Iraq had only accused the West of economic warfare. Further, the Bush administration's vague commitment to Kuwait's territorial integrity, the ambassador's talk of U.S. reluctance to intervene; and the U.S. government's leniency over Iraq's human rights and other transgressions—along with Arab appeasement—seem to have created a feeling in Baghdad that Washington would take no drastic action over a few miles of Kuwaiti sand and an oilfield.[110]

Why, then, did Saddam not play it safe, staying in Kuwait's northern part? If Iraq's main purpose was to seize a harbor to replace the closed Shatt al-Arab, a far less risky option was to occupy the two islands and develop the Umm Qasr and Mina Bakr ports. But such a mini-invasion, even if including the South Rumayla oilfield, would not have solved Iraq's acute cash-flow problems. In fact, it could worsen them by pushing Kuwait and other Gulf states to overproduce oil again. By taking all Kuwait, however, Saddam could hope to terrorize the Gulf Arabs into total submission, become a hero to most Iraqis and many other Arabs, and, most important in the short run: control Kuwait's huge economic assets. Iraqis estimated Kuwait's assets in the West as $220 billion.[111] But Saddam was also sure that the Kuwaitis, being Bedouins like himself, retained the tradition of keeping a huge stockpile of gold in the vaults of their National Bank. (There is much evidence that he himself did, indeed, retain that tradition.[112])

On the night of the invasion Saddam sent helicopter-borne commando units to three sites: to Kuwait airport, to secure landing facilities for the invading troops; to the emir's palace, in the hope that, in the absence of a legitimate Kuwaiti ruler, Iraq could establish an "interim government" that would siphon Kuwait assets abroad to the Iraqi accounts; and finally he sent a unit, equipped with all the necessary gear, to break into the National Bank. The unit was able to enter the vaults but, to its dismay, found there only relatively small quantities of gold.[113]

All these potential gains were, in Saddam's eyes, big enough to dwarf the risk. But then, Saddam also thought the risk as relatively low, given his conviction that America feared going to war and that the Saudis would not change their historic policy of appeasing radical Arabs to invite U.S. troops.[114] As pointed out above, he thought he had adequately prepared the ground for U.S. and Egyptian inaction. While his understanding of Iraq's internal scene was always superb, Saddam's comprehension of other Arab and Islamic countries was far less impressive.

Saddam thus discounted the likelihood of war, economic sanctions, or a strong Arab front against him resulting from the invasion. He was ready to risk diplomatic confrontation even with the world's sole superpower given the high stakes, but hoped that when faced with a fait accompli, it would make a deal. If Iraq gained Kuwait's full oil production, together they would pump over 5 million barrels a day, 21% of OPEC's total production, letting them force the West and its Arab allies to accept Iraq's dictates. It will be remembered that, in their post-invasion conversation, Saddam suggested to Joseph Wilson that, in return for a commitment not to invade Saudi Arabia or "harm American interests" elsewhere and to guarantee an undisturbed flow of oil at reasonable prices, the U.S. government would recognize Kuwait's new status and accept him as protector of the Gulf.[115]

Why did Iraq not advance into Saudi territory to seize oilfields as a bargaining card or, later, to attack arriving U.S. forces before they dug in? To claim, as Saddam did, that he was restrained by his 1989 nonaggression pact with Saudi Arabia is unconvincing. More likely, Iraq's leaders were sure the United States would fight to defend Saudi territory. An attack on Saudi Arabia, let alone on the American troops there, would start the war with America that Saddam hoped to avoid.

Aside from his rational thinking, Saddam's decisions are also explained by his entourage's fear of contradicting the leader once his mind was made, and by Saddam's psychology. His self-image was as an invincible warrior and empire-builder, a reincarnation of Gilgamesh, Sargon the Akkadian, Nebuchadnezzar, Salah al-Din, and even the Sumero-Akkadian god Dumuzi-Tammuz.[116] He had invaded Iran only 14 months after becoming president. Saddam became trapped in his own myth. Having emerged as the leading regional power from the Iraq-Iran war, Saddam was eager to win another victory that would provide him with the leaping stone to far greater ambitions. As emerges from his conversation with Joseph Wilson, he intended to become the Gulf's hegemonic power. As he demonstrated in the Baghdad May 1990 Arab summit, as well as in many of his speeches before and after the invasion, he planned to turn himself into the pace-setter for the whole Arab world. Finally, as implied in a few of his speeches following the invasion, using these economic, strategic, and political leverages, his ambition was to become the most influential leader of the Third World. Beyond the immediate rewards of money and an excellent harbor, then, the long-term stakes were global power and glory.

CONCLUSION:
WHERE DID SADDAM GO WRONG? [117]

A number of Saddam's calculations did prove correct. In the first place, he was right in his conviction that his army could easily conquer Kuwait before anybody intervened. Saddam also gained political support from some of the radical Arabs and Jordan. While the Arab regimes supporting him (Libya, Algeria, Yemen, Sudan, and Jordan) did not endorse the annexation of Kuwait, their efforts to prevent war and remove the international embargo objectively helped Baghdad. On the popular level, too, in the Arab world Saddam received mass support in North Africa and Sudan, from Israeli and Palestinian Arabs, and in Jordan. Saddam also managed to launch missile attacks on Israel without provoking an Israeli nonconventional reprisal. Indeed, Israel did not respond at all, but this, if anything, was a disappointment: Saddam planned on a limited

Israeli response that would split the Western-Arab coalition against him. Yet, although his missiles failed to split the coalition, he at least won much Arab admiration for being the only Arab leader in half a century to have struck Tel Aviv and to have sent the Israelis fleeing the city.

In the last analysis, however, most of Saddam's calculations were wrong. The Arab radicals gave him little real help. His hope that the masses in countries that opposed him would rise against their rulers proved extremely naive. The main demonstrations occurred in Pakistan, Morocco, and Algeria—all places irrelevant to events in the Gulf—and even there no one was toppled from power. To be sure, revolutions against the pro-Western Arab regimes are still possible, but Saddam needed such revolutions before and during the Gulf War. His wish that Palestinian organizations would sow havoc in Europe and America through terrorism and thus help stop the war proved unrealistic.

Saddam's hope that—in return for cash and a promise of future handouts—Egypt would accept Kuwait's occupation was also wrong. Viewing itself as the Arab world's proper leader, Egypt would not accept Iraqi hegemony. As pointed out earlier, the Saudis, too, disappointed him. Turkey, also, saw Iraq's ambitions as so threatening that it took a strong stand against Saddam.

Saddam was hopeful that Iran would support him against the American "great Satan." To his dismay, he found out that all he could expect from the Iranians was sympathetic rhetoric and some food supplies at inflated prices. At the war's end Iran helped the Shi'a and Kurdish revolts against him and did not even return the 138 Iraqi warplanes flown by pilots who had taken refuge there.

Saddam also miscalculated the Soviet stance as Moscow cooperated with Washington almost fully. There was some sympathy from Soviet conservatives, especially after the start of the bombing campaign, but the Soviet Union was too weak to make any difference. Saddam's hope, fueled by Paris's highly equivocal policy, that France would extricate him from his predicament also proved a mirage.

More important, Saddam completely misunderstood the U.S. and British positions. For a man who only five months before the invasion had warned Arabs of the American danger to blunder in such a way was, indeed, extraordinary. The U.S. government was ready to tolerate hysterical Iraqi threats against Israel and to some extent threats against the Gulf Arab states; nor would it have fought over a limited border change.

But it had no choice but to go to war over the whole of Kuwait, because acquiescing to an Iraqi occupation would, in effect, mean accepting Iraq's hegemony in the Gulf. Saddam's greatest miscalculation, then, was his failure to predict the U.S. response to an Iraqi occupation of Kuwait. Taking at face value the popular post-Vietnam perception in the Third World of America as a paper tiger, Saddam did not believe that it had the stamina to fight a costly war against him. Whether this perception was right, he was certainly wrong in his assumption that any war against him would be costly for the Americans.

Having invaded Kuwait and realized that the Americans might retaliate, Saddam still had the option of withdrawing from most of the country while retaining the two islands and disputed border areas. At first, Iraq did promise an early departure, but the invasion and ensuing annexation had created a new reality. Now that "the branch has returned to the trunk" and "the baby has returned to its mother's lap," as Iraqi spokesmen put it, withdrawing was extremely difficult. This was particularly so in view of Saddam's suspicion that the Americans were bluffing.

Even on January 15 Saddam still could not believe the United States would fight. The ambiguous positions of France and the Soviet Union, antiwar demonstrations in the West, and a pilgrimage of ex-world leaders to Baghdad helped convince him that there was no need to hurry. Surrounded by yes men, Saddam was isolated from the real political atmosphere in Washington and London. No wonder that the war came to him as yet another surprise. Finally, Saddam wrongly believed that, in the ground campaign, his soldiers would still fight to the death and inflict enough casualties on the coalition to deadlock the war. This belief, too, was in error.

NOTES

This study was assisted by research grants from the U.S. Institute of Peace; the Bertha Von Suttner Special Project for the Optimization of Conflict Resolution; and Mr. Irving Young of London. I am also grateful to my assistant, Mr. Ronan Zeidel, for his help.

1. In interviews in London (January 1990) and Haifa (July 1991), Iraqi-born Jews educated in Arab schools in the Shi'a south in the 1940s told the author that teachers promised, to the enthusiastic acclaim of their pupils, "Iraq will conquer [*yahtall*] the Gulf, and make order [*yusawi*] in the Fertile Crescent."

2. See report by General Khalil Sa'id, commander of the planned operation, *al-Thawra*, August 21, 1992.

3. On the history of the Ottoman-Kuwaiti and Iraqi-Kuwaiti border issue, see Richard Schofield, *Kuwait and Iraq: Historical Claims and Territorial Disputes* (London, 1991).

4. See Muhammad Heikal, 'Abd al-Nasir's adviser, in *Illusions of Triumph: An Arab View of the Gulf War* (London, 1992), p. 30, reporting a conversation

between 'Abd al-Nasir and Nikita Khrushchev in 1958, following Qasim's coup. Khrushchev urged Nasir to tell Qasim to assure the West that Iraq's oil would continue to flow and all oil agreements would be respected. "If they feel the oil is threatened they will fight," said Khrushchev. Qasim followed the Soviet-Egyptian advice.

5. Baghdad Radio, July 18, 1990, *Foreign Broadcast Information Service* (*FBIS*), July 18, 1990, p. 23. According to Tariq 'Aziz, military hardware cost $102 billion and losses from lower oil sales was $106 billion. The official Iraqi figure for casualties was 100,000 dead. According to *Alif Ba*, 52,948 Iraqis died in Faw alone. The same figure appears on a monument in Faw commemorating the casualties. See *al-Thawra*, April 17, 1992. Casualties in each of the Basra, central, and northern fronts could not have been lower.

6. *Mahdar muqabalat al-sayyid al-ra'is saddam husayn ma'a al-safira abril klasbi yawm 25.7.90* (Minutes of the Meeting Between President Saddam Hussein and Ambassador April Glaspie on July 25, 1990), p. 4. Iraq's embassy in Washington published the text in September 1990. Western sources vary in their assessment of the debt. According to the *Financial Times* (September 8, 1989), by mid-1989 it was somewhere between $65 and 80 billion, half of it to the Arabs and half to countries outside the Middle East.

7. Interview with a representative in Iraq of a large European bank, London, November 15, 1988.

8. It later used these reserves to pay for the Kuwait war and domestic expenses after August 2, 1990.

9. See Iraq's housing minister confirming that rebuilding Basra and Faw was exorbitantly costly, *al-Thawra*, April 13, 1992.

10. See, for example, Saddam's interview promising a multiparty system, *al-Sharq al-Awsat* (London), March 8, 1989, in *FBIS*, March 14, 1989, pp. 29-30; and the joint meeting of the Revolutionary Command Council and the party's Iraqi Regional Leadership, the country's most important institutions, discussing a multiparty system and other democratizing steps, *al-Yawm al-Sabi'* (Paris), January 22, 29; February 5, 12, 19, 1990.

11. In June 1989, 150,000 troops from the First Special Army Corps were released (*Iraqi News Agency* [*INA*] June 22, 1989, in *FBIS*, June 22, 1989, p. 14).

12. Baghdad Radio, April 2, 1990, in *FBIS*, April 3, 1990, pp. 33-34.

13. Iraq spent roughly $5 billion in 1988, or 40% of export earnings on the military. Phebe Marr, "Iraq in the Year 2000", in Charles F. Doran and Stephen W. Buck, *The Gulf, Energy and Global Security*, (Boulder, Colo., 1991), p. 52. In 1989, with the war over and Iran at a clear military disadvantage, Iraq still spent $1.9 billion on arms imports alone (excluding expenditures on its nuclear arms industry). See U.S. Arms Control and

Disarmament Agency, *World Military Expenditures and Arms Transfers 1990*, p. 37.

14. *INA*, December 13, 1990, in *FBIS*, December 14, 1990, p. 16.

15. For Saddam comparing himself favorably with Egypt's 'Abd al-Nasir see, for example, his talk with 'Arafat, *al-Muharrir* (Paris), May 8, 1990, p. 3 (in *FBIS*, May 9, 1990, pp. 4-5).

16. Phebe Marr, "Iraq in the '90s," *Middle East Executive Report* (June 1990), p. 13.

17. *Al-Thawra*, May 13, 1990; *Hurras al-Watan*, May 20, 1990.

18. Consequently, the annual Army Day parade on January 6, 1989, was canceled. Interviews with Western officials in Washington, D.C., February-July 1989, and in London, October-December 1989.

19. Members of the Shi'a opposition told the author, in London in March 1990, that Saddam ordered that his internal security personnel view videotapes of Ceaucescu's demise to show them the danger.

20. See Saddam's complaint and U.S. Ambassador April Glaspie's personal apology, her denunciation of the general treatment of Saddam by the American media and her reference to a formal U.S. apology for the Voice of America broadcast, in the Iraqi transcript of her meeting with Saddam on July 25, 1990, *Mahdar al-muqabalat*, p. 4; and partial text in the *New York Times*, September 23, 1990, p. 19.

21. See, for example, *al-Thawra*, October 7 and November 17, 1989; February 6, 1990; *al-Jumhuriyya*, February 6, 1990.

22. Baghdad Radio, August 12, 1990, in *FBIS*, August 13, 1990, pp. 48-49.

23. "Minutes of . . . Geneva meeting," *Baghdad Observer*, January 20, 1992.

24. Iraqi foreign minister Tariq 'Aziz's letter to the secretary-general of the Arab League, Baghdad Radio, July 18, 1990, in *FBIS*, July 18-19, p. 21; *INA*, July 24, 1990, in *FBIS*, July 24, 1990, p. 24; and interviews with U.S. officials, Washington, D.C., January-August 1989.

25. Interview with Western official in the United States, January 28, 1992.

26. See Saddam's visit, *al-Jumhuriyya*, April 18, 1989; For Spot Image, see *Financial Times*, January 11, 1991.

27. *Al-Thawra*, February 8, 1989, cited by *INA*, in *FBIS*, February 8, 1989, pp. 21-22. For meetings between Iraq's leaders and Kuwaiti guests see ibid., pp. 19-21.

28. *Meeting Between President Saddam Hussein and American Chargé d'Affaires Wilson on 6th August 1990*, Iraqi Embassy, Washington, D.C. (September 1990), p. 2.

29. See, for example, 'Aziz's letter to the Arab League's secretary-general, ibid., p. 23.

30. See, for example, the Iraqi affront to Kuwait in a Gulf football championship there, the *Economist Intelligence Unit (EIU)-Country Report, Iraq*, no. 2, 1990, p. 11.

31. "Saddam Hussein Addresses Officials", *INA* in Arabic, February 19, 1990, in *FBIS*, February 20, 1990, pp. 2-3. The Gulf Cooperation Council (GCC)

representative at the conference, Sayf Ibn Hayil al-'Askari, timidly implied support for the Iraqi demand for an American withdrawal (ibid., p. 2). See also Saddam's speech to the heads of states, *Jordan TV,* February 24, 1990, in *FBIS,* February 27, 1990, pp. 1-3.

32. Interview with a U.S. official, London, March 8, 1990.
33. *EIU-Country Report, Iraq,* no. 2, 1990, p. 11.
34. Tariq 'Aziz to Milton Viorst, *The New Yorker,* June 24, 1991, p. 65.
35. See report in the *Financial Times* reproduced in *Ha'aretz,* November 13, 1992, of postwar British government encouragement to BSA Tools and Matrix Churchill to export to Iraq machine tools that could be used for arms production. Interview with a senior British official, London, November 16, 1989.
36. See, for example, *Middle East Economic Digest (MEED),* May 18, 1990, p. 16.
37. *Al-Muharrir* (Paris), May 8, 1990, p. 3.
38. CIA Chief Robert Gates, reported in *Ha'aretz,* May 10, 1992.
39. *Iraqi Television* and Baghdad Radio, April 2, 1990, in *FBIS,* April 3, 1990, pp. 32-36.
40. Lt. General Muzahim Sa'b Hasan, *Hurras al-Watan,* April 22, 1990.
41. Interview with Major General Avraham Tamir, ex-director general of Israel's Foreign Ministry (Tel Aviv, April 3, 1992). See also *Yediot Ahronot* (Tel Aviv), February 15, 1991. This was not the first such meeting. In 1987 Nizar Hamdun, Iraqi's ambassador to Washington, met two other Israeli generals—Maj. Gen. Avi Yaari and Maj. Gen. Ori Orr (later head of the Knesset Committee on Foreign and Security Affairs)—on study leave at Harvard for an informal discussion at a private home and later met one of them again. (Both interviewed by the author in 1988.)
42. Report on UN-sponsored International Atomic Energy Agency (IAEA) inspection team in Iraq, UN Security Council, *Note by the Secretary-General,* July 25, 1991, pp. 3-4.
43. *The New Yorker,* June 24, 1991, p. 65.
44. Bob Woodward, *The Commanders* (New York, 1991), pp. 202-203. Saddam received his assurance a few days later.
45. *MEED,* April 13, 1990, p. 18.
46. *Al-Thawra,* April 17, 1990, p. 3.
47. *MEED,* April 13, 1990, p. 18.
48. *Middle East News Agency (MENA)* (Cairo), April 8, 1990.
49. Interview with a British official, May 2, 1990, and a senior U.S. official, May 7, 1990. On similar Arab responses, see *MEED,* April 13, 1990, p. 22.
50. Radio Monte Carlo, April 22, in *FBIS,* April 23, 1990, p. 13.
51. Baghdad Radio, June 18, 1990, in *FBIS,* June 19, 1990, p. 21. Saddam spoke similarly at the Baghdad Arab summit in May. See Baghdad Radio, May 28,

1990, in *FBIS*, May 29, 1990, p. 5, and Saddam's interview in the *Wall Street Journal*, June 28, 1990: "If Israel attacks one [Arab] country and there is no response, then the second country to be attacked surely would be Iraq."

52. *Al-Muharrir*, May 8, 1990, in *FBIS*, May 9, 1990, pp. 4-5.

53. *EIU-Country Report, Iraq*, no. 2, 1990, p. 11.

54. *Al-Siyasa*, May 10-11, 1990, in *FBIS*, May 14, 1990, p. 14. Tariq 'Aziz in Radio Amman, May 15, 1990, *FBIS*, May 15, 1990, p. 8; for Iran's positive response, see Radio Muscat, May 13, 1990, in *FBIS*, May 14, 1990, p. 15.

55. *Al-Siyasa* (Kuwait), June 18, 1990; *Associated Press* from Kuwait, June 18, 1990; and *al-Jazira*, June 19, 1990. In early July it became clear that while Iraq was interested in an early summit meeting, Iran wanted detailed ground-work beforehand; while Iraq wanted direct talks, Iran insisted on UN mediation. Finally, while Iraq tried to skirt UN Resolution 598 specifying the order of priority, Iran wanted to follow that resolution. See *al-Sharq al-'Awat* (Riyadh) and *Ha'aretz*, July 8, 1990.

56. See, for example, Tehran Radio, August 6, 1990, in *FBIS*, August 17, 1990, p. 20.

57. *Mahdar muqabalat*, p. 14. For Iran's view, see *Le Figaro*, August 13, 1990.

58. See *al-Thawra, al-'Iraq, Qadisiyya*, June 10, 1990, in *FBIS*, June 14, 1990, pp. 24-25.

59. *INA*, May 30, 1990.

60. Ibid.

61. Mubarak's speech, *MENA* (Cairo), May 28, 1990; the king's speech, *INA*, May 28, 1990.

62. Shadhli al-Qulaybi to the Arab foreign ministers in Baghdad, *INA*, May 22, 1990, in *FBIS*, May 23, 1990, p. 2.

63. The May 30, 1990 speech was broadcast only after the Iraqi-Kuwaiti dispute became public. See *FBIS*, July 19, 1990, p. 21.

64. Interview, September 10, 1990, with a Shi'a opposition leader; and February 5, 1992, with an ex-senior U.S. official; *Komsomolskaya Pravda*, January 5, 1991.

65. After the Cairo Arab Summit of August 10 denounced Iraq's invasion, Iraq invoked the Baghdad Summit resolutions and demanded that, as they backed Iraq against all "foreign threats," the Arab League should denounce the anti-Iraqi concentration of foreign armies. See Salah al-Mukhtar, *al-Qadisiyya*, February 3, 1992.

66. 'Aziz in *al-Thawra*, September 9, 1990, in *FBIS*, September 12, 1990, p. 30.

67. 'Aziz protested to Klibi Kuwait's "procrastination" on Iraq's offer of a water pipeline. See *INA*, July 24, in *FBIS*, July 24, 1990, p. 23. This was strange, bearing in mind that the official Iraqi position had been that it was doing Kuwait a favor.

68. The emir to the editor of *al-Ahram*, published in *Liwa al-Sadr*, August 18, 1991.
69. 'Aziz to *The New Yorker*, June 24, 1991, p. 66.
70. Woodward, *The Commanders*, pp. 205-206.
71. Baghdad Radio, July 17, 1990, in *FBIS*, July 17, 1990, pp. 22-23.
72. Baghdad Radio, July 18, 1990, in *FBIS*, July 18, 1990, pp. 21-24.
73. See, for example, *Yediot Ahronot*, July 24, 1990; *al-Thawra, al-Qadisiyya*, July 19, 1990; the National Assembly's statement on Kuwait and the UAE, *INA*, July 19, 1990, in *FBIS*, July 20, 1990, pp. 17-18; *Qadisiyya*, July 20, 1990, accuses Kuwait and the UAE of "a large degree of hatred against Iraq's progress."
74. Interview in Washington, D.C., October 1992, with a U.S. official basing this conclusion on interrogation of senior officers who became prisoners of war.
75. As suggested by Ofra Bengio, "Iraq," in Ami Ayalon, *Middle East Contemporary Survey* (Tel Aviv University, The Moshe Dayan Center) vol. 14, 1990.
76. See his "Open Letter" to President Bush, Baghdad Radio, August 16, 1990, in *FBIS*, August 17, 1990, p. 21; Baghdad Radio, September 5, 1990, in *FBIS*, September 6, 1990, pp. 27-29; for "Jesus Christ . . . is the prophet of God and . . . he is an Arab . . . like [all] the [other] prophets from the land of the Arabs," Saddam's Christmas message, *INA*, December 31, 1990, in *FBIS*, January 3, 1991, p. 22.
77. Baghdad Radio, August 10, 1990, in *FBIS*, August 14, 1990, pp. 32-33.
78. *October* (Cairo), March 31, 1991, p. 3.
79. *Middle East Economic Survey*, July 23, 1990, pp. D7-D9.
80. *Kuwait News Agency* (*KUNA*) July 20, 1990, in *FBIS*, July 23, 1990, p. 15.
81. *INA*, July 24, 1990, in *FBIS*, July 24, 1990, p. 24. *Al-Thawra*, July 22, 1990, in *FBIS*, July 23, 1990, pp. 29-30.
82. Cairo Radio, August 8, 1990, in *FBIS*, August 8, 1990, p. 7.
83. Baghdad Radio, August 10, 1990, in *FBIS*, August 14, 1990, p. 33. While admitting the deadlock in Jidda, Hammadi, Iraq's leading expert on the dispute with Kuwait, apparently unaware of Saddam's intention to invade Kuwait, disclosed that meetings would continue in Baghdad "in accordance with the agreement reached by . . . President Saddam Hussein and President Husni Mubarak . . . and King Fahd" (*INA*, August 1, 1990, in *FBIS*, August 2, 1990, p. 25). This indicates that Mubarak's version was correct. *INA*, July 24, 1990, in *FBIS*, July 25, 1990, p. 23. Also *MENA* July 24, 1990, in *FBIS*, July 24, 1990, pp. 26-27.
84. Information in author's possession.
85. *INA*, July 27, 1990, in *FBIS*, July 30, 1990, p. 19.
86. *The Observer*, July 29, 1990.
87. Iraqi official spokesman, *INA*, July 27, 1990, in *FBIS*, July 27, 1990, p. 27.

88. *Al-Jumhuriyya*, July 28, 1990, in *FBIS*, July 30, 1990, pp. 19-20. See also *al-Thawra*, July 28, 29, 1990; *al-Qadisiyya*, July 29, 1990; *al-Jumhuriyya*, July 29, 1990; and *al-Thawra*, August 1, 1990, in *FBIS* August 2, 1990, p. 25.

89. *Ha'aretz*, July 19, 1990; *International Herald Tribune*, July 28-29, 1990.

90. *New York Times*, March 21, 1991.

91. *Washington Post*, October 21, 1992.

92. *New York Times*, March 21, 1991.

93. See, for example, *New Republic*, August 5, 1990; *Washington Post*, October 21, 1992.

94. U.S. analysts were puzzled since Iraq had not carried out exercises, as in the previous war; radio communications were far too low; and logistical preparations seemed inadequate. Woodward, *The Commanders*, pp. 205-12. But these expectations were wrong. Iraq did not need intensive training or large-scale logistics, since the enemy was only Kuwait. Iraq also had already underground logistical centers and telephone lines in the area, kept operational since the Iraq-Iran war.

95. Leslie Gelb, *New York Times*, April 5, 1992; *Washington Post*, October 21, 1992.

96. Cited by USIA, Norman Holmes, "Freedom of Navigation in Gulf Important to US," Washington, D.C., July 26, 1990, p. 1.

97. Elaine Sciolino, *New York Times*, September 23, 1990, p. 18; Woodward, *The Commanders*, pp. 213-15.

98. *Meeting Between President Saddam Husayn and American Chargé d'Affaires Wilson on August 6, 1990*, pp. 1-6. (The Iraqi Embassy, Washington, D.C., 1990).

99. Interview with a Soviet expert, December 13, 1990; *INA*, July 28, 1990, in *FBIS*, July 30, 1990, p. 23. There are indications that Iraqi leaders expected the Soviet Union to veto any anti-Iraqi Security Council resolution. Tariq 'Aziz expressed deep frustration that Soviet leaders refused to do so. See *al-Thawra*, February 14, 1992.

100. *Al-Jumhuriyya*, July 28, 1990, in *FBIS*, July 30, 1990, p. 19. Also *al-Thawra*, July 28, 1990, in ibid. p. 20; *al-Jumhuriyya*, July 29, 1990, in ibid., p. 22; *Meeting Between President Saddam Husayn and American Chargé d'Affaires Wilson*, p. 3.

101. See, for example, *al-Qabas*, *al-Watan*, *Kuwait Times*, *al-Ra'y al-'Amm*, July 26, 1990, in *FBIS*, July 26, 1990, p. 18.

102. See, for example, *KUNA*, citing the Iraqi press, July 26, 1990, in *FBIS*, July 26, 1990, p. 18; Woodward, *The Commanders*, pp. 216, 218.

103. Interview with a senior Shi'a opposition figure, September 10, 1990.

104. Saddam's interview to *Hurriyet*, February 10, 1992, in *FBIS*, February 13, 1992, pp. 22-23.

105. Radio Monte Carlo, August 1, 1990, in *FBIS*, August 1, 1990, p. 20.
106. 'Aziz to Viorst, *The New Yorker*, pp. 64-67; 'Aziz in *Milliyet*, May 30, 1991, *FBIS*, June 4, 1991, pp. 13-14.
107. Saddam's interview to *Hurriyet*, February 10, 1992, in *FBIS*, February 13, 1992, pp. 22-23.
108. *Mahdar muqabalat*, p. 18.
109. 'Aziz to Viorst, *The New Yorker*, pp. 64-67.
110. In 1989 Iraq received $1.1 billion in loans and loan guarantees for buying American foodstuffs, part of which was sold for arms. In 1990 the Bush administration approved half of the $1 billion loan guarantees Iraq requested over the objection of officials investigating the $3-4 billion Banco Nazionale del Lavoro fraud; and of officials at the Export-Import Bank because Iraq defaulted on some repayments. Iraq also received U.S. intelligence at least until May 1990, three months after Saddam criticized the U.S. presence in the Gulf. See *Washington Post*, April 28, 1990; *New York Times*, April 4, 1992; Mark Hosenball, *The New Republic*, June 1, 1992, p. 27. According to the *Statement of Henry B. Gonzalez, Chairman of [the House] Committee on Banking, Finance and Urban Affairs, Before the Senate Committee on Banking and Urban Affairs*, October 27, 1992, "U.S. export licensing policy toward Iraq permitted . . . licenses for conventional military uses. . . . In addition, while many export licenses were denied, the decision to treat Iraq as a close ally of the U.S. made it practically impossible to stem the flow of weapons useful technology to Iraq, despite ample evidence showing that Iraq used . . . U.S. technology for nonconventional weapons purposes" (p. 7).
111. Sa'd Qasim Hammudi, *al-Thawra*, March 16, 1992. In fact, these assets were closer to $100 billion. Immediately after the invasion, Saddam set up a puppet regime. Only on August 8, 1990, when it was clear this regime would be denied access to Kuwait's financial assets abroad, did he announce the annexation.
112. See, for example, his payment in gold that was delivered to Amman for a huge Australian wheat shipment (an interview with a senior Australian diplomat, Haifa, November 11, 1992). Before the invasion the Iraqi media announced that the new presidential palace would be very richly decorated with gold, which had been accumulated from Iraqi women's (compulsory) contributions during the Iraq-Iran war.
113. Based on an interview with an Israeli intelligence officer after the Gulf War.
114. Woodward, *The Commanders*, pp. 224-32. A well-informed Arab source told Viorst (*The New Yorker*, p. 67) that this was Saddam's view. According to Woodward, *The Commanders*, p. 229, General Norman Schwarzkopf had

similar expectations of the Saudis and was surprised when they decided to invite the Americans.

115. *Meeting Between President Saddam Husayn and American Chargé d'Affaires Wilson*, pp. 1-6.

116. For details see Amatzia Baram, *Culture, History and Ideology in the Formation of Ba'thist Iraq 1968-1989* (New York, 1991).

117. For details and sources see Amatzia Baram, "The Kuwait Crisis and the Gulf War August 2, 1990-February 28, 1991: Saddam's Calculations and Miscalculations," in Alex Danchev and Dan Koehane, *International Perspectives on the Gulf Conflict* (London, forthcoming).

2

Iraq's Army: Military Weakness, Political Utility .

Mark A. Heller

The 1991 Gulf War was, to a large extent, the result of Western exaggeration of Iraq's military capability. After the invasion of Kuwait in August 1990, Saddam Husayn could have been persuaded to withdraw only by the unambiguous threat of certain military action. That message's credibility, however, was undermined by the nature of the public debate in the West.

Predictions that Iraqi resistance would produce high allied casualties led many prominent participants in that debate to argue against a military response. Right up to the expiration of the UN Security Council deadline there was, therefore, still some doubt whether the U.S.-led coalition would indeed attack, and this ambiguity enabled Saddam to believe—or at least to hope—that he could avoid a war without withdrawing.

While some of the debate may have been informed by purposeful pessimism, the fear of casualties was for the most part genuine, based on Iraq's imposing arsenal and order of battle. Appreciations of Iraqi strength, however, tended to ignore the history and social-political role of an Iraqi army that consistently performed badly against foreign adversaries. A better understanding of these factors might still not have prevented war, but it would at least have prevented the overestimation of Iraq's combat effectiveness that so complicated American efforts at coercive diplomacy.

The purpose of this chapter is to analyze the persistent gap between Iraq's military potential and the actual battlefield performance of its army. The analysis proceeds from an assessment of the Iraqi state system and political order and of the army's role as both primary prop and fundamental threat to any regime. It then reviews the measures adopted by Iraqi governments to ensure the army's effectiveness as an instrument of state and regime maintenance and demonstrates that these very measures undermine its professionalism and operational capability. In short, the Iraqi army's domestic political centrality and military incompetence are intimately and inevitably related because they stem from the same source: the army's indispensability for state and regime maintenance in a barely legitimate, inherently fragile polity.

THE IRAQI ARMY AS INSTRUMENT
OF REPRESSION AND WAR

Certain features of Iraqi society explain important patterns in the country's political system, regardless of the regime's ideological inclinations. Of particular salience is the heterogeneous character of Iraq's population, which necessitates a semblance of sensitivity to the values of various ethnic and confessional groups while also compelling governments to assert strong central authority lest these groups' centripetal tendencies lead to the country's disintegration.[1]

There have been important differences among the regimes ruling Iraq since independence in 1932. For one thing, there has been a qualitative leap in the brutality employed by every successive regime in dealing with dissident Kurds, Shi'a, and other religio-ethnic communities, and even with political opponents from within the dominant Sunni Arab community.

Until 1958, the monarchy dealt harshly with its opponents (especially Communists) but nonetheless practiced a degree of self-restraint in the political arena that was notably absent in later years. The military regimes of 'Abd al-Karim Qasim and the 'Aref brothers treated their domestic opponents with considerably more ruthlessness, but it was applied inconsistently and interspersed with frequent acts of leniency. Under Ba'th party rule—during most of

1963 and since 1968—the violence and finality in dealing with political opponents grew by several orders of magnitude.

Notwithstanding the increasing cruelty of political life, however, some features of the Iraqi state system have persisted throughout all the different regimes—monarchical, officer clique, and Ba'th party. One of these—the army's centrality in politics—has been widely documented. Less frequently noted, though even more relevant to the international politics of the Middle East, is the consistently poor performance of Iraq's armed forces when tested against foreign military establishments.

Since independence in 1932, the Iraqi armed forces have functioned best as a domestic security force. Indeed, one critic argues that "the only army successes have been against tribesmen and defenseless civilians, events that have formed the mentality of the Iraqi officer corps in a very specific way."[2]

The army has consistently suppressed every sort of resistance to Sunni Arab control. The very first army "campaign" after 1932 was a pogrom against Assyrians who had asserted their loyalty to Britain and opposed the grant of independence. In 1935-1936, the army and air force put down a revolt of southern tribesmen (largely inspired by the institution of conscription) and since then has brutally crushed other manifestations of Shi'a discontent and waged war against recurrent Kurdish insurrections, winning almost every campaign though never quite managing a conclusive, permanent victory. Even in 1991, immediately after the very extensive damage suffered in the war against the U.S.-led coalition, the army was able to suppress fairly quickly the partially-simultaneous revolt of Shi'a in the south and Kurds in the north.

The army's effectiveness as an agent of internal repression stands in sharp contrast to its generally poor performance against foreign forces. In May 1941, the Iraqi army offered no serious resistance to a small British force sent to undo a coup by pro-German officers and politicians; despite German air support and superiority in numbers, Iraqi troops were routed at Falluja because they "simply did not have the stomach for a fight," and hostilities ended a few days later.[3]

Iraqi intervention forces in Arab-Israeli wars fared little better. In 1948-1949, Iraq dispatched almost one-third of its entire fighting force against Israel, and these troops' mere presence did affect the ultimate demarcation of the Israel-Jordan armistice line.[4] Nevertheless, the Iraqi army's passivity evoked much ridicule among Palestinians, who professed to believe that its standing orders were *maku awamir* (no orders).[5]

In 1967, the army again avoided any real engagement. In 1973, however, a fairly substantial force of over three divisions was sent to the Golan Heights to help stiffen Syrian defenses and was quickly decimated in its first contact with the Israel Defense Forces. Against Iran, its uninspiring performance in border clashes in 1969 and its clear inferiority afterward forced Saddam to concede terms on the Shatt al-Arab in 1975 that all prior Iraqi governments had resisted tenaciously. And though the Iraqi army enjoyed decisive superiority in technology, firepower, mobility, supply and support services, and even in numbers in important categories, most analysts found its battlefield performance during the war against Iran altogether unimpressive until well into 1987-1988. Finally, in 1990, Iraq made short work of the inconsequential Kuwaiti army, but its subsequent defeat at the hands of the U.S.-led coalition, though hardly unexpected, was nevertheless stunning in its speed and lopsidedness.[6]

In each instance, of course, the result can be explained, at least partly, by mitigating circumstances. In 1941, for example, the army itself was divided in its loyalty to Rashid 'Ali's "Government of National Defense." In 1948 and in 1967 the government was unenthusiastic about fighting Israel and sent a force largely for symbolic purposes. In 1973, intervention was on a more significant scale, but the lack of prior planning or coordination for an improvised expedition was a major handicap.

In the war against Iran, Iraq's army fought not just another army but a revolution whose zeal and capacity for self-sacrifice compensated somewhat for its logistical and professional shortcomings. Moreover, it has been argued that the army's performance in the war's early years did not reflect its true capacity because it was restrained by a political leadership fearful of high casualties and/or the irrevocable alienation of Iran.[7] And in 1991, the Iraqi forces, including the command-and-control systems, faced a technologically superior adversary and were subjected to almost six weeks of intensive aerial bombardment before fighting on the ground ever began.

In most of these cases, however, the "explanation" itself requires explanation. Why was the army divided about fighting Britain in 1941 and the government ambivalent about fighting Israel in 1948 and 1967? Why was a government that killed domestic opponents with such abandon so worried about casualties in the war with Iran, and why was the army unable for so long to bring its massive superiority in firepower to bear? Why was the performance of the air force and air defense in 1991 so poor that the ground war's outcome was a foregone conclusion, and why, even given total allied air supremacy, did Iraqi resistance on the ground collapse so quickly and completely?

The regular appearance of some intervening variable suggests that the explanation for the relative incompetence of Iraq's armed forces lies in some deeper structural cause, that is, in the same social-political pattern that produces other constants in the Iraqi state's behavior. The most basic of these causes is the fact that the state itself could be created, and its governments' authority subsequently sustained, only by the massive application of armed force against substantial sectors of Iraq's own people, who viewed both state and government as fundamentally illegitimate.

THE IRAQI STATE AND CIVIL-MILITARY RELATIONS

The circumstances surrounding the creation of modern Iraq need not be recounted here. It is sufficient to recall that an Iraqi national identity did not exist before the Ottoman Empire's destruction during World War I and that the mere demarcation of Iraqi borders could hardly eliminate the mutual suspicions and antipathies of its major constituent groups. Indeed, the formalization of British mandatory rule in 1920 was accompanied by a large-scale tribal revolt that could be suppressed only by massive force, especially air power. These operations' cost meant that some formula other than military occupation was necessary to preserve British interests, and the formula adopted was "the Arab solution"—indirect rule through the Hashemite monarchy.[8]

Faysal and his entourage of veterans from the anti-Ottoman Arab revolt were barely acceptable to the ex-Ottoman establishment and leading families of the Sunni heartland, who viewed them as "penniless parvenus and opportunists."[9] But they appealed even less to Iraq's other main religio-ethnic communities: the Shi'a, who viewed the new regime as an instrument for perpetuating Sunni control as under the Ottomans, and the Kurds, who feared the "Arabism" of a regime dominated by Sunni Arab nationalists or the ex-Ottoman officials and officers (mostly Sunni Arab) who soon joined it. For the "Arab solution" to work, an Iraqi army would have to be built that could enforce the central government's authority in Baghdad as effectively as the British army had done.

The British army, as agent of an external power, however, was basically indifferent to Iraq's domestic politics, provided Britain's own strategic interests were preserved. Its ability and willingness to sustain government authority were functions of British policy and society, and its "loyalty" from the point of view of Iraqi governments could therefore be taken for granted.

The Iraqi army was just as indispensable to the state's unity and the regime's maintenance, but its reliability was far less assured. Unlike the British army, it grew out of Iraqi society, potentially exposed to all the country's communal enmities, ideological currents, and political fluctuations; hence, it was far more dangerous to the very regime it was intended to protect. Iraqi governments therefore had to pay close attention to the army's political disposition (especially that of the command structure) as well as to its operational activities (especially to potentially threatening deployments of coup-capable forces). The solution to the challenge of state and regime maintenance was threefold:

1. to ensure the army's ability and willingness to suppress Communal challenges by building an officer corps whose composition mirrored that of the urban Sunni Arab ruling elite;
2. to intensify the army's political loyalty by more focused means, including purges of suspect officers and reliance on party or kinship ties in selection and promotion; and
3. to limit the opportunities for dissident unit commanders to act independently and perhaps turn their guns against the political leadership, by adopting a highly centralized command system.

This pattern of government-army relations was put in place during the British Mandate period, when authority and control were progressively transferred to Iraqi governments. By the time independence was formally granted in 1932, the army's organizational structure and its officer corps' ethos were already fully formed.[10]

The most striking dimension is the composition of the officer corps. About 640 ex-Turkish officers (mostly Sunni Arabs from Baghdad and Mosul) were commissioned following the creation of the army in 1921, and this communal bias was perpetuated, following the establishment of the Military College in 1924, through a system of direct commissioning of secondary and law school graduates, already steeped in the ultranationalist, xenophobic ethos of the government education system. In 1925, only about 25% of officers were of tribal origin, although tribesmen made up 75% of the rank-and-file.

A decade later, the imbalances were at least as pronounced; in a sample of 61 officers from a total of 84 with rank of commander or above in 1936, 90% were from the major cities (of which three-quarters were from Baghdad), and 58 were Sunnis (most of whom, given their urban origin, were presumably Arabs); there were only two Christians and one Shi'a, although 70% of the force was still made up of tribal levies.[11] For the next 20 years, more Shi'a and Kurdish officers were recruited, but, according to one observer, Shi'a and Kurdish representation in the elite was actually higher during the monarchy's last decade than it has ever been since then.[12]

This system of officer recruitment ensured that the army remained an effective instrument for suppressing tribal revolts and other manifestations of Kurdish or Shi'a discontent, but it could not insulate the army from other dimensions of civilian politics. For Iraq's military elite, and indeed for much of its Sunni Arab political class (many of whom themselves had military backgrounds), the army was not just a security force, but also a means of asserting and guaranteeing the nation's independence, an instrument of nation-building, and a carrier of the nation's virtues and goals (that is, an incarnation of the Arab nationalist idea).[13]

Officers arrived in the army already imbued with the spirit of militaristic hypernationalism fostered by the first two directors of the educational system, the militant Pan-Arab ideologues Sati'al-Husri and Sami Shawkat. These officers therefore viewed themselves as the legitimate interpreters of the "true" national interest, especially after the Assyrian massacre in 1933—engineered to assert its integrity, honor, and independence—led to the glorification of senior commanders and the army as an institution by the nationalist press and adoring crowds in Mosul and Baghdad.[14]

These attitudes, combined with the manifest ineffectiveness and unpopularity of almost all Iraqi governments, produced a climate of intrigue and contempt for the compromises of civilian parliamentary politics. Government leaders, of course, were aware of the threat posed to them by a politicized officer corps, but they were unable to dispense with the support of the army, both as an instrument to maintain the state's integrity and as a prop in their internecine power struggles.[15]

Instead, they tried to ensure the loyalty of the military establishment by relying on affective ties, especially family relationships, and by insisting on tight, centralized control of information and operations. In mid-1936, for example, Prime Minister Yasin al-Hashimi benefited from the fact that his brother, Taha, was chief of the General Staff.[16] For similar reasons, 'Abd al-Salam 'Aref recalled his brother 'Abd al-Rahman from retirement after overthrowing Qasim in February 1963, and when he eliminated the Ba'thists in November, he had 'Abd al-Rahman appointed acting chief of the General Staff.[17]

Such measures, however, could not compensate for the government's fundamental vulnerability. When political leaders failed to satisfy military expectations or otherwise offended its sensitivities and when circumstances (such as Taha's temporary absence from the country) permitted, factions in the army intervened, in the first wave (1936-1941) by replacing objectionable civilians with more pliable alternatives and, at a later stage, by taking power themselves (in 1958, twice in 1963, and in 1968).

THE ARMY UNDER SADDAM:
SUBORDINATE BUT STILL FLAWED

The major change since the Ba'th takeover in 1968, and especially under Saddam Husayn, has been the successful demilitarization of politics. Non-Ba'thist collaborators in the 1968 coup were ousted within two weeks, and even Ba'thist officers were subsequently eliminated from leading positions of power in the Revolutionary Command Council, party, or government.[18]

The army was effectively subjugated to civilian rule and became less vital to preserving the regime as alternative control mechanisms—the party and security services—grew in strength and sophistication. Nevertheless, the army was still the ultimate barrier of the Sunni Arab minority against potential state-breaking opposition by Kurds and Shi'a, and it remained a potential threat to the ruling Ba'th elite. Consequently, the Ba'th regime continued to rely on the same methods as its predecessors to maintain the state by preserving an officer corps that is, in religio-ethnic terms, an extension of the political leadership and to ensure its political loyalty by emphasizing affective ties.

The demilitarization of politics, however, did not mean the depoliticization of the military. On the contrary, the Ba'th regime went much further than any of its predecessors in thoroughly penetrating the army. Thus, it became a capital offense for anyone in the armed forces to engage in any political activity or to belong to any political organization apart from the Ba'th party itself.[19] A Military Control Directorate (reminiscent of the Main Political Administration of the Soviet armed forces) was made part of the General Staff, and political officers were interspersed throughout the command structure; indeed, party approval was required before many important orders could be carried out.[20]

At the same time, the system of military control retained the quasi-nepotistic features characteristic of previous regimes, not just through the Tikriti town connection (which has included such key figures as Chief of Staff Husayn Rashid and former Air Force commander Hamid Sha'ban), but even more so through direct family ties. Saddam packed the internal security apparatus with relatives, such as his half brothers Barzan al-Tikriti and Sab'awi Ibrahim and his cousin 'Ali Hasan al-Majid (later appointed defense minister), and the military establishment was controlled through the appointment of such people as former defense minister and chief of staff 'Adnan Khayrallah, a brother-in-law and cousin, and the former defense minister Husayn Kamel, the husband of one of Saddam's daughters.

Finally, the centralization of command reached unprecedented proportions. According to one report, for example, General Headquarters (GHQ) in 1990 had direct control over I through VII Corps, I Special Corps, the Republican

Guard Forces Command, various other General Headquarters troops and reserve divisions, and army aviation.[21]

Such measures preserved the army's effectiveness as an instrument of state maintenance and reduced the threat it posed to the political leadership; that is, they improved the army's regime-maintenance performance. But they also perpetuated the Iraqi army's deficiencies as a professional military force. In particular, they contributed to poor morale because of the religio-ethnic gap between officers and other ranks, purchased loyalty at the expense of competence in the officer corps, encouraged lack of initiative because of overcentralization, and hampered interservice coordination because of excessive secrecy.

These defects were exposed in most of Iraq's military confrontations with foreign forces before the Ba'th came to power, and except for a brief period toward the end of the Iran-Iraq war, they have been evident since then as well. Despite the co-optation of some prominent individual Shi'a to senior command positions, the disproportionate representation of Sunni Arabs in the officer corps and corresponding overrepresentation of Shi'a in the ranks has remained; according to one source, Shi'a made up as much as 85% of the rank-and-file in the early 1980s.[22]

Given the state of Sunni-Shi'a relations following the execution of many prominent Shi'a and the deportation of hundreds of thousands of other during the 1970s and 1980s, it would be surprising if relations between officers and enlisted men had changed much since the early 1930s, when a British intelligence report remarked, with characteristic understatement, that officers "only see their men on parade and are not in close sympathy with them."[23] Poor motivation and low morale, indicated by desertions, defections, and the very large number of Iraqi prisoners taken by both the Iranians and the U.S.-led coalition, undoubtedly stemmed, at least in part, from the religio-ethnic gap separating the officer corps and the common soldiers.[24]

Second, the politicization of the command structure continued to have a detrimental impact on the professional competence of officers. By almost every account, the constant purges, the emphasis on party and/or kinship ties, and the pervasive presence of political control elements (spies) either robbed the army of qualified leaders or at least stifled those who remained.[25]

Moreover, centralization of command and political interference induced qualified individuals in positions of command to subordinate their military judgment to political considerations; that is, it robbed them of flexibility and initiative. Officers were not only afraid to fail, which is a condition common to many armies even if the disincentives to failure under Saddam were rather extreme[26]; they also were afraid to succeed too much, since the prominence conferred by success could easily be interpreted as a challenge to the leadership.[27]

Finally, the centralized command structure and excessive secrecy hampered effective interservice coordination. This had a particularly strong impact on the air force, which historically played a critical role in facilitating or frustrating coups.[28] Thus, the air force had its own staff separate from GHQ and air bases were kept under regional commands, rarely receiving timely information from division commanders or passing it on to them. The result was very poor coordination between the ground and air forces. One consequence was the construction in 1984 of a 17-kilometer-long Iranian pontoon bridge in the marshes east of Basra without any interference by Iraq's air force.[29]

It is worth adding that the Iraqi Air Force, for reasons that are not altogether clear, has historically failed to press home its attacks even under favorable circumstances and has preferred to avoid battle altogether when faced with any resistance. In an incident in May 1936 that prefigured air force performance 55 years later, tribesmen in the south shot down two aircraft and so damaged morale among Iraqi pilots that the government pulled the entire air contingent back from Diwaniya to Baghdad.[30]

In 1991, the Iraqi air defense included protected, redundant command and control systems, 600 surface-to-air missile launchers, 300 interceptors, and 9,000 to 10,000 antiaircraft guns. Its performance was so listless that the result cannot be attributed solely to the skills and technical sophistication, however impressive, of the American and allied air forces.[31]

Some analysts suggest that the operational defects inherent in the organization of the Iraqi armed forces were so dangerous, given the nature of the Iranian threat, that Saddam Husayn was forced in the early 1980s to restructure the army on the basis of professional military considerations. Beginning in 1982, the officer corps was purged of "political hacks," political interference in operational decisions was scaled back in 1983 as party commissars were eliminated from command councils, competence was stressed in appointments and promotions, the command structure was decentralized, and Saddam removed himself from intense involvement in planning and operations.[32]

The result was a qualitative improvement in Iraqi performance. Talented commanders emerged during the course of the fighting and were given greater latitude to conduct operations independently as the war progressed. Depoliticization at lower levels produced pockets of professionalism, especially in logistics, which resulted in the strikingly effective management of defensive battles after the mid-1980s and made Iranian attacks futile and increasingly costly. Combined with Iraq's advantages in firepower, mobility, and technology, these changes ultimately forced Ayatollah Khomeini to drink the "cup of bitter poison" and agree to end the war.

Nevertheless, Iran's defeat was in many respects self-inflicted, and the fact that it was so ambiguous and took so long in coming is itself testimony to the flawed competence of Iraq's military. Even the "elite" Republican Guard was so badly mauled during Iran's 1986 victory in Faw that it had to be withdrawn and completely overhauled. And notwithstanding total Iraqi air supremacy, the subsequent recapture of Faw in 1988 was possible, according to some reports, only because of the direct and active assistance of Egyptian special forces.[33] Finally, the consistency of Iraqi military performance before and since the end of the war with Iran still show that Iraq's uninspiring military history is not explained solely by the unpredictable fortunes of war.

CONCLUSIONS

Every government would like to have an army that is both loyal and competent, a security force that is effective against both domestic and foreign adversaries. In principle, these objectives are not mutually exclusive. But in the circumstances of Iraq, there is an inherent contradiction between the requirements of state and regime maintenance and the cultivation of military professionalism and competence.

There are numerous other states—including several in the Middle East—with conditions sufficiently similar to Iraq's to justify a comparative analysis that tests the correlation and might yield some generalizable propositions. Such an analysis, however, requires the development of some indicators to measure state legitimacy, political centrality of armies, and military competence.

The challenge is to understand the implications of the correlation for the future behavior of Iraq, and perhaps of other states in similar circumstances. Iraqi governments have generally had no choice but to give priority to state and regime maintenance, and military competence has inevitably suffered. This contradiction cannot be resolved until an all-embracing Iraqi national identity and formula for political legitimacy emerge that permit the state and its governments to survive without reliance on the army. There is little to suggest that Iraq is heading in this direction.

Of course, what matters is not some abstract degree of military competence, but rather the relative military capabilities of potential adversaries. For Iraq, these adversaries are regional (Third World) actors who are either strong enough to resist the effective military power that Iraq can generate, given the constraints of its polity, or valuable enough to be protected by more powerful (First World) allies.

The consequence is that conventional military forces will continue to be of inherently limited utility to Iraqi governments bent on a foreign policy of grandeur. One alternative—to moderate international ambitions—is unappealing, and it is therefore not surprising that Saddam has chosen the other: to build up a deterrent and/or coercive capability based on long-range delivery systems and weapons of mass destruction. Compared to a regular army, this type of capability can be operated through a highly centralized chain of command with a small, elite force virtually isolated from the crippling distortions of Iraqi society and politics. The Iraqi army's poor showing since 1969 impelled Saddam to pursue this capability. The outcome of the Gulf War of 1991 undoubtedly reaffirmed the validity of the decision for him. It may well have driven others to the same conclusion.

NOTES

1. See, for example, Christine Moss Helms, *Iraq: Eastern Flank of the Arab World* (Washington, D.C., 1984), pp. 7-9, 200-204.

2. Samir al-Khalil, *Republic of Fear: the Inside Story of Saddam's Iraq* (New York, 1989), p. 21.

3. Ibid., pp. 179-80.

4. Dov Tamari, "The Influence of the Peripheral Arab States on Arab-Israeli Wars," in Joseph Alpher, Zeev Eytan, and Dov Tamari, *The Middle East Military Balance, 1989-1990* (Tel Aviv, 1990), p. 66.

5. Rosemary Sayigh, *Palestinians: From Peasants to Revolutionaries* (London, 1979), p. 79.

6. By one early reckoning, 42 of 68 divisions were rendered "combat ineffective" and 80 to 90% of Iraq's main battle tanks, other armored fighting vehicles and artillery were destroyed. "After the Storm," *Jane's Defence Weekly* 15, no. 4, April 6, 1991, pp. 529-30. Later damage estimates were lower, but still very substantial.

7. See Anthony H. Cordesman, *The Iran-Iraq War and Western Security 1984-87: Strategic Implications and Policy Options* (London, 1987), pp. 70-71; and Efraim Karsh, *The Iran-Iraq War: A Military Analysis*, Adelphi Paper 220, London (Spring 1987), pp. 34, 54.

8. The cost of the British garrison in Iraq amounted to £32 million in 1920-1921 and £23.4 million in 1921-1922. Philip Ireland, *Iraq: A Study in Political Development* (London, 1937), p. 312.

9. Paul P. J. Hemphill, "The Formation of the Iraqi Army, 1921-33," in Abbas Kelidar, ed., *The Integration of Modern Iraq* (London, 1979), p. 88.

10. Ibid., p. 105.

11. Ibid., pp. 98-99; Mohammad A. Tarbush, *The Role of the Military in Politics: A Case Study of Iraq to 1941* (London, 1982), pp. 78-79.

12. Phebe A. Marr, "The Political Elite in Iraq," in George Lenczowski, ed., *Political Elites in the Middle East* (Washington, D.C., 1975), p. 139.

13. Hemphill, "Formation of the Iraqi Army," p. 90; Tarbush, *Role of the Military in Politics,* p. 73.

14. Hemphill, "Formation of the Iraqi Army," p. 106; al-Khalil, *Republic of Fear,* pp. 170-71.

15. Even in the early 1920s, British advisers were aware that these currents of thought existed, but they took a generally lenient approach, hoping (along with the Iraqi government) that the army could help propagate "the national spirit" and arguing that "a political foundation is necessary for army personnel if they are to rise above the condition of mere mercenaries." Great Britain, Colonial Office, *Report...on the Administration of Iraq for the Period April 1922-March 1923,* Colonial no. 4, p. 110. For more on the effects of British "advice and guidance," see Mark Heller, "Politics and the Military in Iraq and Jordan, 1920-1958: The British Influence," *Armed Forces and Society* 4, no. 1 (November 1977), pp. 77-86.

16. Tarbush, *Role of the Military in Politics,* p. 118.

17. Majid Khadduri, *Republican Iraq: A Study in Iraqi Politics Since the Revolution of 1958* (London, 1969), pp. 199-200, 229n.

18. Marr, "Political Elite in Iraq," pp. 125-26; Amatzia Baram, "The Ruling Political Elite in Ba'thi Iraq, 1968-1986: The Changing Features of a Collective Profile," *International Journal of Middle East Studies* 21, no. 4 (November 1989), pp. 447-93.

19. "In July [1978] the RCC enacted a blanket decree making non-Ba'thist political activity (such as reading the Communist Party newspaper) illegal for all former members of the armed forces, with the death penalty prescribed for offenders. In a country with universal conscription, this provision meant that any adult male discovered engaging in non-Ba'thist political activity was liable to be sentenced to death. . . . " Marion Farouk Sluglett and Peter Sluglett, *Iraq Since 1958: From Revolution to Dictatorship* (London, 1987), p. 186.

20. Al-Khalil, *Republic of Fear,* pp. 26-27.

21. Gordon L. Rothman, "Saddam's Juggernaut or Armed Horde? The Organization of Iraq's Army," *International Defense Review* 23, no. 11 (November 1990), p. 1240.

22. Stephen C. Pelletiere and Douglas V. Johnson II, *Lessons Learned: The Iran-Iraq War* (Carlisle Barracks, Pa., 1991), p. 11. The Kurds were more successful at avoiding conscription.

23. Cited in Tarbush, *Role of the Military in Politics,* p. 119.
24. According to the U.S. Defense Intelligence Agency, 150,000 Iraqi soldiers defected during the course of the fighting. American and Saudi officials estimated the number of Iraqi prisoners at 60,000 by the end of the war. *New York Times,* June 5, 1991, p. A5.
25. For example, Marr, "Political Elite in Iraq," pp. 127-28; Karsh, *The Iran-Iraq War,* p. 11; Rothman, "Saddam's Juggernaut or Armed Horde," p. 1242.
26. After the withdrawal from Khorramshahr in 1982, two generals and a field commander were reportedly executed for "treasonous action." Helms, *Iraq,* p. 193.
27. This appears to have been the case with one of the war's most successful and famous battlefield commanders, General Mahir 'Abd al-Rashid, who was retired after the fighting ended.
28. According to one historian of Iraqi politics, it was an air strike on Mosul that crippled the Shawwaf revolt against Qasim in March 1959 and an air strike on the presidential palace that paralyzed pro-Qasim resistance in February 1963. Khadduri, *Republican Iraq,* pp. 110, 192.
29. Nick Cook, "Iraqi Air Power," *Jane's Soviet Intelligence Review* 2, no. 10 (October 1990), pp. 435-37.
30. Tarbush, *Role of the Military in Politics,* p. 114.
31. "After the Storm," p. 530.
32. Pelletiere and Johnson, *Lessons Learned,* pp. 11, 42-50; "The Lessons from the War with Iran," *The Economist* (January 12, 1991), p. 36.
33. See Adel Darwish and Gregory Alexander, *Unholy Babylon: The Secret History of Saddam's War* (New York, 1991), pp. 69-70.

3

Iraq's Shi'a and Kurdish Communities: From Resentment to Revolt[1]

Ofra Bengio

In 1932, when Iraq was about to gain independence, King Faysal warned the government of its extreme weakness vis-à-vis the population. Government forces, he revealed, possessed only 15,000 rifles compared to the 100,000 held by the populace. The king described the difficulty the army had in crushing the 1931 Kurdish revolt and raised severe doubts about its ability to cope with two rebellions at the same time. To rectify this imbalance, Faysal called for building an army strong enough to crush such uprisings.[2]

Faysal's vision became reality some 60 years later, when the Shi'a and Kurds rebelled almost simultaneously at the end of the Gulf War to challenge the regime and the state itself. Although the same immediate causes and short-term goals set in motion the two uprisings, their deeper basis and long-term objectives differed widely. Likewise, for the regime each rebellion represented a completely distinct problem and it responded differently to them.

Discussion of the Shi'a issue has been taboo in Iraq for many years.[3] So sensitive has it been that the word Shi'a itself was all but effaced from the lexicon of Iraq's media, literature, and history books. When absolutely necessary to allude to it, the more neutral term al-Ja'fariyya (the fifth school of Islamic Jurisprudence) was mentioned. The Shi'a themselves, over whose heads hovered the accusation of sectarianism, willingly went along with these silencing policies. As a result, very little information on the Shi'a, their grievances, and their aspirations traveled to the outside world.

An important attempt to break through this curtain was made in 1989 by Hasan al-'Alawi's book, published outside Iraq, entitled *The Shi'a and the Nation-State in Iraq (Al-Shi'a wal-dawla al-qawmiyya fi al-'Iraq 1914-1990).*[4] Al-'Alawi, a Shi'a journalist who had served under the Ba'th from 1968 to 1981, challenged various axioms and much conventional wisdom about the problem. First, he attacked British-Sunni collusion, which in the state's early days had given the Arab Sunni minority a monopoly of power, an act he views as the source of all evil in Iraq.

Second, he refuted Sunni insinuations and accusations that the Shi'a have been inadequately loyal to Iraq. He asserted that the contrary is true, as the Shi'a have carried the banners of Iraqi independence since the "great Iraqi revolution" of 1920, the uprising against the British in which the Shi'a 'ulama and tribes played a leading role.

Most important of all, al-'Alawi aired deep-seated Shi'a grievances. To preserve its monopoly of power, the Sunni government perpetuated all kinds of discriminatory policies against the Shi'a majority; accordingly, al-'Alawi maintained, they, and not the Shi'a, should be accused of sectarianism.

Shi'a members of the establishment lent their hand to this discrimination, with the result that the Shi'a were deprived of any real representation in the centers of power. Nor did al-'Alawi shield the Shi'a rank and file themselves from his sharp criticism, blaming them for living in the past instead of the present, for accepting the situation, and for assisting thereby in the entrenchment of dictatorship in Iraq. In his opinion, the only way to break the vicious circle is to bring about a radical change in the power system whereby the Shi'a would become the political majority.

To sum up, the Shi'a have never challenged the territorial integrity of the state and their main demands have revolved around their inadequate representation in Iraq's political system. Further, not since the crushing of Shi'a tribal rebellions in the 1930s has a serious religious or political movement emerged among the Shi'a to press for such demands.

The Kurdish problem is entirely different. The clash here has been between two nationalities, Kurdish and Arab; hence its intensity and long duration. In contrast to the Shi'a, who accepted "submission" (*musalma*), the Kurds have sustained their struggle intermittently for 70 years, and the tribal uprisings of the 1930s and 1940s have evolved into a more or less organized national movement. Further, although the Kurds have usually refrained from raising the slogan of independence, their very demand for autonomy has been tantamount to challenging the state's territorial integrity.

Their cooperation with Iran during the Iran-Iraq war was another trait differentiating them from the bulk of Shi'a, who on the whole remained loyal to Iraq. And whereas the Ba'th stood as a rock against any radical change in the power system of Baghdad, it did give in to Kurdish demands and granted them an autonomy that became, as it were, the Ba'th's original sin.

Since the formation of the Iraqi state in 1920, political maneuverings have largely resulted from the interplay of the Sunni-Shi'a-Kurdish triangle, with the Sunnis having the major role. The peculiar thing about this triangle is that the Shi'a and the Kurds have no common nationality or religious affinity, though they faced a common problem with the Sunnis in power.

To perpetuate their predominance, the Sunnis had to balance their two foes against each other or, at least, to keep them apart as far as possible. History has shown that although the Shi'a and Kurds were united by enmity toward the Sunni government, they made little effort to join forces with a view to changing this balance of power. This long-standing situation, although jeopardized by the March 1991 uprising, survived that threat. For many reasons, therefore, this uprising offers a good case study of the turbulent history of relations among Sunnis, Shi'a, and Kurds in Iraq.

THE OPPOSITION'S STRUCTURAL WEAKNESS

The March 1991 uprising was unique in a modern Iraqi history rich with revolts and uprisings because it was swift and spontaneous, engulfed the Shi'a south and Kurdish north simultaneously, indirectly involved more than one neighboring country as well as the allied forces, and presented the most serious challenge to the state's integrity since the 1930s.

The story of the uprising itself is easily told. It began in early March, immediately after the end of the Gulf War, lasted barely one month, and left the Ba'th firmly in power. The details of the picture, however, are much more intricate, for the event reached into the very heart of the Iraqi society and polity.

The way the Gulf War ended—in the Iraq army's near destruction and the regime's near collapse—seemed to give Iraq's opposition a golden opportunity to take power. In reality, though, the important question was whether the opposition had become strong enough to overcome the regime even in its extreme weakness.

The term Iraqi opposition covers a wide variety of antigovernment groups inside and outside the country. By far the Kurdish and Shi'a groupings were most important: among the Kurds, the Democratic Party of Kurdistan (DPK) and the Patriotic Union of Kurdistan (PUK); among the Shi'a, al-Da'wa, Munazzamat al-'Amal al-Islami (Islamic Action Organization), and the Supreme Assembly of Islamic Revolution in Iran (SAIRI).[5] In addition there are the Iraqi Communist party and other small groupings.

Taken as a whole, the opposition—as it knew—was extremely weak at the time Iraq invaded Kuwait. Muhammad Taqi al-Mudarrisi, leader of the Munazzamat al-'Amal al-Islami, analyzed this weakness's root causes as a lack of self-confidence, extreme dependence on outside forces, disunity and fragmentation, weak or non-existent contact with the Iraqi masses, and helplessness against the government's repressive machinery.[6]

The lack of unity was very acute among the numerous—17 to 27 by various estimates—opposition groups. Even more acute was the ideological and political gulf among them. Whereas the Kurds acted along national-secular lines, the Shi'a acted along Islamic-Shi'a lines; while the former saw their problem's solution as genuine Kurdish autonomy within a democratic Iraqi system, the latter regarded establishing an Islamic republic as the best solution to all of Iraq's problems. The Shi'a groups were no more tolerant of the notion of Kurdish autonomy than was the government itself. They viewed with jealousy any Kurdish achievement of this kind from fear that it would jeopardize their own standing.

Ideological differences between the Shi'a and Kurds were reflected, too, in their respective links with other groups—especially the Iraqi Communist party—which, though quite weakened, still retained a certain appeal. The Kurdish parties and the Communists had a love-hate relationship since both sides tried to attract the Kurdish people to its camp. The Kurdish movement gave shelter to the persecuted Communist party, while the latter helped Kurdish guerrillas fighting against government forces.

In contrast, the Shi'a groups regarded the secular Communist party not just as a rival but as a real enemy against which they should fight relentlessly. The Shi'a's fear of secularism meant that this opposition was largely masterminded by religious leaders or parties. There was no significant Shi'a secular force. Some limited cooperation between the fundamentalist Shi'a opposition and Barazani's Kurds notwithstanding, this lack of an all-Iraqi, universal platform raised a high barrier between the Shi'a opposition and potential supporters not just among the Sunnis but also among the secular part of the Shi'a population itself. As if this ideological division were not enough to weaken the opposition, there were other difficulties and drawbacks. First, there were rivalries among the Shi'a groups, as well as between the two main Kurdish ones. Cooperation between Kurds and Shi'a was hampered because of the physical separation between the Kurdish north and the Shi'a south in Iraq, due not just to geographical factors but also to the fact that the Sunni Arab sector of the population in central Iraq acted as a kind of buffer zone between the Kurds and Shi'a. The government also did its best to block any contacts between different parts of the opposition within the country.

Years of repression and persecution had compelled all the organized groupings either to be clandestine or to abide outside Iraq. In fact, most of their leaders and many of the members were in Iran, Syria, Britain, or scattered elsewhere. As a result, day-to-day contact with potential supporters in Iraq was severely hampered. Nor did a charismatic leader emerge to unify all parts of the opposition. Deprived of a secure income, groups had to rely on outside support, severely restricting their independence and often turning them into their supporters' pawns.

In the vital areas of military and organizational capability there was, once again, a vast difference between the Kurdish and the Shi'a oppositions. The former had long-standing experience in both fields; the latter, very little. Neither, however, seemed to have acquired influence or following in the most important power center—the army. The government's occasional implementing of the death penalty for any non-Ba'th groups attempting to infiltrate the army did not make the task any easier.[7]

To crown its difficulties, the opposition was unable to gain influence in the international arena. The West looked on Shi'a fundamentalist groups with the same aversion and suspicion as the Islamic Republic of Iran, considered their mentor. The Kurdish cause aroused some sympathy in the world media, but little else. No Western country, certainly not the United States or Britain, wanted to open a Pandora's box by granting legitimacy to the Kurds in any international forum. Nor were these quarters any more eager to question the legitimacy or wisdom of Britain's 70-year-old decision to confer power on the Arab Sunni minority, thereby perpetuating the imbalances in the Iraqi society and polity.

THE GOLDEN OPPORTUNITY

Iraq's invasion of Kuwait seemed to have changed the picture overnight. Emboldened by the regime's difficulties, the opposition started intensive efforts to unite, to present a better or more viable alternative to the government, and to initiate contacts with the anti-Iraqi coalition. But uniting its forces was more easily said than done. Long before the occupation of Kuwait, different opposition groups had initiated moves in London designed to bring about a rapprochement among the groups in exile there.

It was only at the end of December 1990, and after increasing pressure from Syria, that exile groups, conferring in Damascus, agreed on a joint platform.[8] The long months of debate showed the depth of rivalry and ideological differences among the groups as well as to their inability to agree on constructive goals. What emerged from the discussions was that they were united only in their wish to oust the Ba'th regime, but little else.

The 12-point resolution these groups issued did present some goals, such as the introduction of a new constitution and the establishment of a democratic system.[9] But such points seemed designed more to interest the Western allies than to represent the opposition's intentions. Worse still, beneath the facade of this joint platform lay deep ideological and political differences among the parties over Iraq's future political system and distribution of power. The debate on whether to open official announcements with the Fatiha (the opening verse of the Qur'an) was symptomatic of a whole range of problems.[10]

Crucial questions confronted the opposition: whether the Shi'a and Kurdish movements could coexist; whether the establishment of an Islamic republic in Iraq would provide a solution to the Kurdish problem; and whether the Shi'a majority would impose its views and policies on the Kurds in any future coalition government or whether it would acquiesce to their demand for autonomy.

To overcome these problems, a five-man steering committee was appointed: two Shi'a, one Kurd, one Ba'thi, and one Communist, each having veto power.[11] This semblance of unity encouraged contact between the Iraqi opposition and various members of the anti-Iraq coalition, which now included Saudi Arabia and Turkey in addition to their traditional supporters, Iran and Syria.

The Western media granted unprecedented coverage to the opposition, its leading personalities and views. The multiplicity of outside "supporters," however, did not enhance cohesion within the opposition since each country supported different groupings and sought to mold them according to its own views and interests.

Indeed, very much like the Iraqi factions themselves, the countries supporting them were united in their enmity of the Ba'th but had little in common in their view of who would replace it. For example, Syria supported the unity efforts of different factions because its chief desire was to see the Iraqi Ba'th ousted from power and replaced by a pro-Syrian government. Iran, on the other hand, ideologically and politically more inclined to the Shi'a groups acting under its auspices, regarded the Islamic solution as the best alternative. Saudi Arabia, the newcomer in this field, encouraged the activities of various Iraqi ex-officers.[12]

One of these was 'Abd al-Rahman al-Dawud, who had masterminded the July 17, 1968, Ba'thi coup and became defense minister in its first cabinet, only to be ousted two weeks later. Another was the ex-deputy chief of staff, Hasan Mustafa al-Naqib, who had fallen out of favor with the Ba'th in 1978 and ever since had been attempting to forge different alliances to oust it. An innovative move on the part of the Saudis involved attempts to establish contact with the heads of Shi'a tribes in the south, whose political influence had long been considered dead.[13] Turkey seemed to have restricted its contacts to Kurdish group since its main concern was the fate of the Iraqi Kurdish north and the repercussions on Turkey's own Kurdish minority.

It is not known what kind of support these countries granted the opposition in the prewar period; but this probably included organizational, financial, and moral support, although not substantial military assistance. Certainly, these countries did not expect the opposition to be able to oust the Ba'th and prevent the war. Rather, they used these groups as a ploy in their propaganda and psychological war against Iraq. At the same time, they tried to prepare the ground for the postwar period. The United States, chief arbiter of Iraq's fate, kept aloof from the opposition. Even after the war began on January 16, 1991, it was reluctant to establish significant contacts with such parties.[14]

At the beginning of 1991, three clandestine opposition radio stations began broadcasting: Voice of Free Iraq, Voice of Rebellious Iraq, and Voice of the People of Kurdistan.[15] The existence of a separate Kurdish station indicated their separate role from the Shi'a opposition groups, a fact later echoed in the uprising. While addressing the Iraqi people as a whole, these clandestine stations' broadcasts urged the army to act against the Ba'th and thus spare Iraq's people another terrible war.

The repeated appeals to the army indicated that the opposition carefully distinguished between the regime's civilian and military sectors, upholding the latter as a national symbol. It also implied that the opposition felt itself too weak to be able to change the regime by itself but was willing, if the army would join it, to use violence.

The occupation of Kuwait and the ensuing crisis presented the opposition with a dilemma. On the one hand, regarding the regime's demise as its own victory, it both sought the anti-Iraq coalition's support and offered to help it. On the other hand, a "blatant" alignment with this coalition would brand the opposition as a traitor to the country and nation. Its way out of this impasse was to condemn both the occupation of Kuwait and the war against Iraq.

This dual stance was not insincere. As on other occasions, the opposition was torn between its desire to see the regime beaten and a genuine fear that in achieving that goal, the Iraqi people would pay a heavy price. Its task was especially difficult because under the Ba'th, the dividing line between regime and state was indistinct. This predicament repeatedly forced the opposition to align itself with Iraq's enemies, while the regime always emerged or posed as Iraq's patriotic defender against both enemies. Anxious to avoid this bind, the opposition decided this time to defer its open anti-Ba'th activities until the very end of the Gulf War.[16]

THE SHI'A AND KURDISH INTIFADAS

The first signs of unrest appeared in mid-February 1991, when anti-Ba'th demonstrations took place in Basra and then in Diwaniyya where protesters raised anti-Saddam slogans and reportedly killed a number of Ba'th officials. Only after the unofficial ceasefire at the end of February did the Shi'a uprising start. This time the signal was given from the south, not surprising since the land battle had been fought there and potentially supportive coalition forces were close. The uprising, which engulfed most Shi'a towns and the countryside, was so intense and violent that it would not be an exaggeration to depict it as a civil war.[17]

The two Shi'a holy cities, Najaf and Karbala, joined the uprising, and government forces were willing to attack even the holiest shrines. This episode opened Shi'a wounds that had seemed long healed. The last Sunni military action of this scale against Shi'a holy places had occurred in 1843, when Muhammad Najib, Sunni Ottoman governor of Baghdad, had forcibly suppressed a Shi'a rebellion in Karbala. A contemporary historian reported that Najib's army had stormed the holy mosque of al-'Abbas and killed most of the people seeking refuge there.[18]

Spokesmen for the Shi'a opposition described the uprising as a popular, spontaneous intifada initiated and led by the people themselves, with no outside support.[19] There is little reason to doubt the uprising's spontaneity and popular nature since it spread within hours, feeding on new and old grievances of social and economic deprivation, political oppression, and national humiliation. The rebels reportedly used the light arms that the government had earlier distributed among the people to defend itself against the coalition.[20] They were also aided by individual soldiers and small units defecting to their side.[21]

Nevertheless, it seems certain that other elements were involved as well. Little is known about the intervention of the Saudis or other Gulf countries. It is quite possible that, having realized the uprising's direction and fearing spill-over effects on themselves, they preferred to keep aloof.

The Iraqi government blamed Iran for the uprising. Indeed, it appeared that Iran was the main foreign element involved, as the rebellion gave it new chances to realize a long-standing aspiration of expanding Islamic revolution to Iraq. Even before the uprising, it was reported that Iran had prepared two divisions to help change Iraq's political system. The first of these, *al-tawwabin* (the repentants), consisted of Iraqi war prisoners who stayed in Iran after the prisoner exchange between the two countries in 1990.

The second, the al-Badr division, was composed of Iraqi Shi'a exiles who had fled or been expelled by the Ba'th over the years. At one point, the head of SAIRI boasted that he could mobilize 100,000 persons for the Badr corps, a figure that appears greatly exaggerated. It is not known when or how these groups entered Iraq, but some of them—and probably Iranians too—acted as liaison officers coordinating the uprising in the south. Iran also provided some logistical and political support.[22]

The uprising in the Kurdish north started on March 4, not because of prior coordination with the Shi'a but because the Kurdish leadership had been waiting for the opportune moment. Even so, the leadership asserted that the uprising's beginning had been spontaneous.[23] The Kurdish movement, with its long experience of struggle against Iraqi governments, began preparing the ground for an uprising immediately after Iraq's occupation of Kuwait. The task was made easier by the government's pressing need to reduce its forces in the north to send them to the Kuwait front.

The Kurdish guerrillas, the Peshmerga, having suffered at the government's hands after the Iraq-Iran war, subsequently began to build bases again in Kurdistan. They relied on existing infrastructure and organizational links, in contrast to the Shi'a opposition, which had to start from scratch because it had no guerrilla or paramilitary organizations. Moreover, whereas the Shi'a had to rely almost solely on Iran's support, the Kurds could rely on Syria and Iran as well as on Turkey's tacit approval.

Months before the uprising, the Tigris River became the main crossing point into Iraq for Kurdish guerrillas and activists. One Kurdish leader maintained that guerrilla activities started in Kurdistan shortly after the occupation of Kuwait but stopped on the eve of the Gulf War. Even before the uprising began, pro-government Kurdish auxiliaries, called Juhush (donkeys), started joining the Kurdish movement. By mid-March, some 60,000 soldiers had reportedly changed sides, bringing their military equipment.[24]

The Kurds' main weaponry was said to be booty taken from the army. As in the south, the vacuum in the Kurdish area just after the ceasefire encouraged the uprising's quick spread throughout Kurdistan. Emboldened by initial successes, Kurdish leaders took an unprecedented step: capturing Kurdistan's main cities formerly garrisoned by Iraq's army. Within days, Sulaymaniyya, Irbil, and Dohuk fell to Kurdish fighters, as did the oil city of Kirkuk, a prime source of contention between Kurds and the government since the early 1970s. This spectacular success could be attributed mainly to the government's urgent need to withdraw forces from northern Iraq to protect Baghdad and put down the Shi'a rebellion.[25]

DIVIDE AND RULE

The euphoria of March did not last into April. Encircled by a double ring of internal and external enemies, the Ba'th pulled itself together in trying to win at least the internal war. Herein lies a paradox that led to a miscalculation of the regime's enemies. It is quite possible that the uprising's very eruption helped unite the Sunni section of the population around the ruling group, strengthening its cohesiveness, since any alternative regime might have jeopardized the entire Sunni group's privileged status. The miscalculation was that the Ba'th would fail as badly in combatting internal rivals as it had with its foreign enemies.

As to the intriguing question of how the regime weathered the crisis, the most obvious answer is its superior force and organization plus long experience in repressing any sort of dissent. The mobilization of Saddam's "ruling family" was remarkable. As early as March 6, the tough Hasan 'Ali al-Majid, Saddam's cousin, was made minister of the interior, an act that in itself could instill fear in the opposition. Another cousin was made governor of al-Ta'mim (Kirkuk) while brothers and other cousins, notably Minister of Industry and Military Industrialization Husayn Kamil, played an important role in suppressing the uprising.

The government also mobilized ex-generals who had retired or been punished—such as Hisham Sabah al-Fakhri and Mahir 'Abd al-Rashid—and appointed six high-ranking officers as governors of rebellious provinces. Against this determination must be weighed the insurgent forces' relative weakness. The regime's task was greatly facilitated by Iran's qualified support of the opposition and the coalition's vacillation between a desire to see the Ba'th ousted from power and its fear of the alternative government.

The victorious coalition's tacit approval for Iraq's government to use helicopters was critical to the regime's success in crushing the uprising. Besides its military importance, however, it had political significance, signaling the Ba'th and Saddam that the United States did not wish their fall but, on the contrary, wanted them to defeat the opposition. These signals reportedly discouraged high-ranking military officers from joining the uprising and ousting the Ba'th.[26]

The structural weakness of the Ba'th's internal enemies also aided it greatly. Although they acted simultaneously, they were far from unity or even cooperation. The Beirut conference they hurriedly set up in mid-March to assess the situation and discuss the future government revealed deep differences among the participants. The Ba'th knew only too well how it could divide and rule.

Aware of its inability to handle two uprisings simultaneously, the regime chose to start by crushing the Shi'a revolt. The logic was that this front looked more dangerous but was also easier to manage. Baghdad's proximity to the Shi'a battlefield and the capital's own Shi'a majority raised the specter of an uprising engulfing the seat of government. Possible intervention by coalition forces or Iran was equally worrisome. The regime had to regain control of the area as fast as possible and obstruct any attempt by outside forces to intervene. The hope was that quickly suppressing the Shi'a uprising would discourage the Kurds or at least give the government time to reorganize its troops and move them north, where difficult terrain and the rebels' experience made the military challenge far stronger.

In breaking the Shi'a uprising, the government used extremely harsh measures. No doubt, the regime had been surprised and infuriated by the event since—in contrast to the Kurds who had worked with Iran against Iraq during the Iran-Iraq war—the Shi'a had been loyal throughout. There was, however, a big difference between that war and the Gulf crisis, as far as the Shi'a were concerned.

After the Iran-Iraq war, Iraq posed as victorious, the regime looked stronger than ever, and Iran was licking its own wounds and did not seem able or willing to encourage a Shi'a uprising in Iraq. This was not the case, of course, after the Gulf War. Nevertheless, Iraq's elite force, the Republican Guard, had emerged with most of its power still reserved, while the Shi'a who confronted it were, by contrast, a far inferior, inexperienced, and unorganized force.

By mid-March, the government had triumphed. But revelation of such anti-government acts as destroying pictures of President Husayn, looting and burning government buildings, and executing officials were shocking proof of the depth of animosity toward a regime that still lacked legitimacy after 22 years in power.[26]

Accordingly, along with the uprising's suppression, the Ba'th took steps to appease the Shi'a majority and buy its goodwill, including intensified contacts with different Shi'a tribal leaders whom the Ba'th had formerly considered "reactionaries" but who were now badly needed to help pacify the Shi'a.[27]

The episode proved that old tribal loyalties were still entrenched in Iraqi society and that Saddam was willing to manipulate tribal chiefs much as the British had done during the 1920s.[28] The mid-March meeting between President Husayn and the Shi'a Grand Ayatollah Abu al-Qasim al-Kho'i, during which the Shi'a leader reportedly denounced the uprising, was another attempt to rebuild bridges.

By far the most important act of pacification, though, was the cabinet reshuffle of March 23, 1991, when for the first time in 22 years of Ba'thi rule, a Shi'a—Sa'dun Hammadi—was made prime minister.[29] This was another stalling tactic rather than a change fostering true Shi'a representation at the center of power. Hammadi was ousted from office in September and his replacement, Muhammad Hamza al-Zubaydi—though a Shi'a, too—was far less influential. (He was known, though, to have good ties with the Shi'a tribes.) Even during Hammadi's brief tenure, decision making continued to be the monopoly of Saddam and his close associates.

Baghdad's preoccupation with the Shi'a had led the Kurds to believe that the regime was too weak to mount a similar operation against them. Their victory festivals continued almost to the end of March, when Jalal Talabani, who began assuming the mantle of a Kurdish national hero, returned triumphantly to Kurdistan after two years in exile. As quick as the victory had been, however, so was the defeat that followed.[30]

Having secured relative quiet in the south, the government could now divert most of its energy to the Kurdish area. By early April, defeated, demoralized Kurds began an unprecedented exodus of up to two million people. The regime did not directly provoke the migration, but its 1988 use of chemical weapons on the Kurds surely encouraged flight. The Iraqi army's extensive use of phosphorous shells was probably designed to spread terror and panic among the Kurds, who mistook them for chemical bombs.[31] The Kurds' flight served both Iraq's immediate and long-term goals, robbing the guerrillas of logistical support and changing Iraq's demographic balance in favor of the Sunnis, a long-standing Ba'thi goal.[32]

Ironically, soon afterward, Iraq's government began autonomy negotiations with the Kurds, motivated by the need to blunt international pressure, gain time, and split the opposition. For its part, the Kurdish leadership went to the negotiating table to try to recoup something from the debacle. One thing is certain: Shi'a-Kurdish unity was shattered to the Baghdad regime's gain.

THE BALANCE OF WEAKNESS AND STRENGTH

Iraq remained intact as a state despite severe challenges from internal and external forces.[33] But the regime's attempt to use foreign adventures as a kind of crucible in which to create an Iraqi nation failed dismally with the Kurds. Instead of increasing their patriotism, wars gave them a chance to try to realize their own national aspirations. The Kurds had no qualms about cooperating with Iraq's enemies to achieve their aims.

Further, the government's harsh measures against them enhanced the Kurds' separate identity at the expense of the Iraqi one. As for the Shi'a, their behavior cast doubts on their commitment to the nationalism disseminated from Baghdad. The rulers' performance in office hardly inspired loyalty or belief in their competence.

The government, as in the past, possessed more power than all the opposition groups combined. Thus, the opposition's failure to oust the regime at its moment of greatest weakness showed the army's involvement was crucial for any successful revolt. And this point, in turn, highlighted the vicious circle in which the Iraqi state has been moving since its inception n 1920.

The anomaly of a Sunni Arab minority ruling a Shi'a and Kurdish majority can be maintained only by force. Since all means of coercion remain in this minority's hands, however, the chances of changing the situation peacefully are remote. Little wonder, then, that the 70 years of Iraqi statehood show a steady decline toward an increasingly totalitarian and dictatorial system.

One secret of the Ba'th's survival is that the civil war barely touched Baghdad, the center of power.[34] As in many past encounters with the Shi'a and Kurds, the more remote areas were the battleground. The government's command of the periphery has always been more precarious; on the other hand, the fact that the conflict was largely restricted to them bettered Ba'thi chances of triumphing in the end. To change things, the opposition would have to either win support from people at the center or muster a force currently beyond its capacity.

When King Faysal issued his warning in 1932 about the ruler's extreme weakness vis-à-vis the ruled, he reflected the reality of those days. Things have changed dramatically since then. Indeed, under the Ba'th, the ruling machinery in Iraq has become so overpowering, and the people so helpless, that very little can be done to check the rulers. The people have become victims of the most absurd wars and ventures.[35]

Saddam Husayn, the creator and product of this new reality, epitomizes the malaise of Iraqi society. No other Iraqi ruler has brought such catastrophes upon his own people and no other has escaped their judgment for such a long time.[36] So far, Saddam's adeptness at surviving has defeated all precedents. He emerges like a phoenix from the rubble of each new war.[37]

NOTES

1. A somewhat different version of this chapter was published as a research memorandum by the Washington Institute for Near East Policy in February 1992. Thanks to Barry Rubin for his incisive input into this paper and for his gracious hospitality in Washington while I was preparing this study.

2. Quoted in 'Abd al-Razzaq al-Hasani, *Ta'rikh al-wizarat al-'iraqiyya*, part 3 (Sidon, 1939), pp. 189-95.

3. Even following the Shi'a uprising of March 1991, Deputy Prime Minister Tariq 'Aziz denied categorically the existence of any Shi'a problem in Iraq. He did admit, however, to the existence of a Kurdish problem. Radio Algiers, April 27, 1991, in *Foreign Broadcast Information Service (FBIS)*, April 29, 1991.

4. Hasan al-'Alawi, *al-Shi'a wal-dawla al-qawmiyya fi al-'Iraq 1914-1990*, 2nd ed. (N.p., 1990). During the uprising, 'Alawi's name was mentioned as one of the opposition's leaders acting outside Iraq.

5. For historical background, see Amatzia Baram, "The Impact of Khomeyni's Revolution on the Radical Shi'i Movement of Iraq," in David Menashri, ed., *The Iranian Revolution and the Muslim World* (Boulder, Colo., 1990), pp. 131-55. For a detailed discussion of the fundamentalist groups, see *al-Shira'*, March 11 and 18, April 1, 8, 15, 29, and May 9, 1991.

6. Muhammad Taqi al-Mudarrisi, *al-'Iraq wal-haraka al-islamiyya*, London, 1988), pp. 32, 41-42, 77, 81-83.

7. Middle East Watch, *Human Rights in Iraq*, (New Haven, Conn., 1990), p. 28.

8. There were 15 groups according to the *New York Times*, December 30, 1990; 21 according to *The Economist*, January 5, 1991; *Middle East International* (*MEI*), January 11, 1991.

9. For the text see, Voice of Iraq (Damascus), December 29, 1990, in *FBIS*, January 2, 1991.

10. The Islamic movement had the upper hand in this debate, as the 12-point statement did start with the Fatiha. That the slogan of democracy was a mere tactic for placating the West could be deduced from one of al-Da'wa's leaders who declared later in the year that democracy could not blend (*mazj*) with Islam. In August Muhammad Baqir al-Hakim declared that his movement's aim was to establish the Islamic Shari'a in Iraq. *Al-'Alam*, January 26 and August 10, 1991.

11. *MEI*, January 11, 1991.

12. Jalal al-Talabani, the leader of PUK, stated in a February 1991 interview that Iranian support of the Kurds had been resumed, but did not go into details. *Kayhan* (London), March 7, 1991, in *FBIS*, March 20, 1991.

13. The chief of the Samawa tribes was quoted as saying that if war broke out, the tribes would "aim [their] fire at the regime." *'Ukaz*, January 13, 1991 in *FBIS*, January 17, 1991.

14. An opposition leader later complained that the only two embassies in Damascus that were not permitted to contact the Iraqi opposition were, ironically, the U.S. and Iraqi embassies.

15. The Voice of Free Iraq was said to be operating with the help of the Central Intelligence Agency. It used transmitters in Saudi Arabia, Egypt, Bahrain and the United Arab Emirates. Its manager, Salah 'Umar al-'Ali had been a

leading Ba'th party member in the cabinet of 1969. *New York Times,* April 16, 1991. The Kurds had been operating a clandestine radio station of their own on and off since the early 1960s.

16. Baqir al-Hakim, for example, emphasized the opposition's reluctance to mount anti-Ba'thi activities during the war in order not to play into American hands. *Al-'Alam,* January 19, 1991.

17. Opposition groups claimed that by March 10, the rebels held 29 cities and hundreds of towns and villages from the Kurdish north to the Shi'a south. *International Herald Tribune (IHT),* March 11, 1991.

18. 'Abbas al-'Azzawi, *Ta'rikh al-'Iraq bayn ihtilalayn,* part VII, (Baghdad, 1955), pp. 64-69. 'Azzawi commented that this event was due to the feebleness of the government of the time, though he also emphasized that in his own day, Karbala still needed a strong hand to govern it. See also Juan R. I. Cole and E. Moojan Momen, "Mafia, Mob and Shiism in Iraq: The Rebellion of Ottoman Karbala 1824- 1843," *Past & Present,* no. 112 (August 1986), pp. 112-43.

19. The term intifada for popular uprising had been used in Iraq back in 1952. The Kurdish uprising in 1987, which predated the intifada of the Palestinians, also used this term.

20. The distribution of arms was probably made by way of the Popular Army (al-Jaysh al-sha'bi), originally the Ba'th party militia. After the uprising the Ba'th decided to dissolve the popular army.

21. It is noteworthy that desertion occurred even in the Republican Guard. A military communiqué of March 8 called on "deserters" of all eight corps including the Guard to join their units within a week. *Al-'Iraq,* March 9, 1991.

22. *Al-Shira',* March 18, 1991; *IHT,* March 21, 1991.

23. According to Talabani, the leadership of the Kurds (and of the Shi'a) did not order the uprising: "The Peshmerga were outside the towns and only later did we decide to support the demonstrators." *Wochenpresse* (Vienna), April 11, 1991, in *FBIS,* April 16, 1991.

24. *Agence-France Presse,* March 12, 1990, in *FBIS,* March 18, 1990.

25. *New York Times,* March 13, 1991; *al-'Alam,* April 6, 1991. U.S. Senate Committee on Foreign Relations, *Civil War in Iraq* (Washington, D.C., May 1991), p. 1.

26. U.S. Senate Committee on Foreign Relations, *Civil War in Iraq,* p. 15.

27. On these events, see *Alif Ba,* March 27, 1991; *Financial Times,* April 15, 1991.

28. *Al-'Iraq,* March 4, 14, 19, and 24, 1991; *Babil,* April 22, 1991. (Babil is an Iraqi daily that began publication at the end of March 1991, edited by Saddam's son, 'Uday). In a speech later in July, Saddam Husayn stated: "You find the morale of tribal chieftains and people who live in rural areas

greater than in the city. Their endurance was greater." *Iraqi News Agency* (*INA*), July 19, 1991, in *FBIS*, July 22, 1991.

29. For British policy, see, Peter Sluglett, *Britain in Iraq, 1914-1932*, (London, 1976), U.S. Senate Committee on Foreign Relations, pp. 239-53.

30. *INA*, March 20, 1991, in *FBIS*, March 23, 1991; *Alif Ba*, March 27, 1991. The opposition claimed that Kho'i was kidnapped and forced to make the statement. Nevertheless, Kho'i, who belonged to the traditionalist trend in the Shi'a movement, was earlier said to have given his tacit support to the Ba'th by opposing a Shi'a revolution along Iranian lines. *Al-Shira'*, April 8, 1991.

31. Commenting on the causes of the "quick collapse" of the Kurdish rebellion, *al-Jumhuriyya* said that the rebels had not fought for a just cause, that they were supported by foreign countries, and that they antagonized the Arab citizens of the cities they occupied. *Al-Jumhuriyya*, April 15, 1991.

32. U.S. Senate Committee on Foreign Relations, *Civil War in Iraq*, p. 10. Western journalists were told so by Kurdish refugees. Iraqi forces also reportedly "staged" chemical attacks, *Ha'aretz*, April 15, 1991.

33. For Ba'thi "demographic disinformation" regarding the percentage of Kurds, see Ofra Bengio, "Iraq," Ami Ayalon, *Middle East Contemporary Survey*, 1989, pp. 396-97; *Hurras al-Watan*, July 15, 1990.

34. One is reminded of Richard Coke's observation at the start of the British Mandate: "The Mesopotamian nation was to be a new experiment in nation building; it was to demonstrate the belief prevalent in the West that there is nothing in the world which cannot, if necessary be made by machinery. No great evidence was forthcoming that the native population of Mesopotamia wanted to be a nation . . . but the League of Nations and the British government conceived it an excellent way of disposing of a country that was threatening to become a nuisance." Richard Coke, *The Heart of the Middle East* (London, 1925), p. 217.

35. As soon as the uprising began, the government promptly started collecting hundreds of thousands of arms that it had earlier distributed among the residents of Baghdad. *Jordan Times*, March 23, 1991, in *FBIS*, March 27, 1991.

36. The number of people killed during the intifadas alone was estimated at between 6,000 to 30,000. *MERIP Reports*, July-August 1991; *al-Ittihad* (Abu Dhabi), August 8, 1991; *Le Monde*, January 13, 1992.

37. Shortly after the uprisings were crushed, the military organ, *al-Qadisiyya*, published a poem in Saddam Husayn's honor: "The land is the body and you are the soul." *Al-Qadisiyya*, April 25, 1991.

The Crisis's Economic
Roots and Repercussions

4

Iraq's Economy and International Sanctions

.

Patrick Clawson

Iraq's economy has much potential. Its resources are excellent to superb. The country has rich agricultural land. Its manpower is relatively extensive and well trained. Iraq's oil resources are the world's second largest, after Saudi Arabia.[1] At 65 barrels per person per year, Iraq's oil production capacity should provide sufficient resources to make the country prosperous; after all, that is a higher level of production than in such Gulf Cooperation Council (GCC) nations as Bahrain and Oman.

Despite these many advantages, Iraq has remained a poor country compared to its GCC neighbors. The tragedy of the Iraqi economy is that such a potentially rich nation has been cursed with a government so uninterested in its people's economic well-being. In particular, successive Iraqi regimes pursued economic policies that put ideology above growth. The two sectors suffering the most have been oil and agriculture.

The antigrowth policies grew worse under the Ba'th party and especially under Saddam Husayn but date back to the pre-1958 monarchy. Iraq has taken an isolationist, confrontational approach to the international oil industry, such as in the long dispute over the Rumayla oilfield.[2] If Iraq had been willing to cooperate with the world oil industry and to use fully foreign technology and expertise, its output could have been twice the actual level.

In agriculture, the Ba'th put first its ideology of state control although it reduced output. Iraq was a food exporter for 3,000 years, until after the 1958 land reforms and subsequent Ba'th actions to reinforce state control over the economy. The output of Iraq's main crops—cereals and dates—was below the 1957 levels.[3] That was a world-class record of failure matched by only two or three African countries.

Tragic as the antigrowth policies have been, Iraq's fundamental economic problem was that government policy wastes the available resources. The most important part of that profligacy has been a massive military machine. Contrast Iraq and Kuwait. Saddam spent $50 billion during the 1980s just on arms imports.[4] During that same decade, Kuwait's government invested $50 billion in its reserve funds. The result by 1990: Iraq had 100,000 to 150,000 dead on the battlefield, while Kuwait had an investment portfolio that had increased in value to $100 billion.[5]

Military adventurism was not the only reason for Iraq's economic plight. Ba'thist economic policy also wasted resources on inappropriate investment, following the classic Stalinist approach of gigantic projects. One example was the transformation of Baghdad in the early 1980s in preparation for the Non-Aligned Summit Meeting, which in the end was not held in Iraq because of the war.

Saddam has a Nebuchadnezzar complex: He wants to build vast towers to his glory. From the data available in the *Annual Abstract of Statistics*, it would appear that Iraq had to invest at least $10 in capital for each $1 increase in output, which is a remarkably low level of capital efficiency. The ration of investment to output (ICOR) in Egypt and Jordan in 1980-87 was 5.6; the newly industrialized countries of southeast Asia have ICORs of about 2.5.[6]

Besides wasting Iraq's resources on inappropriate investment, Saddam imposed such rigid controls on the private sector that much of the nation's productive capacity was underutilized and much of its people's effort was misdirected into fulfilling government directives instead of producing useful goods. Saddam's regime has extraordinary detailed controls over the economy, down to official prices for vegetables. Saddam's "liberalization" program announced with great fanfare in 1988 did little to change the pervasive state presence. As a measure of Iraq's level of repression, one of the liberalization steps was to drop the requirement for a secret police license for each individual typewriter.

Neither Saddam nor his predecessors have been willing to sacrifice the political ideals they hold sacred for economic gain. The true political goals are of course not necessarily those proclaimed, and Saddam's chief priority has been strict control over society. He is not committed to classic socialism. It would be imprudent to assume that Saddam might change course and suddenly give priority to economics over politics or let businessmen gain the independence to ignore government pressure. The historical record suggests that Saddam will not be easily deterred by economic problems.

THE IRAQI ECONOMY 1988-1990

Saddam's claims about Iraq's financial plight before the invasion of Kuwait have received an all-too-receptive ear from many Western observers.[7] Before the invasion, his basic argument was that Kuwaiti overproduction of oil caused an acute crisis for Iraq's economy, already suffering from a heavy debt incurred to defend the Arab cause during the Iran-Iraq war.

To this he added some last-minute claims that Kuwait had been pumping Iraqi oil from a field along the border. The implication was that the Iraq-Kuwait dispute was economic, leading some to speculate that Iraq might leave Kuwait if an attractive financial package could be assembled. In fact, Iraq's claims of economic damage by Kuwaiti action were without much foundation. Kuwait's pumping from the shared oilfield with Iraq was well within international norms (unlike Iraq's wells slanted at a steep angle to take oil from under the border) and Organization of Petroleum-Exporting Countries (OPEC) quotas were hardly inviolable obligations on Kuwait. Iraq claims were used to mask the fundamental failure of the statist economics applied by the ruling Ba'th party.

Contrary to Iraq's claim that it faced an immediate economic crisis, Iraq's short-term economic situation was better in 1990 than it had been for some years. Iraq paid $3.4 billion in debt service in the first three months of 1990, more than it paid in all of 1989 and much more than anyone expected.[8]

In 1990, Iraq paid more on its debt than either Brazil or Argentina did on their much larger debts. In addition, Iraq boosted its allocations for civilian imports by $1.4 billion, or 16%, in July—not exactly the action of a country with an empty wallet.[9]

Imports in the first half of 1990 were running above the 1989 level and at 25% above the 1986 low. Further, despite Saddam's complaints about loss of oil revenue, Iraq's oil income was steadily rising. In 1989, oil earnings were 70% higher than in 1986. Even under a pessimistic price scenario, Iraq's 1990 oil earnings would have equaled the 1989 level, thanks to higher output.[10] Iraq's economic problems are systemic and long term, not a short-term crisis caused by temporary Kuwaiti high oil production.

Before the invasion of Kuwait, Iraqi spokesmen liked to claim their country deserved special consideration because of its heavy debt, which they described as having been incurred defending Arab interests against Iran. In fact, Iraq's debt burden was not so large if one excludes debts to Arab states—debts that no country was then pressing Iraq to repay.[11]

The standard measure of a debt burden is the relation of debt to exports. Before the invasion, Iraq's debt was roughly $40 billion.[12] Iraq's 1989 exports were $15 billion, including non-oil goods ($0.5 billion) and services ($1 billion). The debt-to-exports ratio was therefore 2.7, far below the level for heavily indebted Third World nations.

Consider Turkey, which had about the same debt ($42 billion at the end of 1989) and exports ($19 billion in 1989) as Iraq; Turkey is said to be a success story, not an irredeemable basket case. Egypt before the Gulf crisis had $49 billion in debt and only $10 billion in exports—a ratio of five to one. Five to one is the ratio characterizing countries with real debt crisis, such as Argentina.[13]

The real economic factor behind the invasion was that Saddam Husayn, unwilling to abandon his grandiose policies, was unable to meet public expectations that the ceasefire with Iran would bring prosperity. Saddam's only strategy for growth was to order more and more huge projects. Thus, Iraq's technocrats prepared in 1988-1990 detailed plans for $30 to 50 billion of white elephants: a Baghdad metro, Mosul airport, 1,900 miles of railways, six-lane expressways to Turkey and Jordan, two large dams (Madawa and Badush), an 1800-megawatt power station (Al-Anbar), an oil refinery (near Baghdad), a 1- to 2-million-ton iron and steel complex, a 200,000-ton aluminum smelter, a factory to make 1 million tires a year, plus the multibillion-dollar Petrochemical Plant Number 2.[14]

These plans were far beyond the country's financial capacity unless phased over 20 years. To be sure, Iraq could afford to carry out over the next five years some of these projects, but not the package as a whole. Saddam was unable to set priorities; he insisted on pressing ahead on every front simultaneously, just as he demanded developing simultaneously a broad range of sophisticated weapons.

As a result, resources were wasted in starting so many projects that many were halted half built. More important, so many resources were channeled into large-scale projects that few resources were left for small-scale investments much more vital for growth. The economy would have grown much faster if $1 or $2 billion dollars a year had been transferred from these megaprojects to a free foreign exchange market in which entrepreneurs could have bought the dollars they needed for inexpensive equipment to expand output of simple consumer goods and of vegetables, which were imported (particularly from Jordan) because of the low level of Iraq's output.

Saddam's love for gigantic projects left him dissatisfied with the limited earnings he could expect from Iraq's oil industry. He wanted a continuing flow of many billions, which he would get only by grabbing additional oilfields or by making himself the man who dictated low oil quotas for other producers (with the short-term goal of raising prices and the medium-term goal of increasing Iraq's export opportunities).

He had plans to spend much more than the $18 billion a year he could expect pre-crisis from oil, non-oil exports, and some small borrowing. His announced investment projects, his ministers' promises about imports for the private sector, and his military-industrial program would have taken at least $25 billion a year if not more.

Furthermore, the history of Saddam's rule suggests that he continually enlarged the portfolio of capital-intensive projects to a size Iraq could not afford. He did not want the mere $2.4 billion one-time payment that his ministers mentioned in late July 1990 as compensation for oil Kuwait allegedly pumped from an oilfield overlapping the Kuwait-Iraq border. Saddam was after grand larceny, not petty theft.

The historical record suggests that if Saddam had every penny of Kuwait's revenues, he would have wasted the money and Iraq would still be a poor country, though of course richer than it had been. Give him another $50 billion, and he would spend it on arms (or the arms industry) and inappropriate large-scale civilian development projects.

He would improve the civilian standard of living, if only to assure domestic support, but primarily through transfer payments and government programs that could not be continued unless oil revenues rose ever higher. Saddam would never put Iraq on the path to self-sustained development. The Iraq-Kuwait conflict was a clash between competent and incompetent, not between haves and have-nots.

THE EFFECT OF SANCTIONS AND WAR ON IRAQ'S ECONOMY, 1990-1991

Sanctions caused a substantial drop in the Iraqi standard of living. In the first two or three months, Iraqis did not feel the pain. They benefited from the looting of Kuwait, which led to a tremendous increase in the stock of consumer durables, including perhaps 50,000 automobiles alone. Those lucky enough to steal in Kuwait obviously did well, but so did the ordinary Baghdad consumer.

The streets were said to be full of vendors of goods from Kuwait, goods of a quality and profusion not seen in Baghdad since before the war, if even then.

In addition, some of the refugees fleeing Kuwait sold their possessions at bargain prices to raise money for the trip home.[15] But this windfall gain from the loot of Kuwait was soon gone. Well before the war started in January, sanctions had reduced Iraqi living standards. The bombing and especially the civil war in March-April 1991 was to disrupt supply channels to the point that Iraqis were forced to eat wild plants and to go hungry.[16]

After the war, living standards improved significantly. By June or July 1991, the government was distributing on a regular basis rations providing 1,200 to 1,500 calories per day.[17] These rations cost a family of six about 11 dinars in August 1991, compared to their free market value of 219 dinars. This sum left a family dependent on a typical unskilled laborer's salary with only about 200 dinars per month.[18]

With that sum and given food prices for six cities provided by the United Nation's World Food Program, I estimate a family could have at least 2,000 calories per person per day if they devoted all of one wage-earner's income to food. That was not a good diet and was well below the Iraqi prewar 3,000 calorie-per-day diet, but it was sufficient to sustain life.[19]

Furthermore, this level of rations could be sustained with no more than $600 million a year in imports, based on world market prices for the inputs and the Food and Agricultural Organization's very low estimate of Iraq's domestic food output in 1991.[20] Meanwhile, Iraq imported $1 to 1.5 billion of food in 1991-1992 according to data from suppliers and information given the UN Sanctions Committee by the Jordanian and Turkish governments.[21]

The international and charitable organizations active in Iraq insist, in the words of Jean Dreze and Harris Gadar, that "Iraq's public distribution system is an exemplary one in terms of coverage, equity, efficiency, and the amount distributed."[22] If that is the case, there was little starvation in Iraq since the government imported food at a rate well in excess of what is needed to sustain life.

Industry was greatly affected both by sanctions and by the war damage; the latter mattered mostly through its effects on infrastructure such as bridges, since direct damage to industry was slight. Industrial output fell sharply but factories continued to operate at a reduced level. For example, cement production in the second half of 1991 was forecast in August 1991 to be 610,000 tons, 20% of the 1987 level. The most likely explanation for the low output is the same as for the four factories producing various products visited by Dreze and Gadar: lack of electricity, inputs, and skilled foreign labor, not direct war damage.[23]

Despite limited supplies of spare parts and inputs, industry could operate at low levels using pre-crisis inventories and delaying repairs, partly by relying on cannibalization, since capacity utilization in Iraqi factories was below 50% anyway.

The industries that most concerned Iraq's government were those in which consumers immediately felt any shutdown. Three principal industries fit this bill, and all were operating in August 1991 at levels satisfactory for domestic consumption: oil refineries, electric generating plants, and the water systems. The report of the Secretary-General's Executive Delegate Sadruddin Aga Khan, who visited Iraq in July 1991 with a team of experts, stated that the Baiji, Dora, and Basra oil refineries were producing 460,000 barrels per day, compared to prewar consumption of about 700,000 barrels.[24] This level was probably sufficient to meet demand for most oil products, given that demand dropped because families were using their available income to pay for food.

The Aga Khan report concluded in July 1991, "The power generating capacity has been restored to 25% of the prewar level. As it is operating continuously, electricity production is about 40% of the 1990 level."[25] Given the shutdown of most industries—which consumed much of the prewar electricity—the electricity for consumers was at well over half of the prewar level. Electricity output seemed sufficient to meet all consumer demands other than air conditioning.

The Aga Khan report found that water was being supplied in July 1991 to 85% of the 17 million Iraqis who relied on the government water system prewar.[26] The amounts available varied, but the report estimated that supplies on aggregate·were 40% of the prewar level, (that is, 100 liters per person per day instead of 250 liters). Because of the priority given to pumping water instead of sewage, waste water accumulated in some low-lying areas (especially in Basra) and polluted the Tigris downriver from Baghdad.

Journalists and experts such as those on the Aga Khan team repeated a forecast that Iraqi industrial output would deteriorate from the July 1991 levels because, after the initial recovery from war damage, shortages of spare parts and inputs would be likely to accelerate. In fact, there was no evidence of such problems. Each subsequent team of experts—such as the international study teams assembled by Harvard University activists that visited Iraq in August 1991—found that electrical and industrial production was increasing. It is plausible to argue that the worst was past for Iraq's economy and a slow recovery was under way.

Iraq's medium-term outlook depended mainly on its ability to generate foreign exchange to finance imports. The UN Security Council established procedures under Resolutions 706 and 712 to let Iraq export oil sufficient to generate $933.7 million over six months for humanitarian imports, as well as for reparations and for UN ceasefire and arms control monitoring.

As of January 1992, Iraq had agreed to the UN conditions for oil sales, which were designed to reduce opportunities for Iraq to divert funds from humanitarian imports, including a range of industrial inputs, although the United States blocked permission for imports of anything other than food, medicines, and a limited range of other goods. In any case, Saddam could always have access to $934 million if he felt a need. That he had not agreed to the oil sales suggests that Iraq's foreign exchange position was not so desperate. Let us see why.

Iraq could have generated $2 billion in foreign exchange in 1991-1992 independent of the UN actions, much of it by the private sector or provided by charitable organizations, reducing what the Iraqi government had to spend from its own pocket. The principal sources could have been:

1. Gold sales. The last data provided by the International Monetary Fund on gold holdings was for 1977, when Iraq had 130 tons of gold.[27] Iraq's ambassador to the UN reported that its holdings had not changed in 20 years. In addition, the stock of gold jewelry in Iraq pre-crisis appeared to have been 100 to 300 tons.[28] Private Kuwaitis appear to have had at least 200 and perhaps as much as 400 tons.[29] Disposing of this gold would be no problem, since Turkish jewelers alone buy 100 tons of old jewelry per year.[30] Sales of 50 tons would bring in $500 million.

2. Non-oil exports. Agricultural goods such as lambs and vegetables were said to be flowing into Kuwait, while animal products were being trucked into Jordan.[31] Used goods, including construction equipment, cars and advanced home electronics were reportedly arriving in Iran.[32] Each of these two sources could be worth $100 million a year, or $200 million combined.

3. Oil trucked overland to Jordan. Jordan informed the UN that such oil imports had resumed and would be used only to retire Iraq's debt to Jordan. It took remarkable credulity to accept at face value the statement that Saddam Husayn was shipping oil for the sole purpose of repaying his debt, an activity not known to be high on his priority list. The *London Observer* reported a variety of mechanisms Iraq used to finance imports, including using overinvoicing to divert some of the funds to 'Uday Husayn's use.[33]

Peter Galbraith cited what was widely rumored in the region, namely, that Jordan was extending new credits to Iraq in the exact amount of the old credits being repaid.[34] In addition to the exports to Jordan, several thousand barrels per day were being smuggled into Turkey to take advantage of the price differential between Turkey and Iraq.[35] If Iraq were to truck 100,000 barrels per day as during the Iran-Iraq war (before the opening of the pipeline across Saudi Arabia), then the oil would be worth $500 million a year.

4. Released Iraqi assets. Iraq has provided the UN a list of $3.8 billion in assets in foreign banks as of March 31, 1991, nearly all of which were

frozen. Since then, the British government agreed to release $125 million in association with the freeing of a British citizen held on corruption charges dating from well before the crisis. Credible reports circulate of the release of other funds. It would be quite possible for Iraq to mobilize $200 million a year from this source, if not more.

5. Aid. Iraq received some aid from political allies. For instance, those with access to UN data report that Libya provided $5 million per month in UN-permitted humanitarian goods. More important was humanitarian aid. Various UN agencies—such as the world food program, the UN High Commissioner for Refugees, and UNICEF—estimate provisionally their 1991 spending in Iraq at around $100 million.[36]

6. Loans apparently allowed under UN rules. Iraq is said to be securing rice from Vietnam against promised future oil deliveries. Iraq could have found other interested partners.

Compared to the $16 billion in foreign exchange resources available to Saddam in 1989, the $2 billion cited here is trivial. Nevertheless, Iraq's resources would be more than ample to pay for the $600 million needed to sustain food rations and $100 million for medicine.[37] With $2 billion, Saddam could spend *twice* as much as this minimum on food and medicine and still have enough to provide $100 million for foreign travel and other services, $300 million for industrial spare parts, and $200 million for the military.

As for Iraq's long-term economic prospects, damage from the war has often been exaggerated. The allied bombing campaign hit hard at military and government sites, destroying a number of economic assets (especially electricity distribution and generation stations, oil refineries, communication facilities, and bridges).

In general, allied forces did only that damage necessary to put the facility out of action and then moved on to the next target, though errors produced excessive attacks on electrical generating equipment. The allied aim may have been to close down the most facilities with the least number of bombs, but the effect was to hold down damage. A useful analogy is that shooting the tires immobilizes a car, but the car is not destroyed forever.

The allied ground campaign did far less damage to the economy, taking place in the desert far removed from built-up areas. The March-April 1991 civil war and subsequent fighting in Kurdistan had more impact, but the rebels' light weapons could not inflict much damage on buildings.

The upper limit for damage done to Iraq's physical infrastructure could not exceed its overall value. The rule of thumb is that a country's assets other than land and minerals is equal to 2.5 to 3.0 times its Gross National Product (GNP), in which case Iraq's capital assets at that time were around $125 billion.[38] But many of those assets—such as housing and consumer durables—were little affected, and much of the rest was damaged rather than destroyed. It is hard to imagine damage could have been as much as a quarter of the capital stock, $31 billion. But this still overstates the war's effect on the infrastructure. Infrastructure wears down from ordinary use, so that a certain percentage must be replaced each year. Every piece of equipment and building depreciates at a different rate, so an economy-wide average is difficult. As a rough rule of thumb, a Third World economy at rest may need investment equal to 20% of GNP to sustain its capital stock, which implies an average life span of 15 years (15 years at 20% gives a capital stock of 300% of GNP). So capital replaced because of the war in part would have to be replaced in any case. If Iraq needs $8 to 9 billion of investment each year just to renew capital stock, then over the course of a decade, Iraq would invest $80 to 90 billion for this purpose.

In that context, repairs of wartime damage no longer loom as an insurmountable barrier. Of course, the more rapidly Iraq repairs war damage, the more the cost would be above the normal stream of investment and thus an added burden. For example, if Iraq patches up a damaged electrical generating plant for three years before replacing it, and if that plant had a useful life of ten years left when the war began, then 30% of the replacement cost is ordinary investment and 70% is from war damage. But if Iraq replaced the plant the day after the war, 100% of the cost is attributable to the war.

The Iraqi government's submission to the UN on Iraq's requirements—a document that would be expected to overstate need—put the cost of rebuilding destroyed infrastructure and enterprises "at ID [Iraqi Dinar] 8 billion, 80% of that amount, or ID 6.4 billion [$20 billion], in foreign currency."[39] This estimate seems quite reasonable.

Iraq's ability to recover from the war and sanctions depended on four main factors. First is its level of military expenditures. If the Iraqi government continued the prewar policy of pouring much of its resources into military salaries, weapons purchases, and the military-industrial machine, this would slow recovery.

The most expensive item is foreign arms and military technology. Even at 500,000 men, army salaries at $50 to $75 a month (and that at the official exchange rate, overstating the value by several fold) are not a heavy burden.

Yet much as Baghdad may wish to buy arms and military technology, its access will be limited. Therefore spending will be far below the $3 to $6 billion-a-year level that some estimate for the prewar decade. Iraq also starts out with such a large weapons' inventory that it could have a large force even if it had to rely on dissembling existing weapons for spare parts. A further element holding down Iraq's costs is that the price for the Soviet-style weapons it uses is likely to be much lower in the 1990s than in the 1980s as ex-Soviet bloc nations sell off arms and struggle to find markets for factories no longer needed. The second factor is the economic policies of Iraq's rulers. The experience of development shows that government policies matter a great deal. Pro-growth policies permit more efficient use of investment funds—to the point that $3 or less of capital is needed for each $1 of added output per year, whereas antigrowth policies can force a society to invest as much as $10 or more for each $1 of output. The key concept of pro-growth policies that can make such a difference, according to the World Bank, is to be market-friendly.[40] Government should intervene in the economy reluctantly, stepping in only where markets are demonstrably not working, and should do so subject to rules rather than official discretion. It should create an atmosphere for enterprise, with simple regulations fairly and efficiently administered. It should promote integration with the world economy, especially orienting industry toward world markets and forcing firms to face competition from imports.

On all these fronts, Iraq did poorly and was unlikely to do better, given Saddam's reluctance to allow true independence from his centralized control. On the other hand, Iraq had done rather well on some of the other points emphasized by the World Bank, namely, investing in people and providing a stable macroeconomic foundation.

The third factor is the treatment of Iraqi debt. Few heavily indebted Third World countries are paying their debt as originally scheduled. Countries such as Brazil and Argentina are not paying more than a third of what their debts would have called for, had they been honored on the original terms. Were Iraq to secure similar terms for a debt that is no more than $90 billion, then $5 billion a year would be ample, given 1992 interest rates.

On the other hand, if Iraq were required to set aside from its oil earnings enough to repay the loans fully, interest charges alone would be at least $8 billion and the total bill would have to include some amortization as well. Sanctions gave the UN a way to force Iraq to repay loans as a condition for regaining access to world oil markets, but the Security Council refused any suggestion that it require Iraqi payments on past debt before lifting sanctions.

If that attitude continued, it seems unlikely that Iraq would make more payments than was the norm for other heavily indebted countries. It may refuse to make more than token payments on the grounds that it is a much poorer country now than when the debts were contracted.

The Security Council was more insistent on Iraqi reparations for damage done to Kuwait and to third-country nationals there. The Security Council required that Iraq pay 30% of its oil receipts for such reparations, as well as paying for the UN ceasefire inspections.

Of the initial $1.6 billion in oil sales authorized by the Council, 12% would go for these UN expenditures. The funds available for imports into Iraq would then be 58% of the $1.6 billion, or $933.2 million. It seems likely that the Council will insist for some time that Iraq make substantial payments out of its oil income for reparations and UN activities. Conceivably such demands could run into the billions per year.

The final factor is the oil income. Prospects depend on the world market, since Iraq's oil production and (equally important) its pipelines could be quickly repaired. By early 1992, Iraq's government was claiming that production capacity was close to the prewar level. Expansion beyond that point would come faster if Iraq cooperated with foreign oil firms, a point over which it was often stubborn in the past despite the great potential rewards. Iraq certainly has the reserves to sustain an annual production of 5.0 million barrels per day (mbd). The constraint on sales is more likely to come from the demand side than from the output side.

The world oil market depends on many variables, including the growth of demand, Russian production levels, new technology, and environmental restrictions on consumption. If world demand for oil grows by 1.5 mbd each year (a 2% rate) while production in industrialized nations (mostly Russia) declines by 1 mbd, the market could accommodate Iraqi exports of 4 mbd by the late 1990s. If the price (in 1991 dollars) is $20 per barrel, Iraq would earn $29 billion a year, which could finance $2 billion for the military-industrial complex, service debt at $5 billion a year (a typical Third World level), pay reparations of $3 billion a year, meet its ordinary civilian import needs of less than $10 billion a year (now that foreign workers no longer send money home), and still have $9 billion a year to rebuild rapidly and finance investment for growth.

In other words, if Iraq complied with UN resolutions it could regain prosperity within a decade of the war, a reasonably hopeful outlook. But the Iraqi government's stubbornness about the UN resolutions further impoverished the country in the war's aftermath.

NOTES

1. Reserve figures have been manipulated by many countries in the region (especially Iran) as part of a bid to get large OPEC quotas, but Iraq's reserves are certainly as high as the 100 billion barrels claimed. Given world reserves of just under 1 trillion barrels, Iraq has 10% of the world's total and Kuwait an additional 9.5%.

2. Iraq could have had much extra revenue from the Rumayla oilfield 30 years ago, but the field sat unexploited from the mid-1950s until the early 1970s, because Iraq would not compromise with the international oil companies. Anyone hoping for Iraqi concessions in the face of low income would do well to study the history of Iraq's oil industry. Each major development came after literally decades of tough Iraqi demands, on which Iraq refused compromise despite a dire need for cash.

3. To remove the effects of weather variations, multiyear averages were calculated. From 1953 to 1957, cereal output averaged 2.15 million tons, while the 1986 to 1989 harvests averaged 2.10 million tons. (Data from the U.S. Department of Agriculture based largely on Iraqi data reported to the UN's Food and Agriculture Organization.)

4. Arms Control and Disarmament Agency (ACDA), *World Military Expenditures and Arms Transfers,* various issues, and author's estimates. In some years, ACDA data have shown substantial increases going back for several years.

5. Estimates of Iraqi battlefield deaths vary greatly; this figure is from U.S. government sources. Estimates of the Kuwaiti portfolio also differ, because some of the funds are held in worthless loans and stocks to Kuwaiti and Arab institutions while other funds are in Western real estate and stocks that have gone up in value. This estimate is the author's.

6. World Bank, *Trends in Developing Economies 1990* (Washington, D.C., 1990) reports the ICOR in the tables for each country accompanying the description of data in that country.

7. For instance, Zbigniew Brzezinski advocated in the *New York Times,* October 7, 1990, adjudication of "the Iraqi financial and territorial claims (not all of which were unfounded)." According to the Iraqi version, U.S. ambassador April Glaspie made similar remarks to Saddam on July 25, 1990.

8. Trade Minister Muhammad Mehdi Saleh, *Middle East Economic Digest (MEED),* June 22, 1990, p. 18.

9. Trade Minister Mohammed Mehdi Saleh, *MEED,* July 27, 1990, p. 19.

10. The mid-1990 price was $15 per barrel. Exports were at least 2.5 million barrels per day; 2.8 million was allowed under the OPEC production quota of 3.14 million. That produces a revenue of $13.7 billion a year, slightly above the $13 billion earned in 1989. By contrast, 1986 revenue was $8 billion.

11. For instance, Kuwait's foreign minister stated in an interview that Kuwait offered in late July to forgive all of Iraq's debt (*MEED,* August 31, 1990).

12. From the post-crisis data, it would appear that Iraq owed $27 billion to Western industrial countries, $9 billion to the ex-Comecon members, and $5 billion to Third World countries. The breakdown for major Western nations (*MEED,* September 7, 1990) includes, among others: $10.8 billion

to Italy ($5 billion for military debt, $3 billion for civilian government-guaranteed debt, and $2.8 billion for Banco Nacional de Lavoro); $3.7 billion to other Western banks excepting loans guaranteed by Western governments; $3 billion to Japan; $2 billion each to Germany and the United States; and $1.7 billion to the United Kingdom. The breakdown for ex-Comecon members is: $5 billion to the Soviet Union (*Izvestia,* March 1, 1990); $2 billion to Bulgaria; and $1.7 billion to Romania (*Financial Times,* February 1, 1991). The breakdown for the Third World was: $2 billion to Turkey (*Financial Times,* January 28, 1991); $1 billion to Brazil; $500 million each to Argentina, India, and Jordan. By comparison, Iraq's government informed the UN that its total foreign debt on December 31, 1990, was $42.1 billion, a figure that probably includes some debt to GCC nations. Permanent Mission of Iraq to the UN, *Financial Obligations and Basic Requirements of Iraq,* submitted to the Secretary-General, April 29, 1991.

13. All data except Iraq from World Bank, *World Tables 1991* (Washington, D.C., 1991). The comparisons are biased to make Iraq's situation look worse than it is, because the data for other countries do not cover all short-term debt, which is at times substantial.

14. *MEED,* March 31, 1990, summarizes the development program.

15. *New York Times,* September 15, 1991.

16. Jean Dreze and Harris Gazdar write, "Most of the 'indicators' that are now recognized in the economic literature as being commonly associated with famine situations were discernible in Iraq during the war." *Hunger and Poverty in Iraq 1991,* Development Economies Research Programme Discussion Paper No. 32, Suntory-Toyota International Centre for Economics and Related Disciplines of the London School of Economics and Political Science, p. 42.

17. Report to the secretary-general dated July 15, 1991, on humanitarian needs in Iraq prepared by a mission led by Sadriddin Aga Khan, executive delegate of the secretary-general (hereafter Aga Khan Report), UN Document s/22799, annex on rations, provides data for June-August. See also Dreze and Gadar, *Hunger and Poverty in Iraq.*

18. Calculations by Dreze and Gadar, *Hunger and Poverty in Iraq,* pp. 15-24, of the value of the ration basket and of the average wage.

19. On the politics and science of what level of food intake is needed to sustain life, see Dennis Avery, *Global Food Programs 1991,* (Center for Global Food Issues at the Hudson Institute, 1991).

20. The FAO, in the Aga Khan Report and subsequently (personal communications to this author), estimated Iraqi 1991 wheat and barley output combined at the implausibly low level of 1.2 million tons.

21. Personal communication from 45 government sources.

22. Dreze and Gadar, *Hunger and Poverty in Iraq*, p. 4.

23. Ibid., annex on visit to factories.

24. Aga Khan Report, p. 39.

25. Ibid., p. 13 and appendix 8.

26. Ibid., pp. 17-22.

27. Iraq has returned to Kuwait the Kuwaiti gold seized during the invasion. *MEED*, August 30, 1991.

28. Gold Field Mineral Services, *Gold 1980* through *Gold 1990* (London, 1981-1991).

29. Economist Intelligence Unit, *IMA*, no. 4, 1990.

30. *Gold 1990.*

31. Peter Galbraith, *Kurdistan in the Time of Saddam Hussein*, Staff Report to the U.S. Senate Committee on Foreign Relations, November 1991, p. 11, on mineral products to Jordan; U.S. government sources on the agricultural products.

32. "Luxury saloons [cars] were fetching up to $30,000 when sold in Iran, and the cars were often driven to the border filled with stolen electronic cable, steel wire, and goods looted from Kuwait." *MEED*, December 13, 1991. See also Galbraith's graphic account of the construction equipment offers for sale at the Haj Oman border station. Galbraith, *Kurdistan in the Time of Saddam Hussein*, p. 10.

33. *London Observer*, August 20, 1991.

34. Galbraith, *Kurdistan in the Time of Saddam Hussein*, p. 10.

35. Among other press reports, see Agence-France Presse, December 13, 1991, in *Foreign Broadcast Information Service (FBIS)*, #NES-91-241, December 16, 1991, p. 47.

36. Based on data provided the author by UN Disaster Relief Organization, January 1992.

37. While Iraq insisted to the Aga Khan team that it needed $460 million in drugs and medical supplies—$23 per capita—the UN Development Program (UNDP) reports, "between 1.5 and 2.5 billion people still have little or no regular access to essential drugs.... Basic and essential drugs cost around $1.00 per person" per year. UNDP, *Human Development Report 1991*, p. 63.

38. For instance, for the United States, net fixed reproducible tangible wealth averaged 2.7 times GNP in the 1980s (*Statistical Abstract of the U.S.*, various issues). Iraq's GNP is difficult to measure in dollars, given the variation in exchange rates between the official rate (ID .33 per dollar) and the market rate (ID 4 to 6 per dollar pre-crisis). An upper-bound estimate for 1989 GNP is $45 billion.

39. Permanent Mission of Iraq to the UN, Financial Obligations and Basic Requirements of Iraq, April 29, 1991, p. 4.

40. World Bank, *World Development Report 1991: The Challenge of Development* (New York, 1991), pp. 1-10.

5

Iraq and the World Oil Market: Oil and Power After the Gulf War

Robert J. Lieber

What were the implications of the Gulf War for the world oil market and for global energy security? Some observers found little cause for concern. Three separate factors contributed to such a conclusion.

First, Iraq suffered a devastating defeat, which suggested that military threats to oil supplies can be minimized. Second, the producing and consuming countries managed to cope with the purely oil-related components of the Gulf crisis so that both the supply and price of petroleum appeared manageable. Third, there is the argument that, in any case, elasticities of both supply and demand ensure that world energy markets can and will cope with potential disruptions.

An assessment of oil and power in the aftermath of the Gulf War, however, can also lead to other, more sobering conclusions. This interpretation rests not only on analysis of the Gulf crisis itself, but also on the lessons of the two oil shocks of the 1970s, as well as on evidence from the following decade. In this light, each of the above three arguments can prove less reassuring.

In the military realm, the U.S.-led coalition's extraordinary victory in the war has given rise to a virtual consensus on both the coalition's invincibility and the inevitability of its triumph. However, cases both old (the British debacle at Gallipoli against Ottoman Turkish forces in 1915[1]) and contemporary (the failure of Desert One, the U.S. effort to rescue the Iran-held hostages in April 1980[2]) suggest that the triumph of the forces of modern Western powers over those of less-advanced Middle East regimes cannot simply be taken for granted.

Moreover, timing was crucial. Had Saddam Husayn's forces continued their August 2, 1990, invasion and occupation of Kuwait by driving into Saudi Arabia, the Saudis and Americans would have lacked the military means to stop the Iraqi dictator's hundreds of thousands of troops and thousands of armored vehicles. At best, this might have triggered a longer, less successful and far more costly war. At worst, Saddam might have controlled the Saudi Gulf coast and major Saudi oilfields, leaving the United States with two unwelcome options: to mount a military campaign without the benefit of the Saudi ports and facilities, risking the destruction later seen in Kuwait on a bigger scale in Saudi oilfields, or to accept Iraq's control of almost half the world's proved oil reserves and domination of the remaining Gulf oil producers.

Coping with the cutoff of Kuwaiti and Iraqi oil from world oil markets proved successful. Saudi Arabia increased its own oil production by more than 3 million barrels per day (mbd)—about equal to the amount previously supplied by Iraq—and other countries more than made up the shortfall caused by the loss of Kuwait's production. On the demand side, members of the International Energy Agency (IEA), led by the United States, eventually took measures to show their ability and will to reduce demand and release oil from their strategic stocks. Yet, even with the supply and demand effects largely under control, initial uncertainties and market psychology caused oil prices to more than double, to a high of $40 per barrel in the early autumn of 1990, before they fell back to the $20 per barrel range.

Markets did work, but the temporary run-up of prices proved costly in terms of inflation and in tipping a weakening U.S. economy into recession. Moreover, the 1973-1974 and 1979-1980 oil shocks showed that markets often overshoot and that inelasticities of both supply and demand for energy can make the adjustment process long and very costly.

In sum, the experience of the Gulf crisis—as well as the evidence of the past two decades—leaves little reason for complacency, and the case deserves careful examination.

OIL AS A PROBLEM IN POLITICAL ECONOMY

A reliable understanding of the role of oil in international politics and political economy has proved elusive. A principal reason for this is that too many observers approach the subject through perspectives that are narrowly economic or, conversely, mostly political. These interpretations, in their most pristine forms, can be considered as "ideal types."

From the vantage point of the exclusively economic perspective, it is simply assumed that the market mechanism will provide an eventual equilibrium for supply and demand. Thus, if shortages of oil develop, prices will rise until the available supply matches demand. Higher prices will have the effect of causing additional supplies of oil and other forms of energy to be developed and brought to market. At the same time, higher prices will result in reduced demand, as buyers seek to economize by conserving or by switching to other forms of energy.

From this perspective, policies aimed at protecting energy security are seen as largely irrelevant and the risks of energy crises as minimal. Moreover, the economic perspective points to both the unintended consequences and to the failures of deliberate government policies. For example, oil and gas price regulation and allocation policies largely failed during the 1970s and were ultimately discarded. So too was the Carter administration's expensive synthetic fuels program.

The economic perspective itself, however, remains seriously deficient when used in isolation. It tends either to minimize the importance of the Organization of Petroleum-Exporting Countries (OPEC) in shaping the world oil system or else to suggest that long-term market factors make it largely impossible for OPEC to have a lasting impact. Moreover, this approach tends to overlook the implications of geography, particularly the fact that 63% of proved world oil reserves are located in the Persian Gulf region. In addition, market imperfections and barriers to market entry, in terms both of cost and time, are minimized. Yet, regardless of market signals, it costs many billions of dollars and takes many years to find and develop a new oilfield or build a nuclear power plant. Finally, an exclusively economic perspective does not successfully explain, given the costly and disruptive cases of the 1973-1974 and 1979-1980 oil shocks, why a repetition of such disruptions may not occur.

Conversely, analyses of oil that are essentially—or even exclusively—political also provide only a one-dimensional perspective. These approaches tend to minimize the role of market phenomena altogether. They thus have overstated the threat of oil embargoes, exaggerated the relationship between world oil supply and the Arab-Israeli conflict, and inflated the fundamental power of individual oil-producing countries. After each of the 1970s oil shocks, the political approach tended to assume that oil prices would continue to rise indefinitely.

To be sure, many of the prevailing economic (or political) interpretations are more complex than these ideal types convey. For example, one of the more sophisticated market-oriented interpretations, which sees economic forces tending to push oil prices lower over the long term and tends to downplay the risk of future oil shocks, nonetheless incorporates policy recommendations for the United States that go well beyond merely letting the market take its own course. Thus, Eliyahu Kanovsky urges that the United States take steps to limit its vulnerability to Middle East supply disruptions through actions such as incentives for Third World states to pursue oil exploration and development, as well as the introduction of fiscal and regulatory policies to encourage domestic energy efficiency and conservation.[3]

In reality, oil can be understood most effectively through integrating insights from both economics and politics. Without this synthesis, as Robert Gilpin has noted, political scientists tend to overlook the role of markets, while economists often neglect the importance of power and the political context of events.[4]

Oil issues in the Persian Gulf and Middle East take on a broader significance because of the way they encompass both political and economic dimensions and because they often have consequences spreading far beyond regional confines. Under certain, very specific, circumstances, events in the Gulf can reverberate halfway around the world almost instantaneously.

The most dramatic (though least common) pattern is that of an oil shock, defined as a profound disruption of the existing supply and price system. However, two major phenomena must be present simultaneously for such an event to take place. One is the existence of a tight or precarious balance between supply and demand, in which available world oil supplies only just manage to satisfy world oil demand and there is little or no additional unused production capacity. The second component is some major event (war or revolution, most probably), which triggers a disturbance in existing supply patterns. When these two circumstances intersect, and only then, the result is an oil shock.

The political economy of world oil thus entails an integrated world system. All countries that import or export petroleum are linked to it. Developments occurring anywhere in the system—whether political or economic—that have a bearing on the demand or supply for oil affect that system's overall balance. Hence, when a serious disequilibrium occurs, the effects are felt globally. For example, even if the United States imported little or no Middle East oil, the fact that it imports oil—and that it does so in order to provide almost 50% of its total petroleum supplies—means that it is almost instantly affected.

IRAQ AND PERSIAN GULF OIL

Prior to the outbreak of the Gulf crisis and war, Iraq was producing 3.4 million barrels of crude oil per day.[5] This represented a 20% increase over average output for 1989 and meant that Iraq had regained its level of peak production set in 1979—the last full year prior to the Iran-Iraq war. Even at the July 1990 figure, however, Iraq's oil output accounted for just 5.7% of world production.[6]

By another measure, however, Iraq's importance to the world oil system is significantly greater. In terms of proved oil reserves, Iraq is second only to Saudi Arabia. (See Table 5.1.) Set against a world total of just over 1 trillion barrels, the Saudis, with 255 billion barrels, hold approximately 25% of the world total. For its part, Iraq has 100 billion barrels, equivalent to 10%, and is followed closely by the United Arab Emirates (UAE, 98 billion barrels), Kuwait (95 billion barrels), and Iran (93 billion barrels). By contrast, the next largest group of producers, Venezuela, the Soviet Union, and Mexico, fall in the 56 to 59 billion barrel range. The United States has just 26 billion barrels, less than 2.5% of world proved reserves.

The significance of Iraq's threat in the crisis thus becomes more evident. As of August 2, 1990, Iraq controlled both its own and Kuwait's reserves—some 20% of the world total—while directly menacing Saudi Arabia. Combined with the oil of the rich but militarily weak UAE, Iraq was in position to dominate—directly or indirectly—55% of the world's proved reserves.

The importance of Gulf and OPEC oil, along with variations in their significance, is due to a phenomenon that one analyst has called "the OPEC multiplier."[7] Oil-importing countries, for a combination of political and economic reasons, have tended to rely on OPEC oil as a last resort. They prefer, where possible, to use domestic oil and energy resources. If they must resort to imports, they next seek supplies from non-OPEC countries. But when these other avenues are no longer available or are fully utilized, they must turn to OPEC suppliers. Consequently, changes in the demand for OPEC oil tend to be disproportionate.

When world demand falls, the reductions thus affect OPEC to a greater extent than other suppliers. In the case of the United States, where total oil demand fell by more than 3.6 mbd—or almost 20%—between 1978 and 1983, domestic oil production continued at levels near full capacity, and imports of non-OPEC oil actually increased. At the same time, U.S. imports of OPEC oil fell sharply, dropping from 5.7 to 1.8 mbd (a reduction of 68%).[8]

The OPEC multiplier, however, can work in the opposite direction as well. During the last half of the 1980s, a combination of economic growth, cheaper

Table 5.1
Proved Oil Reserves

Country	Billion barrels
Saudi Arabia	255
Iraq	100
United Arab Emirates (UAE)	98
Kuwait	95
Iran	93
Venezuela	59
Soviet Union	58
Mexico	56
United States	26
China	24
Libya	23
Nigeria	16
Norway	12

Estimated as of January 1, 1990, based on reserves recoverable with present technology and prices. Data from *Oil and Gas Journal*, December 25, 1989.

oil prices, and gradual decreases in U.S. oil output caused an upsurge in world oil demand. At the time, most of the non-OPEC suppliers were producing at or near capacity, and so demand for OPEC oil rose rapidly. In the case of the United States, imports of OPEC oil increased by 2.5 mbd, to a level of 4.3 mbd. For the world as a whole, demand for OPEC oil surged from a low point of 16.6 mbd in 1985 to 24.3 mbd by the spring of 1990. At the time, OPEC still possessed several mbd of unused capacity, but much of this was concentrated within Saudi Arabia and other nearby areas in the Gulf.

IRAQI—AND SAUDI—OIL IN THE GULF CRISIS

In the weeks following the Iraqi invasion of Kuwait, the UN embargo against Iraq's oil exports removed approximately 4.0 to 4.3 mbd from world supplies of crude oil.[9] World oil markets, reacting initially to the threat of war in the

Gulf and then to the loss of oil from Iraq and Kuwait, saw a dramatic run-up in prices for crude oil. As a result of growing tensions in the region, prices, which had been as low as $13 per barrel for Saudi light crude oil in June 1990, had already climbed to $20 by mid-July. By August 2, the day of the invasion, oil reached $24 per barrel. Not surprisingly, prices moved steeply higher in the following weeks, peaking at $40.42 on October 11.[10]

Set against world oil production of some 60 million barrels per day, Iraqi and Kuwaiti pre-crisis oil exports amounted to approximately 7% of the global total. A shortfall of this magnitude, had it not been offset by production increases elsewhere, would have been in the same range as that which triggered the 1973-1974 oil crisis and would have been larger than the 4% shortfall during the second oil crisis in early 1979.[11]

Moreover, even without a supply shortage materializing, the economic impacts of sharply higher oil prices threatened to be significant. Thus, had oil remained at an average price of $30 per barrel for 1991 as a whole (instead of receding to $20 by late January), the industrial democracies of the Organization for Economic Cooperation and Development (OECD) would have seen 2 percentage points of additional inflation, 0.5% reduction in Gross National Product growth, and an adverse $90 billion shift in the balance of trade.[12] By themselves, these figures were less damaging than the results of the 1970s oil shocks (the numbers for inflation and balance of trade, for example, were only one-third those of the earlier period[13]), but were nonetheless potentially significant factors in tilting the world economy into recession. Moreover, even the relatively brief price "spike" that did occur caused serious economic problems in Eastern Europe and parts of the Third World, as well as damaging certain industries (such as aviation and automobiles) in the more prosperous Western countries.

In reality, despite the loss of Iraqi and Kuwaiti crude oil and fears that terrorism or war could further reduce supplies of oil from the Gulf, sufficient oil production increases were made available to offset the potential shortfall. Almost 80% of this production came from Persian Gulf states and from other member countries of OPEC, with smaller amounts from producers elsewhere around the world. However, Saudi Arabia proved to be, by far, the greatest source of increased production.

Based on comparisons between December 1989 and December 1990, Saudi production of crude oil rose by nearly 2.9 mbd, to almost 8.6 million barrels per day. (See Table 5.2.) In other words, while a great deal of added activity took place elsewhere—production increases, efforts to curtail or defer demand, and a January 1991 pledge by the 21 International Energy Agency member states to withdraw 2 mbd from their reserves[14]—more than two-thirds of the reduction in oil from the Gulf was covered by Saudi Arabia's increased production alone, with less than 20% coming from outside the Middle East.[15]

Table 5.2
Production of Crude Oil
December 1989 Versus December 1990
(partial list)

Producer	December 1989	December 1990	Change
Iraq	3.000 mbd	0.425 mbd	-2.575 mbd
Kuwait	2.090	0.075	-2.015
Total loss:			**-4.590**
Estimated Net Loss (Less Domestic Consumption):			**-4.0/4.3**
Saudi Arabia	5.696	8.570	+2.874
Iran	2.900	3.300	+0.400
Libya	1.201	1.500	+0.299
Algeria	1.110	1.210	+0.100
Qatar	0.395	0.370	-0.025
UAE	2.406	2.400	-0.006
Net Additions from Persian Gulf:			**+3.642**
Venezuela	1.977	2.340	+0.363
Mexico	2.476	2.660	+0.184
Indonesia	1.434	1.550	+0.116
Nigeria	1.854	1.950	+0.096
Total of Other Major Net Additions:			**+0.759**
Other Totals by Category:			
Arab OPEC	15.897	14.550	-1.347
Persian Gulf	16.529	15.182	-1.347
Total OPEC	24.605	24.280	-0.325
World	61.320	60.449	-0.871

Source: Author's calculations from data in *Monthly Energy Review* (Washington, D.C.: U.S. Department of Energy, Energy Information Administration, March 1991), pp. 118–19.

Elsewhere, net additions to world supplies came from Iran (0.4 mbd), Venezuela (0.36), Libya (0.3), Indonesia (0.1), Algeria (0.1), Nigeria (0.1), and lesser amounts from a variety of other producers around the world. One important factor worked in the opposite direction, however, due to a continuing decline in Soviet production. As of December 1990, the reduction compared to a year earlier amounted to more than 1 mbd.

In total, world oil production in December 1990 was 60.4 mbd. Despite the Gulf crisis, this was just 0.9 mbd below the figure of a year earlier. With a reduction in world demand of some 1 mbd in response to the sharply higher price of crude oil, as well as the subsequent decision by the United States and other IEA countries to make available additional oil from stocks (OECD stocks would have been sufficient to provide 2 mbd for an additional four and one-half years),[16] world oil supplies remained adequate.

In sum, no real oil crisis developed. The shortfalls from Iraq and Kuwait were offset. By mid-January 1991, oil prices fell below $20 per barrel, thus returning more or less to their pre-invasion levels and then fluctuating in a narrow range around that figure during the Gulf War and its aftermath. A potentially destabilizing loss of supply from two major producing countries was absorbed with no major crisis, while the accompanying surge in oil prices subsided within five months. Given this result, as well as the post-crisis commitment of the Saudis to maintaining high production levels, the gradually increasing flow of Kuwaiti oil, and the prospect that some amount of Iraqi oil will eventually be exported again, there might appear to be grounds for complacency. A closer look, however, suggests reasons why this ability to weather a crisis without severe disruption cannot be taken for granted. The single most important factor is the role of Saudi Arabia. Had the Saudis been unable or unwilling to respond as they did, the history of the Gulf crisis would have been far different. An Iraqi invasion of Saudi Arabia in August 1990 would have been beyond the ability of the Saudis themselves—or of U.S. forces in their initial deployment—to repel. Saudi oilfields are concentrated near Ras Tanura, less than 200 miles from the Kuwaiti border, and they could have been seized by a determined Iraqi assault. In such circumstances, even had the Saudis retained any kind of nominal independence, it is unlikely they could have been in a position to do anything except acquiesce to whatever demands Saddam would have placed upon them and their resources.

As for the United States, the ability to mount a military operation would have been extremely problematic. Actual U.S. deployments succeeded because they had the full cooperation of the Saudi government, access to Saudi ports, and the use of a vast infrastructure of modern airbases. Without these prerequisites, a U.S. military effort aimed at driving the Iraqi invaders out of both

Saudi Arabia and Kuwait would have been exceptionally difficult and costly, even in the event the Bush administration had opted to attempt it. The widespread diplomatic, political and military support that the U.S.-led coalition enjoyed would also have been far more difficult to assemble under circumstances in which Saddam's triumph looked self-evident and the costs of reversing it unsustainable.

The subsequent Iraqi destruction and burning of Kuwait's oil wells in the midst of the allied military triumph also suggests that even a successful U.S. assault on the Iraqi forces in Saudi Arabia would have resulted in unprecedented destruction of oil facilities. The threatened reduction, or actual disappearance, of 8.5 million barrels in oil supply (as measured against Saudi Arabia's December 1990 oil production) would have triggered a disastrous crisis in world oil supplies resulting in shortfalls of petroleum for the world economy, staggering price increases, alliance disarray, and political blackmail.

As a consequence, by mid-August, Saddam Husayn would have been in a position to exercise control over the oil resources of Kuwait and Saudi Arabia, along with those of Iraq. With 45% of the world's proved reserves of crude oil subject to his direct dictate, and with his Gulf neighbors painfully aware of his ability to use any means at his disposal, the Iraqi president would have gained access to a vast source of present and future wealth. Moreover, based on the record of the past two decades, there is every reason to believe that these resources would have permitted him to purchase the most modern forms of technology and arms, including missiles and nuclear weapons technology.

The sobering conclusion of this scenario is that oil-importing countries and Iraq's Middle East and even European neighbors have been fortunate in what did *not* happen after August 2. Despite Iraq's shattering military defeat and the destruction of much of its most dangerous weapons, the avoidance of disaster was by no means inevitable.

IRAQ AND WORLD OIL: PAST AND FUTURE PATTERNS

Saddam Husayn's seizure of Kuwait had multiple causes, not least the Iraqi leader's characteristic of overreaching with disastrous consequences. Nonetheless, important economic considerations are quite evident as well. During the 1980s, Iraq had spent approximately $100 billion on its military. By 1990 the country had accumulated an international debt of $80 billion, on which interest payments amounted to some $8 billion per year.

With world oil prices at $20 per barrel, exports of 3 mbd would generate less than $20 billion per year in revenue. Moreover, by June 1990, with both Iranian and Iraqi oil exports having increased after their bloody war ended in 1988, oil prices had slipped as low as $13 per barrel. At that level, Iraq would earn about $14 billion a year—barely enough to cover debt service and imports of necessities. Given the costs of reconstruction following the Iran-Iraq war, the needs of Iraq's economy and popular expectations, and Saddam's continuing, grandiose military spending predilections, the Iraqi leader sought ways to increase his country's revenues. The resources and income of Kuwait, as well as the prospect of exerting leverage over Saudi Arabia and hence influence over world oil prices, offered a tempting target.

After the Gulf War, with continuing UN sanctions on oil exports, Iraq's economy had an acute need for oil revenues. This situation gave some chance for external actors to influence Iraq's conduct. Whenever Iraq resumed oil exports, however, the amounts involved could grow quickly. It has been estimated that within three months after restrictions are lifted, Iraq could be producing 1 mbd. With investment of about $1 billion in repairing damaged facilities, output could reach 2.7 mbd.[17]

Given Iraq's debts, estimated costs of $30 billion to repair destruction from the war, and UN-mandated reparations of as much as $50 billion to pay for destruction and looting in Kuwait,[18] Iraq will continue to have a pressing, long-term need for export revenue. This will motivate Saddam or his eventual successors to encourage higher world oil prices and thus give Iraq good reason for seeking to intimidate its neighbors. Apart from efforts to shape oil production and pricing policies, such pressure could include demands for aid (in less polite terms, blackmail), influence over defense and foreign policies, and changes in the internal regime of adjacent states.

As long as the United States remains committed to regional security, this potential Iraqi intimidation will not have much effect in light of the U.S. role in opposing Iraq's takeover of Kuwait, in orchestrating UN condemnation and sanctions, and finally in leading an international coalition to defeat Iraq. However, if the United States proves unable to sustain a long-term commitment or if regional states are unwilling or unable to help maintain it, Iraq will eventually find ways to reassert strength in the region. Under such circumstances, and as long as the regime of Saddam Husayn (or a successor regime with comparable interests and values) continues in power, there will be a threat both to regional stability and to the prevailing Persian Gulf oil regime.

The oil-related dimension of this incorporates two distinct elements. One is that Iraq—having earlier attacked four nearby states (Iran, Kuwait, Saudi Arabia, Israel) and having bitter quarrels (Syria) or uneasy relations with others

(Turkey)—could again find itself in a war. If so, the danger to oil facilities is omnipresent. Alternatively, if Iraq succeeds in regaining regional power and influence, this may lead to an attempt (whether or not sustainable) to manipulate oil production in order to increase world prices. To be sure, the economic and market-related dimensions of the political economy of oil make it uncertain whether Iraq could succeed. The experience of the OPEC countries in the 1980s suggests this is a difficult task. On the other hand, Iraq might manage to exert control over its neighbors or intimidate them.

Moreover, the interplay among politics and economics means that if Iraq can regain economic strength and loosen sanctions, oil revenues can again be translated into offensive military power jeopardizing regional security. Unless a UN embargo on weapons, exports can be sustained and rigorously enforced, at least some states will seek markets for their tanks, aircraft, missiles, chemical weapons, and nuclear weapons technology. The pressing financial predicament of emergent East European economies, the problems of Latin American manufacturers such as Brazil and Argentina, and the behavior of China make this a long-term problem.

Indeed, *post*-Gulf War accounts of a Czech decision to supply T-72 tanks to Syria, of China's shipment of M-9 missiles to Syria and construction of a nuclear "research" reactor in Algeria, and of an ongoing Argentine Condor II surface-to-surface missile program financed by Iraq[19] provide evidence that any sustained effort to control the export of advanced offensive weapons to the region will face great difficulties.

CONCLUSION

The principal developments in world oil over the past two decades have come largely as surprises, and many of these have run directly counter to conventional wisdom among practitioners, analysts, and scholars. Such cases include the tightening world oil market after 1970, the 1973-1974 and 1979-1980 oil shocks, the oil gluts (and accompanying price reductions) of 1976-78 and especially of the mid-1980s, and Iraq's August 1990 invasion of Kuwait.

The long-term pattern of oil supply and price, along with the stability of the Persian Gulf and Middle East, depends on a complex interplay of elements that are economic, political, and military. Such factors as the fate of the Ba'th regime of Saddam Husayn, the availability of oil revenues to finance a rearming of Iraq, the durability of the U.S. commitment to regional security, the role of Saudi Arabia and the stability of its regime, the pattern of long-term oil and energy demand outside the region, declining oil production in the former Soviet

Union, the inability of the United States to implement an energy policy that would reverse its rising dependence on imported oil, and the risk of renewed warfare within the region can all interact. In other words, economic and energy variables partially determine political and military outcomes—and vice versa.

In sum, the fact that the first great crisis of the post-Cold War era did not produce a severe oil shock should not be grounds for complacency. A reconsideration of the three optimistic but widely shared notions cited at the start of this chapter suggests grounds for caution.

First, despite the crushing defeat of Iraq and the destruction of much of its military infrastructure, Saddam Husayn survived the war and managed a bloody suppression of uprisings by Shi'a in southern Iraq and Kurds in the north. Although subjected to a continuing oil and weapons embargo, the durability of these restraints is problematic over the long term. Without a change of regime, Saddam and his Ba'th leadership could eventually pose a renewed regional threat. Moreover, the crisis that began in August 1990 could have had a far more dangerous outcome if Saddam had sent his forces into Saudi Arabia immediately or had the United States been less skillful in gaining United Nations support, in assembling an unprecedented international coalition, and in ultimately winning congressional approval for its actions.

Second, the ability of oil producers and consumers to weather the crisis owed a great deal to the willingness and ability of Saudi Arabia to increase production. However, had Saudi Arabian oil facilities been disrupted by the crisis, or had its leaders decided not to boost production—or had they been prevented from doing so—the economic and political consequences of the crisis would have been far more serious.

Third, while the market mechanism functioned successfully, both in the recent crisis and in moderating the policies of OPEC countries during the past decade, the market does have its limits. For example, markets tend to overshoot. Thus, in the aftermath of Iraq's seizure of Kuwait, and despite the factors that allowed producing and consuming countries to avoid serious disruption, panic buying resulted in a temporary doubling of prices, to more than $40 per barrel. Moreover, markets by themselves cannot change geography—in this case the distribution of almost two-thirds of the world's proved oil reserves in the Gulf area alone. These supplies remain potentially vulnerable to military or political events that have nothing to do with markets, but that can have a potentially enormous impact on oil supply and price.

Indeed, even though markets can and do have a benign effect in regulating supply and demand for oil and energy, market imperfections have consequences as well. These include the role of OPEC in influencing (though by no means determining) world oil supply and price, as well as time delays before markets regain equilibrium. While it is true that the price "spikes" of 1973-1974 and 1979-1980 ultimately proved reversible, it is also true that the damage done to Western—and developing country—economies during these two shocks was quite serious. By one estimate the Group of Seven industrial counties lost $1.2 trillion in economic growth as a result of the two oil shocks.[20] For their part, the developing countries' grave problems of indebtedness, that have plagued their economies and societies during the 1980s and early 1990s, are also a legacy of these "temporary" oil price disturbances.

While the picture that emerges of Iraq and the world oil system in the aftermath of the Gulf crisis and war can provide reassurance, there is at the same time reason for caution. An awareness of the interrelated political and economic dimensions of the problem, and a willingness to draw lessons from the 1990-1991 crisis (as well as those of 1973-1974 and 1978-1979) is essential if future threats to energy security are to be avoided.

NOTES

1. A recent and detailed account of the Gallipoli expedition and debacle can be found in David Fromkin, *A Peace to End All Peace: The Fall of the Ottoman Empire and the Creation of the Modern Middle East* (New York, 1990), pp. 150-87.

2. See, for example, Gary Sick, *All Fall Down: America's Tragic Encounter with Iran* (New York, 1985), pp. 296-302.

3. See Eliyahu Kanovsky, *OPEC Ascendant? Another Case of Crying Wolf* Policy Paper No. 20 (Washington, D.C., 1990), pp. x and 53-56. See also an earlier paper by the same author that argued that competition for market share and revenue needs of oil exporters, along with advances in oil exploration and production, energy efficiency, and the conclusion of the Iran-Iraq war, would hold down oil prices for the foreseeable future. Eliyahu Kanovsky, *Another Oil Shock in the 1990s? A Dissenting View.* (Washington, D.C., 1987.) Also see the discussion of Kanovsky's approach by Hobart Rowen, *Washington Post,* May 12, 1991, p. H16.

4. Robert Gilpin, *U.S. Power and the Multinational Corporation: The Political Economy of Direct Foreign Investment* (New York, 1975), pp. 4-5.

5. *Monthly Energy Review,* U.S. Department of Energy, Energy Information Administration, Washington, D.C. (March 1991) Table 10.1a, p. 118.

6. Percentage calculations throughout this chapter are those of the author. World crude oil production in 1990 amounted to 60.072 mbd. See *Monthly Energy Review,* March 1991, Table 10.1b, p. 119.

7. For elaboration of the concept, see Bijan Mossavar-Rahmani, "The OPEC Multiplier," *Foreign Policy* 52 (Fall 1982), pp. 136-48.

8. In 1978, "petroleum products supplied" (that is, total demand for petroleum) in the United States amounted to 18.847 mbd. By 1983 the figure had declined to 15.231. Data from *Monthly Energy Review,* March 1991, p. 17.

9. Note that as of December 1989, Iraq had been producing 3.0 mbd and Kuwait 2.1. By December 1990, these figures had fallen to 0.425 for Iraq and a mere 0.075 for Kuwait. Allowing for domestic uses of various kinds, the combined reduction of nearly 4.6 mbd was, however, greater than the two countries' net exports. Together, these have been estimated in the range of 4.0 to 4.3 mbd.

10. With the exception of the June figure, all other prices are for light sweet crude oil quoted on the New York Mercantile Exchange. See *New York Times,* October 12, 1990, and March 1, 1991.

11. Robert J. Lieber, *The Oil Decade: Conflict and Cooperation in the West* (Lanham, Md., 1986), especially pp. 13-43.

12. Data from *The Economist* (London), August 11, 1990, p. 23.

13. The increased wealth transfer at $30 per barrel from the OECD countries would have been on the order of 0.6% of GNP, whereas in each of the 1970s oil shocks, the figure was 2.0%. In addition, compared with a hypothetical OECD inflation increase of 2% for 1991, the actual increase for the group of seven leading industrial countries (G7) in 1974 was 6.1% (that is, rising from 7.9% in 1973 to 14.0% in 1974). In the second oil shock, the inflation rate of the G7 increased by almost 6 percentage points. See *The Economist,* August 11, 1990, p. 23.

14. *New York Times,* January 29, 1991.

15. Note that figures for oil supply from the Gulf and OPEC, as well as world figures, often vary depending on the particular source quoted, differing time periods, and other factors. For reasons of consistency, except when otherwise noted, data used in this chapter come from the *Monthly Energy Review* of the Energy Information Administration, U.S. Department of Energy.

16. Data on stocks from International Energy Agency, reported in *The Economist,* August 11, 1990, p. 21.

17. *New York Times,* April 28, 1991.

18. *New York Times,* May 15, 1991, p. A16.

19. The Condor II project was a secretive program organized by the Argentine air force over which government officials have had little control.

20. Daniel Yergin, "Crisis and Adjustment: An Overview," in Daniel Yergin and Martin Hillenbrand, eds., *Global Insecurity: A Strategy for Energy and Economic Renewal* (Boston, 1982), p. 5.

PART II

IRAQ'S FOREIGN RELATIONS

The Arab World and Iraq

6

Kuwait: Confusing Friend and Foe

Joseph Kostiner

Kuwait's relations with Iraq played an important role in Iraq's invasion of Kuwait. The crisis, after all, arose partly from the two states' interactions and mutual perceptions, leading to the questions of whether Kuwait's policies stimulated Iraq's invasion and why Kuwait failed to recognize or better defend itself from Iraq's aggressive intentions.

We should not, however, underestimate the astuteness and resourcefulness of Kuwait's leaders, which often helped them steer their country safely through surrounding dangers.[1] Their policies challenging Iraq should therefore not be attributed to mere incompetence or ignorance of Iraqi politics. Rather, they stemmed from a view of Kuwait's own national goals and security interests.

By attempting to fulfill its national interests, Kuwait rivaled and challenged Iraqi interests. Kuwait's problems in state-building formed the foundation for these goals. Kuwait originated from a chieftaincy, a loose tribal confederacy based on nomad groups and townsmen. The town-based al-Sabah family played a leading role, with other groups enjoying a considerable amount of political independence.[2]

Kuwait's course of state-building evolved according to two principles. First was a trend toward government centralization, essential for establishing stability among nomadic and town-based groups. After the al-Sabahs established their borders in the 1920s, they developed an administration to run Kuwait and a military force to defend it. By using British assistance and oil wealth, the al-Sabahs succeeded in controlling Kuwait's territory, devising a successful petroleum and commercial economy. From the 1950s, they started vigorously developing towns and infrastructure.[3]

The other principle, in keeping with tribal traditions, was the distribution of benefits among citizens to maintain internal social stability. The government subsidized business enterprises and the citizens' welfare, including rights for almost free education, free health insurance, and no income taxes. A "distributive coalition of Kuwaitis widely sharing Kuwaiti wealth" (to apply Mancur Olsen's phrase) evolved.

The government focused on improving the position of the rich merchant families by treating them the way elders had once been treated in the tribe. They were given chances to engage in finance, trade, and real estate businesses. Following some fierce encounters with the authorities in 1921 and 1938, they also gained the right to advise and even criticize the government. This prerogative was institutionalized after Kuwait's independence in 1961 in the National Assembly, a 50-member elected, advisory body that functioned from 1962 to 1976 and again from 1981 to 1986.[4]

The 1980s brought security and economic crises that challenged Kuwait's state-building principles and the government's control of the country. Despite the government's efforts, Kuwait was beset by repeated acts of Shi'a terrorism perpetrated by foreign, professional hit squads and occasionally by Kuwaiti citizens. There were also continuous, mostly Iranian attacks on Kuwaiti oil tankers in Gulf waters. It became evident that the government had a hard time defending Kuwait and keeping the Iran-Iraq war from spilling over onto its territory.[5]

The government's resources and control also was affected by the mounting oil recession of the 1980s which brought a decline in Kuwait's (and other oil-states') production and income. The government was both forced to cut its own economic and development activities and face a recession. Thus, the development budget in 1986 was only 694 million Kuwaiti dinars (1 KD = c. $3.20 U.S.) of a total of KD 3.4 billion; in 1988, the overall budget deficit was KD 1.4 billion.[6] In the mid-1980s declining international interest rates also cut by 17% the earlier high Kuwaiti income from its huge foreign investment (KD 1.7 billion in 1980-1981).[7]

Political and economic problems also affected the business elite, challenging Kuwait's other main state-building principle, social stability. Businessmen were hit by a crash in the unofficial stock market (suq al-Manakh) in 1982; a decline in the activity of government-employed contractors; a fall in the rent values of real estate; and losses resulting from overextended loans in bank investments.[8]

In the face of burgeoning security and economic problems, the government decided to disperse the National Assembly in August 1986, dealing a direct blow to the elite, whose members from different political convictions had constituted its majority. Motivated by a sense of political deprivation, former leading assembly members formed a "parliamentary movement" and, when the Iran-Iraq war ended in September 1988, demanded the assembly's restoration.[9]

However, the immediate postwar period saw a serious attempt to recover from the previous crises and reestablish effective state-building strategies. This period offered new opportunities and brought about an atmosphere of optimism and vigor.

Kuwait developed several avenues to improve its economic situation. The relative improvement and stability in oil prices (that is $17-$18 per barrel compared to $15 in the mid-1980s) enabled the oil minister, 'Ali Khalifa al-Sabah, to breach the oil quotas of the Organization of Petroleum-Exporting Countries (OPEC) for Kuwait by producing considerably higher quantities to compensate for the former lean years. Already in 1989, Kuwait produced about 500,000 barrels per day above OPEC's quota. The government's oil revenue in 1989 was $9.3 billion, the highest since 1983 and 66% higher than in 1988.[10] At OPEC's meeting in Vienna in November 1989, Kuwait received 6.79% of OPEC's production, equivalent to a quota of 1.5 million barrels per day (mbd) but Kuwait kept exceeding that limit to a level of 2.03 mbd. (Kuwait announced a reduction of about 200,000 barrels a day for May 1990.)[11]

Higher oil revenue promoted economic activity in other areas. The government was especially keen to improve Kuwait's traditional sources of wealth, namely, trade and financial business, and to turn Kuwait once more—as it had been until 1982—into the main Gulf business center.[12] Non-oil revenues for 1989 were estimated at KD 228.5 million, up by KD 176.5 million over the previous year.[13]

While the official budget deficit was up by 11%, in early 1990 government spending increased by 7%—the highest level in three years. In April 1990, the Central Bank manager, 'Abd al-Salim al-Sabah, expressed Kuwait's confidence in public investment to stimulate economic activities.[14]

The policy of investment and increased public spending was mainly aimed at enhancing sociopolitical integration and tranquility. The "private sector"— that is, wealthy businessmen—were offered tempting investment terms and urged to invest in Kuwait's economy. In December 1989, 1,350 of the main debtors of the al-Manakh collapse (about 54% of all debtors) whose debts had been covered by collateral were allowed to write off up to KD 250,000 of debt to let them resume activities and enter new business enterprises.[15]

The government also aimed at integrating other echelons in society: In July, expatriates were permitted to invest in Kuwait through local representatives acting on their behalf; non-Kuwaiti shop owners and craftsmen were permitted to conduct business without a Kuwaiti partner.[16] Subsidies for food, education and health insurance were kept up to protect "the peoples' needs," namely, to keep the lower strata, notably the Shi'a, pacified.[17]

The government accompanied these measures by strengthening its rule and control of the Shi'a community. Thus, it occasionally cracked down on Shi'a to prevent terrorist activities. But after the war—as relations with Iran gradually improved—Kuwait's leaders also tried to mend fences with local Shi'a. In June 1990, for example, a state security court acquitted four Shi'a accused of plotting to overthrow Kuwait's political system.

During 1989 the government increased its effort to strengthen its grip on the country by appointing new governors and provincial councils to Kuwait's five provinces.[18] When members of the elite demonstrated demanding restoration of the national assembly and new elections, however, the government forcefully dispersed these gatherings and arrested participants. However, in April 1990, the emir, Jabir al-Ahmad, tried to meet the elite halfway, by announcing that a new national assembly would be elected on June 10 to include 25 appointed and 50 elected members. This plan fell short of the elite's expectations but signified the authorities' intentions to ease tensions.[19]

What should therefore be kept in mind is that during the Gulf War's aftermath, Kuwait was trying to rehabilitate its economy and ensure control over a society shaken by the events of the last decade. Rising economic opportunities met rising expectations for higher living standards. Kuwaiti authorities, keen to utilize their economic resources to the utmost and exert full control of their territory, were therefore inclined to refuse Iraqi demands for Kuwaiti territorial and economic concessions.

In late 1988 and throughout 1989, Iraq insisted that Kuwait cease pumping oil from the disputed Rumayla oilfield on the border and lower oil production to the OPEC quota to reduce the world oil glut and to increase prices, and hence Iraqi profits. Yet Kuwaiti leaders deemed an economic upswing vital for social cohesion and were eager to take advantage of what they considered to be an era of "prosperity and growth."[20]

Oil production was the key to this process. Kuwaiti leaders such as former minister of oil 'Ali al-Khalifa regarded the oil-quota system, which set a limit to Kuwait's production, as outdated. When asked about his OPEC colleagues' different view, he replied, "I am not paid to make everybody happy."[21] Kuwait also disagreed with Iraqi territorial demands. It was reluctant to give up economic assets (such as Rumayla) or strategic ones such as Bubyan Island. Iraq wanted to take over or lease this mostly unpopulated island due to its location at the Gulf's northern end, but Kuwaiti authorities then redefined Bubyan as a new development region. The government planned to build a new city, al-Sabiya, and link it through a causeway to the mainland. In 2015, it was supposed to have 250,000 people. By 1990, its planning had begun and a power station was built.[22]

KUWAIT'S SECURITY:
THE ATTITUDE TOWARD IRAQ

Kuwait's attitude toward Iraq also was shaped by security considerations. Its leaders' basic assumption was that the aftermath of the Iran-Iraq war presented no danger of a new full-scale war since both protagonists, having suffered so heavily, were incapable and uninterested in resuming military activities.

Crown Prince Sa'd 'Abdallah stressed that the superpowers and international community had produced a ceasefire between Iraq and Iran and would continue to guarantee peace in the Gulf.[23] This perception was widely shared, and echoed by an academic, 'Abd al-Reda Assiri, in his 1990 book predicting Iran and Iraq would be preoccupied with reconstruction. Assiri concluded that they posed only "minimal direct threats to the Gulf States in the short and medium terms. As a result, no hegemonic power may appear in the Gulf in the immediate future."[24]

Given this basic assumption, Kuwaiti leaders believed neutralism the security strategy best suited for the postwar situation. In principle, Kuwait had been following this approach for three decades. Being a small state (17,500 square kilometers) with only 40 percent indigenous population (of a total 2 million before August 1990), Kuwait had to keep good relations with all its bigger, more powerful neighbors. This attitude developed into a nonaligned policy among the superpowers and a strategy of mediation in Arab affairs. Kuwait's neutralism was active, utilizing its financial abilities and its leaders' shrewdness.[25]

Moreover, Kuwait's tilt toward Iraq during the Iran-Iraq war was no complete change of Kuwait's neutralism. In Kuwait's perception, Iraq was worth supporting as an essential security buffer against Iranian expansion but not as a full ally. Kuwait could not afford to take a totally pro-Iraqi partisan policy that would provoke Iran into retaliation. It thus tried to be cautious in assisting Iraq: taking a pro-Iraqi line in its media; using its ports to import and deliver to Iraq essential supplies and export small amounts of Iraqi oil; giving Iraq about $14 billion; and resisting Iranian-backed Shi'a terrorism. But Kuwait did not join a defense pact with Iraq and maintained diplomatic relations with Iran for most of the war's duration. Kuwait joined in founding the Gulf Cooperation Council (GCC) in 1981 because its leaders were determined not to be an Iraqi satellite.[26]

When the war ended, Kuwait wanted to return to a balanced neutralism. Its leaders believed Kuwait could best benefit by getting along with all regional states, including Iraq and Iran, and mediating among them. Already in February 1988, Kuwaiti Ambassador to Washington Sa'ud Nasir al-Sabah tried to dissociate Kuwait from Iraq's current offensive against Iran by declaring "We are playing the role of a mediator between Iraq and Iran and we have never taken sides with one Islamic country against another."[27]

In spring 1988, Minister of State Sa'ud al-'Usaymi played down the aid to Iraq: "We are giving aid to 64 Third World countries. Why not Iraq?"[28] Kuwait went on to normalize relations with Iran, restored to ambassadorial level in September 1989.[29] Moreover, a high-ranking Kuwaiti delegation visiting Baghdad in February 1989 suggested to its hosts that the GCC states could bring Iran and Iraq together and stimulate postwar reconstruction.[30]

Kuwait also took other mediation tasks: leading Arab arbitration efforts among Lebanese factions; playing go-between for Turkey and Bulgaria over the expulsion of Muslims from Bulgaria. Kuwaiti leaders believed these activities would make their country so highly valued and well connected as to enhance its security. In Assiri's words, Kuwait's survival depended "on a combination of domestic support and its external role as donor/mediator. Kuwait's political support for a variety of Arab causes, its political structure, its financial capabilities and its sense of mission make it a candidate to mediate interregional disputes, simultaneously neutralizing foes and acquiring friends."[31]

Kuwait's strategy of neutralism thus reinforced its assessment that there was no immediate serious danger. Iraq seemed no threat, Kuwait's leaders reasoned, because—like themselves and Iran—it was too weak to embark on a new military adventure and had no reason to do so. They saw Baghdad's main emphasis as economic growth facilitated through regional cooperation.

Moreover, rather than viewing Iraq as a potential regional leader, Kuwait's suggestions for regional economic cooperation show that its leaders thought Iraq needed its help and thus did not want to antagonize Kuwait. At worst, Iraq might provoke a petty border dispute. But such issues were considered soluble through the same methods Kuwait was applying elsewhere—inter-Arab mediation in a spirit of compromise. A Palestine Liberation Organization (PLO) official, Khalid al-Hasan, called this approach "the old, Arab Bedouin way."[32] Kuwait believed that any problem it might have with Iraq could be handled by relying on neutralism and Arab solidarity.

KUWAITI RESPONSES TO IRAQ'S DEMANDS

Thus, Kuwait's premises reflected several principles. First, it was not ready to accept Iraq's territorial and economic demands. Second, while Kuwait objected to Iraq's demands, it did not express a final refusal to negotiate the issues involved. This practice was in keeping with the common "Bedouin way" permitting both sides to bargain and yet stick to their policies without fearing serious escalation. Third, Kuwait offered Iraq cooperation in economic projects as a means of showing friendship to all regional states.

Kuwait's responses to Iraq's demands in 1988 and 1989 succeeded in fending off these pressures without provoking Iraqi retaliation. During this period, Iraq focused particularly on renting or obtaining the islands of Warba and Bubyan and on writing off its financial debt to Kuwait. Kuwait answered by asking Iraq for a comprehensive border settlement (during Sa'd 'Abdallah's visit in Baghdad in February 1989) and by announcing the development of al-Sabiya. Iraq, unprepared to give up any territorial demands, refused to make a comprehensive border settlement, and the issues were left pending.

Kuwait also raised plans for development projects: the above-mentioned proposal of Iran-Iraq cooperation with the GCC states and a plan signed in March 1989 (set during Sa'd 'Abdallah's visit in February 1989) to supply Kuwait with fresh irrigation water from the Shatt al-'Arab. Kuwait undertook to finance the $1.4 billion pipeline to carry the water.[33] According to some reports, Kuwait also continued providing Iraq with some financial aid—albeit far less than during the Iran-Iraq war—into 1989.[34]

In Kuwaiti eyes, the mix between postponing the border dispute, proposing economic projects, and maintaining some economic help for Iraq seemed to be working. During the Emir Jabir al-Ahmad's September 1989 visit to Baghdad, he inaugurated the water project and was awarded an Iraqi medal for Kuwait's assistance during the war. The border problem was not even mentioned during his visit.[35] Kuwait felt so confident that it did not even conclude a nonaggression agreement with Iraq, like the Iraq-Saudi agreement of February 1989.

Iraq started escalating its pressure on Kuwait in Spring 1990. Now no longer satisfied with asking the Gulf states to cancel its debt to them, it demanded from Kuwait an additional $10 billion. Iraq also accused Kuwait of waging economic warfare by overselling its OPEC quota in order to swamp the market with cheap oil and rob Iraq of needed income. Iraq also demanded $2.4 billion for Kuwait's alleged theft of its oil from Kuwait's side of the vast Rumayla oilfield.[36]

Kuwaiti responses during this period indicate only small tactical shifts but no strategic sea changes. Kuwait kept viewing its dispute with Iraq as soluble according to the "Bedouin way," and responded accordingly. The Kuwaitis thus gave only partial responses, avoiding a definite reply to Iraq's demands and refusing to concede territories or forego loans.

Yet Kuwait still avoided delivering a final refusal, and Jabir promised negotiations with Iraq once it officially recognized Kuwait's sovereignty. In addition, Kuwait announced in May a reduction of about 200,000 barrels per day in its oil production (which had been 2.03 mbd, 500,000 over the quota), but its oil minister al-Amiri further stated in July that Kuwait would propose scrapping the quota system altogether at OPEC's October 1991 meeting.[37]

Kuwait's perception of the dispute, even after Iraq made it public and official, also tallied with the traditional Arab outlook. In a cabinet meeting two weeks before Iraq's invasion, Kuwait's ministers stated that Iraq was either making threats merely in order to extort money, or, at worst (as Sa'd 'Abdallah asserted) aiming to send troops into Kuwait in disputed border areas, namely, into Warba and Bubyan islands or the Rumayla oilfield.[38] They thought in terms of traditional border disputes, not envisioning a full-scale occupation.

Kuwaiti response to Iraq's mounting threats (and, after July 24, its heavy military buildup on the border) also reflected the perception that a common border dispute should be resolved through negotiations in a traditional inter-Arab framework. Kuwait first labored to display its inclination to Arab solidarity. Before Iraq made public the dispute, Kuwait defended Iraqi actions against non-Arab parties, such as the execution for alleged spying of the British journalist Bazoft in March, or Saddam Husayn's threat in early April to destroy half of Israel.[39]

After Iraq went public on its conflict with Kuwait, the latter stressed its generous contribution "to Arab causes, notably against Iran during the war without expecting anything." Kuwait equally stressed "the need to adhere to the principles of consultation and understanding and holding a dialogue."[40] Kuwaiti leaders and newspapers urged Iraq to resolve problems through a peaceful dialogue.[41] Kuwait thereby tried to set the rules as its leaders had perceived them.

In practice, the Kuwaitis appealed for mediation to other GCC states, Arab League secretary-general Shadhli al-Qulaybi, UN secretary-general Perez de-Cuellar, and individual Arab states such as Egypt. Kuwait tended to rely on Saddam Husayn's promise to President Mubarak of Egypt to avoid any attack as long as Iraq and Kuwait negotiated, and it put great hope on resolving the conflict at a July 31 meeting in Jidda.[42]

Although Kuwaiti cabinet members still disputed Iraq's charges of stealing oil from Rumayla or waging economic warfare and did not agree to write off Iraq's debt, they also did not reject any concessions officially and finally.[43] Hence, according to the "Bedouin way," the Jidda meeting was perceived in Kuwait as a start for a long process of bargaining, displaying intransigence, and perhaps making some concessions.

Kuwait did show some flexibility at Jidda. It did not send Foreign Minister Sabah al-Ahmad, whose hard line toward Iraq made Baghdad denounce him as "an American agent." Sa'd 'Abdallah later recounted that he, as head of the Kuwaiti delegation, agreed to write off Iraq's debt and to lease Iraq the island of Warba (but not Bubyan).[44] He attributed the breakdown to the fact that Iraq's delegation came only to deliver an ultimatum, repeat all the old Iraqi demands, and insist on total surrender in order to prepare the ground for an invasion.[45]

It seems logical that Kuwait—which kept believing that talks would continue and that bargaining was legitimate—was trying at the last minute to pull Iraq into a border agreement. Iraq, however, played according to different rules by delivering nonnegotiable demands and when its delegates were dissatisfied with the results, walking out. On August 2, one day after the Jidda meeting ended, Iraq invaded Kuwait.

To what extent did Kuwait provoke Iraq into the invasion? The "provocation" argument is not convincing.[46] Kuwait's sovereignty gave it a right to refuse Iraq's demands.[47] Moreover, Kuwait's stand was not shaped by mere caprice but by what it considered essential state interests and objectives. In addition, accusations of Kuwait's provocation, when later made by Iraqi opponents such as former foreign minister Tariq 'Aziz, focused on Kuwait's style rather than Iraq's demands: delays on writing off the loan or the effort to change OPEC's quota rules.

'Aziz further explained that the Kuwaiti policy of waging "economic warfare," that is, overproducing oil became acute for Iraq only in December 1989.[48] Hence, even from an Iraqi viewpoint, Kuwait's policy of overproduction was too short-lived to be really damaging. Hence, Kuwait's policies were an irritant to Iraq but were partly changeable and accommodating. Kuwaiti policies can hardly be regarded a cause for Iraq going to war.

Iraq's decision to occupy Kuwait grew out of its belief that this would bring the financial and strategic assets needed to solve its economic and strategic problems. The fact that Kuwait refused to meet Iraq's demands was not the cause of the invasion but only a pretext for it.

Why did Kuwait fail to prepare for an Iraqi invasion? Kuwait believed that Iraq preferred economic development to foreign adventures; that its security strategy of neutralism was effective; and that its reliance on negotiations, Arab mediation, and abstention from military preparations would avoid war and invasion. Following these assumptions instead of the evidence, Kuwait was strategically surprised, like the Soviet Union in June 1941, the United States in December 1941, or Israel in October 1973.

Kuwaiti post-invasion statements attest to this blunder. To give one example, Defense Minister Nawwaf al-Sabah said, "We simply could not imagine that the Iraqi head of state would lie to Egypt's President . . . [and] Jordan's King . . . furthermore, we did not want to inflame Saddam with a mobilization of our troops."[49]

In Kuwait's defense, most Arab parties shared its expectation that Iraq would not attack and that the "Bedouin way" would work. Even after Iraq's occupation, its allies and apologists continued to state this line. After all, never in the Arab League's history had one Arab state simply occupied another. A limited Iraqi-initiated skirmish was expected, but a full-scale invasion was Saddam's real surprise, which cost Kuwait its independence.[50]

Finally, although Iraq later claimed that Kuwait had planned to bring in U.S. forces to fight it, Kuwait's abstention from any such alliance and overreliance on neutralism and mediation was the factor that left it unable to deter or rebuff an Iraqi attack.

NOTES

1. H. A. Al-Ebraheem, *Kuwait: A Political Study* (Kuwait, 1975).

2. P. S. Khoury and J. Kostiner, "The Complexities of Tribes and State Formation in the Middle East," in P. S. Khoury and J. Kostiner, eds., *Tribes and State Formation in the Middle East* (Berkeley, Calif., 1990), pp. 1-24; J. Ismael, *Kuwait: Social Change in Historical Perspective* (Syracuse, N.Y., 1982), pp. 17-80.

3. Ismael, *Kuwait*, pp. 59-101.

4. J. E. Peterson, *The Arab Gulf States: Steps Toward Political Participation*, The Washington Papers no. 131 (Washington, D.C., 1988), pp. 27-61.

5. On the atmosphere of declining security in Kuwait, see M. Viorst, "A Portrait at Large (Kuwait)," *The New Yorker,* May 16, 1988, pp. 43-79.

6. *Financial Times,* February 11, 1985; February 25, 1986; *al-Anba'* (Kuwait), April 26, 1988; *Kuwait News Agency (KUNA),* June 26, in *Foreign Broadcast Information Service (FBIS),* June 27, 1988.

7. *Financial Times,* February 22, 1984.

8. *Al-Anba',* April 26, 1988.

9. *Financial Times,* November 28, 1989.

10. *Economist Intelligence Unit (EIU)-Country Report, Kuwait,* no. 2, 1990, pp. 8-9; *Middle East Economic Digest (MEED),* April 27, 1990.

11. *EIU-Country Report, Kuwait,* no. 1, 1990, p. 11; *EUI-Country Report, Kuwait,* no. 2, 1990, p. 11; *Financial Times,* March 13, 1990.

12. *International Herald Tribune,* May 3, 1989.

13. *KUNA,* July 3, 1989, in *FBIS,* July 6, 1989.

14. *EIU-Country Report, Kuwait,* 1990, no. 2, p. 9; *MEED,* April 27, 1989; al-Sabah's interview, *al-Anba',* April 14, 1989.

15. *Financial Times,* March 13, 1989.

16. *Arab Times,* January 22 and July 24, 1989.

17. Finance Minister Jasim al-Khurafi's interview, *al-Ra'y al-'Amm,* July 30, 1989.

18. *Al-Sharq al-Awsat,* September 27, 1989.

19. *KUNA,* April 23, 1990, in *FBIS,* April 24, 1990.

20. Sa'd 'Abdullah's interview, *Arab Times,* December 12, 1989.

21. *Financial Times,* March 13, 1990.

22. *Al-Qabas,* March 25, 1989; *al-Siyasa,* February 7, 1990; *al-Qabas,* March 17, 1990.

23. Sa'd 'Abdullah's interview, *al-Watan al-'Arabi,* January 27, 1989.

24. 'Abd al-Reda Assiri, *Kuwait's Foreign Policy* (Boulder, Colo., 1990), p. 199.

25. Ibid., pp. 32-91; Viorst, "A Portrait at Large."

26. On Kuwait-Iraq relations, see Assiri, *Kuwait's Foreign Policy,* pp. 69-98; R. K. Ramazani, *Revolutionary Iran* (Baltimore, 1988), pp. 76-80, 126-30; G. Nonneman, *Iraq, The Gulf States and the War* (London, 1986).

27. *KUNA,* February 3, 1988, in *FBIS,* February 16, 1988.

28. Viorst, "A Portrait at Large."

29. *KUNA,* September 29, 1989, in *FBIS,* September 29, 1989.

30. *Al-Anba'* (Kuwait), February 8, 1989, quoted by Assiri, *Kuwait's Foreign Policy,* p. 135.

31. Assiri, *Kuwait's Foreign Policy,* p. 133.

32. *Newsweek,* November 5, 1992.

33. *Middle East Economic Survey,* March 20, 1989; *al-Siyasa,* September 13, 24, 1989.

34. See G. Nonneman, "Iraq and the Arab States in the Gulf: Modified Continuity Into the 1990s." Paper presented at the Royal Institute of International Affairs, May 9, 1990, p. 13.

35. *Al-Siyasa,* September 13 and 24, 1989.

36. See R. Schofield, *Kuwait and Iraq: Historical Claims and Territorial Disputes* (London, 1991), pp. 126-28; M. Viorst, "Report from Baghdad," *The New Yorker,* June 24, 1991.

37. *Financial Times,* March 13, 1990; *EIU-Country Report, Kuwait,* no. 2, 1990, p. 11; *al-Qabas,* July 16, 1990.

38. *Financial Times,* August 18-19, 1990.

39. *Iraqi News Agency,* March 19 (quoting Kuwait's minister of information, Dr. Jabir Mubarak, March 22); *al-Ra'y al-'Amm,* June 29, 1986.

40. *KUNA,* July 18, 1990, in *FBIS,* July 19, 1990; *al-Qabas,* July 21, 1990.

41. *KUNA,* June 24, 1990, in *FBIS,* July 25, 1990.

42. *KUNA,* July 26, 1990, in *FBIS,* July 26, 1990.

43. *Financial Times,* August 18-19, 1990.

44. Ibid.

45. *Financial Times,* August 18-19, 1990; Minister of Defense Nawwaf al-Sabah's interview, *Der Spiegel,* September 24, 1990.

46. This argument was raised, though not as a central theme, in Viorst, "Report from Baghdad."

47. U. Dann, "The Iraqi Invasion of Kuwait: Historical Observations," The Moshe Dayan Center for Middle Eastern and African Studies, Shiloah Institute, August 1990.

48. Viorst, "Report From Baghdad."

49. Nawwaf's interview, *Der Spiegel,* September 24, 1990.

50. Viorst, "Report from Baghdad."

7

Saudi Arabia: The Bank Vault Next Door

Jacob Goldberg

Some U.S. officials justified the tanks deal with Saudi Arabia
on the grounds of a possible military threat from Iraq. We
would like to stress that the fraternal ties, based on mutual respect and good-neighborliness, between Saudi Arabia and
Iraq are very strong. They are growing stronger at all levels
thanks to President Saddam Husayn's wisdom, farsightedness
and understanding of the conditions of the Arab nation, and
because of his honesty and patience.

—Statement by a Saudi official, November 15, 1989[1]

Saddam Husayn used chemical weapons against his own
people and executed thousands of Muslim scholars. . . . This
insane terrorist squandered the wealth of the Iraqi people and
now wants to loot other Arab countries. . . . The bloodthirsty
monster, who follows in the footsteps of Hitler, committed

the most vile aggression in the Arab nation's history. . . . . He
has to go because the fate of states and people cannot depend
on a traitor who lost his sanity.

—Editorials in the Saudi press, August 12-17, 1990[2]

These two Saudi references to Saddam Husayn represent the metamorphosis
of Saudi policy toward Iraq after the invasion of Kuwait. They also reflect
the two most extreme poles of Saudi reaction to the Iraqi threat: appeasement
and conciliatory statements on one hand, confrontation and resort to U.S.
military protection on the other. With the wisdom of hindsight, it seemed as if
the two preceding decades merely set the stage for inevitable collision between
the two countries.

Iraqi-Saudi rivalry did not originate with the 1968 Ba'th coup in Baghdad.
Some of its basic ingredients are geopolitical and go back to the ancient
symbiotic relations between fertile Mesopotamia and the arid Arabian Peninsula. Since the inception of Hashemite-ruled, modern Iraq in 1920, Saudi-Iraqi
relations were dominated by the historic hostility between the House of Saud
and the Hashemite family, which held power in both Iraq and Transjordan.

While Iraq's 1958 revolution overthrew the Hashemites there, the radical
regime that emerged viewed the Saudi government as representing the last
vestiges of Western imperialism that had to be removed. The Ba'th party
takeover of Iraq a decade later compounded the deep hostility. It is hard to
conceive of two regimes whose ideologies, interests, agenda, and world view are
more diametrically opposed than Iraq's Ba'th regime and the Saudi royal family.
Such conflicts, however, were tempered by pragmatic considerations forcing
both countries to prefer expediency over ideology. Saudi-Iraqi relations thus
went through four distinct periods between 1968 and 1990.

1968 TO 1970

After the Ba'th coup, Iraq shifted its leadership aspirations from the Fertile
Crescent to the Persian Gulf. This coincided with Britain's withdrawal from
the Gulf and the decline in Nasir's influence among the Gulf Arabs following
his defeat in the 1967 war. Iraq's desire to fill the vacuum and play a central
role in Gulf affairs alarmed the Saudi royal family.

Expecting a confrontation with Iran, however, the new Iraqi regime sought to
forge closer ties with Saudi Arabia. Thus, in September 1968 and in February and

May 1969, Baghdad tried to promote Gulf security cooperation with the Saudis, suggesting a military compact and creation of a joint deterrent naval force. Saudi leaders, however, were anxious about the new regime's revolutionary ideology and commitment to radical social and economic change. Thus, Riyadh preferred a Gulf security alliance with Iran, not Iraq, despite strained relations with Tehran over the Shah's claims to Bahrain. Iranian-Saudi talks to that end were held during the Shah's visits to Riyadh in November 1968 and April 1970, though no formal defense pact was ever signed.[3]

Not surprisingly, this created tension in Saudi-Iraqi relations and led Baghdad to accuse "the reactionary Saudis [of] complicity in the plans of American imperialism and Iranian reactionary forces to carve out spheres of influence in, and eventually take over, the Arab Gulf." As Iraq's foreign minister stated: "There is a regrettable struggle and war between the two sister states."[4]

1970 TO 1975

Failing to obtain Saudi cooperation against Iran, Baghdad reassessed its policy. Considering a U.S.-backed Saudi-Iranian Gulf security arrangement a threat to its vital lifeline, Iraq began ideological confrontation with Saudi Arabia and the other Gulf states and sought Soviet support. Saddam Husayn explained: "We cannot have a normal relationship with a state which relies on a foreign country [that is, non-Arab Iran] and uses the forces of that country against our people. We shall establish a normal relationship with any state which shows concern for the soil of the Arab homeland and the Arabism of the homeland in the Gulf."[5]

Iraqi-Saudi relations deteriorated as Soviet-Iraqi cooperation increased, peaking in April 1972 with a 15-year Treaty of Friendship and Cooperation between them. Straining relations further was Iraq's support for the People's Democratic Republic of Yemen (PDRY) and radical elements in North Yemen, the Dhofar Liberation Front in Oman, and the Popular Front for the Liberation of the Occupied Arabian Gulf. Iraq seized a Kuwaiti border post in March 1973 and claimed Kuwait's Warba and Bubyan islands. In addition, Saudi leaders believed that Iraqi pilots had flown the PDRY's MiG-17s that violated Saudi airspace that month.[6]

The Ba'th party's activity, supported by Iraq's resources, in the Gulf Arab states was seen in Riyadh as both "subversive" and as encroaching on the traditional Saudi sphere of influence. Bilateral relations were strained and the Saudis cultivated even closer relations with Iran as a counterweight to Iraqi pressure.[7]

In March 1973 Saudi opposition members started a publication in Baghdad by the name of *Sawt al-Tali'a* (Voice of the Vanguard). Iraqi influence was obvious since the term was commonly used in the Ba'th party's vocabulary. Two months later, a Saudi opposition group inaugurated a radio station broadcasting from Baghdad. Iraq's regime was clearly providing Saudi opposition groups the means to express themselves and to disseminate their propaganda.[8]

Differences over oil policy also strained bilateral relations. Iraq did not subscribe to the plan of the Organization of Arab Petroleum Exporting Countries (OAPEC) after the 1973 war to reduce production. Baghdad protested that it omitted any reference to an embargo against the United States, arguing that it was "essential to differentiate between hostile countries, which should be boycotted, and friendly states, which should be assured of normal oil supplies." The Saudis viewed the Iraqi position as a direct challenge to their leadership of Arab oil producers.[9]

In short, the Saudi kingdom at this time considered Iraq's regime as the most dangerous threat it faced. This view was reinforced in January 1974 when the Ba'th party proclaimed: "Iraq, being the largest Arab country in the region and the most advanced, carries the main burden in safeguarding the area whose national importance and the dangers facing it cannot be overemphasized."[10] Against this backdrop, Saddam's promise "to fight off Soviet forces, if they were to occupy a Saudi territory, even before the Saudi army" did not impress any Saudi leader.[11]

Attempting to counter Iraq's growing threat, Saudi Arabia enhanced coordination with Iran. The special U.S.-Iran relationship was a useful deterrent toward Iraq but implied some danger of a U.S.-backed Iranian drive for hegemony in the region. The Saudis sought, therefore, to cement their own relations with the United States independently of Iran. They also began building a big military city in Hafar al-Batin, facing their border with Iraq.

1975 TO 1979

In this era, Iraq softened its radicalism and advocated détente based on "noninterference in the internal affairs of neighboring states." The eighth Ba'th party Congress stated: "It is absurd imagination to assume that Iraq has plans to undermine the Gulf states and their regimes."[12] A more accommodating attitude toward Riyadh led to less tension, exchanges of visits among leaders, and a resolution of their border disputes.

Iraq's cooperation and coordination with the Gulf states increased markedly. In late 1974 Saddam Husayn expressed interest in exchanging visits and improving relations with the Saudis. Iraq also renewed its proposal to create a joint naval force in the Gulf to protect Arab interests. In February 1975 the Iraqi foreign minister visited Riyadh and suggested that the two countries start negotiations to resolve their border disputes.[13]

Saudi Arabia was also becoming concerned over Iran's role in the Gulf and growing involvement in the affairs of some Gulf countries, especially the stationing of Iranian troops in Oman. Saudi leaders sought, therefore, to seize on the change in Baghdad's policy and use Iraq to frustrate the Shah's schemes for an Iranian-dominated Gulf defense pact. Other motives for Saudi-Iraqi detente included Riyadh's alarm over alleged U.S. plans to seize Arab oilfields, desire to reduce Iraqi reliance on the Soviet Union, and a more confident posture following the oil boom.[14]

The conclusion of the Iraqi-Iranian Algiers accord in March 1975 pleased Saudi leaders. They thought it might weaken the Soviet position in the Gulf; signal the end of Iraqi-supported subversive activity in the region; and prove Iraq's ability to cooperate with conservative monarchies. Hence, the Saudis responded to the Iraqi overtures, and on March 27 the new Crown Prince Fahd expressed the kingdom's desire to cultivate brotherly relations if Baghdad was ready to resolve a number of bilateral disputes, such as border delineation, the "neutral zone," tribal migration, and smuggling.[15]

Consequently, in April 1975, Saudi and Iraqi officials agreed to partition the disputed "neutral zone" between their countries. On June 10-12 Crown Prince Fahd, Foreign Minister Sa'ud al-Faysal, and Oil Minister Yamani visited Baghdad, and, on July 2, the "neutral zone" border agreement was signed. The two countries decided to rebuild the 800-mile Najaf-Medina road, considered important for Iraqi pilgrims to the holy shrines. Riyadh was reported to have loaned Iraq $200 million. Saudi leaders also tried to mediate Iraqi disputes with other Arab states, notably with Syria over the use of the Euphrates River's water.[16]

In April 1976 Saddam Husayn paid an official visit to Riyadh, in the course of which he described Saudi-Iraqi relations as "growing and being consolidated in all spheres." In April 1977 Iraq's Interior Minister 'Izzat Ibrahim visited Riyadh and signed with Prince Na'if, his Saudi counterpart, an agreement regulating border control, tribal migration, smuggling, exchange of criminals, and other administrative matters. In April 1978 Saudi Defense Minister Sultan went for talks in Baghdad with President Bakr and Saddam, declaring there were "no points of disagreement on any topics discussed."[17] The close relations peaked with Saddam Husayn's visit to Riyadh in October 1978.

Such cooperation notwithstanding, Iraq did not change its view of the Gulf monarchies. Though it reportedly stopped attempts to subvert the conservative regimes, Iraq still made propaganda, aided opposition groups, and remained the Saudis' rival in competing for hegemony on the Gulf Arab coast. Saudi Arabia therefore continued rejecting Iraqi overtures for joint cooperation on Gulf security and defense. It preferred to work with other Gulf states.[18]

Another area of Iraqi-Saudi controversy was oil policy. In the December 1976 meeting of the Organization of Petroleum Exporting Countries (OPEC), Saudi Arabia opted for a 5% increase in oil prices while Iraq demanded a 10% increase. Baghdad was very critical of the Saudi position and accused the kingdom of "serving imperialism and Zionism."[19]

Still another dispute arose over the Saudi-mediated Egypt-Syria reconciliation in December 1976. Given its old rivalry with Damascus, Iraq was frustrated at Syria's achievement and angry at the acceptance of virtual Syrian hegemony over Lebanon and basing Syrian troops there as a disguised "Arab Deterrent Force." With the Egyptian-Syrian-Saudi axis as the Arab world's dominant force, Iraq's status was reduced.

1979 TO 1988

In this period, Iran's revolution, the Egypt-Israel peace, and the Soviet invasion of Afghanistan created a unique convergence of Saudi and Iraqi interests. The U.S. failure to save the Shah made Saudi leaders doubt the credibility of its commitment to defend their kingdom. Disenchanted also with the U.S.-sponsored Camp David accords, Riyadh sought to distance itself from Washington.

Iraq sought to seize this opportunity by projecting a moderate image to gain the Saudis' confidence. Baghdad wanted to weaken U.S.-Saudi military ties and ensure Saudi membership in the Iraqi-led anti-Sadat coalition. The Saudis were pleased that Iraq had broken its close ties to South Yemen's Marxist regime and supported North Yemen instead. They also were glad that Baghdad had edged away from Moscow's embrace and criticized Soviet actions in Afghanistan, South Yemen, and Ethiopia. Finally, they noted reduced Iraqi support for revolutionary movements.[20]

But the critical factor was a common fear of Iranian-backed Islamic fundamentalism subverting their own and regional stability. Both Iraq and Saudi Arabia were alarmed at the prospect of unrest among Shi'a communities wooed by Tehran. In late January 1979, immediately after the Shah's fall, Iraq's Interior Minister 'Izzat Ibrahim rushed to Riyadh. After seven days of extensive discussions on the revolution's repercussions, Iraq and Saudi Arabia announced a project agreement to cooperate on internal security that could possibly be expanded to a larger Gulf mutual defense pact.[21] A few weeks later Saddam Husayn declared that Iraq would never allow Saudi Arabia to be occupied by the Soviet Union.[22]

Creating a whole new framework for Iraqi-Saudi relations to reflect the new common interests, Saddam stated that the two countries should abandon "differences over secondary issues" and unify efforts over four major dangers threatening the Arab world: "American and Soviet penetration, Iranian expansionism and the breakdown of Arab consensus due to Sadat's peace with Israel."[23]

The Iran-Iraq war finally turned Saudi Arabia, for the first time, into a major supporter of Iraq on which Baghdad had to depend for crucial assistance. According to "well-informed sources in Saudi Arabia," Riyadh was fully behind Iraq's invasion of Iran in September 1980. During Saddam Husayn's visit to Riyadh on August 5—his first as Iraq's president—the Saudis reportedly committed themselves to support Iraq once war began. They feared that Iran was planning to use the October pilgrimage to incite rebellion against the royal family.[24] Another source claims that two days before war began, Saudi Arabia, the United Arab Emirates (UAE), Qatar, and Bahrain signed an agreement with Iraq, pledging to supply all military and non-military requirements needed for the Iraqi war effort.[25]

Other works disputed such assertions, claiming it was inconceivable that Saddam Husayn, a secretive operator by nature, would have disclosed his decision to invade Iran to the Saudis, in what could have amounted to a major security breach. Moreover, they cited a report that when Saddam later complained to the Saudis about insufficient support, Saudi leaders replied that Iraq should have told its Arab brothers in advance about its moves and thus sought their support beforehand.[26]

The Saudis viewed Iraq's invasion of Iran as an attempt to preempt any spread of fundamentalism and take advantage of the chaos in Iran in order to assert Iraqi domination over the area. Riyadh was quite concerned lest Iraq win the war and assert hegemony in the Gulf. But once it became clear that Iran was gaining the upper hand, Saudi leaders decided that it represented a far greater danger and began supporting Saddam's war effort.

From Iraq's perspective, the destruction of its southern port and oil-exporting facilities, the closure of the Syrian pipeline, and the sharp drop in revenues all created heavy dependence on the Gulf monarchies for crucial financial and other aid. Thus, what started as mere Saudi-Iraqi cooperation against a common adversary, Iran, turned into a vital strategic, political, and economic alliance against a major threat to their very security and existence.

Saudi support of Iraq during the war consisted of five principal areas.

Financial Assistance

In mid-April 1981, Saudi Arabia pledged $6 billion as part of a $10 billion Gulf package for Iraq. During much of 1981 and 1982, Saudi Arabia and the Gulf states provided Iraq with $1 billion per month. According to a Western source, Gulf support for Iraq between March 1981 and March 1982 reached $22 billion. One study put Saudi assistance to Iraq in 1980 to 1983 at $20 billion. Finally, an American source suggested that by the end of 1982, Saudi aid had reached $30 billion. In a speech hours before the U.S. attack on Iraq in January 1991, King Fahd revealed that Saudi assistance to Baghdad during the Iran-Iraq war had totaled $25.7 billion.[27]

Oil Sales

In 1981 Saudi Arabia and Kuwait began giving Iraq the income from the daily sales of about 300,000 barrels of oil produced in the Saudi-Kuwaiti "Neutral Zone." It was estimated that Iraq received about $9 billion by this means between 1983 and 1985 alone. The sharp decline in oil prices, however, cut this income from about $4 billion in 1981 to $1.8 billion in 1987.[28]

Oil Pipeline

Given Iraq's loss of the Gulf as an outlet for its oil and closure of the pipeline going through Syria, the construction of Iraqi pipelines through Turkish and Saudi territory became critical. The vulnerability of the Turkish pipeline and the need to export more oil forced Iraq to accord priority to the Saudi pipeline. In late 1983 Riyadh and Baghdad reached an agreement to build a 400-mile pipeline connecting Iraq's southern oilfields to the Saudi east-west Petroline. In 1985 it became operational, enabling Iraq to export 500,000 barrels of oil a day. The project's second phase involved an independent 600-mile Iraqi pipeline, which went into service in 1989, able to carry 1.15 million barrels a day to a Red Sea terminal at Yanbu'.[29]

Port Facilities

Military supplies were sent to Iraq via Saudi Red Sea ports. The first shipment of 100 T-55 tanks was reportedly sent from Poland starting in December 1980. The Saudis allowed Soviet arms to be unloaded at the small port of Qadima north of Jidda and transported across their territory to Iraq, even though they had no diplomatic relations with Moscow and did not like close ties between the Soviet Union and any Arab country. Thus, by the fall of 1981, Saudi Arabia became Iraq's most critical arms import channel with more weapons reaching Iraq through its territory than by any other route.[30]

Military Assistance

Beginning in 1986, the Saudis provided a military transport link of another kind when they apparently allowed Iraqi aircraft to land and refuel after striking at Iranian oil facilities in the far reaches of the Gulf.[31]

Despite Saudi-Iraqi cooperation against Iran, there were also considerable frictions. Saudi Arabia was reluctant to give Iraq direct military support, in contrast to Jordan, Egypt, and Sudan, which sent troops and military hardware. Indeed, Iraq periodically complained about the "insufficient" level of assistance from Gulf states whose backing of Baghdad was less than "complete" when compared to Jordan's. As early as the summer of 1981, Saddam Husayn said there was "some bitterness in the hearts of the Iraqis" over the lack of Arab support. This bitterness reached its peak in Saddam's speech following the Iraqi withdrawal from Khoramshahr in June 1982.[32]

Such displeasure intensified after 1983 as declining oil prices made Gulf states decrease aid to Iraq. In early 1983 Iraq's Deputy Premier Tariq 'Aziz told *Le Monde* that "Iraq's Arab brothers virtually stopped helping us for the last twelve months." At that time, there was a sense in Baghdad that the Saudis had edged back toward neutrality and the position of a mediator.[33]

A major source of controversy was Iraq's exclusion from the Gulf Cooperation Council (GCC) when the grouping was formed in May 1981. It was argued that Saudi Arabia and the five GCC states were anxious not to be seen as "ganging up" on and antagonizing Iran, a perception that would have been generated by Iraq's membership.[34] The main reason for Iraq's exclusion, however, had to do with the basic Saudi perception of the Iraqi regime, which did not change despite the common enmity toward Islamic Iran.

Saudi fears of Iraqi domination did not diminish given that state's superior size and power as well as radical ideology. By omitting Iraq, Saudi Arabia intended the GCC to institutionalize and highlight a distance between Baghdad and its Gulf Arab neighbors. The GCC charter stressed the Gulf regimes' homogeneity, explicitly referring to "the special relations and similar political and economic orientations of the Council members." Obviously, the Iraq Ba'th regime did not fit in such a grouping.

Finally, Saudi Arabia sought to use its leadership of the GCC to reassert its position and influence in regional affairs following the setbacks caused by Iran's revolution, the attack on the Mecca Mosque, the Camp David peace process, and increasing insecurity in the Gulf area. Iraqi membership in the GCC would have made it impossible for the Saudis to play a leadership role there. Badly in need of Saudi Arabia's assistance and goodwill, Iraq merely expressed deep disappointment at being left out of the GCC. Saddam argued that any formal pact among Arab states should be signed within the framework of the Arab League. Iraq later expressed readiness to join the GCC if invited. Iraqi spokesmen even described the GCC as "the model for any future effort" to resolve the problem of Gulf stability and security.[35]

Differences between Baghdad and Riyadh surfaced on other issues as well. Iraq opposed the initial Saudi decision in the fall of 1980 to permit the stationing of U.S. surveillance aircraft (AWACS) on Saudi territory. It was also critical of Riyadh's subsequent decision to purchase the AWACS in view of Washington's assertion that the aircraft was intended as much against Iraq as against any other threat to Saudi Arabia. On oil issues, Iraq was displeased with the Saudi stand at OPEC's June 1981 meeting opposing price fixing and production cuts for the rest of the year. Finally, it was obvious that Iraq was unhappy with the Fahd Middle East peace plan announced in August 1981.

But in all these instances, Baghdad couched its criticism of Saudi Arabia in mild language. Alluding to the Fahd Plan, Saddam Husayn explained that Iraq did not favor unilateral initiatives: "We do not seek an alternative that is only relatively better than Camp David or any other plan. . . . The soundest stand is that agreed on by all the Arabs." When the Fahd Plan was put on the agenda of the November 1981 Fez Arab summit, however, Iraq joined Syria and the PLO in opposing it, and Saddam refused to attend the summit.[36] This revealed once again the Saudis' limited leverage vis-à-vis Iraq, even at a moment when Baghdad was beholden to Riyadh for crucial economic and political aid.

Saddam must have realized that Saudi Arabia also benefited from the Iran-Iraq war's continuation. The quarrel between the two major Gulf powers stopped either of them from expanding their influence and threatening the Saudis. The Saudis also gained from the fact that reduced Iranian and Iraqi oil production caused by the war helped ease a world petroleum glut, thus checking a further deterioration in oil prices.

1988 TO 1990

Despite the considerable potential for confrontation, Iraq-Saudi relations did not reach a point of no return, largely due to Baghdad's realization that it could not yet successfully challenge Saudi Arabia. From Riyadh's perspective, the turning point in Saudi-Iraqi relations occurred after the Iran-Iraq war ended in 1988, followed by Ayatollah Khomeini's death a year later. Without Britain or the Shah policing the Gulf and protecting the weak Arab states, and with Iran considerably weakened, the Saudis feared that Saddam had decided he was free of the constraints traditionally curbing Iraqi aspirations in the Gulf area.

The Saudis were especially apprehensive about the formation of the Arab Cooperation Council (ACC) in February 1989. Saddam's growing regional power seemed further enhanced by the inclusion in the Iraqi-led ACC of North Yemen, a country the Saudis viewed as within their orbit, and Jordan, previously dependent on Saudi Arabia. The Iraq-Bahrain defense pact signed in December 1989 added to Saudi anxieties that Saddam was encroaching on what the Saudis considered their sphere of influence. Finally, Saddam's threats in the February 1990 ACC Amman summit and his aggressive speech at the May 1990 Baghdad summit followed by his blunt threats against Kuwait and the United Arab Emirates put the Saudis on the spot.

Except for rushing to Baghdad to sign a nonaggression pact with Iraq in April 1989, King Fahd devised no strategy to deal with a potential Iraqi attack. There was no attempt to mobilize an Arab front against Saddam or to improve U.S.-Saudi coordination to deter Iraq. It seemed as if Saudi leaders feared such defensive steps would anger Saddam and provoke him into hostile acts. The Saudis must have underestimated Saddam's readiness to challenge both his former Arab allies and Washington. They also seemed to have been caught off balance by Iraq's quick reorientation of its policy.

It is often asked whether Saddam really intended to invade Saudi Arabia's Eastern Province after he occupied Kuwait. If so, he could have made a historical claim like the one he made on Kuwait: that the district (*sanjaq*) of Hasa [the Saudi Eastern Province] was an integral part of the Ottoman province (*vilayet*) of Basra, which Great Britain helped the Saudis conquer in 1913.[37] In one respect, Iraq's claim over Hasa was the stronger one. Whereas Kuwait had acquired some distinct status because the al-Sabah family had been ruling there for over 200 years, no political features of a distinctly local nature existed in Hasa.

Whether or not Saddam intended to invade Saudi Arabia, the Saudi royal family was certain that he was about to do so in August 1990. This conclusion was reinforced by three small Iraqi military incursions onto Saudi territory on August 4 and 5. As the Saudi ambassador in Washington, Prince Bandar, later recalled, these infiltrations prompted the Saudis to activate a "hot line" phone with Iraq's army. At first the Iraqis apologized but later they refrained from responding, so that the Saudis "became persuaded that behind the smoke screen, an invasion was imminent."[38]

In a speech to his people five months later, King Fahd stated that "after the aggression against Kuwait," Iraq was preparing for "an aggression against Saudi Arabia." Fahd placed Iraq's plans in a wider context: "Saddam wanted to expand to the Gulf states, starting with Kuwait, then the Kingdom of Saudi Arabia, Bahrain, Qatar, the United Arab Emirates and Oman; we have signs indicating this." In his "victory speech" on March 5, 1991, Fahd stated that Saddam wanted "to swallow Kuwait and part of Saudi Arabia too."[39]

The point, however, is that Iraq did not need actually to invade Saudi Arabia to subordinate it. With hundreds of thousands of Iraqi troops massed on the border threatening the kingdom, which had no means to stop them, King Fahd knew Iraq could dictate Saudi policy and destroy the country's independence.

There were two options to deal with this situation. One was the traditional Saudi technique of buying goodwill with generous financial assistance. According to a "top-secret American intelligence report," the royal family discussed offering Saddam several billion dollars if he withdrew Iraqi forces from the border and respected the kingdom's sovereignty and integrity.[40] But King Fahd knew that if he did not want to remain Saddam's hostage, he had to counterbalance the Iraqi threat with Western protection. And once he was assured of massive U.S. support, the road was open for inviting U.S. troops to Saudi Arabia.

In the final analysis, it appeared that after the Iran-Iraq war and eight years of cooperation with Saddam, Saudi Arabia began to harbor some illusions about a possible compatibility of Iraqi and Saudi interests. After the invasion of Kuwait, King Fahd repeatedly stressed how the Saudis were surprised:

> We never believed nor imagined that one day matters could lead Iraq to occupy Kuwait and plan an aggression against Saudi Arabia. . . . We never thought that Saddam would deliberately destroy all Islamic ties and conventions, as well as the kinship between two Arab countries, and take over an independent Arab homeland, a member of the Arab League and the international community.[41]

But the Saudis were not the only ones surprised by Saddam's moves. Academic works written throughout the 1980s show that a great many Western scholars harbored the same illusions about Iraq and about Saudi-Iraqi relations as well.[42]

Yet no matter how they cooperated temporarily, the two countries were in serious conflict on at least ten points:

1. The balance of forces in the Gulf made weak, oil-rich Saudi Arabia a tempting target for a militarily superior Iraq.

2. Iraq's ruling ideology was committed to destroying "reactionary," pro-U.S. regimes and monarchies like Saudi Arabia.

3. Iraqi ambitions in the Arabian Peninsula and Gulf Arab coast posed a direct challenge to the traditional Saudi wish for hegemony there.

4. Riyadh saw Iraq's irredentist claims in Kuwait, involvement in Yemen (both North and South), and subversive activities in Oman and other Gulf states as destabilizing and undermining Saudi security.

5. Iraq's desire to play a central role in any Gulf security system collided with a Saudi determination to exclude it from such arrangements, a collision reflected in the GCC's formation.

6. Iraq's close relations with the Soviet Union ran fundamentally counter to the Saudi regime's anti-Soviet policy.

7. Likewise, the "special relations" between Saudi Arabia and the United States were anathema to Iraq's ideology and policy.

8. Saudi Arabia preferred a political solution to the Arab-Israeli conflict; Iraq took an uncompromising stance on the issue.

9. As major oil producers and members of OPEC and OAPEC, Iraq and Saudi Arabia promoted conflicting policies on production and price levels as well as divergent concepts regarding the employment of oil as a political weapon.

10. There were some disagreements over delineating the border and "neutral zone" between the two countries.

Such fundamental differences notwithstanding, several analysts thought that the two state's positions converged on several issues:

1. Both were concerned about superpower rivalry in the Gulf.

2. Both were interested in increasing and protecting the value of their oil revenues.

3. Both opposed, though for distinct reasons and to different degrees, the Camp David accords and the Egypt-Israel peace.

4. Both were deeply concerned with Iran's revolution and saw its fundamentalist ideology as a direct threat to their stability.

5. Both opposed Moscow's invasion of Afghanistan.[43]

A closer glance at each similarity, however, shows that convergence was limited, confined to a tactical level:

1. As for the superpower presence, Iraq saw the United States as an imperialist threat; Saudi Arabia as a protector.

2. Baghdad and Riyadh favored different policies on oil production and prices to protect their interests.
3. They shared opposition to the Camp David process but had diametrically opposed perceptions and goals on the Arab-Israeli peace process. For example, Saudi Arabia accepted Arab sanctions and took a militant stand against Egypt only after subjected to Iraqi and Syrian threats at the March 1979 Baghdad summit.
4. The concern with Iran's revolution did not result in any long-term, joint strategy toward the new regime in Tehran.
5. The rejection of the Soviet invasion of Afghanistan also prompted different reactions: the Saudis offered extensive help to the Afghan rebels; the Iraqis refrained from any intervention.

The pattern of Iraqi-Saudi relations, then, indicates some important and recurring themes.

First, Iraq, not Saudi Arabia, set the tone and determined the course of bilateral relations. While Baghdad held the initiative, Riyadh merely reacted, usually adopting a defensive posture, in response to Iraqi actions. Thus, any improvement or deterioration in relations was primarily a function of changes in Iraqi priorities rather than a shift in Saudi policies.

Second, Saudi leverage vis-à-vis Iraq and ability to redirect its ideology or policy was limited even when Iraq was weak, as during its war with Iran. Unlike other recipients of Saudi aid, oil-rich and militarily powerful Iraq was less susceptible to the financial and diplomatic pressures of Riyadh.

Third, the Saudis were aware of their strategic weakness vis-à-vis Iraq and saw their position in the Gulf as largely a function of the balance of forces between Baghdad and Tehran. Both were thought to be evil forces able to damage Saudi security or interests. The only question was which was more dangerous at any given time. After 1968, Iraq's Ba'th regime was viewed as a greater evil than the Shah; after 1979, Islamic Iran was seen as far more threatening, paving the way for an alliance with Saddam Husayn.

Fourth, even when Saudi Arabia and Iraq shared a common hostility toward Iran, Riyadh still viewed Baghdad as its political rival in the struggle for influence on the Arab side of the Gulf. Hence, the Saudis were determined to exclude Iraq from the GCC.

Fifth, numerous instances of Saudi-Iraqi rapprochement showed that Saudi leaders were ready to cooperate with radical Arab regimes, even those ideologically bent on their own destruction, if such cooperation was self-serving and reduced pressures on Riyadh.

Finally, in defending itself against Iraq, Saudi Arabia employed a variety of means. It tried to appease Iraq and "join" with Baghdad whenever possible, as was the case after Egypt had made peace with Israel. It forged a front with Iran as a counterweight to Iraq. It strove to create a joint front with its small Gulf "sisters" under Saudi leadership and excluding Iraq. It sought a credible military deterrent against Iraq by constructing its largest military compound in Hafar al-Batin, facing that border. Although it refused to subscribe to the "Carter Doctrine" and to Reagan's "Strategic Consensus," Saudi Arabia was always in a position to invoke its "special relationship" with the United States, as well as the "over the horizon" military presence, as deterrence. As a last resort, it could turn to Washington and ask for protection.

As war against Saddam became imminent in early 1991, Saudi perceptions of Iraq focused on several principles.

Saudi leaders wished to see "Iraq's military capability to wage offensive war and to engage in future aggression" ended but opposed wrecking Iraq's army since it might then be unable "to play its traditional balancing role in the Gulf." Such a vacuum would upset the regional power balance and create "undeterred military supremacy of Iran in the east and of Israel in the west."[44]

They favored the preservation of Iraq's independence and territorial integrity and "will do the utmost to prevent any attempt to carve up its territory." They vehemently rejected the formation of a Shi'a entity in southern Iraq, and they strove to prevent a group of Iraqi Shi'a dissidents living in Iran from gaining influence in Iraq in the postwar era.[45]

They wished to see Iraq purged not only of Saddam Husayn himself but also of all the "hypocritical pillars of the Ba'th dictatorship." Only such a change could "guard against a new tyrant [and] ensure that the same experience would not be repeated." But the task of "imposing the will of the Iraqi people" was not up to outside states. Rather, the Arab countries that had helped Saddam must "exert pressure on the Iraqi regime and . . . abandon it, forcing it to leave matters to the Iraqi people," or "persuade Saddam to relinquish power and save the country."[46]

Such statements notwithstanding, in early 1991 Saudi Arabia quietly began assembling former Iraqi political and military officials to form a potential government-in-exile that could fill a power vacuum in Baghdad if Saddam was ousted. The Saudi leadership was eager to have a voice in shaping the political future of Iraq in general and to have a government in Baghdad that was friendly to Riyadh.[47]

Even after the war, however, Saudi Arabia was no closer to achieving this goal than it had been earlier. Its leaders were frustrated at their inability to influence Iraqi politics and fearful about Iraq's military arsenal and the future threat it might pose the Saudi kingdom.[48]

NOTES

1. Saudi Press Agency, November 15, 1989, in *Foreign Broadcast Information Service* (*FBIS*), November 17, 1989.
2. Editorials in *al-Madina*, August 12, 1990; *al-Jazira*, August 14, 1990; *al-Riyad*, August 15, 1990; '*Ukaz*, August 17, 1990.
3. Tim Niblock, "Iraqi Policies towards the Arab States of the Gulf, 1958-1981," in Tim Niblock, ed., *Iraq: The Contemporary State* (London, 1982), pp. 142-43; Edmund Ghareeb, "Iraq in the Gulf," in Frederick Axelgard, ed., *Iraq in Transition: A Political, Economic and Strategic Perspective* (Boulder, Colo., 1986), pp. 66-67.
4. Ibid.; Amatzia Baram, "National Integration and Exclusiveness in Political thought and Practice in Iraq under the Ba'th, 1968-1982," Ph.D diss., Hebrew University of Jerusalem, 1986, pp. 176, 180.
5. J. M. Abdulghani, *Iraq and Iran: The Years of Crisis* (London, 1984), p. 80.
6. David Holden and Richard Johns, *The House of Saud: The Rise and Rule of the Most Powerful Dynasty in the Arab World* (New York, 1981), p. 376.
7. Ghareeb, "Iraq in the Gulf," p. 67.
8. Alexander Bligh, "The Interplay Between Opposition Activity in Saudi Arabia and Recent Trends in the Arab World," in Robert Stookey, ed., *The Arabian Peninsula: Zone of Ferment* (Stanford, Calif., 1984), pp. 73-74.
9. *Middle East Economic Survey,* October 26, 1973, p. 4.
10. Richard Nyrop, *Iraq: A Country Study* (Washington, D.C., 1979), p. 216.
11. Abdulghani, *Iraq and Iran,* p. 80.
12. Baram, "National Integration and Exclusiveness," p. 176.
13. *Middle East Economic Digest* (*MEED*) November 29, 1974; *al-Hawadith,* December 27, 1974; Baram, "National Integration and Exclusiveness," p. 177.
14. Abdulghani, *Iraq and Iran,* p. 159, and notes 40 and 41 on p. 173.
15. Ghareeb, "Iraq in the Gulf," p. 70; Nadav Safran, *Saudi Arabia: The Ceaseless Quest for Security* (London, 1988), p. 266.
16. Ghassan Salameh, *Al-Siyasa al-Kharijiyya al-Sa'udiyya mundhu 1945* [Saudi Foreign Policy since 1945] (Beirut, 1980), pp. 75-76; Naomi Sakr, "Economic Relations Between Iraq and other Arab Gulf States," in Niblock, ed., *Iraq,* p. 154.
17. *Arab Report and Record,* April 1-15, 1976, p. 214; *al-Nahar,* April 26, 1977; *al-Siyasa* (Kuwait), April 19, 1978.
18. Ghareeb, "Iraq in the Gulf," p. 71; Safran, *Saudi Arabia,* p. 266.

19. *Arab Report and Record,* December 16-31, 1976, p. 754.
20. Ghareeb, "Iraq in the Gulf," p. 72; Abdulghani, *Iraq and Iran,* pp. 194-95.
21. *New York Times,* February 8, 1979; *al-Nahar,* February 26, 1979.
22. *The Guardian,* April 11, 1979. (Saddam made a similar statement in 1974; see note 11.)
23. Interview in *al-Watan al-'Arabi,* February 1, 1980.
24. Sakr, "Economic Relations," pp. 150-51; Alan R. Taylor, *The Arab Balance of Power* (New York, 1982), p. 88.
25. Edgar O'Ballance, *The Gulf War* (London, 1988), p. 52.
26. M. S. El-Azhary, *The Iran-Iraq War: An Historical, Economic and Political Analysis* (New York, 1984), p. 82.
27. *Al-Ra'y al-'Amm,* April 16, 1981; Ghareeb,"Iraq in the Gulf,"p. 76; *Financial Times,* March 26, 1982; Gerd Nonneman, *Iraq, the Gulf States and the War* (London, 1986), pp. 95-97; *Business Week,* December 6, 1982; *Ha'aretz,* January 17, 1991.
28. Eliyahu Kanovsky, "Economic Implications for the Region and World Oil Market," in Efraim Karsh, ed., *The Iran-Iraq War: Impact and Implications* (Tel Aviv, 1987), p. 237; Ghareeb, "Iraq in the Gulf," p. 76; Nonneman, *Iraq,* pp. 102-103.
29. Frederick Axelgard, "War and Oil: Implications for Iraq's Postwar Role in Gulf Security," in Axelgard, ed., *Iraq in Transition,* pp. 10-11; Kanovsky, "Economic Implications," p. 238.
30. *MEED,* November 28, 1980; *Financial Times,* February 6, 1981; William Quandt, *Saudi Arabia in the 1980s* (Washington, D.C., 1981), p. 21; Nonneman, *Iraq,* p. 39.
31. Frederick Axelgard, *A New Iraq? The Gulf War and Implications of U.S. Policy* (New York, 1988), p. 75.
32. Ibid.; *al-Mustaqbal,* July 25, 1981; Radio Baghdad, June 20, 1982, in *FBIS,* June 22, 1982.
33. *New York Times* and *Le Monde,* January 8, 1983; Baram, "National Integration and Exclusiveness," p. 182.
34. Sakr, "Economic Relations," p. 152.
35. Nizar Hamdoon, "Iraq-U.S. Relations," *Arab-American Affairs* 14 (Fall 1985), p. 96.
36. Claudia Wright, "Neutral or Neutralized? Iraq, Iran and the Superpowers," in Shirin Tahir-Kheli and Shaheen Ayubi, eds., *The Iran-Iraq War: New Weapons, Old Conflicts* (New York, 1983), pp. 182-84.
37. For details see Jacob Goldberg, "The 1913 Saudi Occupation of Hasa Reconsidered," *Middle Eastern Studies* 18, no. 1 (1982), pp. 21-29.
38. *New York Times,* October 4, 1990.

39. Saudi TV, January 12 and March 5, 1991, in *FBIS*, January 14 and March 6, 1991, respectively.

40. Bob Woodward, *The Commanders* (New York, 1991).

41. Saudi TV, January 12, 1991, in *FBIS*, January 14, 1991.

42. In 1981, William Quandt wrote that "Saudi leaders hope that Iraq would continue its policy of non-alignment and curtail its disruptive actions in countries of special interest to Saudi Arabia—Yemen, Oman and Kuwait. The Saudis believe that Iraq can be lured away from its Soviet connection and that a strongly pragmatic streak lies behind Saddam's Ba'thist rhetoric" (Quandt, *Saudi Arabia*, p. 146).

In the mid-1980s, Edmund Ghareeb observed that "Iraq's relations with the Gulf states are better than they have been at any time in recent history, and not simply as a result of regional concerns about the Gulf war and the Iranian revolution. Rather, Iraq's foreign policy in general and its Gulf policy in particular have become more tactful and less rigid than before. In the Gulf, Iraq's pragmatism and use of skillful diplomacy combined with political expediency to produce a convergence of interests with those of the other Gulf states. . . . The evolution in the thinking of Iraqi leaders is in essence the conceptualization of foreign policy as an instrument to achieve regional accommodation rather than to pursue regional ideological transformation" (Ghareeb, "Iraq in the Gulf," pp. 76-77).

Frederick Axelgard argued that Iraq's oil pipelines across Saudi Arabia suggested that "aside from a common fear of Iran, the two countries could be partners in long-term cooperation." Criticizing those who "jarred a wide array of cynical assumptions about the longevity and underlying strength of Iraqi relations with the Gulf states," Axelgard made the following prediction: "In the postwar period, the pipeline would involve Iraq constructively in the life of the Gulf and presumably help dampen any remaining vision Iraq might have of imposing hegemony there. The pipeline locks Saudi Arabia into a vital association with a country whose revolutionary, secular outlook has for decades been the antithesis of its own" (Axelgard, *A New Iraq?* pp. 76-77).

43. Quandt, *Saudi Arabia*, p. 21.

44. Saudi officials quoted in the *Washington Post*, November 11, 1990, and the *New York Times*, January 9, 1991.

45. *New York Times*, February 22, 1991; Saudi Press Agency, March 17, 1991, in *FBIS*, March 18, 1991.

46. Editorials in *al-Bilad*, March 16, 1991, and *'Ukaz*, March 17, 1991.

47. *New York Times*, February 22, 1991.

48. Saudi officials quoted in the *Washington Post*, November 11, 1990.

8

Jordan's Relations with Iraq: Ally or Victim?

Joseph Nevo

Jordan's unequivocal backing for Iraq, one of the more intriguing expressions of the Kuwait crisis and Gulf war, was the result of a special relationship that was first developed in the late 1970s.[1] During a decade or so, this link made Jordan economically, politically, and militarily dependent on Iraq. The developments of that period provide some explanation for Jordan's strong support for Iraq between August 1990 and February 1991.

Nonetheless, an examination of Jordanian-Iraqi ties in a wider historical perspective unfolds far more frequent fluctuations, from cordiality to animosity and vice versa. A search for a pattern suggests that both constant and variable elements contributed to shaping that relationship.

HISTORICAL SETTING

The lack of symmetry so salient in the bilateral relations originated not only in Iraq's greater size, population, and natural resources. Iraq also enjoyed historical continuity around a territorial nucleus since the days of pre-Islamic, even biblical, empires. The demarcation of the Iraqi state—established after World War I encompassing the former Ottoman villayets of Basra and Baghdad and part of Mosul—seemed almost obvious and "natural."

Jordan, on the other hand, had never been a unified administrative or political entity. The territory that in the 1920s became the Emirate of Transjordan was controlled in the past (when it was controlled) simultaneously from several different external centers, such as Baghdad, Damascus, Medina, and Palestine.

The family ties between the two ruling houses flavored relations between Iraq and Transjordan (since their foundation in 1921) with a certain uniqueness. Yet the situation of two neighboring political entities ruled by brothers—'Abdallah and Faysal—who were both "imported" into their respective realms did not guarantee friendship and cooperation. Both of them had, first of all, to gain the confidence and legitimacy of their new subjects. In that situation the ruling brothers occasionally developed conflicting political interests and vied for the same territory.[2]

The common familial framework, however, did have an effect on bilateral relations, even when personal relations were not always amicable. "Iraq and Jordan had more in common than any other two Arab states."[3] Even after a three-generation-long Hashemite rule in Iraq had been violently ended, it seems that King Husayn still had a special attitude to that country. He sometimes gave the impression of feeling more at ease in Baghdad than in Damascus or Riyadh, for example, even when Jordan-Iraq relations were not at their best.

Both rulers worked in the 1920s to enhance their own position at home by building and consolidating their respective nations. By the early 1930s, they were struggling over control of Syria. Each ruler opposed his brother's ambition for the "crown of Damascus" and to his endeavors to unite Syria with his own country.[4]

After Faysal's death, that competition continued between his offspring in Iraq and 'Abdallah in Transjordan. In the second half of the 1930s, following the army's growing intervention in Iraqi politics, the royal house's role in governing there was markedly diminished. The radicalism and anti-British attitude of the army officers in Baghdad also did not contribute to improved relations with Transjordan.

When, in April 1941, a nationalist coup took over in Baghdad and challenged the Hashemites, they sought (and found) refuge at the court of Emir 'Abdallah in Amman, the family's senior member. They eventually returned to Baghdad after the British had crushed the rebellious Iraqi army. The British were helped by Emir 'Abdallah's troops, whose motive in entering that venture was more than merely family solidarity.[5]

The Hashemite comeback under the protection of British bayonets alienated them from Iraqi and Arab nationalists. It did enhance, however, relations between the regimes in Transjordan and Iraq. Even the competitive Arab unity schemes designed by Emir 'Abdallah and Nuri al-Sa'id during World War II ('Abdallah's Greater Syria scheme and Nuri's Fertile Crescent unity) did not cast a heavy shadow over the strengthened friendship.

Following the end of that war and the foundation of the Arab League, a new division emerged, splitting the Arab world into two blocs: Egypt and Saudi Arabia on one side and Iraq and Transjordan on the other. The formation of the first bloc, to which Syria was closely affiliated, served as an incentive for closer relations between Transjordan and Iraq. The failure of 'Abdallah's attempts to foster his Greater Syria scheme also facilitated the improvement of Iraq-Transjordan relations and yielded, in 1947, a ten-year treaty of alliance.[6]

At that period 'Abdallah focused his intentions more and more on Palestine, which he wished to annex to his domain. Under pressure, he was also ready to acquiesce to Palestine's partition and to settle for annexing parts of it. Iraq's considerable support for 'Abdallah's ambitions in Palestine stemmed not only from solidarity with a neighboring Hashemite regime. Some Iraqi politicians, chief among whom was Nuri al-Sa'id, would rather have seen 'Abdallah consume his political energy in the struggle for Palestine and leave Syria for their own ambitions.

One of the exceptions in Iraq's supportive position toward Jordan's policy in Palestine was its prompt recognition of the All-Palestine Government in Gaza in October 1948. Iraqi support of this anti-Jordanian venture did not indicate a policy shift but merely reflected the efforts of the new government in Baghdad to improve relations with the Arab world and especially with Egypt, which backed the Gaza administration. Practically, however, it had no impact on Iraq's de facto recognition of the authority of Jordan's military governors in Palestine, including the areas held by the Iraqi army.

It was also Iraq that managed to defuse the crisis between Jordan and the Arab League in 1950. It provided the formula that put an end to Jordan's negotiation for a peace treaty with Israel in return for a de facto temporary Arab recognition of Jordan's annexation of the West Bank.[7]

In his last years King 'Abdallah of Jordan was toying with the idea of a union with Iraq both as a personal ambition and as an attempt to deal with the problem of succession in Jordan. Disappointed in his son and heir apparent Talal, he dreamed of a union of the two countries with himself on the throne, to be succeeded by Faysal II, the Iraqi crown prince.[8]

Syria remained a bone of contention between Iraq and Jordan, and only 'Abdallah's murder in 1951 removed the Syrian issue from the central position it had occupied in bilateral relations. By discarding Jordan's hitherto traditional claim for Syria, 'Abdallah's successors ceased to pose a threat to Iraq's external ambitions. Jordan's importance for Iraq, either as a threat or as an ally, had considerably declined.

Indeed, the possibility of a Jordanian-Iraqi union was somewhat intensified after 'Abdallah's sudden death. Both Britain and Iraq feared Jordan's disintegration following the king's murder. A union with Iraq seemed a reasonable way to secure Jordan's integrity. Later, however, the question of a union was mentioned intermittently but usually in a low key, rather out of inertia than as a practical option. In that era, the subject was raised almost exclusively from the Iraqi side.

In his first years on the throne, King Husayn developed a certain ambivalence toward Iraq, part of which still prevails. On the one hand, he suspected Iraq's intentions regarding his kingdom. On the other, he felt neglected, if not deprived, by his affluent and powerful relatives. Iraq's power was not transformed in relations with Jordan into political backing or economic aid. Iraq had not even gone out of its way to coopt Jordan into the Baghdad Pact. On the contrary, Iraq's efforts in this respect were suspiciously modest.[9]

There was, however, a gradual improvement in bilateral relations during 1956, stemming from the growing common worry about the Egyptian regime of Gamal 'Abd al-Nasir. The two kings had an official meeting; diplomatic ties were raised to ambassadorial level, and, fearing an Israeli attack, Jordan invited Iraqi forces to defend it. In 1957 when Husayn's regime was threatened by a radical prime minister, a mutinous chief of staff, and a hostile Syria, Iraq (and Saudi Arabia) backed Jordan militarily and politically. Iraq warned Syria not to meddle in Jordan's affairs.

The final period of Hashemite rule in Iraq was accompanied by the establishment of a nominal federation with Jordan. Iraq was reluctant to accept Husayn's proposal for a union. As in previous unity bids, Jordan had little to offer Iraq either economically or strategically to counterbalance its liabilities.[10] Yet the change of the regional strategic balance following the formation of the Egypt-Syria union was stronger than any other consideration. For the first time in their history, the family tie between the two ruling houses produced a formal connections of their countries.

The violent end of Iraq's Hashemites in 1958 removed an important dimension from bilateral relations. Thereafter they were dominated by the conventional factors shaping regional relations. Yet past sentiments did not wane entirely, at least on Husayn's part.

If, in the mid-1950s, Husayn was sometimes hesitant whether to side with Iraq or Egypt, by 1959-1960 he found himself once again between these two countries, trapped between the hammer and the anvil. The new Iraq regime of 'Abd al-Karim Qasim urged the Palestinians in the West Bank to challenge Jordan and to form their own entity and own army.

After two years of open hostility, Husayn sought to reestablish diplomatic relations with Iraq. That move was depicted by Benjamin Shwadran as "Perhaps the most difficult adjustment Husayn made in his inter-Arab politics."[11] Yet it was the only feasible way to break the isolation imposed on Jordan by Nasir. The resumption of diplomatic relations (October 1960) led toward a comprehensive Iraq-Jordan rapprochement. Bilateral normalization was hardly hampered by Jordan's support of the integrity and independence of Kuwait against the Iraqi claims in 1961. Even the temporary coming to power of the Ba'th in Iraq in early 1963 brought about no major change. Following the abortive attempt for a tripartite union among Syria, Iraq, and Egypt that excluded Jordan, both Syria and Iraq—disillusioned by 'Abd al-Nasir—eagerly strengthened ties with Jordan, which they expected to side with them in their new quarrel with Egypt.[12]

During the 1967 Arab-Israeli war, Iraqi forces entered Jordan at its request, a sign of the two states' trust and cooperation. The tension and cooling-off of bilateral relations in the following years occurred not so much because of the 1968 Ba'th takeover in Iraq but rather because of Jordan's September 1970 showdown with the PLO. After that conflict, the 25,000-strong Iraqi forces in Jordan went home. In July 1971 when the PLO was totally beaten and expelled from Jordan, Iraq, like Syria, closed its border with Jordan.

A gradual improvement in bilateral relations began only after the October 1973 war. Since the mid-1970s relations were fairly stable and mainly economic. Iraq's leading role in organizing Arab opposition to the 1978 Camp David accords enhanced its relations with Jordan and reintroduced the political dimension. Iraq was courting Jordan and offering economic aid mainly to prevent it from joining the U.S.-Egypt-Israel peace talks. The politicization of relations also coincided with President Bakr's resignation and the succession of Saddam Husayn. Jordan welcomed Iraq's overture since its relations with Syria were deteriorating.

After the outbreak of the Iran-Iraq war, Jordan immediately sided with Iraq. Jordan was not only the first Arab state to support Iraq publicly, but it also worked to achieve a unanimous Arab backing for it. Jordan placed its whole transportation infrastructure and communication system at the disposal of Iraq's war effort. In 1982 it even sent a few thousand volunteers (the Yarmuk forces) to Iraq as a token of its identification with Iraq's war aims.

Relations remained close and cordial even after the war. Iraq rewarded Jordan for its stand during the war by providing a large amount of weapons captured as booty and by deepening political ties.[13] Bilateral connections were then characterized by increasing military cooperation and coordination of regional policy. Both Jordan and Iraq (together with Egypt and North Yemen) were founding members of the Arab Cooperation Council (ACC) in early 1989. Jordan tended to support Iraqi views regarding the ACC's policy and goals which were markedly different from those of Egypt. The trials and tribulations that Jordan-Iraq relations underwent since the early 1920s were shaped by many factors. The most influential among them were the nature of the two countries and regimes, the asymmetry of their relations, and the impact of some inter-Arab issues.

THE NATURE OF THE COUNTRIES AND REGIMES

Iraq was far richer and stronger than Jordan in terms of its size, population and natural resources as well as its military power. The difference between the size and quality of their armies stemmed not only from different resources but was also a matter of policy and priorities. In 1967 the Iraqi and Jordanian armies were almost the same size: 56,000 and 55,000 men respectively[14]. In just over 20 years Jordan's army doubled in size while Iraq's army became almost 20 times larger. This difference in power is the basic explanation for the fact that Iraq was the senior partner in its connections with Jordan.

Distinct histories and geographies also produced two types of regimes. In Jordan, despite being a newly created, vulnerable entity, a peculiar kind of political stability evolved. The lower level of development and cohesion of Jordanian society—and hence the relatively weak political community it produced—allowed the emergence of a rather authoritative regime.

During the last 70 years, political decisions in Jordan were made by two persons (if one ignores the Talal interlude): the kings 'Abdallah and Husayn. Throughout that time Jordan was characterized as a pro-Western, nonradical monarchy. In those same seven decades, however, Iraq underwent several political metamorphoses, reflecting the more complex nature of its society. Power there was shared by scores of rulers and leaders. Since King Husayn came to rule in 1953, Jordan was governed by a single ruler and regime, while Iraq experienced at least three different types of regime and about a half-dozen different heads of state.

Since 1958, when Iraq's monarchy was overthrown, an ideological rift opened between the two countries. It widened a decade later when the Ba'th party took over in Iraq. King Husayn's commitment to his Hashemite heritage, his pro-Western stance (which also included, for most of the period, an anti-Communist ingredient), Jordan's special position regarding the Palestinian problem, and the role of Islamic values in Jordanian society as promoted by the regime all often clashed with the military or Ba'th party regime in Baghdad.

The Iraqi Ba'th, however, had demonstrated a rather pragmatic flexibility as political and economic interests were sometimes used to bridge this ideological gap. In certain cases, therefore, Iraq evolved a two-level attitude toward Jordan. In 1976-1977, while the two countries enjoyed an upgrading of economic ties, the Iraqi media was unfriendly, if not hostile, toward Husayn's regime.[15]

Eventually ideology gave way to pragmatism. Not only did the verbal attacks on Jordan stop, but, in the late 1970s, Iraq initiated closer relations and courted Jordan. Saddam Husayn tried to persuade his Jordanian counterpart and namesake that Iraqis were realistic and thus ideal allies for Jordan.[16]

In addition to basic ideological differences, in the late 1980s, the regimes' political systems became even more different. While Jordan was experiencing since 1988 an ongoing democratization process, including free elections, the Iraqi regime's grip on its citizens was very tight. But these differences had no impact on bilateral relations, which reached a record high in mid-1990.

THE ASYMMETRY OF RELATIONS

The imbalance in the two countries' economic and military potential was reflected in their relationship. Jordan's regional policy has always sought to overcome its basic inferiority vis-à-vis its neighbors and most Arab states. Jordan therefore became one of the most ardent spokesmen for Arab solidarity and cooperation as well as a keen advocate of Arab summit meetings. In addition, it constantly looked for support and protection from an Arab ally.

Even when Jordan enjoyed cordial relations with a strong, influential Arab state such as Egypt, it still sought special ties with one of its three Arab neighbors: Saudi Arabia, Syria, or Iraq. On the face of it, friendship with Iraq seemed the most advantageous. While Saudi Arabia had abundant money and Syria enjoyed considerable armed might, Iraq had both. Once the irrelevance of the ideological factor was established and Iraq convinced Jordan of its pragmatism, bilateral relations steadily moved from stability to cordiality and almost to a de facto federation in 1990.

The turning point was Saddam Husayn's installation as president in 1979. Since then "Iraq has projected the image of a powerful, self-confident and ambitious state."[17] That image made it a most suitable ally in Jordan's eyes, especially when Iraq encouraged a rapprochement. The timing was also appropriate from Jordan's point of view, since its own relations with Syria were then deteriorating. As indicated earlier, King Husayn developed a special sentiment, even a sort of a sense of responsibility toward Iraq, which up to 1958 had been ruled by his kinsmen.[18]

While Jordan's forces were rarely stationed on Iraqi soil (the Yarmuk forces of 1982 were the most prominent exception), Iraqi forces came to Jordan more frequently, for longer times and in larger numbers than any other Arab army. Due to Jordan's location, Iraqi troops had to cross it on their way to Palestine in 1948 and, again, heading to the Israeli border during the 1967 war. Iraqi forces were sent to Jordan also to protect the regime from external or internal threats. Such was the case in 1957 and also from 1967 to 1970, under both the Hashemite and radical Ba'th regimes.

In return for political support to Iraq—especially after Iran's revolution—Jordan expected to enjoy its neighbor's economic, military, and political power. First, Jordan hoped to make their economic relations more balanced. Indeed, from the late 1970s Iraq became an important market for Jordan's products (in 1979 Jordanian exports to Iraq were valued at $39 million) and a source of substantial financial aid. Iraq literally bought Jordan's amity. In 1980 it gave Jordan a $190 million loan plus a $60 million grant, the latter designated mainly for the expansion of Aqaba's port and improvement of the road to the Iraqi border.[19]

Jordan also considered Iraq as a strong and reliable partner to consolidate an Eastern Front against Israel. On the other hand, Jordan expected Iraqi diplomatic backing in case of its future participation in any form of Arab-Israeli peace talks. Iraq, for its part, hoped to prevent Jordan from joining the peace talks between Egypt and Israel. Yet Iraq was eager, as much as Jordan, to form an Eastern Front.

The fear of revolutionary Iran cemented the ties between the two countries and promoted them to the highest level since 1958. The Iranian threat, according to King Husayn, put Iraq and Jordan on equal footing. While Jordan stood firm along its western border that constituted the confrontation line with a non-Arab "aggressor" (Israel) posing a threat to the whole Arab world, Iraq was facing a similar responsibility along its eastern border (with Iran). Saddam Husayn shared the same view and entirely agreed with this Jordanian concept.[20]

Iraq regarded Jordan as an important potential ally mainly due to its geographical assets. Jordan could provide Iraq with an outlet to the sea. In a crisis or war, Iraq's access to the Persian Gulf—its only maritime outlet—could be easily blocked, as actually happened from 1980 to 1988 and from 1990 to 1991. Jordan's port of Aqaba and road system became invaluable for Iraq's imports and exports.

Another reason Iraq preferred Jordan as an ally was because the latter was less doctrinaire than their other Arab neighbors—Ba'thi Syria or Islamic conservative Saudi Arabia—which, unlike Jordan, took a stand toward Iraq influenced by their respective ideologies. Another advantage of Jordan's friendship from Iraq's viewpoint was that the former's weakness would guarantee Iraq's dominant position in the bilateral relationship. Moreover, Jordan's record as a pro-Western state might serve as a channel for Iraq's rapprochement with the Western bloc.

Iraq's invasion of Iran in September 1980 and the ensuing eight-year war introduced a new dimension to Jordan-Iraq ties. Basically, the war strengthened existing patterns in the bilateral relations, such as enhancing political, military, and economic cooperation. Yet it also created, for the first time, a certain Iraqi dependence on Jordan.

That reliance, however, was by no means equal to Jordan's continuing dependence on Iraq. Jordan could neither threaten its neighbor nor dissolve their relationship; such an option remained exclusively open to Iraq. Jordan could, on the other hand, extract from Iraq some additional economic and political benefits, and this it certainly did. Nevertheless, the war's end again reduced Iraqi dependence on Jordan's logistic facilities.[21] The sharp reduction in the amount of Iraqi goods sent through the port of Aqaba contributed to the plunge of Jordan's economy in the late 1980s.

King Husayn, hoping that his support for Iraq would assure Jordan an increased importance in the inter-Arab arena, worked hard to organize an Arab consensus to back Iraq in its conflict with Iran. Jordan's media claimed that Iraq was fighting a war for the sake of the whole Arab nation, to defend it from a non-Arab predator. The dispatch of Jordanian volunteers to Iraq in 1982 was depicted as an Arabization of the war.[22]

Once having committed itself to support Iraq's war effort, Jordan gained tremendous economic advantages. But the prosperity had a price: Jordan's economic dependence on Iraq increased; its freedom of choice on other aspects of bilateral relations decreased. The more the tide turned in Iran's favor, the more Iraq demanded from Jordan. Jordan had practically no alternative but to comply. Iraq's defeat would mean an economic disaster for Jordan and its exposure to Iran's wrath.

For Iraq, the effort invested in courting Jordan in the late 1970s seemed to pay back every penny during the war, and with interest. Aqaba became Iraq's indispensable lifeline. Jordan also provided various military services (see below) and served both as a mouthpiece and a loudspeaker of Iraqi propaganda. Saddam Husayn made no secret of the reason for his attitude toward Jordan, explaining that their special relations stemmed from several geographic and historic factors.[23]

The Iran-Iraq war had underlined (but certainly did not create) Jordan's dependence on Iraq and the asymmetry of their bilateral relations. These were most conspicuously manifested in the economic field. As already indicated, improved economic relations between Ba'thi Iraq and Jordan preceded the political alliance. As early as 1977 (when the Iraqi media were still attacking the Jordanian regime), a ten-year agreement granting Iraq a free-zone area in the port of Aqaba was concluded.

Just as Jordan's 1973 to 1982 economic boom was due partly to its exports to Iraq, the drop in that trade—given Iraq's exhaustion from the war—helped account for Jordan's tremendous foreign trade deficit in 1983.[24] To cut its losses, Jordan was compelled to grant Iraq a very generous credit. Thus, by the time the war ended, Iraq owed Jordan $835 million. This fact partly explains Jordan's support of Iraq in the Kuwait crisis. The only chance of retrieving at least part of their investment, so the Jordanians believed, was to side with Iraq.

Jordan became the victim—even a hostage—of its own policy. In the middle of 1990, 70% of the cargo arriving in Aqaba was bound for Iraq; 25% of the cargo exported from Aqaba originated in Iraq. Three-quarters of Jordan's industry produced mainly for the Iraqi market; 80 to 90% of Jordan's oil needs came from Iraq.[25]

The Iran-Iraq war also paved the way for greater military cooperation between Iraq and Jordan. Jordan let Iraq use its military facilities. Iraqi fighter planes reportedly landed on Jordanian airfields, using them as a safe haven out of range of Iran's bombers. Iraq financed a $200 million Jordanian arms deal with the Soviet Union.[26]

This cooperation bore fruit mainly after 1988 and during the Gulf War. In early 1990 there were reports of the establishment of Jordanian-Iraqi joint military units, a joint air squadron, and of Jordanian pilots being trained by Iraqi airmen.[27] Iraqi officers reconnoitered along the Jordan-Israel border and Iraqi aircraft flew over it. During the Gulf War, Jordan assisted Iraq with military intelligence, its air-defense warning systems were at Iraq's disposal, and Jordanian instructors had trained the Iraqis in operating surface-to-air Hawk missiles.

THE IMPACT OF INTER-ARAB ISSUES

As already indicated, Jordan's position in the inter-Arab system influenced its search for an ally and patron. It had frequently found itself caught between two regional powers. Iraq, usually, was one of them. Sometimes Jordan had to take sides, at other times it became the victim of such regional encounters.

Syria has always played a unique role in Jordan's bilateral relations with Iraq. During King 'Abdallah's reign, Syria was a source of tension in that relationship and the subject of a latent competition between the two countries. When a possible Iraq-Syria union was discussed in 1949, 'Abdallah threatened to use force to block it.[28] Later, positions were switched and Jordan became the object of Syrian and Iraqi ambitions.

On various occasions, from the late 1950s onward, two of the three countries either formed or entered a coalition against the third: In 1958, Jordan and Iraq formed the Arab Federation against the United Arab Republic (UAR) of Syria and Egypt. In 1963, the scheduled tripartite union among Iraq, Syria, and Egypt had excluded Jordan. In 1976, when its union with Syria proved futile, Jordan moved into the Iraqi orbit. During the Syria-Jordan tension at the end of 1980, Iraq offered Jordan military assistance against Syria.

In the late 1980s, however, Husayn attempted to put an end to that sort of vicious circle. Taking advantage of his position between the two Ba'th regimes, he made painstaking conciliatory efforts that yielded a "historical" meeting in Jordan between Saddam Husayn and Hafiz al-Asad in April 1987.

Another Arab issue on which the two countries did not always see eye to eye was the Palestinian problem. In 1948, Iraq supported the Palestinian rivals of 'Abdallah, and, in 1949, it refused to make an armistice agreement with Israel. Iraq's proposal for a Palestinian entity in 1959 threatened to deprive Jordan of the reason for its own existence as a sovereign state by turning its own Palestinian population against the Hashemite regime. The Iraqi forces stationed in Jordan after the 1967 war supported the PLO there and even facilitated their penetration into Jordan disguised as Iraqi soldiers.[29]

Iraq tried to mediate between Jordan and the Palestinian organizations during their occasional clashes throughout 1970, but its thousands of soldiers stationed in Jordan did not intervene in the fighting that September. Iraq not only continuously committed itself to the Palestinian issue and recognized the PLO but, like other Arab states, exploited the Palestinian struggle for its own ends by sponsoring its own Palestinian organization—the Arab Liberation Front—and later supporting and hosting Abu Nidal and his group. Despite all this, Jordan estimated that Iraq, unlike Syria, would not consider Jordanian control of the West Bank as a threat to its own national interests.[30] Thus, in a nutshell, the Palestinian issue was less crucial in Jordan-Iraq relations than in Jordan's bilateral relations with other Arab states.

Since the late 1970s, Iraq's dominant position in relations with Jordan was clearly reflected in the inter-Arab system. Jordan unequivocally supported Iraq in Arab forums, such as summit or ACC meetings, lobbying to mobilize Arab support for Iraq and endorsement for its policy.

CONCLUSION

The only constant factor in Jordan-Iraq relations—the lack of symmetry in assets—led to Jordan's dependence on Iraq. The other factors are variable. The Iraqi regime changed several times, but its political and ideological identity did not automatically decide the nature of the bilateral relationship with Jordan. Since Saddam Husayn's ascendancy, those relations were constantly enhanced. Despite Jordan being the weaker, dependent partner, Iraq initiated and encouraged closer relations no less than Jordan. The ideological gap placed no serious obstacle on the path of friendship, due to the Iraqi regime's pragmatism. Ba'thist Iraq and royalist Jordan enjoyed much closer and much more cordial relations than they had when both were Hashemite monarchies. As relations became closer, however, Jordan was gradually deprived of its freedom of choice. On the other hand, those relations reached such a peak that any further development (save a union between the two countries) would be considered a setback.

Such a setback indeed followed the Gulf War. Iraq's isolation heavily influenced its relationship with Jordan. King Husayn, for his part, was not too sad to get rid of the dependent component of bilateral relations, particularly when it became apparent that his regime was able to cope with those domestic forces that vehemently and vociferously supported Saddam Husayn even after Iraq's military defeat.

Jordan, however, had a harder time finding substitutes for the benefits it had enjoyed from past relations with Iraq: economic support, a strong ally and/or a friendly neighbor. Nevertheless, the relatively quick absolution granted Jordan by the United States for its role during the Gulf War, its smooth readmission into regional activity, and its role in the Arab-Israeli peace process indicated that there can be suitable alternatives.

NOTES

1. One of the most interesting forms of support was given to Iraq by Jordan's media. Yet besides the "conventional" pro-Iraqi stance expressed through editorials, news bulletins, or commentary, Jordanian TV waged a sort of psychological warfare against the West. During August 1990 its English-speaking channel intensively screened documentary and feature films that showed the white Christian civilization's mistreatment of other races. They

included, for example, pieces on Martin Luther King; the American abuse of the Indians; South African apartheid, and the seventeenth and eighteenth century slave traffic from West Africa to America.

2. Yehoshua Porath, *In Search of Arab Unity 1930-1945* (London, 1986), pp. 18-19.

3. Muhammad Ibrahim Faddah, *The Middle East in Transition: A Study of Jordan's Foreign Policy* (London, 1974), p. 184.

4. Porath, *In Search of Arab Unity,* pp. 18 ff.

5. Isma'il Ahmad Yaghi, *Al-Alaqat al-Iraqiya al-Urduniya 1941-1958* (Cairo, 1988), p. 7.

6. Saad Abubaker, "Iraq and Arab Politics: The Nuri as-Sa'id Era 1941-1958," Ph.D. diss., University of Washington, 1987, pp. 173-175; see also Bruce Maddy-Weitzman, "Jordan and Iraq: Efforts at Intra-Hashemite Unity," *Middle Eastern Studies* 26 (1990), p. 65.

7. Barry Rubin, *The Arab States and the Palestine Conflict* (Syracuse, N.Y., 1981), p. 212.

8. Maddy-Weitzman, "Jordan and Iraq," pp. 66-67.

9. Elie Podeh, "The Quest for Hegemony in the Arab World: The Struggle Over the Baghdad Pact, 1954-1958" Ph.D. diss., Tel Aviv University, 1990 (Hebrew), p. 256.

10. Maddy-Weitzman, "Jordan and Iraq," p. 65.

11. Benjamin Shwadran, "Husain Between Qasim and Nasir" *Middle Eastern Affairs* 11 (1960), p. 343.

12. Uriel Dann, *King Hussein and the Challenge of Arab Radicalism: Jordan 1955-1967* (New York, 1989), p. 135.

13. *Middle East Contemporary Survey (MECS)* 12, 1988, p. 532.

14. Samir Mutawi, *Jordan in the 1967 War* (Cambridge, Mass., 1988), pp. 42, 45.

15. *MECS* 1, 1976-1977, pp. 414, 437; Amatzia Baram, "Ba'thi Iraq and Hashemite Jordan: From Hostility to Alignment," *Middle East Journal* 45, no. 1 (Winter 1991), pp. 53-54.

16. Baram, "Ba'thi Iraq and Hashemite Jordan."

17. *MECS* 4, 1979-1980, p. 582; Asher Susser, *Between Jordan and Palestine: A Political Biography of Wasfi al-Tall* (Tel Aviv, 1983), (Hebrew), p. 183.

18. Valerie Yorke, *Domestic Politics and Regional Security: Jordan Syria and Israel. The End of an Era?* (Aldershot, 1988), p. 263.

19. Baram, "Ba'thi Iraq and Hasemite Jordan," p. 56.

20. See *MECS* 4, 1979-1980, p. 198; Hasan Bin Talal, *Search for Peace* (New York, 1984), p. 1. For Saddam Husayn's views see *MECS* 12, 1988, p. 533.

21. *MECS* 12, 1988, p. 607.

22. Yorke, *Domestic Politics and Regional Security,* p. 263; *MECS* 4, 1979-1980, p. 22. See also Baram, "Ba'thi Iraq and Hashemite Jordan," pp. 59-60.

23. *MECS* 4, 1979-1980, p. 198.
24. Yorke, *Domestic Politics and Regional Security,* pp. 54-55, 63.
25. Baram, "Ba'thi Iraq and Hashemite Jordan," pp. 67-68.
26. *MECS* 6, 1981-1982, p. 688.
27. *Ittihad* (Abu Dhabi), January 26, 1990; *Middle East Journal* 44 no. 3 (Summer 1990), Chronology, for February 20, 1990, p. 473.
28. Michael Eppel, "Iraqi-Syrian Relations 1945-1958," Ph.D. diss., Tel Aviv University, 1989 (Hebrew), p. 154.
29. James Lunt, *Hussein of Jordan* (London, 1989), pp. 169-70.
30. Baram, "Ba'thi Iraq and Hashemite Jordan," p. 56. Syria apprehended that an agreement over the West Bank might be reached on the account of a settlement of the Golan issue. Moreover, Syria considered a stronger and friendly to Israel Jordan, a potential threat for its regional ambitions. It was particularly unhappy regarding the possibility that the Palestinian issue might be excluded from its control.

9

Iraq and the PLO: Brother's Keepers, Losers Weepers

Barry Rubin

Yasir 'Arafat once unconsciously, unintentionally revealed the essence of his relations with the Arab states. The PLO, he said, would fight on like the Spartan troops at the ancient battle of Thermopylae who defended Greece "until at last the rest of the Greek forces arrived."[1]

True, the Spartans struggled bravely, but the other Greek cities never sent their armies to help. The Spartans were wiped out. For two decades, Iraq had trampled on the PLO's interests. Yet 'Arafat, who had unsuccessfully tried periods of Syrian, Jordanian, and Egyptian patronage in the 1980s, turned toward Iraq in the 1990s.

To judge from the Arab states' propaganda, they have been totally devoted to the Palestinian cause and PLO. In fact, however, they always pursued their own interests, refusing to fight Israel or the West on the PLO's behalf and often treating that people and organization with contempt. A history of bitter experiences should have taught the PLO that it could not rely on any Arab regime, since, as one veteran put it, "virtually every Arab state has stabbed them in the back at one point or another." Yet the Palestinians and PLO could not break their addictive expectation of finding an Arab ruler to be their savior. In 1990, President Saddam Husayn of Iraq became their latest great Arab hope.[2] A key factor underlying Iraqi-PLO relations was the lack of an Iraq-Israel border combined with Iraq's ambition to lead the Arab world. Consequently, while Baghdad was long a vocal, militant player in the Arab-Israeli conflict, it was also generally a secondary one.

'Arafat turned toward Saddam Husayn as his patron at the moment Iraq's dictator was making his bid to rule the Persian Gulf and command the Arabs. The PLO leader broke his own precept against becoming too dependent on any one Arab state and paid for it dearly as Iraq was first isolated in the Arab world, then defeated by a Western-Arab coalition.

Like other Arab rulers, Saddam put his own interests first and those of the Palestinians second. Yet Saddam's pursuit of Iraqi interests twice pushed the Palestinians to the bottom of regional priorities: in the Iran-Iraq war of the 1980s and the Kuwait crisis of the 1990s. Thus, 'Arafat's turn toward Saddam stands out as the worst among many bad decisions made by the PLO leadership.

THE PLO'S PROBLEMATIC ARAB POLICY

Iraq and other Arab states were far stronger than the PLO, controlling large territories, economic resources, armies, and populations far exceeding the total number of Palestinians, even if that dispersed people were to be reassembled. 'Arafat had some assets of his own—mainly the prestige and popularity of the Palestinian cause—but the Arab states usually saw the PLO as a useful tool to manipulate or dominate. Only in exceptional cases—Jordan briefly in 1969 and 1970; weak, divided Lebanon from the mid-1970s to 1982—did 'Arafat gain the upper hand over a state.

Generally, however, Arab aid had strings attached to it. For the two decades following 1948, the Palestinians subordinated themselves to the states, believing Arab unity would bring them liberation. But when Fatah took over the PLO after the 1967 war, its claim to be the vanguard in the struggle against Israel and for Arab unity threatened the Arab states' sovereignty.[3]

Arab states never considered the PLO an equal partner, neither consulting it nor respecting its interests when setting their policy toward Israel or the United States. A PLO intelligence chief estimated that the Arab states were responsible for three-quarters of Palestinians killed in the struggle.[4]

Thus, 'Arafat walked a tightrope, balancing each favor with a tilt in the opposite direction, preserving his independence by using it only sparingly. A sympathetic historian writes, "Few independence movements have been so heavily dependent on external assistance," and the PLO's survival was conditioned on maintaining "unity at any price."[5]

'Arafat tried to preserve the PLO's autonomy by attempting to avoid a single patron's control or conflicts with Arab states that would make them revoke his license as the Palestinian leader. He understood that having some Arab rulers as enemies would necessitate having others as masters, and vice versa. In contrast, the smaller PLO groups, out of weakness and ideology, often became clients of Arab regimes.

From the late 1960s into the 1990s, 'Arafat traveled in perpetual motion among the Arab capitals, patching connections, making deals and conspiracies. Conflicts among Arab states gave him maneuvering room. When Jordan attacked the PLO, 'Arafat took refuge with Syria; when Syria assaulted the PLO, he turned to Jordan and Egypt. Falling out with the moderates, 'Arafat accepted Iraq's patronage; being abused by the radicals, he appeared again on the moderates' doorstep.

Like other aspects of PLO strategy, its Arab policy promoted the organization's survival while simultaneously blocking its progress. On the contrary, from the PLO's standpoint the Arab states went backwards over the decades: from refusing to wage war for the Palestinians' sake to waging war against the PLO itself or even refusing to give it money. But when, for example, Egypt announced plans to rebuild the ancient Alexandria library in early 1990, the United Arab Emirates, Iraq, and Saudi Arabia immediately offered $20 million each. A pro-PLO newspaper commented, "We only wish that these Arab leaders would demonstrate equal generosity in supporting the intifada."[6]

IRAQ AND THE ORIGINS OF THE PLO

In his rivalry with Egypt and Jordan, Iraqi dictator 'Abd al-Karim Qasim gave a December 1959 speech proclaiming that the Palestinians were victims of Jordan and Egypt as well as of Israel. He urged them to regain their own territory from these "three thieves."[7] At the January 1964 Arab summit meeting, Iraq again tried to embarrass its rivals. If they were really Arab patriots, it suggested, Jordan and Egypt would support a Palestinian government in the West Bank and Gaza. It was then that Nasir raised the ante. The Arab states would show even more dedication to the cause, he replied, by establishing a Palestine Liberation Organization and a Palestinian army. This event led directly to the PLO's creation.

The new movement gained great influence in the refugee camps of more tolerant Lebanon and Jordan but was kept under tight control in Iraq. Still,

Iraq always stood in the wings as an alternate, more radical patron. So extreme was its posture that Iraq was the sole Arab country that preferred to withdraw its troops from the front in the 1948 war rather than sign a ceasefire with Israel. But Iraq's rhetorical militancy was often a substitute for direct engagement. In 1970, an Iraqi division in Jordan did nothing while King Husayn crushed the PLO. While Baghdad talked of sacrificing itself on the altar of Palestine, Saddam was soon openly proclaiming that Iraq and its own concerns came first.

Saddam also played rough in his direct dealings with the PLO. He maintained puppet Palestinian groups inside and outside the organization, subsidizing the Democratic Front for the Liberation of Palestine (DFLP) and controlling both the Arab Liberation Front (ALF) and the Palestine Liberation Front (PLF) of Muhammad Abu al-'Abbas. Palestinian refugees in Iraq were restricted and mistrusted. Even those active in pro-Iraqi groups were so closely watched by the secret police that Iraqi citizens feared to befriend them.

The PLO's rapprochement with Syria made Iraq jealous. In the late 1970s there was a mini-war in which Baghdad hired the anti-'Arafat Palestinian terrorist Abu Nidal to assassinate PLO men. During the first half of 1978, his group killed the PLO's representatives in London, Kuwait, and Paris—plus four people at its office in Pakistan. The PLO retaliated by attacking Iraqi officials in Britain, France, Pakistan, and Lebanon; Iraq countered with more killings of 'Arafat supporters.[8]

But after Egypt began negotiating peace with Israel, Iraq aligned with the PLO once again as they became the backbone of the rejection front that expelled Cairo from Arab counsels and totally rejected the Camp David treaties.

THE PLO AND THE IRAN-IRAQ CONFLICT

Iran's shah was overthrown in February 1979 by Ayatollah Ruhollah Khomeini, a supporter of the PLO who hated the United States and Israel. For 'Arafat, the new Iranian leader was both an ally and an inspiration. If Khomeini could rise from obscurity and exile to lead a small group in conquering a seemingly mighty foe, so could he.[9]

'Arafat arrived uninvited in Tehran in February 1979, a few days after Khomeini's forces took over. As his plane approached Tehran's Mahrabad airport, 'Arafat said, "I felt as if I was landing in Jerusalem." His entourage carried Khomeini's picture and chanted, "Today Iran, tomorrow Palestine." Symbolically, the new Iranian government gave the PLO the former Israeli embassy. After over two decades of struggle, this was the first piece of Israeli real estate 'Arafat had captured.[10]

Envisioning himself as the organizer of an Arab-Iranian alliance battling Israel and America, 'Arafat announced that Iran's revolution had shifted the strategic balance decisively against his enemies. "Iraq can now throw its army fully into the battle against the Zionist enemy. And there is no Persian pressure any more on Saudi Arabia and the Gulf states."[11] But both Iran and Iraq had their own quarrels that took priority over any struggle to liberate Palestine. 'Arafat's attempts to mediate between Baghdad and Tehran made both sides angry.

Iran cut off support to the PLO, advising 'Arafat to turn toward Islamic fundamentalist doctrine instead of nationalism. And when, in August 1980, Iraq invaded Iran to start an eight-year war costing a million casualties. Saddam also pressured 'Arafat to support him.[12]

Iraq's interests also had a tremendous effect on the PLO's fortunes on another front. An Iraqi intelligence colonel, who served as deputy to the anti-'Arafat terrorist Abu Nidal, led a three-man hit team that seriously wounded Israeli Ambassador Shlomo Argov in London on June 3, 1982. This assault was designed as a diversion to give Iraq a way out of its own disastrous war with Iran. By provoking an Israeli attack on Lebanon against Syrian and PLO forces, whom Israel blamed for the attack, Iraq would weaken Syria, Iraq's enemy and Iran's ally. The same crisis gave Baghdad an excuse to demand that Iran make peace and unite with the Arabs against Israel.[13]

"I was standing in Tyre, Lebanon, when the Iranian revolution took place," 'Arafat later recalled, "and I declared that the PLO's strategic depth extends from Tyre all the way to Iran. Then came the Iran-Iraq war." By 1983, with the PLO besieged by Syria, "the huge strategic depth of the PLO shrunk to the size of a few kilometers."[14] Preoccupied by the Iran-Iraq war, the Arab states neglected the PLO even more. The Arab world was so disorganized and divided it was incapable even of holding a summit meeting between September 1982 and November 1987. And when the Arabs again convened in Amman, they focused on the war, largely ignoring the Palestine question.

As long as Iraq was fighting Iran—between 1980 and 1988— its needs conflicted with those of the PLO. In a bid for U.S. support in the mid-1980s, Iraq's ambassador to Washington, Nizar Hamdoun sent American journalists and policymakers full-color copies of a captured Iranian map showing that Tehran's eventual goal was to capture Jerusalem and destroy Israel. The Iraqis were thus inviting the United States to support them as the de facto protector of Israel.

At a small dinner party in Washington during a 1985 visit, Iraq's foreign minister, Tariq 'Aziz, explained that the Iran-Iraq war was his country's principal problem. A drunken American columnist was outraged. "You must tell Secretary of State Shultz," he shouted, "that the Arab-Israeli conflict is your main concern!" The somewhat shaken diplomat tried to calm his guest. "Of course, the Arab-Israeli issue is important but that is not my mission's purpose." But the enraged American went on chastising the startled Iraqi leader for failing to live up to his expectations of proper Arab behavior.[15]

'Arafat, too, had expectations of what Iraq should do. He claimed that the war's end would make Baghdad and the other Arab states devote themselves to supporting the Palestinian cause. Once more, Saddam seemed to be a valuable ally, the victor over Iran and master of ample oil wealth and a one-million-man army. The Palestinian uprising and Iraq's victory, the PLO official Nabil Sha'th claimed, "changed the balance in favor of the Palestinian cause." Having already developed missiles and chemical weapons that could hit Israel, Iraq was busily building nuclear and biological arms as well. With the Soviet Union no longer giving the Arabs a nuclear umbrella and a superpower alternative to the United States, the PLO and many other Arabs were seeking a local replacement.[16]

'ARAFAT'S TURN TOWARD IRAQ

In December 1988, 'Arafat spoke words no PLO leader had ever dared utter in the quarter century since that organization's founding. At a dramatic press conference in Geneva, Switzerland, 'Arafat claimed to recognize Israel's right to "exist in peace and security" and to "totally and categorically reject all forms of terrorism." "Our desire for peace is strategic and not a temporary tactic," he proclaimed. "We are committed to peace, and we want to live in our Palestinian state and let others live."[17] The speech was the product of a year of Palestinian revolt, secret U.S. diplomacy and open debate in the PLO.

A few hours later, Secretary of State George Shultz announced the opening of a U.S.-PLO dialogue. The history of the Arab-Israeli conflict—indeed, the direction of the whole Middle East—seemed at a turning point. The achievement of a Palestinian state and an end to the long and bloody Arab-Israeli conflict appeared to be within reach.

Yet this did not happen. No matter how blame is apportioned for the collapse of the 1988 to 1990 peace efforts, the PLO was the big loser. The lack of practical gains after three years of intifada demoralized the Palestinians. They now turned to an external savior. If the PLO could not help them, Saddam could. Suspicious of U.S. intentions and weary of Egyptian demands for more moderation, 'Arafat moved closer to Iraq in 1989. The PLO shifted some offices from Tunis to Baghdad and began holding many top-level meetings there. 'Arafat went monthly to Iraq's capital to be greeted with all the pomp due a head of state. Iraq gave him a huge Palestinian embassy and his own private jet.

'Arafat also was looking to Saddam to replace the lost Soviet support for the PLO after Gorbachev's policy shift removed the PLO's main source for political support, arms, and training, both direct and through its Arab allies. Moscow's permission for hundreds of thousands of Soviet Jews to emigrate helped Israel; East European countries stopped aiding the PLO and become friendly to Israel.

Thus, when Saddam threatened to "burn half of Israel" with chemical weapons in April 1990, the Palestinians saw him as a liberator in the same way they had viewed Nasir in the 1950s and 1960s. 'Arafat considered Saddam the region's new strongman and, at the May 1990 Arab summit in Baghdad, helped Iraq's dictator try to crown himself as the Arabs' leader. Calling Saddam a "noble knight," 'Arafat claimed that Baghdad's missiles and chemical weapons gave Arabs the strength "to achieve liberation from Baghdad to Jerusalem and from al-Faw [southern Iraq] to Gaza." Yet despite 'Arafat's lavish praise, Saddam neither pressed for increased aid to the PLO nor even insisted on mentioning it in the meeting's final communique.

On May 30, 1990, a 16-man terrorist force left Libya by sea on their way to attack Israel's coast. They were former Fatah fighters whom the PLF had recruited with Iraq's assistance and trained with Libya's help. It was a major Jewish holiday and the beaches were packed with families. The force's orders were to kill civilians in Tel Aviv's tourist district, proceed to the Sheraton Hotel, murder as many people as possible, and attack the seaside U.S. embassy.

But they were intercepted by Israeli forces, which sank some of the terrorists' boats, killed four of the men, and captured the other 12 on the beach moments after they landed. The PLO refused to criticize or punish the attack. Despite U.S. efforts to salvage the U.S.-PLO dialogue, the Bush administration felt compelled to suspend it on June 20. Iraq, the PLF's patron, probably sponsored the operation in order to destroy the peace process.

By following Iraq rather than Egypt at that critical juncture, 'Arafat was making a fundamental choice. Egypt was the most important Arab regime and the patron most likely to guide the PLO toward a negotiated solution. Cairo's triple status as a U.S. ally, leading Arab state, and the sole Arab country at peace with Israel gave it tremendous advantages as a mediator. The choice between Egypt and Iraq represented the difference between a road to moderation and peace and the way of extremism and war.

The PLO not only supported Iraq, it also opposed Egypt's interest. For example, 'Arafat fought against the return of Arab League headquarters from Tunis to Cairo. Egypt was livid about Iraq "stealing" the PLO away from it and upset about 'Arafat's lack of cooperation in the peace process. In the summer of 1990, Cairo's government-controlled press attacked 'Arafat's "betrayal." In retaliation, a PLO leaflet issued on August 1, 1990, called Egypt an American "puppet" and "an obedient tool in the hands of the American administration."

The next day, Iraq invaded Kuwait and 'Arafat leaped to support what he thought was the victorious side. An East Jerusalem Palestinian newspaper even suggested that Iraq should send its troops to the West Bank, "where they would be welcome." But 'Arafat and the Palestinians would prove to be badly mistaken. As an Arab journalist sighed, "God save this nation from its heroes!" For Iraq's invasion and annexation of Kuwait again divided the Arab world and diverted attention from the Palestinian struggle.

THE COSTS OF ALLIANCE WITH IRAQ

Kuwait had once been 'Arafat's home, and it was there that he founded Fatah. Now he was helping to destroy the country that had once given him refuge and riches. Certainly, many of the 300,000 Palestinians there did have grievances. They had lived and worked in Kuwait for decades without ever being granted equal rights. Saudi Arabia tried to keep Palestinians out of the country altogether. If Palestinians had become, as they liked to say, the "Jews of the Middle East" in their dispersion, they also filled that group's historic role as target of antipathy and hostility. "In the Gulf," claimed a Palestinian intellectual, they were "treated like third-rate human beings."[18]

Thus, the Palestinians, including those living in Jordan and Kuwait, loudly cheered Saddam for his anti-Israel and anti-Kuwait efforts. By supporting Saddam, Palestinians were following 'Arafat's pro-Iraq policy. But they were also acting on a belief that their own leaders had failed and that they needed someone else to follow. Yet by calling Iraq's leader "the Arab Bismarck" or a new Nasir, Palestinians implied that a future Palestine would merely be a province in an Iraq-dominated Middle East and, thus, that the separate nationalism represented by the PLO would have no function.

While some Arab states gave limited support to Iraq, only the Palestinians' collective interest still called for the kind of Pan-Arabism that Saddam claimed to represent. This distinction further isolated them. All the other Arabs were increasingly preoccupied with their own nation-state's perspective. Arab commentators pointed out that Saddam seized Kuwait's loot for Iraq's benefit, Saudi Arabia sought U.S. help to protect its independence, Egypt and Syria acted in their own national interests in opposing Baghdad's aggression and bid for regional domination.

The PLO's alignment with Iraq unleashed an unprecedented storm of criticism from Saudis, Kuwaitis, and Egyptians. *Al-Ahram* called 'Arafat's embrace of Saddam "prostration" before the man who plunged "his poisoned dagger in the Arabs' back." A Saudi official wrote that 'Arafat "not only abandoned Kuwait but also lauded its butcher!" An Egyptian journalist asked, "How can one blame the Gulf states now for not sympathizing with the organization and with the Palestinian intifada, some of whose leaders sent a cable to Saddam calling his invasion of Kuwait the first step to Jerusalem and the liberation of Palestine?" A leading Kuwaiti intellectual wrote, "The day will come . . . when you will see with your own eyes that there is no longer any need for you or your organization." Another Egyptian writer noted, "If Iraq has the right to take over Kuwait . . . what, then, prevents Israel from taking over Palestinian and Arab land?" Losing his temper at all this criticism, 'Arafat called the strongest PLO supporter among Egyptian editors an Israeli agent.[19]

These Arab countries severely punished the PLO. Kuwait's government-in-exile, Saudi Arabia, and other Arab oil-producing states cut off all money to it as well as direct donations to West Bank schools and hospitals, $35 to $50 million a year. An estimated 300,000 Palestinians in Kuwait were thrown out of work by the crisis, no one collected their 5% tax to the PLO ($120 to $125 million annually), and they could not send money (about $80 million a year) to their own families on the West Bank. The sharp fall in the value of Jordan's currency impoverished Palestinians in Jordan and the West Bank. Tens of thousands of Palestinians in the Gulf were fired as a potential fifth column.[20]

'Arafat's policy also damaged the PLO's international standing and diplomatic prospects. Iraq could not, of course, mediate between the PLO and the United States or Israel. Saddam had no stake in furthering the peace process and a great deal of reason to sabotage it.

On matters of principle, too, PLO actions weakened its case. 'Arafat had supported a country's seizure by force of another people's land and contested the Kuwaitis' right to self-determination, exactly the things he decried in terms of Israel's occupation of the West Bank and Gaza.

As the disastrous consequences of supporting Iraq became clear, a few Palestinians criticized 'Arafat's strategy. Jawad al-Ghusayn, chairman of the Palestine National Fund, who was seeing Arab states' contributions vanish, branded Iraq's occupation "illegal" and claimed the PLO supported Kuwait. Nonetheless, virtually all the small PLO groups—the PFLP, DFLP, and the Iraq-sponsored ALF and PLF—backed Saddam, publicly offering to commit anti-American terrorism on his behalf.

After four days of meetings, the PLO came up with a new, confusing position on August 19 by proposing an "Arab solution" that seemed likely to result in Iraq's keeping Kuwait. Gulf Arabs were not impressed with this new "neutral" stance. A Saudi diplomat said the PLO was doing nothing while "a giant is murdering a little child." Exiled Kuwaitis asked 'Arafat in an open letter, "Don't you remember how many years you spent in Kuwait and the continuous Kuwaiti contributions and support to the Palestinian revolution?"

Equally important was the disillusionment of some Israelis who had advocated negotiations with the PLO. The spectacle of 'Arafat urging Iraq to attack Israel with missiles and chemical weapons did not seem to presage moderation. The prospect of an independent Palestinian state some day inviting Iraqi troops to help it attack Israel also did not encourage a belief in the stability of such a diplomatic settlement.

Yossi Sarid, the most important Israeli politician endorsing talks with the PLO and a Palestinian state, strongly criticized the PLO leaders for having made "every possible mistake." "Over the past two years," he noted, "the PLO had been trying to convince [Israeli public opinion] that it is a different PLO, 'accepting Israel's existence and renouncing terror.' Now the PLO has kicked the pail and all the moderation has spilled out." After moving "from bed to bed—and there is no Arab ruler who did not share his couch with them—they have learned nothing. Won't Saddam, who is prepared to sell his own mother, sell them?"[21]

The damage done to the PLO's situation on all fronts, then, was enormous. Saudi Arabia and Kuwait stopped financial aid, denounced 'Arafat, and took other reprisals. The pro-Saudi newspaper *al-Hayat* summed up the situation: "With one blow," 'Arafat had antagonized the Arab oil-producing states, "his major source of money"; Egypt, "his link with the world"; the Soviet Union, his international sponsor; the United States, "which he had tried so hard to engage in a dialogue"; and moderate Israelis, through whom he tried to address that society.[22]

Iraq's halfhearted call to link the Kuwait issue and Palestinian question also did not help the PLO. Essentially, it was a trick to buy time and make Saddam seem the Arab world's leader and champion. Obviously, he had not annexed Kuwait in order to free Palestine. If everyone was tied up in knots trying to deal with the Palestinian question first—an issue still unresolved after a half century and with no solution in sight—they would never be able to force Iraq out of Kuwait.

Whatever attempts Saddam made to link the Gulf and Arab-Israeli conflicts, the Kuwait crisis still reduced the intifada to a sideshow. By switching patrons from America's best friend in the Arab world—Egypt, to its worst enemy—Iraq— 'Arafat forfeited whatever diplomatic gains still remained from earlier years. The PLO's new radical phase removed any U.S. incentive to bring it into a peace process. While the Bush administration spoke of the importance of trying to resolve peacefully the Arab-Israeli conflict, it was in no mood to do favors for 'Arafat.

The United States rejected linkage but tried to counter Baghdad's propaganda through its own public relations' effort. President Bush turned the issue around with his UN speech in October 1990. It was Saddam's fault, he said, that no progress was being made on the Arab-Israel issue. Only after Iraq pulled out of Kuwait could something be done for the Palestinians. The United States also voted for some UN resolutions condemning Israel.

The United State's Arab allies in the anti-Saddam venture—Egypt, Saudi Arabia, Kuwait, and Syria—were relatively indifferent to the Palestinian issue and far more concerned with protecting themselves against Iraqi aggression. A Saudi writer said the PLO needs new leaders, "who can speak to the world in more civilized way and who oppose any kind of aggression and occupation, if it is by Israel, Iraq, Palestinian terrorists or others."[23]

Moreover, all the talk about linkage did nothing material for the PLO or Palestinians. In the absence of any willingness by Arab states to make peace with Israel—and with the PLO allied to anti-American Iraq—no peace process existed, no progress could be made, and nothing had happened to make the conflict any more resolvable than it was the day before Iraq seized Kuwait.

The only top PLO leader willing to speak out about the extent of Iraq's and 'Arafat's mistake was Abu Iyad, generally considered the organization's second most important figure. "We are opposed to the invasion and annexation of Kuwait," he said flatly. "We cannot revolve in Iraq's or any other state's orbit." On January 15, 1991, however, Abu Iyad was assassinated in Tunis by a supposed defector from Abu Nidal's organization. While it cannot be proven, it seems possible that Saddam might have eliminated his most outspoken critic in the PLO leadership.[24]

THE GULF WAR'S EFFECT ON THE PLO

Throughout the crisis, the PLO took a hard pro-Iraq, anti-American line, accusing the United States of "cowardly aggression" against Iraq and warning that "blood, catastrophe and destruction" will sweep the world" if America attacked Saddam. 'Arafat said that the United States wanted to seize control of the oilfields. Identifying with Saddam, the PLO claimed, "We are all exposed to aggression when [Baghdad] is bombed."[25]

For the PFLP and DFLP—as well as the ALF and the PLF—the crisis was a chance to reclaim the PLO's revolutionary traditions and advocate anti-American terrorism. The former pair took this position even though their old patron Syria supported the anti-Iraq coalition; the latter two were Iraqi puppets.

Frustrated by the inability of the intifada or PLO to gain through militancy or negotiations, rank-and-file Palestinians also hailed Saddam as a liberator. In doing so, they repeated previous mistakes: making the fate of the West Bank and Gaza dependent on those outside the territories, subordinating the Palestinian future to Arab rulers, and backing a military rather than diplomatic option. As one Palestinian put it, "Our fate now is in the hands of Iraq." But adulation for Saddam implied that 'Arafat had failed and again gave the Palestinians an image in the West as a radical, anti-American, destabilizing force.[26]

Iraq's aggression put the PLO's issue on the back burner, as its war with Iran had done during the 1980s. By cheering Iraq and urging it to attack Israel, Palestinians disillusioned some Israeli doves and American advocates of their interests. The PLO's radical phase ended any U.S. incentive to bring it into the peace process; the PLO's support for Saddam turned several key Arab states against it.

'Arafat often compared his group to the phoenix, a mythical bird periodically immolating itself only to rise from the ashes. Certainly, the PLO showed a great capacity to set itself afire through miscalculation and misdeeds, then survive the ensuing disaster. Yet the self-inflicted debacle in the Gulf crisis set a new record. The last time the Palestinian nationalist movement supported the losing side in a war against the United States and Britain was World War II. The international reaction to this behavior was a factor in Israel's creation and a defeat the PLO was never able to reverse or revenge.

Had 'Arafat backed Kuwait and asked to join the coalition, the PLO would have greatly strengthened its hand. Instead, PLO leaders attacked the "aggression against Iraq," urged a resolution to Iraq's advantage, and babbled about American cruise missiles being fired from Israel, Israeli planes attacking Iraq from Turkey, and an impending Israeli invasion of Jordan.[27]

The main Arab political and financial powers—Egypt, Syria, Saudi Arabia, and Kuwait—saw 'Arafat's alignment with Saddam as treason. They rejected linking the Gulf and Arab-Israeli conflicts, viewing this as an Iraqi stalling and distracting tactic; their attacks on the PLO reached new heights. Secretary of State James Baker told a Palestinian delegation in Jerusalem in March 1991 that no Arab leader even wanted to meet 'Arafat. The eight Arab coalition members at their March 1991 Cairo victory meeting did not mention the PLO in their final communiqué.

The most prosperous Palestinian community, in Kuwait, was in disarray. Many fled and were not allowed to return. Hundreds were arrested as collaborators with Iraq. Other Gulf states fired or deported them. Financial losses were enormous as Arab states stopped donating money to the PLO and Palestinian institutions in the West Bank and Gaza. Palestinians working in the Gulf lost their jobs and could no longer send remittances to their families. Having sided against the United States in a war made U.S. policy seek to exclude the PLO from the peace process. The Arab states assisted a variety of non-PLO Palestinians, including Islamic fundamentalists and anti-'Arafat radicals.

In Israel, where both government and public opinion already rejected bargaining with the PLO, Palestinian cheers for Iraqi missiles and chemical weapons against Israeli cities, the harrowing scenario in which a Palestinian state might have welcomed Iraqi missiles and soldiers to the West Bank, and the sight of 'Arafat praising Saddam and urging an apocalypse fortified that consensus.

The PLO had thus allied itself to a country that cared little for its interests and would have ruthlessly subordinated the organization if Saddam had won. Baghdad did little for the PLO either before or after the invasion of Kuwait. 'Arafat's move thus seems to be based largely on ideology and wishful thinking rather than on any sophisticated calculation of forces. He simply had to believe that Saddam was going to triumph. In the aftermath of Iraq's defeat, 'Arafat only gradually and incompletely retracted his support and the PLO made no self-criticism or reevaluation of its own behavior.

Judging from Iraq's media and leaders' speeches, Baghdad never put a high estimate on the PLO's support nor treated it as a favored client. While a few Palestinian gunmen might have helped in the occupation of Kuwait, there was no serious terrorist offensive nor even any extensive Iraqi propaganda on the PLO's behalf. 'Arafat had not just bet on the losing side, he had made an altogether bad deal with Saddam. Yet, ironically, this defeat became a factor both persuading and forcing him to make peace with Israel in 1993.

NOTES

My research on the PLO was supported by grants from the U.S. Institute of Peace and the Henry F. Guggenheim Foundation, for whose help I am grateful.

1. *Journal of Palestine Studies* 2, no. 2 (Winter 1973), p. 176. See also Barry Rubin, *Revolution Until Victory?: The Politics of the PLO* (Cambridge, Mass., 1994).

2. Yezid Sayigh, "Fatah: The First Twenty Years," *Journal of Palestine Studies* 13, no. 4 (Summer 1984), p. 115.

3. Ibrahim Ibrash, "The Palestinians and Arab Unity: From the Disaster of 1948 through Today," *al-Mustaqbal al-'Arabi*, July 1984, pp. 39-57.

4. This includes the 1967 and 1973 wars, the 1971 and 1974-1975 disengagement agreements, and the 1978-1979 Camp David accords.

5. Alain Gresh, *The PLO: The Struggle Within* (London, 1985), p. 246. See also Walid Khalidi, "The Asad Regime and the Palestinian Resistance," *Arab Studies Quarterly* 6, no. 4 (Fall 1984), p. 265.

6. *Al-Quds al-Arabi*, text in *Middle East Mirror*, February 15, 1990. Muhammad Milhim called the Arab states' support "peanuts" in comparison to their resources. *Filastin al-Thawra*, February 1, 1986, pp. 14-15.

7. Department of State, 784.00/2-2259, Jernegan to Herter, December 22, 1959.

8. Abu Nidal's real name was Sabri al-Banna. U.S. Department of Defense, *Terrorist Group Profiles* (Washington, D.C., 1988). U.S. Department of State, *Abu Nidal Organization,* (Washington, D.C., 1988), pp. 5-8.

9. On the common factors in the nature of Third World dictators and their realms, see Barry Rubin, *Modern Dictators: Third World Coupmakers, Strongmen, and Populist Tyrants,* (New York, 1987). On the Iranian revolution and its relationships with the United States, see Barry Rubin, *Paved with Good Intentions: The American Experience and Iran,* (New York, 1980).

10. Christos Ioannides, "The PLO and the Iranian Revolution," *American-Arab Affairs* (Fall 1984), pp. 89, 95.

11. Ibid.

12. Ibid.

13. Ian Black, "Iraqi Intelligence Colonel Led Terrorists in bid to Kill Envoy," *The Guardian,* March 7, 1983.

14. *Al-Hawadith,* March 1, 1985.

15. The author witnessed this incident.

16. Voice of the PLO (Baghdad), October 16, 1989, in *Foreign Broadcast Information Service (FBIS),* October 17, 1989, p. 6.

17. Text, Voice of the PLO (Baghdad), December 15, 1988, in *FBIS,* December 15, 1988, p. 3; *Washington Post,* December 15, 1988.

18. Abu Za'im, *al-Watan,* April 18, 1986; Fouad Moughrabi, "The Palestinians After Lebanon," *Arab Studies Quarterly* 5, no. 3, (Summer 1983), p. 211. Walid Kazziha, *Palestine in the Arab Dilemma,* (Totowa, N.J., 1979), pp. 15-19.

19. The Saudi Ambassador to Bahrain in *al-Sharq al-Awsat,* November 9, 1990 (text in *Middle East Mirror,* November 9, 1990, p. 25). Mahmud 'Abd al-Mun'im Murad, *October* in *Middle East Mirror,* August 21, 1990, p. 20; Dunia al-'Issa, *al-Qabas International* August 21, 1990.

20. *The Economist,* September 22, 1990, p. 48; Hazem Saghiyeh, *al-Hayat,* August 21, 1990, in *Middle East Mirror,* August 21, 1990, p. 20. The tax payments, however, were later restored.

21. *Ha'aretz,* August 17, 1990, text in *Middle East Mirror,* August 17, 1990, p. 7.

22. Saghiyeh, *al-Hayat.*

23. Yusuf Hasin, *al-Nadwa,* October 1, 1990.

24. Sayigh, "Fatah: The First Twenty Years."

25. *Washington Post,* January 18, 1991. *Vjesnik,* December 8, 1990, in *FBIS,* December 13, 1990, p. 1.

26. Karen Laub, "Palestinians Fearful of Attack, But Proud of Iraq for Targeting Israel," Reuter, January 18, 1991.

27. For example, *FBIS,* November 13, 1990, p. 1.

10

A Modus Vivendi Challenged: The Arabs in Israel and the Gulf War

Ilan Pappe

The Arabs of Israel had little effect on the Gulf crisis, but they, like the rest of the Palestinians, were greatly affected by it. This chapter first sketches the parameters in which Arab Israelis have lived and acted since 1948 in order to find out whether these factors changed as a result of the war. Second, we shall inquire whether a new set of rules or principles in Arab-Jewish relations emerged in the wake of Arab behavior during the crisis. Finally, we shall provide our own analysis and explanation on the Arab mode of behavior during the war.[1]

THE GOLDEN MEAN—THE ART OF SURVIVAL

The 160,000 Palestinians who found themselves under Israeli rule after the 1948 war, contrary to common belief, adapted swiftly and sensibly to the new situation imposed on them. In the first years of statehood, Israeli policy and the behavior of the Arab community shaped the framework of Palestinian existence in Israel.

From the early years of statehood, the main parameters in which the Arab community could operate and basic constraints under which it had to live became obvious to the government of the majority and the community of the minority. The constraints are still imposed, and some are self-imposed, on the Arab population in of spite the abolition of the military regime in 1966.

The first striking characteristic of the Arab community in Israel—in 1948 and today—is the absence of strong centralized leadership. It is impossible to single out a leader or even group of leaders of the Arabs in Israel. This is a unique situation in comparison with other minorities around the world. There were candidates for that post, but those aspiring to it failed to win the community's allegiance. A related feature—and probably an explanation—was the heterogeneous character of its politics, a spectrum stretching between advocacy for complete submission to the Jewish state (to the point of assimilation) and, on the other extreme, total rejection of Israel's right to exist.

Israel's Arab policy during the years of the military rule (1950-1966) can serve only as a partial explanation for these phenomena. The policy in those days was a curious mixture of discrimination based on security grounds coupled with an attempt to preserve the country's democratic character. The Arabs were encouraged to assimilate and become full citizens while at the same time were still suspect as a fifth column within the state.

Israeli ambivalence created an atmosphere of uncertainty among the Arabs. On the one hand, they were living under a very severe military regime. At the same time, they were entitled to vote and to be elected and enjoyed a fair measure of free press. The crux of the matter was that all these privileges could be denied, pending developments in the Arab-Israeli conflict.

The response by a minority uncertain of its ruler's real ambitions and policy is to tread very cautiously and carefully on the political path. There was no need for open resistance as the military regime was declared a temporary measure, and many voices within Israel itself called for its abolition. The Israeli self-image as a democratic society promised an ostensible effort on Israel's part to allow full citizenship for the Arab minority.

On the other hand, there was no room for complacency. The security factor would always exist until there is peace. Under the security clause, land could be confiscated, curfews imposed, and tolerance toward contrasting Arab opinions strained. The ideological nature of Jewish nationalism also did not promise a full integration or an easy relationship with the government.[2]

The "golden mean" between total submission and outright resistance as a way of life and form of national identity was tested periodically by the community. Political activists who objected to this cautious way served as testers for the rest of the population. They probed the tolerance of the Israeli consensus, security forces, and society's perceptions of morality.

In the treacherous path of trial and error, it transpired that the Israelis would not tolerate total identification with Palestinian nationalism (in the form of the PLO) or with Pan-Arabism (the Nasirist or the Ba'thist variety). Nevertheless, the Israelis would accept a cosmopolitan Marxist position, even if it concealed nationalistic ambitions, advocating the creation of a Palestinian state as a Communist, not as a Palestinian. Those who insisted on expressing themselves in a nationalist or Pan-Arabist manner paid dearly but showed the rest of the community the limits of political existence.

During the years up to 1967, the initial Israeli phobia about its Arab citizens withered away. Full citizenship was unattainable but a worthy cause whose pursuit by the Arabs did not fundamentally antagonize the relations between them and the majority. Democracy for Arabs in Israel was conditional pending changes in the security situation or in the behavior of the Arabs themselves. There was therefore an vested Arab interest in peace and keeping the modus vivendi. An Arab consensus emerged which asserted that nothing should be done to aggravate the situation. The Arabs could protest specific abuses and policies but not the basic situation: namely their existence as an Arab minority in a Jewish state.

There was no reason to deviate from this mode of behavior as long as the future did not seem to offer dramatic changes in the status quo. Nasir's rhetoric and actions in May 1967 had led some activists to believe that the situation would be transformed. These predictions, however, were no more than wishful thinking and those who acted militantly on that expectation were arrested or exiled from the country. As we shall see, Saddam Husayn—who by no means won the same support in the Arab world as Nasir had—would succeed in luring much larger segments of the Arab community in Israel to believe that they were witnessing the breaking of a new dawn in the Middle East.

THE POST-1967 ERA: CHALLENGES TO THE GOLDEN MEAN

The year 1967 could have undermined the delicate fabric of Arab-Jewish relations in Israel. For the Arabs in Israel this was a significant year both due to the war and subsequent abolition of military rule. Arabs in Israel were still discriminated against on security grounds and as a result of the state's Jewish nature. The only significant change was the granting of freedom of movement, which had been suspended during the military years.

But that year had been meaningful in other ways. After 19 years of separation two large Palestinian communities were reunited. The reunion could have potentially endangered the relationship that had been worked out in Israel, but, in the final analysis, it was disappointing for both groups. The way the Arabs in Israel expressed their nationalism was not accepted by the rest of the Palestinian community, especially since the emergence of a Palestinian guerrilla movement. Very early on, even the two Communist parties—in Israel and in the West Bank—accepted that cooperation was unworkable.

What remained was a bond among themselves that still characterizes the attitude of Arab Israelis. This bond is probably equivalent to the Zionist consensus among the Jews. The Arabs in Israel decided consciously to retain their own particular way of expressing their nationality: a mixture of Israeli citizenship, religious identity, and Palestinian nationalism. In practical terms it meant supporting the idea of a Palestinian state while, at the same time, expressing a desire to remain Israeli citizens should such a Palestinian state ever be born.

Within this consensus enough room was left for those who wanted to join Zionist parties, non-Zionist parties, or even vote for ultra-orthodox Jewish parties. The challenge to this consensus came from five developments: the emergence of a nationalist leadership outside the Communist party leading to the "Day of the Land"; the success of the nationalist Progressive Party for Peace to attain legal status as a nationalist Arab party in spite of the Israeli Security Service's objection; the intifada; the emergence of the fundamentalist movement; and, finally, Arab behavior during the Gulf War.

The organization of local heads of councils in protest against Israel's land policy led to the first ever Arab national day of protest. However, this "Day of the Land" (Yawm al-Ard)—apart from 1976 and 1988—did not deviate from the consensus sketched above. Half a day of strike, demonstrations and marginal violence are actions tolerated by any democratic system.

Muhammad Mi'ari's success in running for parliament on a platform supporting a Palestinian state—without burying it in a cosmopolitan frame-work—was another test case. His ideology advocated coexistence, but he ultimately lost most of his Jewish partners. His party and 'Abd al-Wahab Darawshe's Arab Democratic Party became national, non-Jewish parties.

Nevertheless, these parties' platforms are legitimate in the eyes of Israeli public opinion, even when they openly accepted the Algiers 1988 PLO's Declaration of Independence. Support for a Palestinian state in some segments of the Zionist left has also helped to legitimize the new Arab parties. Hence their emergence does not constitute a deviation from the game in the eyes of the Israeli center (Likud and Labor).

The intifada called upon the Arabs in Israel to examine whether verbal support for Palestinian nationalism is enough. This became a dilemma, particularly when the nature of Israeli actions in the territories was portrayed as brutal and ruthless by not only Palestinians but also the Western media and the Israeli left. The Yawm al-Ard of 1988 reflected these strains, being a violent day when angry Arab youths blocked many of the main roads in the country's north and center. Yet Israeli authorities did not take preemptive actions before the next Land Days and the National Committee of Local Arab Councils (NALAC), a consensual nonpartisan body, prepared these commemorations in a way that fit the unwritten contract between the state and its Arab citizens. The intifada's affect on the Arabs in Israel is still an ongoing process that has strained the relationship between Arabs and Jews in Israel.

In the late 1980s, other factors contributed to an uneasy coexistence. The recession in Israel also hurt the Arab community. The scarcity of jobs matching the young Arab generation's higher educational level added to the misery of the unemployed. Poor management and irresponsible fiscal policies by local Arab governing councils intensified the problem. The arrival of waves of new Russian Jewish immigrants in 1990 and 1991 accentuated the predicament. The Arabs in Israel perceived the need to provide the new immigrants with housing and employment as a direct threat on their livelihood and existence.

Communism's decline, disappointment with secular Palestinian nationalism for its failure to produce any change in the situation, and economic hardship pushed a sizable section of the population into the hands of the Muslim fundamentalists. It should be stressed, however, that so far (and this includes the Gal'ed affair[3]) the Islamic movement's leaders, in their behavior and policy, acted within the accepted rules. These events did not undermine the coexistence of the Jewish-Zionist or Arab-Israeli consensus in Israeli society. The Gulf War, on the other hand, almost succeeded in shuffling the political cards.

THE GULF WAR—THE INVASION OF KUWAIT

The onset of the crisis itself did not constitute a particular challenge to the Arabs in Israel. Iraq's aggression was widely condemned in Communist, nationalist, and Muslim newspapers.[4] In spite of long-standing Palestinian antipathy toward Kuwait's rulers, a sister Arab state's right to exist was never questioned.

The Arab press in Israel stressed the logical link between condemning Israel's occupation of Palestinian and Arab territories on the one hand and objecting to Iraq's invasion on the other. Kuwait's small size also became a point of sympathy, given the projected small size of the coveted Palestinian state.

The Communist party had a particular ax to grind when it came to Saddam Husayn, who had fiercely repressed their Iraqi counterparts. On the other hand, the party's leaders were aware that many radicals in the Arab world justified Saddam's geopolitical claims. His demands were therefore supported but his resort to force was totally rejected.[5]

The Muslim movement also was not swayed by Saddam's ostensibly religious behavior. They regarded him—as they did other Ba'th party leaders—as a modern Jahili (pagan).[6] Moreover, like the Communists, Muslim activists were well aware of his punishment and execution of their Iraqi compatriots.

By mid-August, however, the declaration of Operation "Desert Shield" changed this attitude. Pro-Saddam rhetoric forcefully appeared in the newspapers and here and there symbolic acts of support for Iraq could be seen the streets. We shall provide our own interpretation for this support after following the Arabs' own explanations through a chronological survey of the crisis.

THE NEW CRISIS—SADDAM AL-DIN

The first article in Iraq's favor appeared in the official organ of the Muslim movement, *al-Sirrat,* on August 17, 1990. A new war had started, declared the editorial, "a war against the honor and integrity of the Arab people," waged by U.S. imperialism.

Within two weeks, Saddam's occupation was rehabilitated in the Arab newspapers. This was done, however, in two different ways. The Communist party and its partners in the Democratic Front for Peace took a more cautious line and still objected to Saddam's use of force; the other Arab parties acted more like Saddam's allies in countries such as Yemen and Jordan.

The Communist stand was formulated amid strong internal divisions. The majority in the leadership persisted in condemning the occupation while a small group—probably reflecting the rank and file—demanded a more vigorous show of solidarity with Iraq. The U.S. countermeasures were condemned, but official Soviet policy was accepted and followed. In lower echelons, national sentiments led to a stronger identification with Saddam, but grass-roots pressure did not succeed in changing the official line. The party's policy can be fairly described as adopting a neutral stance toward a struggle between an Arab leader and the mightiest Western power.

The Communists' competitors in the Arab community, deciding to attack the neutral position, stressed their wholehearted support for Saddam to portray the Communists as betrayers of the Arab cause. Such taunts opened the split within the Communist party on a national basis. The party's Arab organ, *al-Ittihad*, gave vent to the hidden nationalism of its grass-roots members; the Jewish paper, *Zo Ha-Derech*, very faithfully echoed Moscow's cautious policy. This included support not only for a swift diplomatic solution to the conflict but even a grudging acceptance of the UN resolutions.[7]

Hence the Muslim movement, the Progressive List for Peace, the Democratic Arab Party, and Abna al-Balad unequivocally supported Saddam's policy. Abna al-Balad, an extreme political movement inspired by the rejectionist factions in the PLO, was especially vociferous in endorsing Saddam's polemics, including his specific threats to destroy the Jewish state.

From mid-August on, these parties began publicly accepting Iraq's claims over Kuwait. Various newspapers enumerated Iraq's "justified" historical and moral claim over Kuwait. Iraq's invasion was described as an act of defiance against the artificial borders created by the West after World War I (which in Kuwait's case, incidently, was historically inaccurate since its borders were determined much earlier by an Ottoman-British agreement).[8]

Saddam was also portrayed as a warrior against Arab decadence. 'Abd al-Wahab Darawshe advocated unifying of Iraq and Kuwait as part of a struggle against the rich oil-producing monarchies that had failed to contribute their share to the general Arab cause.[9] This line of argument featured very strongly in Saddam's own polemics. Muhammad Mi'ari saw Saddam's move as a first step on the way to Arab unification, notwithstanding his own preference for unification in peaceful means.[10]

This verbal support for Saddam did not endanger the modus vivendi in Israel as long as Iraq's threats were confined to words alone. When missiles began striking Israel, however, open endorsement of a ruler vowing to burn the Jewish state with chemical weapons could have tainted the whole community. This precarious situation worsened during the war itself, when support for Saddam reached a crescendo toward the end of January 1991.

THE OUTBREAK OF THE WAR—SADDAM THE MARTYR

The war's quick pace and the power of U.S. air attacks caused perplexity and confusion among Arab polemicists and political activists in Israel. This general quandary narrowed the gap between the Communists and the rest of the Arab parties. In the second half of January 1991, therefore, a unified reaction could be read and heard in the Arab press and street.

While opinions diverged on Iraq's right to annex Kuwait, almost everyone regarded the Americans as the intransigent side in the conflict responsible for failure to reach a peaceful solution. The war broke out due to a U.S. refusal to compromise with Saddam. The widely held conspiracy theory that the Americans had induced Saddam to occupy Kuwait so they could attack and destroy him was especially highlighted in the Communist newspaper, *al-Ittihad*.[11]

All the Arab parties stressed Saddam's willingness to compromise and the Soviet Union's mediation effort. The stiffening U.S. position was taken as proof of Washington's premeditation in this war. Muhammad Mi'ari, writing in *al-Sinara*, was this theory's main spokesman, but the idea was shared by the Muslims and the rest of the Arab parties.[12]

The Muslim movement's official organ also claimed that the attack on Iraq had little to do with the occupation of Kuwait.[13] The fundamentalists' discourse and rhetoric, of course, differed from the other groups in that it portrayed the Americans as Mongols and Crusaders. The presence of the Americans on the Muslim land of Saudi Arabia and their "debasement" of a state containing Islam's holiest shrines featured widely in the Muslim press.

The real U.S. goal was said to be control of Iraq's oilfields. This alleged economic motivation was especially emphasized in the Communist party's organs.[14] According to *al-Ittihad*'s editor, economic recession was the main force driving America to a military confrontation. Judging from letters to the editor, many readers also saw the situation analogous to the 1956 Suez crisis in which Britain, France, and Israel tried to overthrow Nasir.

News of the destruction from the bombing produced even more militant rhetoric. The newspapers in this instance, probably more than before, reflected faithfully the feeling of many Arab Israelis. Nevertheless, the fate of Israelis hit by the Scuds and the danger of Arab citizens becoming victims mitigated this wrath. While the newspapers at the start of February 1991 were still full of bitter anti-American protests, by that month's end this mood subsided to be replaced by growing concern for the postwar era.[15]

Saddam's image also changed during February, from that of Salah al-Din reincarnated to that of a martyr. He was portrayed as someone who dared against all odds to cut the long chain of humiliations inflicted by Western imperialism on the Arab world since Napoleon's invasion of Egypt. The Arab press reported, quite accurately one presumes, that the view of Saddam as martyr was that of the man in the street.[16] Even greater admiration was shown to the Iraqi people for their Sumud (steadfastness) in the face of constant U.S. bombing.[17]

On this score, the official leadership, the NALAC, took a clear stand condemning the U.S. use of force against civilians. But Arab Israeli leaders and institutions generally preferred to safeguard relations with the Jewish majority, despite pressures from their own constituents.

Thus, the Arab Israeli response was mostly verbal. The only actual protest during the war related to the situation in the occupied territories. The long curfew imposed there strengthened feelings of solidarity with the Palestinians. Consequently, money as well as food was collected and sent to the West Bank and the Gaza Strip in order to ease the situation there.[18]

BACK TO THE MODUS VIVENDI

On January 23, a missile fell near an Arab village, symbolizing the joint fate of Jews and Arabs in Israel. The dilemmas of daily survival began to supersede national pride and aspirations. That day, Emil Habibi said, "Every household in this country, both Jewish and Arab, must be made aware of the perception that we all share a common fate and both peoples should leave the sealed rooms with a vow never to return to them."[19]

Like other colleagues with Arab friends, my phone was flooded with offers of asylum in the Galilee, considered to be safer from missiles. Israeli newspapers were full of such stories. Local Arab councils made official invitations to Jewish schools, families, and whole settlements to spend the time in Arab villages.

The sense of a common experience shared by Arabs and Jews during the war helps explain the former's retreat from full support for Saddam. Israel's population as a whole, Arabs and Jews alike, went through the surrealistic ordeal of waiting in sealed rooms with gas masks on their faces almost every day of the war. The Arabs, insisting they be given the same protection as the Jewish community, had to confront the contradiction between demanding full citizenship and supporting Saddam. Their need to be shielded from the new Arab savior showed up the absurdity of their situation. One presumes that Israeli self-restraint and the decisive U.S. victory also contributed to this process of retraction.

In the last days of January, cautious behavior reemerged in attempts to explain to the Israeli Jewish public the motives behind the Arab position during the war. The editor of *al-Sinara* told Israeli Radio that support for Saddam did not mean backing Iraq against Israel. It was merely a solidarity with an Arab leader who was combatting Arab tyrants, explained Lutfi Mash'ur.[20]

On February 15, NALAC officially signaled a return to normal by condemning the firing of missiles at Israel. In March, faint pro-Saddam voices could still be found in the press, but the next month was devoted to analyzing the new world order and the PLO's deteriorating image in world public opinion as a result of the war.

ANALYSIS AND CONCLUSIONS

In viewing the political behavior of Arab Israelis from 1948 to the Gulf War, one is impressed by the realistic, pragmatic viewpoints expressed by political activists and communal leaders. A salient feature in their self-analysis has been a resignation to the status quo, an assumption that fundamental change cannot be expected.

Moreover, the Arabs in Israel do not have the ability to change the situation. They can only contribute to a better understanding between Israel and the Arab world—a role in which their initial efforts were highly disappointing—or hope for a momentous war that will reshuffle the region's political cards. The latter hope was a strong incentive to deviate from the usual pattern of behavior in support of Saddam Husayn.

The Arab newspapers between August and December 1990 expressed a recurrent hope for a political earthquake to be generated by the Gulf crisis. Saddam was both courageous enough—and quite probably insane enough, in the eyes of Arab Israelis—to risk an open confrontation with the United States. If America was forced to change its policy, Arab Israelis hoped, U.S. pressure on Israel could force a withdrawal from the territories. Saddam had the ability to upset a system that they did not find satisfactory.

Since Sadat's visit to Jerusalem—an initiative that had weakened the Arab ability to unite against Israel—no one, including the PLO, Asad, or Qadhafi, had been able to attract as much international attention as Saddam did. It should also be remembered that Saddam's scenario of linking the Kuwaiti and Palestine problems was accepted by France and the Soviet Union and was not rejected by the rest of the Arab world.

Thus, some important segments of the Arab Israeli political activists and public thought Saddam's rhetoric and acts had the power to change the status quo fundamentally. Most Arab states did not agree, even if they sympathized with Saddam as an alleged victim of the West. But Arab Israelis were willing to view him as a savior—misjudging the international and regional situation in the process—because of their own political despair, economic hardship, and social frustration.

Some of the leaders genuinely shared this popular feeling. Others, especially among the Communists' opponents, were driven by more cynical motives.

Their ostensible enthusiasm for Saddam was an opportunistic attempt to gain some of the Communists' supporters. In hindsight it seems a reckless gamble that endangered the community as a whole. In fact it was largely due to the Communists' behavior that the modus vivendi with Jewish Israelis was kept alive. The Communist party remained in the Israeli establishment's eyes the leading Arab force in the country. Therefore, its cautious policy was seen as a continued adherence to rules accepted by both sides. Emil Habibi in March 1991 compared his party's behavior in the war to the Communists' attitude in 1948: "In 1947-48, in spite of the general atmosphere, and notwithstanding the injustice incurred in the partition resolution, the Marxists [sic] withstood the stream of fanaticism and adhered to a rational position."[21] Whether this attitude reflected the rank and file's position is doubtful but it was the view of the cosmopolitan activists in the party leadership, and thus the party line.

Another factor helping to mend fences by the end of the crisis was that Arab Israelis limited their support for Saddam to words alone. This stands in sharp contrast to the behavior of the West Bank and Gaza Palestinians who passionately demonstrated in favor of Iraq.[22]

The main protest of the time within Israel was the NALAC's call for a two-day strike after a large number of West Bank Arabs were killed by Israeli forces during an October 1990 clash in Jerusalem. Although Saddam Husayn linked this incident to the Kuwait crisis, no Arab newspaper in Israel did so. On the contrary, this event deflected everyone's attention for a while from the Gulf.

While Arab Israelis thus managed to preserve the Jewish-Arab relationship in general, the alliance between the Zionist left and Arab parties was damaged. The Peace Now movement demanded that Arab Israelis fully support the U.S. action, criticizing the nationalist component in their identity that made them support Saddam and reject open identification with Israel's government—even in time of war—or U.S. policy.[23]

The most famous condemnation, directed at Palestinians in general, came from member of parliament Yossi Sarid: "If it is permissible to support Saddam Husayn, who murdered tens of thousands of 'opponents of the regime' . . . perhaps it is not so terrible to back the policies of Shamir, Sharon and Rabin. In comparison with Saddam Husayn's crimes, the Israeli government's sins are as white as the driven snow."[24]

Even when enthusiastic support for Saddam subsided, a gap between past partners in the Israeli peace camp remained. It was beyond the conception of most Arab activists why Peace Now in Israel refused to accept the linkage, offered by Saddam, between the Gulf crisis and the Palestinian problem.[25]

Support for linkage became an undebatable point, accepted by everyone in the Arab community. The apolitical chairman of NALAC, Ibrahim Nimr

Husayn, expressed the hope for diplomatic linkage after the war ended. Having only rarely in the past expressed himself in matters beyond municipal problems, he now led the group to issue an official proclamation, in late January, supporting an international conference to solve all outstanding problems in the Middle East.

During the Kuwait crisis, dialogue between the Palestinians and the Israelis on the left was at a standstill. Meanwhile, Arab Israelis moved from parties stressing coexistence to those emphasizing nationalism. The only party, apart from the Communists, with an Arab-Jewish character, the Progressive List for Peace, lost most of its Jewish members.[26]

Generally speaking, one can find in Israel the same factors explaining support for Saddam in the Arab world. Economic, cultural, and political imbalances between the Orient and West since the early 19th century have fueled anti-European and anti-American attitudes. Imperialism only accentuated feelings of frustration and antagonism—emotions that were successfully and cynically utilized by Arab regimes to distract internal criticism and opposition. Economic hardship and torn cultural and social identities have pushed masses of Arabs to seek a hero who would extricate them. Nasir had been such a hero in the past; Saddam succeeded in being one for a while.

The logical explanation for the initial vociferous support for Saddam Husayn among Arabs in Israel must include their satisfaction with the worry the crisis had sown among Jews in Israel. Daily life as an Arab in Israel can be at times a humiliating experience; seeing the dominating majority at its moment of nadir can be rewarding.

Arabs themselves are convinced that concepts of honor and humiliation have an important effect on their policies. As one Arab philosopher explained: "My Arab and Human honor have been sullied by what the Americans are doing today, but on the other hand the Arabs also feel their honor has been vindicated. Iraq fought and survived, a myth has been born, no matter what had happened."[27]

But the need to cope with daily existence in Israel after the crisis forced the Arab community to adopt once more the golden mean as a way of life.

NOTES

1. The Arabs' attitude in Israel was gathered mainly from the Arab press and interviews. Documentation for such a contemporary subject is of course difficult. It may well be that this is no more than an elite analysis, but the elite has so far faithfully reflected other segments of the Arab population in Israel.

2. Ilan Pappe, "The Golden Mean—The Unique Version of Palestinian Nationalism in Israel, 1948-1958," in Ilan Troen and Noah Lucas, eds., *Israel: the First Decade—Independence* (New York, 1994).

3. In February 1992, four supporters of the Islamic movement murdered three Israeli soldiers in the camp of Gal'ed. The movement's head denied any association with the perpetrators and condemned the act.

4. Sarah and Asa'd Ghanem, *The Arabs of Israel in the Shadow of the Gulf War*, The Institute for Arabic Studies (Givat Haviva, 1991), p. 3.

5. *Al-Ittihad,* February 4, 1990.

6. Emmanuel Sivan, *Radical Islam: Medieval Theology and Modern Politics* (Tel Aviv, 1985), (Hebrew), pp. 32-40.

7. This information was gathered in conversations with members and ex-members of the party who have asked not to be identified.

8. See, for instance, *Kull al-'Arab,* March 15, 1991.

9. *Yediot Aharnot,* August 17, 1990.

10. *Hadha al-Usbu',* August 9, 1990.

11. *Al-Ittihad,* January 1, 1991.

12. *Al-Sirat,* January 15, 1991.

13. *Al-Sirat,* February 11, 1991.

14. Ahmad Sa'd, director of the Emil Touma Institute in Haifa, expressed this view in a symposium held there in January 1991.

15. Salem Jubran in an editorial in *al-Ittihad,* January 27, 1991.

16. *Kull al-'Arab* and *Sinara,* February 1991; Samir Darwish, the mayor of Baqa al-Gharbiyya, *Yediot Aharnot,* February 1, 1991.

17. Ghanem, "The Arabs of Israel," p. 8.

18. Ibid., p. 12.

19. Interview in *Davar,* January 23, 1991.

20. Interview on January 24, 1991.

21. Interview in *Iton 77* (A Literary Monthly), (March 1992), p. 26.

22. On Palestinian activity in the territories see chronology in *Journal of Palestine Studies* 20, no. 2 (Winter 1991), pp. 202-32.

23. See Mattiyahu Peled, "An Israeli View," in *Journal of Palestine Studies* 20, no. 2 (Winter 1991), pp. 106-11.

24. *Ha'aretz,* August 16, 1990.

25. Darawshe in *al-Fajr,* January 15, 1991.

26. The first report on the developments in this party appeared outside of Israel in the *Washington Times,* August 21, 1990.

27. Interview, *Ha'aretz,* March 1, 1991.

11

Syria:
Iraq's Radical Nemesis

Michael Eppel

The development of relations between Syria and Iraq from the establishment of those states after World War I was heavily influenced by their internal weakness as political communities having no common denominator for their heterogeneous populations. Their stability was also undermined by social, cultural, and economic crises resulting from imposed, accelerated modernization and the traumatic encounter with the West.

Given the weakness of national crystallization in both states and their respective regimes' tenuous legitimacy, Pan-Arab ideology—whose vision transcended the borders of individual Arab states—became a weighty factor as a means of achieving legitimacy and enlisting public support for domestic politics and as a way to attain goals in the inter-Arab arena. In Iraq's case, its Pan-Arab vision included an ambition to dominate Syria.

The desire to rule Syria arose during the reign of King Faysal I of Iraq (1921-1933), motivated by the former country's seemingly incoherent nature as well as by Iraq's wish to be the core of a far larger Pan-Arab entity. Iraq's goal directed Syrian-Iraqi relations in the 1930s and early 1940s, when Syria was still under French rule. Fearing the ambitions of Iraq and Transjordan, Syria sought Egyptian and Saudi assistance after World War II.

During the 1940s and 1950s, Iraq was able to intervene in Syrian politics because it had a stronger economy and leadership as well as a well-defined foreign policy. Syria had no reciprocal influence, but its politicians were pleased to receive financial and political assistance from Iraq, as they did from Saudi Arabia and Egypt, to use in their internal political struggles.

In Syrian politics, those forces in opposition to President Shukri al-Quwatli and the Damascus elite adopted a more pro-Iraqi orientation. Syrian politicians who maintained connections with Iraq and sought its assistance—promising to support eventual federation between the two states—came mostly from the northern city of Aleppo, which traditionally had close links with Iraq, belonged to the al-Sha'b (People's) party, and vehemently combatted al-Quwatli and his party, al-Watani (National) party.

Between 1945 and 1949, al-Quwatli tried to minimize tension with Iraq, lest it be exploited by pro-Iraqi forces in Syria. He used the conflict between the branches of the Hashemite family ruling Iraq and Jordan to drive a wedge between them. When Syria seemed threatened by the ambitions of King 'Abdallah of Transjordan, al-Quwatli made a show of rapprochement with Iraq.

The undermining of Syria's internal balance following the March 1949 coup led by Husni al-Za'im made that country an object of competition between Hashemite Iraq and Transjordan, on the one hand, and Egypt and Saudi Arabia, on the other. Initially leaning toward Iraq, al-Za'im even proposed a federation, since he feared Egypt and Saudi Arabia—which had supported al-Quwatli, whom he had deposed—and wanted to avoid a takeover by Transjordan. When he realized that Saudi Arabia and Egypt were ready to accept his rule, provided that he limit Hashemite influence in Damascus and avoid a federation with Iraq, al-Za'im stopped courting Baghdad.

In the wake of another coup less than six months later, in August 1949—this one headed by Sami al-Hinnawi—Syrian public opinion underwent a wave of enthusiastic support for the idea of federation with Iraq. Iraq's regent, 'Abd al-Ilah, politicians linked with the palace, and Pan-Arab nationalist circles all sought to seize what they considered a historic opportunity to establish Arab unity. This was to be implemented in the form of an Iraqi-Syrian federation ruled by Iraq's royal house.

By contrast, Iraq's government under Nuri al Sa'id, who had been the Iraqi politician most actively favoring a unified Fertile Crescent under Iraqi leadership, now displayed a reserved, suspicious attitude toward Syria. Nuri al-Sa'id feared the effect of Syria's erratic politics on Iraqi stability and did not trust the Syrian politicians. He also doubted if a stable federation favorable to Iraq and its regime could be established without broad-based support within Syria, the approval of Great Britain and the United States, and Egypt's consent. During the 1950s, two clear trends were evident in Iraq's policy toward Syria. The regent, the palace, and politicians who sought 'Abd al-Ilah's support sought to establish a federation or union under Iraqi rule. For his part, Nuri al-Sa'id thought the federation a hopeless cause and advocated a more limited goal of gaining dominant influence in Syria to ensure it backed Iraq's policies. Iraq would thus be able to avoid a pro-Egyptian or radical Syrian regime that endangered Iraq's interests.

The December 1949 coup in Syria, led by Adib al-Shishakli, was meant to block any possibility of federation with Iraq and to prevent the loss of Syrian independence. After the al-Shishakli regime fell in early 1954; it was replaced by forces identified with a pro-Iraqi orientation and known to support the establishment of an Iraqi-Syrian federation. Yet these basically conservative forces weakened during 1954, giving rise to a radical leftist-nationalist faction that viewed Iraq as a bastion of reaction and surrender to the West.

Although Iraqi-Syrian relations took place officially on an intergovernmental diplomatic plane, the real power center were direct links between Iraqi Hashemite court politicians and Syrian forces or politicians. Nevertheless, neither Iraq's superior ability to intervene in Syrian affairs nor the financial and political aid it gave conservative Syrian politicians had the desired result. Most of those politicians sought Iraq's assistance to strengthen their own status against the new radical nationalist forces while remaining suspicious of Iraqi domination. Iraq was unable to help form a stable pro-Iraqi regime in Syria that could prevent the rise of radical forces which Iraq's ruling elite perceived as dangerous to their country and themselves.

Between 1955 and 1958, Iraq-Syrian relations took on an ideological dimension following the rise of the Syrian Ba'th party, which sided with revolutionary, neutralist Egypt against monarchist, pro-Western Iraq. This new factor in bilateral relations put Iraq in a position of inferiority relative to both Egypt and the Syrian radical forces, against which Iraq had no effective response.

Iraqi activity in Syria during the 1950s was defensive: to prevent Syria from joining the anti-Iraq, pro-Egypt camp and to keep such antagonistic forces out of power in Damascus. But Iraq's moves—creating the Baghdad Pact, pressing Syria to join the pro-Western camp, and trying to organize a coup in Damascus—all had the opposite effect. Iraq unintentionally accelerated Syria's internal disintegration and helped push it toward union with Egypt in 1958. Iraq's dependence on Syria's declining conservative elite, as well as its inability to win support among the rising new middle class and the dominance of radical officers in Syria's army, doomed Iraq to lose influence in Syria.

The merger of Syria and Egypt into the United Arab Republic in 1958 constituted a historic defeat for Hashemite Iraq and marked the end of its 30-year effort to achieve dominance over Syria or even to establish an Iraqi-Syrian federation.[1] This Iraqi failure, in turn, sped up the ripening of conditions that brought about the overthrow of its own monarchist regime in 1958, leading to the most significant political and social changes since Iraq's creation.[2]

IRAQ-SYRIA RELATIONS UNDER
SADDAM HUSAYN AND AL-ASAD

The rise to power of the Ba'th parties in both Syria (1963) and Iraq (first in 1963 and again in 1968) added a new factor to the rivalry between the two countries: a dispute over the legitimacy of their respective regimes.

The roots of this dispute lay in the struggle within the Syrian Ba'th party from 1962 to 1966 between the older leadership (the "National Command"), headed by Michel 'Aflaq and Salah al-Din al-Bitar, and the party's radical leftist wing headed by young army officers. This wing, called the "Regional Command," reflected the rise of new social forces within the minority groups, the lower classes, and the residents of small towns and villages.

The struggle was decided in 1966. Following an officers' coup headed by Salah Jadid, the radicals held power in the Syrian Ba'th party and in Syria.[3] The older leadership, expelled from Syria after the coup, found a haven with the Iraqi Ba'th party, which assumed power in 1968. The alliance with 'Aflaq and the National Command gave the Iraqi Ba'th, headed by Hasan al-Bakr and Saddam Husayn, legitimacy as the only real Ba'th party.[4] The fact that each of the two Ba'th factions—Syrian and Iraqi—claimed sole legitimacy and represented itself as the focal point around which the Arab nation must rally made the two regimes fierce rivals.

The rise of Hafez al-Asad (in 1969-1970) and Saddam Husayn (the power behind the scenes until becoming undisputed leader in 1979) to leadership of their respective Ba'th parties and, subsequently, of their respective states added a personal dimension to the long-standing rivalry between Iraq and Syria.

The hostility and suspicion that prevailed between the two leaders may have been exacerbated in 1979 by the attempt of several Iraqi Ba'thists to halt Saddam Husayn by forming a federation with Syria.[5] In such an event, Saddam would be pushed down to third place on the leadership hierarchy, after al-Bakr and Hafez al-Asad. Although mutual personal hostility and conflicting regional ambitions played an important role, the basic factors affecting relations between

Iraq and Syria lay in the nature of the two states, the character of their regimes, and the conditions of the inter-Arab arena.

Prior to 1958, Iraq had a stronger ruling elite, more powerful army, and greater economic resources than did Syria, which was then a weak country in a state of utter political disarray. In contrast, during the period of Ba'th rule after 1963 and especially following Asad's rise to power in 1970, Syria transformed itself into a relatively strong state with pretensions to being a regional power.

With Asad's accession in Syria and that of Saddam Husayn in Iraq, both countries gained strong rulers with regional ambitions who were backed by stable, well-entrenched regimes. During the long, relatively stable period of Ba'th rule, Iraq and Syria each developed strong state machinery and tendencies toward national crystallization. Growing segments of the population began to identify with their respective states and rulers.

These nation-building processes are still far from complete, and both states still suffer from basic weaknesses as a direct result of the still-weak national identity of heterogeneous populations, their regimes' tenuous legitimacy, the frustrations of accelerated modernization, and economic difficulties. This internal weakness—which each of the rivals can exploit to undermine the other's stability—obligates both countries to strive for military might and for a central role in the inter-Arab arena.

Given Syria's and Iraq's lack of democratic government and inability to tolerate legitimate opposition activity, forces and individuals acting against the regime of each state found asylum within the rival country. Syria persistently encourages and assists Iraqi groups that oppose Saddam Husayn, such as the Kurds. After Iraq invaded Kuwait, Damascus became a center of activity for those who wanted to oust Iraq's ruler. A meeting of such groups took place in Damascus in December 1990. Syria was a venue for Kurdish, Sunni, Ba'thist, and Communist opposition groups.

Similarly, in the early 1970s, Iraq began aiding anti-Syrian and anti-Asad groups operating in Lebanon. This activity increased Syrian fears that Lebanon's weakness would be exploited to damage the Ba'th regime in Damascus. It was also one of Asad's motives in expanding his country's involvement in Lebanon in the mid-1970s.[6]

Iraq's military expansion began in the 1970s and was given enormous impetus by the war against Iran (1980-1988). By the war's end, Iraq had become the most significant military power among the Arab countries. In contrast, Syria's serious economic difficulties in the late 1970s and the 1980s made it difficult for the Syrian leaders to build their forces.

Saddam Husayn's ambitions of regional power and Iraq's growing military strength were among the factors that led Asad to offer Iran help during its war against Iraq. This move, coupled with Asad's insistence on ostracizing Egypt over the peace agreement with Israel and on supporting terrorist operations against Israel and the West, led to Syria's isolation in the inter-Arab and international arenas. The Iran-Iraq war's end in 1988 increased Syrian fears of Iraq's military machine and Saddam Husayn's ambitions. In February 1991, Vice President 'Abd al-Halim Khaddam of Syria claimed that, ever since the Iran-Iraq ceasefire, the Syrians recognized that Saddam Husayn was preparing for a new adventure in the Gulf.[7]

Fear of Saddam's ambition, Iraq's power, and increased Iraqi activity in Lebanon—plus a desire to escape isolation and dependency on a declining Soviet Union—motivated Asad in 1988-1989 to gradually change Syria's foreign policy toward resuming ties with Egypt and the West. Syria's participation alongside Egypt and Saudi Arabia in the U.S.-led coalition against Iraq was a natural outgrowth of this reorientation.

The development of Iraqi-Syrian relations also had implications for the Arab-Israeli conflict and vice versa. Syria's Ba'th regime has a profound ideological commitment to the struggle against Israel and Zionism. This struggle serves the regime as an important means of earning legitimacy and enlisting support within Syria and as the principal means of attaining leading status in the inter-Arab arena.

In contrast to Syria, Iraq's stand on the Arab-Israeli conflict was more flexible, dictated by inter-Arab politics to a greater extent than by a direct interaction with Israel. When Iraq's principal attention was directed to domestic affairs or to relations with Iran and the Gulf states, its governments tended to reduce involvement in the Arab-Israeli conflict and to moderate their positions regarding Israel and Zionism. When, however, they considered it a useful means to consolidate power within Iraq or combat Arab rivals, these same regimes turned to extremism on the Arab-Israeli conflict.

Under Saddam Husayn, most of Iraq's efforts were addressed to the war against Iran, to reinforcing Iraq's position in the Gulf, and to maintaining internal stability. Yet Saddam's ambition to lead the Arab world moved him to extremism when it came to Israel. For that reason, Iraqi publications and officials were quick to attack any Syrian move vis-à-vis Israel resulting from pragmatic considerations that might be interpreted as moderate or as efforts to refrain from uncompromising struggle.

Thus, Iraq attacked Syria's agreement to a ceasefire in 1973 and to a separation of forces in the Golan Heights in 1974.[8] Iraq repeatedly reminded Asad of his failure to bring about an Israeli retreat from the Golan. Following the split between Syria and the PLO in the early 1980s, Iraq began in 1983 to offer asylum to many Palestinian institutions and training camps.

The protection Iraq gave Palestinian organizations—including help to the most extremist groups—and its public support of PLO positions did not stop it from adopting a stance of relative moderation during the Iraq-Iran war. Iraqi pragmatism went so far as de facto recognition of the Egypt-Israel peace treaty, even dropping a few feelers hinting at a readiness to reach an understanding with Israel.[9] This seeming policy shift was in line with Iraq's urgent need for Western support in its war against Iran, constituting an expression of Iraq's instrumentalist attitude toward the Arab-Israeli conflict.

Iraq's attempts to become the PLO's patron and exploit the struggle against Israel to make Iraq the leading Arab state directly challenged Syria's role and ambition. Both the Syrian and pro-Syrian press in the West eagerly emphasized Iraqi-Israeli contacts to prove Saddam Husayn's hypocrisy and treachery.[10] Similarly, Iraqi newspapers never held back from reporting Syrian-Israeli contacts as an expression of Asad's defeatism.[11]

While power-oriented, pragmatic considerations dominate both countries' policies, they justify their moves with Pan-Arab nationalist ideology to further their domestic legitimacy and regional ambitions. Syria-Iraq relations also reached the crisis level over differing economic interests, such as the question of a pipeline from Iraq to the Mediterranean and the division of water from the Euphrates, the latter leading so far as the massing of military forces on the Iraqi-Syrian border in 1976.[12]

Yet Syria has also needed Iraq to be militarily and economically strong as a potential ally against Israel. Paradoxically, however, when Iraq pursues its regional ambitions, it endangers Syria and its leadership. Syria was and is certainly not first on the list of Saddam Husayn's priorities, yet to realize his goals of power and of regional Arab leadership, Iraq would have to dominate Syria.

SYRIA-IRAQ RELATIONS IN THE GULF CRISIS AND WAR, 1990-1991

Iraq's invasion of the Arab state of Kuwait was, for the Syrians, clear proof of their previous claims regarding the nature and tendencies of Saddam Husayn and his regime. Syria's immediate response to the invasion on August 2, 1990, was to call for the urgent convocation of an Arab summit conference. President Asad discussed this move by telephone with the heads of government in Egypt, Jordan, Libya, and Morocco.[13]

From the crisis's first days, Syria took intensive action in seeking a central role in any preparations taken by the Arab states against Iraq.[14] Syria demanded

Iraq's withdrawal from Kuwait and restoration of the old regime, though emphasizing the need for an Arab solution to the problem. The idea was to prevent intervention in Arab affairs by a foreign power, and thus avoid a war that might be disastrous not only for Iraq but for all Arabs.[15]

Syria's insistent, uncompromising attitude resulted from a fear of Iraqi expansionism and Saddam Husáyn's increased strength should his move in Kuwait prove successful. An Iraqi success in Kuwait would tip the balance of power even further to Syria's disadvantage, endangering the status and survival of Asad's regime and perhaps that of Syria in general. Saddam's justification of the invasion as a step toward "the liberation of Palestine" and attempts to draw Israel into a crisis was received with bitter sarcasm by Syria, whose media derided the notion that Israeli withdrawal could be brought about by invading another Arab state and inciting divisive controversy within the Arab world.[16]

Rejecting Iraq's claim to historic rights in Kuwait, Syria warned that the same sort of argument was being used by the Zionists to justify their rights in Palestine.[17] Similarly, Syria turned down Iraqi requests for reopening an oil pipeline from Iraq to the Mediterranean via Syria, after Iraq's other pipelines were closed as sanctions. Damascus also rejected all Iraqi appeals to unite against the West and Iran as enemies of all Arabs.[18]

That Saddam Husayn had no illusions about the chance of Syria's altering its position is shown by the phrasing of his August 12, 1990, proposal linking resolution of the crisis he had created with the solution not only of the Palestine question but also Syria's withdrawal from Lebanon.

From Syria's standpoint, Saddam's attempt to appear as the Arab leader, heading the struggle against Israel and promoting the Palestinian cause, was extremely injurious to Syria and personally damaging to Asad. By including an Israeli withdrawal from the Golan Heights in his own initiative, Saddam tried to present himself as able of achieving what Asad had failed to accomplish. Moreover, his proposal for the withdrawal of all forces from Lebanon—not only Israeli, but Syrian troops as well—was seen by Syria as an attempt to undermine its status in Lebanon and to reinforce Iraqi influence on anti-Syrian forces there.[19]

Throughout the Kuwait crisis, Saddam Husayn provoked Asad with reiterations of such earlier demands as his February 1990 call that Syria withdraw from Lebanon and Asad apologize to Iraq and the Arab people for supporting Iran and closing the pipeline from Iraq through Syria.[20] At the same time, however, these attacks remained fairly moderate relative to those on Saudi Arabia and Egypt.[21] It appears that although Iraqi leaders saw no chance of cooperation with Syria, they were still careful not to exacerbate relations unduly and thus open another potential military front.

While Syria stressed the vital need for an Arab solution to the Gulf crisis, with no foreign intervention, it responded to Saddam's refusal to withdraw from Kuwait by sending an expeditionary force to Saudi Arabia.[22]

Syrian radio claimed that the invasion of Kuwait was distracting the Arabs from their central, vital struggle against Israel and Zionism.[23] The attack served Israel's interests, Syria said, by letting the Zionists reinforce their hold on the occupied territories and obtain additional arms.[24] Syria's media complained that the invasion had wasted all the Palestinian intifada's gains and pushed the issue off the top of world consciousness and priorities.[25]

The Syrians rejected any linkage between the Gulf crisis and the withdrawals of Israel from the territories and Syria from Lebanon. They ruled out any comparison between Iraq's invasion of Kuwait and the presence of Syrian forces in Lebanon; the latter action, they claimed, was intended to assist the legitimate Lebanese government in accordance with the Taif agreements.[26]

Saddam was accused by Syrian Foreign Minister Faruq al-Shara' of having brought about—by proposing linkage and missile attacks—Israel's involvement in an internal inter-Arab dispute.[27] Saddam's missile strikes on Israel were said to enable that country to obtain antimissile missiles, that it had not previously possessed.[28] Syria hinted that even if Israel retaliated against Iraq, it would remain hostile to Saddam.[29]

Syria's decision to join a U.S.-led coalition created a severe public opinion problem for a government that had built itself an image as the determined opponent of both U.S. imperialism and Zionism. Saddam Husayn's efforts to represent himself as the great Arab and Muslim fighter against the evils of Western imperialism and the fact that Iraq's slogans and justifications were similar to those used to legitimize the Syrian regime created an uncomfortable situation for Asad.

Concern was aroused in Damascus lest Saddam win the sympathy of Syria's people. Indeed, Jordanian and Turkish sources reported in late August 1990 that riots had broken out in Dír al-Zur, Kamishli, and other cities in northeastern Syria close to the Iraqi and Turkish borders, as well as demonstrations among Palestinian refugees and students in Damascus.[30]

High Syrian officials had to go to great lengths to explain this decision to party activists, military officers, and the public, which had for many years been accustomed to consider the United States in highly hostile terms. Now they were being faced with the presence of Syrian troops in the same camp as U.S. forces, fighting against an Arab country whose slogans were similar to those of Syria and whose leader had declared that this was the great battle of the Arab and Muslim nation against the West.[31]

In an effort to justify this policy, the Syrian media blamed Iraq, which, by its invasion of Kuwait, had caused the incursion of foreign military forces onto

Arab soil and forced Syria to place its military power alongside that of the United States.[32] Syrian spokesmen emphasized that the purpose of the Syrian soldiers was to protect the threatened Arab state of Saudi Arabia and to liberate the conquered Arab state of Kuwait.[33]

The commanders of the Syrian army, who were involved in the government's apologetic propaganda effort, stressed that their soldiers would not be fighting the Iraqi army on Iraqi soil and that they were not under U.S. command.[34] In fact, the forces dispatched by Syria were not its best and the significance of their participation in the coalition was more political than military.

But Syria also urged Saddam to withdraw from Kuwait to prevent a war that would bring destruction to Iraq and catastrophe to the Arabs.[35] Beyond the tactical aspect, the wish to avoid war reflected an interest in preserving Iraq's territorial integrity, resources, and military strength as Syria's strategic depth against Israel. On January 12, 1991, Asad appealed to Saddam in a telegram to get out of Kuwait and to save his forces and resources for the struggle against Israel.[36]

Throughout the crisis, the Syrian leaders and media urged Iraq's people to overthrow Saddam Husayn and his regime in order to end their own suffering and to enable the Arabs to unite against the dangers besetting it.[37] If any country had influence over a post-Saddam Iraqi government, Syria preferred that it play that role.

Distinguishing between Saddam Husayn and his regime on one hand and the Iraqi people and army on the other was convenient in terms of propaganda, but it also reflected the complexity of Syria's position, both ideologically and in regard to its potential need for Iraq's help in the future.

In accordance with this attitude, Syria pressured client groups opposed to Saddam, such as the Kurds, to refrain from separatism and to promise to preserve Iraq's sovereignty.[38] This issue was also raised in talks between Syrian and Turkish foreign ministers in February 1991, with Syria urging that Turkey not exploit the situation to obtain Iraq's northern area.[39]

Similarly, Syria did not want Iran to become the dominant force in the Gulf—or within Iraq in the event of a Shi'i revolution there—despite their mutual cooperation against Saddam. The transformation of Iraq into a Shi'i fundamentalist state under Iran's protection would be as dangerous for Syria's rulers as Saddam's rule. It was no wonder, then, that in May 1991, the Iraqi Shi'i oppositionist party, al-Da'awa, which rejected Iran's domination, found support in Syria.

Syria derived great benefit from its policy in the crisis and war. Asad was clearly aware of the importance ascribed to his cooperation by the United States and the coalition. Following the prewar summit conference between presidents Bush and Asad in November 1990, Syria emphasized its insistent demand that, once the Gulf crisis had been resolved, the United States and the West put their main priority on the Palestine problem and Israeli withdrawal from the occupied territories.[40] Syria's possible response was a major consideration in shaping U.S. policy aimed to prevent Israel's direct involvement.

Syria's actions did not result from policy shift but from the continuation of trends evident since 1988. These included détente with Egypt, given a common fear of Saddam's intentions; a search for channels of communication with the United States and Europe; and more openness toward a peace process to resolve the Arab-Israeli conflict. All these trends were given additional impetus by the Gulf crisis, resulting in valuable Syrian gains.

Syria was extricated from the isolation forced on it in the 1980s when it had chosen to support Iran against Iraq. Syria returned to the center of the inter-Arab arena and restored its ability to influence the diplomacy around the Arab-Israeli conflict. The restrictions placed on Syria by the European Community over accusations of Syrian support of terrorism were removed. Diplomatic relations with Britain were resumed.

Despite differences in their basic positions, a U.S.-Syria rapprochement followed talks with U.S. Secretary of State James Baker in Damascus and the Bush-Asad meeting in November 1990. Under cover of the Gulf crisis, Syria ended the rùle of Maronite General Michel 'Awn in Lebanon, reinforcing Syrian hegemony in that country. Generous financial aid from Saudi Arabia, Western Europe, and Japan let Syria improve its own economic situation significantly and financed the resumption of its arms purchases.

The Gulf War of January-February 1991 dealt a severe blow to the military might and international status of Iraq, making Syria the strongest Arab state in the Fertile Crescent. Yet its dilemmas regarding Iraq have by no means been eliminated.

As long as large groups of their people continue to feel alienated and Ba'thist Pan-Arab ideology remains the source of legitimacy for their regimes, Syria and Iraq will be willing and able to engage in mutual subversion. As long as the struggle for power and dominance in the region remains integral for the two regime's stability and ambitions, the potential for rivalry and tension will also exist.

NOTES

1. Michael Eppel, "Iraqi-Syrian Relations, 1945-1958," Ph.D. diss., Tel Aviv University, 1990 (Hebrew).
2. Uriel Dann, *Iraq under Qassem* (Jerusalem, 1969), pp. 19, 24-26.

3. Itamar Rabinovich, *Syria under the Ba'th* (Jerusalem, 1972).

4. Amatzia Baram, "Ideology and Power in Syrian-Iraqi Relations 1968-1984," in Moshe Maoz and Avner Yaniv, eds., *Syria under Asad* (London, 1986), pp. 127-28; Eberhard Kienle, *Ba'th v. Ba'th* (London, 1990), pp. 39-46.

5. Patrick Seale, *Asad of Syria* (London, 1988), p. 355.

6. Itamar Rabinovich, "The Changing Prism, Syrian Policy in Lebanon as a Mirror, a Truce, and an Instrument," in Maoz and Yaniv, *Syria under Asad*; Ofra Banjo, "Iraq," *Middle East Contemporary Survey* 1975-1976 and 1978-1979, p. 573.

7. *Tishrin,* February 12, 1991; Radio Damascus, February 10, 1991.

8. Kienle, *Ba'th v. Ba'th,* p. 81; Baram, "Ideology and Power," p. 131.

9. For overall surveys of news on Iraqi-Israeli contacts, see Moshe Zak, *Ma'ariv* (Tel Aviv), September 19, 1990; Eyal Erlich, *Ma'ariv* (Tel Aviv), February 8, 1991.

10. See, for example, *al-Jumhuriyya* (Baghdad), February 22, 1990.

11. See an article from Damascus published in *Akhir Sa'a* (Cairo), February 6, 1991.

12. *Tishrin,* February 12, 1991; Radio Damascus, February 10, 1991; Kienle, *Ba'th v. Ba'th,* p. 115.

13. Radio Monte Carlo, August 2, 1990.

14. *Al-Hayat* (London), August 21, 1990; *al-Ba'th* (Damascus), August 1990, p. 6.

15. Announcement by the Syrian Foreign Ministry on Radio Damascus, August 4, 1990; *al-Thawra* (Damascus), August 5, 1990.

16. Radio Damascus, August 14, 1990.

17. See statement by Vice President 'Abd al-Halim Khaddam of Syria on Radio Damascus, February 10, 1991; *Tishrin* (Damascus), February 12, 1991.

18. *New York Times,* August 12, 1990; *Washington Post,* August 15, 1990; *Sabah al-Khayr* (Beirut), August 25, 1990.

19. Statement by Syrian minister of information, BBC *Survey of World Broadcasts* (*SWB*), October 19, 1990.

20. Letter from Saddam Husayn to the Speaker of the Jordanian Parliament, *Foreign Broadcast Information Service* (*FBIS*) February 22, 1990.

21. See statement by Taha Yasin Ramadan, *al-Tadamun,* October 29, 1990.

22. Asad in an interview given to the Egyptian press: *al-Ahram* (Cairo), August 12, 1990; *al-Akhbar* (Cairo), August 12, 1990.

23. Radio Damascus, November 2, 1990; BBC *SWB,* November 5, 1990.

24. Radio Damascus, August 26, 1990; *Tishrin,* August 8, 1990; statement by Syria's foreign minister, *FBIS,* February 8, 1991.

25. Radio Damascus, November 2, 1990; Radio Damascus, August 23, 1990.

26. *Tishrin*, August 19, 1990; BBC *SWB*, October 19, 1990; Radio Damascus, October 16, 1990.

27. *Al-Sharq al-Awsat* (London), February 8, 1991; *FBIS*, February 11, 1991.

28. *Al-Ba'th* (Damascus), February 3, 1991.

29. *Al-Diyar*, August 11, 1990, in *FBIS*, August 14, 1990.

30. *Al-Yawm al-Sabi' (Paris), August 27, 1990; al-Nahar*, August 30, 1990; *al-Hayat*, August 31, 1990; *al-Quds* (Jerusalem), August 30, 1990.

31. These public relations efforts were prominent throughout the crisis. See, for example, *FBIS*, August 9 and 30, 1990; *Tishrin*, August 15, 1990.

32. Radio Damascus, August 26, 1990; *Tishrin*, August 15, 1990; Asad's statement, *FBIS*, September 13, 1990.

33. *FBIS*, February 8, 1992.

34. *Al-Hayat* (London), August 13, 1990; BBC *SWB*, October 11, 1990.

35. Radio Damascus, August 12, 1990. See 'Abd al-Halim Khaddam's statement according to Radio Damascus, October 31, 1990; *al-Thawra* (Damascus), November 6, 1990. See also Asad's statement in which he indicated his attempts to save Iraq by appealing for its withdrawal from Kuwait, according to *FBIS*, April 12, 1991.

36. See statement by 'Abd al-Halim Khaddam, Radio Damascus, February 7 and 10, 1991; *Tishrin*, February 12, 1991.

37. *Al-Ba'th* (Damascus), August 31, 1991; *al-Thawra* (Damascus), February 5, 1991; *FBIS*, February 14, 1991; *Al-Thawra* (Damascus), August 24, 1990; Radio Damascus, February 5, 1991; *Al-Thawra*, April 4, 1991.

38. BBC *SWB*, March 23, 1991.

39. *Tishrin*, November 26, 1990; see Asad's statement according to Radio Damascus, November 24, 1990.

40. Radio Damascus, February 11, 1991; *Mideast Markets*, February 25, 1991.

12

Egypt in the Gulf Crisis

Yoram Meital

Those in the Arab world who opposed Egypt's position in the Gulf crisis argued that Egypt's motive was to obtain political and economic benefits from the West and the Gulf states. Thus, they claimed, Egypt never tried to exhaust all chances of reaching a peaceful solution within an Arab framework and thus it contributed to the intervention of foreign armies in the area. Conversely, those siding with Egypt argued that Egypt's stand was grounded in Arab and Islamic principles and values.[1]

In fact, Egypt's stand reflected a basic disagreement with Iraq going back more than two decades. Egyptian policy expressed its leaders' deep conviction that the actions of Iraq and its leader, Saddam Husayn, were geared to undermine the most fundamental interests of the Egyptian state, economy, and society.

Between the 1967 Arab-Israeli war and the Ba'th takeover in Iraq in July 1968 there was a turning point in Egypt-Iraq relations. Since then, relations between the two countries have been marked by basic disagreements around two issues: first, the goals of the Arab-Israeli conflict and means of achieving them: second, relations to the West and mainly to the United States.

After the 1967 war, Egypt sought to further its interests by following a more pragmatic regional and international policy. In the 1970s, it became the foremost Arab country advocating a political solution to the Arab-Israeli conflict, an approach diametrically opposed by other Arab countries, including Iraq.

When Egypt accepted Security Council Resolution 242 and subsequently the diplomatic mission of Gunnar Jarring, it was criticized by Iraq.[2] After seizing power in Iraq, the Ba'th party set an extremist foreign policy based on its radical nationalist Arab ideology and need to legitimatize itself at home. When Egypt accepted the Rogers Plan in July 1970, a U.S. plan for a political solution of the conflict with Israel, Iraq stepped up a vitriolic verbal offensive against Egypt. Nasir responded with a letter to Iraqi president Ahmad Hasan al-Bakr on August 3, 1970, that clearly indicated their disagreements:

> The Egyptian nation does not conduct its struggle from the pulpit, or through political channels. I was astonished by the line taken by the Iraqi Administration, both official or party-related, against [Egypt] . . . and I will not hide the fact that I sometimes ask myself why you do not dispatch your army, whose duty it is to face the enemy to the front? Why did no aircraft of yours bomb the positions [of the enemy]? Why does the enemy not engage your army in battle, and why does he not send his air force to attack you? . . . The war cannot be fought, and liberation cannot be achieved, with slogans.[3]

After Nasir's death and the succession of Anwar Sadat in late 1970, Egypt became increasingly aware that it needed rapprochement with the United States and a diplomatic solution to the Arab-Israeli conflict in order to develop its economy and society. This approach deepened the controversy with Iraq, which maintained a nationalist position on the inter-Arab level and a radical stance on the Arab-Israel conflict and on relations to the West, especially the United States.

President Sadat's historic visit to Jerusalem, the negotiations with Israel and the Camp David Agreement met with unambiguous Iraqi opposition.[4] In response, Egypt cut diplomatic relations with Iraq on December 6, 1977. An Arab summit conference held in Baghdad on November 2 to 5, 1978, following the Camp David Agreements decided to impose sanctions if Egypt signed a peace treaty with Israel. When that document was indeed signed on March 26, 1979, Arab foreign ministers and ministers of finance who convened in Baghdad on March 27 to 31, 1979, decided to sever diplomatic and economic ties with Egypt, suspend Egypt's membership in the Arab League, and move that organization's headquarters from Cairo to Tunis.

In the early 1980s, the tactical needs of Egypt and Iraq brought a gradual reestablishment of cooperation. The underlying factors were Iraq's difficulties in the war against Iran, Syria's support for Iran, Egypt's declaration of neutrality early in the war, and—to a lesser degree—Sadat's assassination and the rise to power of President Husni Mubarak. Iraq needed wide Arab support—political and financial—including the military aid Egypt was prepared to offer, in order to face Iran.[5] At that stage, the change did not involve Iraq's stance on the Arab-Israeli conflict, which remained radical.[6] Egypt believed that aiding Iraq would help it rebuild its leadership position among the Arab states, reestablish diplomatic ties, and renew its Arab League membership. But Egypt took this line without reversing its policy of maintaining peace with Israel.[7]

This process came to a climax at the Arab summit conference in Amman on November 8 to 11, 1987, when Iraq supported Egypt's rehabilitation.[8] Two days afterward, Iraq and Egypt resumed diplomatic relations.[9] Egypt and Iraq continued to develop closer ties and together formed the Arab Cooperation Council (ACC)—along with Jordan and Yemen—in February 1991.

Some bilateral conflicts remained, however, even during this period. Egypt was outraged by the slaughter of hundreds of its citizens who were working in Iraq between October 1989 and February 1990. They were murdered by Iraqis returning from the Iran-Iraq war who resented that over 1 million Egyptians held jobs that they wanted.[10] Iraq was concerned over closer ties between its rival, Syria, and Egypt.[11]

Throughout 1990 essential differences reemerged between Egypt and Iraq over both the United States and the Arab-Israeli conflict. At the 1990 ACC summit meeting in Amman on February 23 to 24, 1990, Saddam emphasized the need to liberate Palestine and combat U.S. influence in the region. In contrast, Mubarak emphasized the importance of peace as the key to stability and security in the area.[12] From March through May, Iraq claimed that Israel was harboring aggressive intentions toward Iraq. Trying to relax the tension, Mubarak visited Baghdad and met with the Iraqi president on April 7, 1990. Despite this effort, differences were not settled and were brought into the open at the Baghdad Arab summit on May 28, 1990.[13] At the meeting, Iraq and the PLO insisted on a motion condemning the United States in the strongest terms, holding it responsible for Israel's policy. Egypt and Saudi Arabia tried to moderate the criticism of the United States. In the end, the two sides compromised, but Egypt-Iraq disagreements persisted.[14]

THE GULF CRISIS

The Gulf crisis confronted Egypt's leaders with a great challenge, which Mubarak called the hardest period of his presidency.[15] The official Egyptian position aimed at two goals: on the one hand, unconditional withdrawal of Iraq's army from Kuwait and reinstatement of the legitimate government; on the other hand, flexibility over the means used to achieve these objectives. Egypt supported the UN Security Council resolution 660 of August 2, 1990, and was one of the first countries to condemn Iraq's invasion. From the start of the crisis, and especially after Baghdad announced its annexation of Kuwait, Egypt was ready to take political and military action in parallel to find a solution. Sometimes Egypt seemed to suggest that part of Iraq's claims had some foundation but needed to be discussed with Kuwait's leaders at the negotiating table. At the same time, Egypt kept the option of military action as a last resort.[16]

Between Iraq's invasion on August 2 and November 29, when the UN authorized military action to free Kuwait, Egypt sought a peaceful solution. To this end, Egypt sent 28 official communications and messages conveyed to Iraq. But in late November, Egypt accepted the use of force to secure Iraq's withdrawal.[17]

To explain Egypt's position, official spokesmen said the invasion of Kuwait damaged both Arab national security and Egypt's leadership role in the Arab world.[18] Defense Minister Yusuf Sabari Abu-Talib remarked: "The defense of Saudi Arabia is in effect the defense of Egypt itself, and the action for the liberation of Kuwait and the restoration of its legitimate government equally defends Egypt's security, which is an integral part of Arab security."[19]

The massive Egyptian involvement in the Gulf crisis has been explained as a matter of necessity in view of Egypt's central leadership role in the Arab world and Saddam's damage to Arab interests.[20] Mubarak stated: "The position adopted by Egypt is the correct Islamic position, and the exact Arab position, and the fundamental, lawful and ethical-cultural position—which relates to Muslim Arab, basic, ethical and cultural Egypt."[21]

One of Saddam's goals was to destabilize Arab countries in the U.S.-led coalition through propaganda or terror. Egypt's leaders were aware of the risk and took action on several levels: refuting Saddam's claims publicly; enlisting the support of the Muslim clergy, of military officers; of leftists and right-wingers supporting the government line; negative media coverage of Saddam Husayn and Iraq's regime; intensive activity within the Arab League and the UN along with ongoing contact with many countries, chiefly the United States, Britain, France, and the Soviet Union.

The publicity campaign in Egypt was exceptional in its scope, including several detailed speeches by President Mubarak and other political, religious, and military leaders. Its objective was to show that Egypt's stance on the Gulf crisis was just and right, reflecting the basic principles of Islam, Arab values, and current ways of thinking, in contrast with the course of action adopted by the Iraqi leader, which was unjust, conflicting with all the aforementioned factors.[22]

Egypt's campaign refuted Saddam Husayn's arguments while exposing his cynical use of Muslim and Arab concepts to reach his megalomanic goals. As the crisis progressed, Egyptian media coverage of the Iraqi leaders was extraordinarily negative, representing Saddam as a bloodthirsty dictator and warmonger who was quite prepared to hurt fellow Arabs, including his own countrymen. Radio analysts in Cairo described Saddam as "the monster from Tikrit" (*al-Wahsh al-Tikriti*) who conducted himself in Hitlerite fashion.[23] Saddam was shown to be an irresponsible leader whose poor judgment had brought on the crisis.[24] But the media dissociated its vilification of Iraq's leaders from its view of Iraq's people, who were "brotherly" (*al-Shaqiq*) but victimized by Saddam and the Ba'th party. This message was vigorously driven home by the media (including cartoons) and official statements.[25]

Negative coverage extended to Saddam's supporters, including King Husayn of Jordan; Yasir 'Arafat, head of the PLO; 'Ali 'Abd Allah Salih, the president of Yemen; and 'Umar al-Bashir, ruler of Sudan.[26] Still, Egyptian public opinion continued to dislike Kuwaitis, Saudis, and others from wealthy Gulf states who had previously treated Egyptians in a condescending, contemptuous manner. The old Egyptian demand for a new and more just distribution of Arab wealth in return for guarantees of Arab national security was widely heard.[27]

Throughout the Gulf crisis, Egypt's government enlisted the support of Muslim clerics from the religious establishment headed by the minister of awkaf (religious endowments), Muhammad 'Ali Mahjub, Sheikh al-Azhar, Jad al-Haqq 'Ali Jad al-Haqq, the mufti of Egypt, Muhammad Sa'id Tantawi, and the elder Muslim dignitaries of al-Azhar.[28]

INTERNAL REACTIONS

It seems that the majority of the public supported the Egyptian government's stance during the Gulf crisis.[29] Still, certain circles voiced criticism—sometimes strong criticism—of the official stance. Egypt's government feared this might develop into a domestic crisis because of the ideological issues it raised and the potential escalation of the opposition's methods. The complex issues, which both the left- and right-wing opposition regarded as fundamental, included: the Arabs' inability to secure a peaceful solution; the massive presence of foreign armies on Arab-Muslim soil; the fact that Arab armies joined forces with non-Arab armies in a military confrontation with Arab soldiers, inevitably with civilian casualties and economic damage.

On the internal level, the government let opposition groups express their views legally, while using emergency legislation to arrest numerous members of Islamic groups and radical left-wing activists.[30] The government's tolerance was said to prove the extent of democratization in Egypt.[31] By allowing a certain level of dissent, the government sought to maintain control of public opinion while giving opponents a safety valve.

The majority of Islamic groups (*al-Jama'at al-Islamiyya*), the force most hostile to the regime, condemned the government's position. As the crisis progressed, there were widespread arrests of persons suspected of membership in radical Islamic groups actively opposing the government's stance. But there were internal disagreements within the Islamic camp, too, and the Muslim Brotherhood renounced Iraq's invasion of Kuwait as early as August 1990, while also criticizing the coalition forces' military operations.[32]

Leftist parties, and especially the al-Tajammu' and the al-Ahrar, denounced the invasion of Kuwait, but focused criticism chiefly at U.S. intervention and Egypt's support for it.[33] The general secretary of the al-Tajammu' party issued a declaration in February 1991 summing up the party's position on the Gulf crisis: "The Egyptian regime ignored the effort made in Arab and non-Arab metropolises to resolve the Gulf crisis prior to the commencement of military operations on land. The stance is detrimental to the image of Egypt."[34] The stance of the al-Tajammu' party was criticized, however, by members of left-wing groups who supported government policy.[35]

But spokesmen of the Nasirist faction complained that Egypt acted in light of local interests instead of giving preference to global Arab interests. It was this wrong approach that, they argued, led to the disaster of massive foreign intervention in the affairs of the Arab nation. Muhammad Hasanayn Heikal, known to be a Nasirite, spoke in this way in a November 1990 interview:

> From the beginning of the crisis I am being asked one single question: Do you side with Saddam? And my answer is No, I do not side with Saddam. Do you side with Jaber? I reply: No, I do not side with Jaber. Are you neutral? And I say that is not true either, I am not neutral. I am an Arab nationalist who had independent views on the problems of the nation. . . . From my point of view the question is not whether or not I condemn, but whether I try to find a way towards a solution…And when I consider the Gulf crisis, I see it in accordance with my wish. And my wish is for an undivided Arab nation. For security. For unity. Within these limits I would say that the mistakes that were made and which led to foreign intervention—everybody has a share in them, including the government of Kuwait.[36]

Although it tried to let opponents voice their reservations regarding its policy, Egypt feared that criticism might gather momentum, escalating from mass street demonstrations to the authorities' loss of control and the erosion of Egypt's stability. This threat seemed to materialize on February 20 to 26, 1991, as disturbances spread from student demonstrations at Cairo University to the universities of 'Ayn-Shams, Zakazik, al-Mansura, and Asyut and reportedly at several faculties of Bani Souyef and Minya.[37] Thousands of students took part demanding that U.S. aggression against Iraq's people and army be stopped, that foreign forces withdraw from the Gulf area, and that Egyptian forces be removed from the battlefield. They also shouted slogans condemning Egypt's regime and its approach to the Gulf crisis. The demonstrators burned U.S. and Israeli flags.[38] It took security forces an entire week to stop the demonstrations, and not before one demonstrator was killed, tens were wounded, and hundreds were arrested.

THE CRISIS'S IMPLICATIONS FOR EGYPT'S ECONOMY

The Gulf crisis both hurt and benefited Egypt's economy. Some benefits were that a large part of Egypt's external debt was canceled, an agreement was made with the World Bank and International Monetary Fund (IMF), and Egypt received special aid from several countries. However, immediate economic damage was caused by a sharp drop in foreign currency holdings, chiefly resulting from the stop of remittances by almost 1.5 million Egyptian workers employed in Iraq and Kuwait, and a dramatic fall in income from tourism and Suez Canal fees.[39] This reduced the balance of payments and increased the current deficit, and probably indirectly increased unemployment and inflation rates.

The United States canceled Egypt's entire military debt of $6.7 billion.[40] Germany agreed in principle to waive $2.5 billion of Egypt's debt.[41] Egypt reported that the United States asked other countries to follow its example.[42] According to Egyptian sources, France canceled $2.8 billion. Saudi Arabia and the Gulf states followed suit, canceling a debt of $6.6 billion.[43] Finland annulled Egypt's entire $78 million debt.[44] The April 9, 1991, agreement between Egypt and the IMF cleared the way to annul in two stages 50% of the $22 billion Egypt owed to the Paris Club; the rest was rescheduled. Through the end of May 1991, almost $25 million of debt was wiped out.

Saudi Arabia reportedly promised to give $1 billion of special financial aid to close the gap in Egypt's balance of payments, as well as $500 million for development projects.[45] In September 1990, the French ambassador in Cairo announced that his country would give $500 million in emergency aid to Egypt.[46] A month later, it was reported in Cairo that Germany was offering $675 million in aid.[47] It was further reported that Japan and South Korea had undertaken to give financial aid to Egypt, Turkey, and Jordan in the amount of $2 billion.[48] It was also reported that the United States would sell Egypt a $1.6 billion package of 46 F-16 fighter planes and 1,600 missiles, including 80 Maverick air-ground missiles.[49]

In Egypt, cancellation of much of the external debt was considered a stepping-stone toward implementing a comprehensive development plan.[50] On December 15, 1990, Mubarak announced a "1000-day plan" to liberate Egypt's economy.[51] Egypt tried to translate the support of Western countries and public opinion into political and strategic gains, including advancement of the Arab-Israeli peace process. While building their main links with the six Gulf states and Syria, Egypt's leaders also tried to reach an understanding with Jordan, Sudan, the PLO, and even Iraq.

NOTES

1. The former camp included Iraq, Jordan, Yemen, Algeria, Sudan, the PLO, and part of the Egyptian opposition. Egypt's supporters were Saudi Arabia, Kuwait, Bahrain, Qatar, the United Arab Emirates, Syria, and most political groupings inside Egypt.

2. *Middle East Record (MER)*, 1967, p. 272; *MER* 1968, pp. 228-29; *MER,* 1969-70, pp. 107-108.

3. Ahram Center for Political and Strategic Studies, *Jamal 'Abd al-Nasir Speeches and Interviews: January 1969-September 1970* (Cairo, 1973), pp. 534-35 (Arabic).

4. Egyptians claimed the reason for this was Iraq's ambition to seize control of the Arab world. Kamal Hasan 'Ali, *Fighters and Negotiators* (Cairo, 1986), p. 351 (Arabic).

5. *Middle East Contemporary Survey (MECS)*, 1979-1980, p. 523.

6. When military aid arrived, Egypt clarified its position: "We have assisted Iraq when we found that it was in distress and that it needed ammunition and arms to defend itself. We have not given Iraq arms to strike out at Iran or to occupy its lands. . . . We have not participated with any military forces." Arab Republic of Egypt, Ministry of Information, *The Egyptian Point of View on International Issues: Egyptian Moves in the International Arena* (Cairo, 1986), p. 52.

7. Along with better relations with Iraq came a marked improvement in Egypt's relations with the PLO and with Jordan. On December 22, 1983, when Arafat was forced to leave Tripoli, Lebanon, he stopped in Cairo to meet Mubarak. In September 1984, Egypt-Jordan diplomatic ties were resumed.

8. In a long editorial, Makram Muhammad Ahmad quoted in detail the position taken by Mubarak at a closed meeting of the Arab summit. Mubarak insisted on Egypt's unconditional return to the Arab League. *Al-Musawwar* 3293, November 20, 1987, pp. 4-6.

9. After the conference, diplomatic relations between Egypt and nine countries were resumed: The United Arab Emirates, Iraq, Kuwait, Morocco, Northern Yemen, Saudi Arabia, Bahrain, Qatar, and Mauritania.

10. CPSS, *The Arabic Strategic Report—1989* (Cairo, 1990), pp. 563-66 (Arabic). See also Samir al-Khalil, *Middle East Report* 168, no. 1 (January/February 1991), p. 15.

11. This rapprochement involved the renewal of diplomatic relations between Egypt and Syria (December 29, 1989) and the summit meeting of Mubarak and Asad in Damascus (May 2, 1990).

12. Jordanian Television, February 24, 1990.

13. Ibid., May 28, 1990.

14. *Ha'aretz,* May 31 and June 1, 1990.

15. For the complete speech, see *Mayo,* March 4, 1991. Some politicians argued, for instance, that Jewish immigration from the Soviet Union was the most dangerous development in 1990. *Al-Ahram al-Iqtisadi,* December 31, 1990, pp. 58-59.

16. See the speech by the Minister of State for Foreign Affairs, Boutros Ghali, at the UN General Assembly (October 4, 1990). *October,* October 14, 1990, p. 44.

17. *Al-Jumhuriyya,* February 27, 1991. See also Mubarak at a news conference in Alexandria, Radio Cairo, August 28, 1990.

18. For an in-depth discussion of the subject, see a special edition entitled "The Invasion of Kuwait and the Collapse of Arab Security," *al-Hilal* (September 1990).

19. Defense Minister Yusuf Sabri Abu Talib, Voice of the Arabs, January 10, 1991.

20. 'Abd al-'Aziz Sadiq, "The Man Who Killed an Arab Nation," *October,* August 19, 1990. Compare with statement by Yusuf Sabri Abu-Talib, Voice of the Arabs, January 10, 1991.

21. *Al-Ahram,* February 12, 1991.

22. Mubarak pointed out that he would have followed the same policy if a similar attack had been mounted against any other Arab country, including Iraq. See Mubarak's speech on the anniversary of the October 1973 war: October 5, 1990, and Mubarak's declaration at the time of his visit to Saudi Arabia. Radio Cairo, October 22, 1990.

23. Ibid., August 11 and 15, 1990. See also interview with 'Abd al-'Azim Ramadan, ibid., January 19, 1991.

24. For a discussion of the military errors committed by Saddam Husayn and his government, see interview with 'Abd al-Ghani al-Jamasi, *October,* March 3, 1991, pp. 12-15, and interview with Hasan Abu-Sa'dah, pp. 14-15. See also Mubarak's address, *Mayo,* March 4, 1991; *al-Jumhuriyya,* February 27, 1991.

25. *Al-Hilal* (September 1990); *October,* March 3, 1991. Mubarak's address, *Mayo,* March 4, 1991. Similar to the ruling party, the National Democratic Party made an announcement (August 14, 1990), Radio Cairo, August 14, 1990.

26. See a blunt article by Mahmud 'Abd al-Mun'im Murad, *October,* March 3, 1991, pp. 8-9. In an article containing sharp criticisms of King Husayn, Ahmad al-Razzaz wrote: "Your Royal Highness, Palestine is the victim of the schemes of many who trade in this problem. And they are all Arabs. As the Palestinian nation is hurting, we address the following questions to these dealers: Was the blow of Black September aimed at supporting the Palestinian problem? Who was the hero of this slaughter? And how many Palestinian victims were sacrificed there? Your Royal Highness knows only too well who the hero of the slaughter is." *Al-Ahram al-Iqtisadi,* February 18, 1991, p. 41. Part of the left in Egypt objected to the criticism voiced against the Palestinian leadership. See *al-Yasar* 14 (April 1991), pp. 9-12, and *al-Adab wal-Naqd* 68 (April 1991), pp. 36-37. See also Khalid Muhammad Khalid, *al-Kuwait* (Cairo, 1990), pp. 15-35, 87.

27. On the need for distribution of income from oil sales as a factor in the relations of the inter-Arab system, see Gad Gilbar, *The Economic Development of the Middle East in Modern Times* (Tel Aviv, 1990), Chapter 8 (Hebrew).

28. *Al-Azhar* (September 1990), pp. 144-45.

29. On the whole, the leading opposition party, the New Wafd party supported the regime. See, for example, interview with Ahmad Taha on behalf of this party, Radio Cairo, August 30, 1990.

30. For a report about the arrests of members of the al-Tajammu' see *al-Ahali,* February 27, 1991. For more details about the arrests of the Islamic groups (*al-jama'at al-Islamiyya*) in Aswan and Fayum, Radio Cairo, March 6, 1991.

31. After the dissolution of Egypt's parliament, general elections were held November 29, 1990, that were boycotted by most political groups including the New Wafd party and the Muslim Brotherhood.

32. Egyptian Muslim Brotherhood General Guide Muhammad Hamid Abu al-Nasir's statement in Ann Mosely Lesch, "Contrasting reactions to the Persian Gulf Crisis: Egypt, Syria, Jordan and the Palestinians," *Middle East Journal* 45, no. 1 (Winter 1991), p. 39.

33. 'Abd al-Sattar al-Tawila, *The Gulf Crisis* (Cairo, 1991) (Arabic). Organs of the al-Tajammu' party frequently stated this view. See *al-Yasar* 14 (April 1991), pp. 9-12. *al-Adab wal-Naqd,* 68 (April 1991), pp. 36-37. The party

organ, *al-Ahali,* expressed this view in almost every issue, for example, its February 27, 1991 headline: "Americans slaughter Iraqis and Iraqi forces." But differences of opinion within leftist circles led to divisions among the parties. Thus, for instance, a group headed by Professor 'Umar Muhyi al-Din, brother of Khalid Muhyi al-Din, left the al-Tajammu' party: See 'Abdallah Ahmad, "Mubarak's Gamble," *Middle East Report* 168, no. 1 (January/February 1991), p. 21. There were also disagreements in the al-Ahrar party, especially between the leader, Mustafa Kamil Murad, who denounced the government's stance on the Gulf crisis, and the group headed by Shaykh 'Abdallah al-Juwabi, who denounced the measures taken by Saddam Husayn and supported Egypt. *Al-Ahram al-Iqtisadi,* February 18, 1991, p. 50.

34. For the declaration's text, *al-Ahali,* February 27, 1991. See also an interview with Ibrahim Shukri, the leader of the Socialist Labor Party, *al-Musawwar,* October 12, 1990.

35. See, for instance, an article by Professor 'Abd al-'Azim Ramadan which argues that *al-Sha'b,* the organ of the al-Tajammu' party, publishes inaccurate, tendentious articles speaking of an American-Arab war while ignoring the crisis' origin: Iraq's invasion of Kuwait. Ramadan points out that the stance of the al-Tajammu' party damaged the interests of Egypt and Egyptian society. *October,* March 3, 1991, pp. 22-23. In another interview, Ramadan defined Saddam's procedure in Kuwait as "Iraqi imperialism" designed to cover up the failure of the campaign against Iran and the damage resulting from it. Radio Cairo, August 30, 1990. Lutfi al-Khuli, another outstanding leftist, also denounced Iraq's invasion, arguing that Egypt's stance resulted from popular pressure from Egypt's people in addition to pressure from Kuwait and Saudi Arabia. *Ha'aretz,* November 1, 1990.

36. *October,* November 4, 1990. Heikal presents his arguments extensively in *The Gulf War* (Cairo, 1992) (Arabic).

37. Whereas semi-establishment newspapers (*al-Jumhuriyya, al-Ahram, al-Akhbar*) briefly mentioned demonstrations while giving prominence to the reactions of government spokesmen, opposition newspapers (*al-Sha'b* and *al-Ahali*) carried long articles describing the marches, listing the names of casualties and emphasizing the security forces' brutal conduct. Compare *al-Jumhuriyya,* February 27, 1991, as against *al-Ahali,* February 27, 1991. Official spokesmen pointed out that the left and the Muslim Brotherhood were behind the demonstrations; security forces exercised restraint, one demonstrator was killed, and a few dozen people were arrested. Left-wing publications claimed that three demonstrators were killed from the security forces' gunfire, dozens of demonstrators were injured, and about 400 were arrested. *al-Ahali,* February 27, 1991. The secretary general of the al-Tajammu' party published a statement denouncing the security

force's brutality in suppressing the demonstration. *Al-Ahali,* March 6, 1991. In addition, the left's spokesmen in Egypt accused the government of taking unfair advantage of the Emergency Laws to suppress the demonstrations and the presentation of views opposed to the government's stance. *al-Yasar* 14 (April 1991), pp. 4-5.

38. *Al-Ahali,* February 27, 1991.
39. According to an Egyptian investigation, the drop in income from tourism from August 1990 through March 1991 amounted to 1.5 billion Egyptian pounds, *al-Musawwar,* February 22, 1991. Another Egyptian investigation assessed damage to the economy resulting from the Gulf crisis at $9 billion. *Al-Ahram al-Iqtisadi,* January 7, 1991, p. 12. According to official reports Egypt earned $1.6 billion from fees for passage through the Suez Canal in 1990—the year of the Gulf crisis. *Al-Musawwar,* December 28, 1990, p. 12.
40. *Al-Ahram al-Iqtisadi* 1158, March 25, 1991, p. 10; U.S. Information Agency, *The Gulf Crisis,* (Washington, D.C., 1991), p. 41.
41. *Ha'aretz,* February 12, 1991. The same article reports that the United States and Gulf states waived $14 billion of Egypt's debt.
42. *Al-Ahram al-Iqtisadi* 1147, January 7, 1991, p. 12.
43. 'Abdallah Ahmad, "Mubarak's Gamble," p. 12.
44. *Al-Ahram al-Iqtisadi* 1155, March 4, 1991, p. 27. In addition, Finland gave Egypt an $85 million aid package for 1991-1994. See ibid.
45. Simon Brindle, "Forever in Debt to You," *The Middle East* (January 1991), p. 30. *Al-Ahram al-Iqtisadi* 1147, January 7, 1991, p. 12.
46. *Al-Ahram al-Iqtisadi* 1146, December 31, 1990, p. 75.
47. Ibid.
48. Ibid., 1147, January 7, 1991, p. 12.
49. *Al-Ahram,* March 8, 1991.
50. Ibid., March 22, 1991.
51. Ibid., December 16, 1990.

The Regional Powers and Iraq

13

Turkey: Iraq's European Neighbor

David Kushner

A n old Turkish proverb says, *Refikin iyi ise, Bagdat yakin olur* ("If your friend is a good one, Baghdad becomes close"), while another proverb has it *Asiga Bagdad uzak degil* ("Baghdad is not too distant for the lover"). Situated far from their capital in an area of little interest to them, in Turkish eyes, Baghdad appears to have become a symbol of remoteness and isolation.

Notwithstanding this image of Baghdad, Turkey and Iraq, once freed of the shackles of the Ottoman Empire, established a relationship marked by considerable understanding and friendship.[1] There was, to be sure, the question of their common border (the so-called Mosul Question), which lingered on for a few years after the conclusion of the Lausanne Treaty of Peace. But by 1926 Turkey approved the border's delineation (the Brussels Line), as confirmed by the League of Nations, and agreed, in return for consenting to Mosul's inclusion in Iraq, to receive 10% of the province's oil royalties.

From then on the absence of a border question let Turkey and Iraq strengthen mutual ties and attain a high level of cooperation. This situation stood in sharp contrast to the relations that would develop between Turkey and its other Arab neighbor, Syria, after the latter attained full independence. In that case, a territorial issue (notably the question of Alexandretta-Hatay), as well as bitter memories of Ottoman repression of Syrian Arab nationalists during World War I, prevented the development of real friendship and confidence between them. Iraq-Turkish relations twice developed into actual alliances aimed at warding off outside aggression. In 1937, Turkey and Iraq, along with Iran and Afghanistan, formed the Sa'adabad Pact (named after the palace in Tehran where it was signed) to "ensure peace and security in the Near East." In 1955, Turkey and Iraq again joined hands—this time against Soviet expansionism—in the Baghdad Pact. This followed years of efforts by Western powers and Turkey to form a Middle East regional alliance with the participation of Arab states. Yet most of them were reluctant to join, reflecting their deep suspicions of Western aims.

Iraq was more aware of a Soviet threat and interested in safeguarding not only its security but also its monarchical political regime. It also hoped to gain a leadership position in the area. The idea of a regional pact, therefore, was abandoned in favor of a "Northern Tier" Alliance, and the resulting Baghdad Pact was to incorporate not only Turkey and Iraq but Iran, Pakistan, and Britain as well.

Three years later, Iraq's pro-Western monarchy was overthrown by Brigadier 'Abd al-Karim Qasim's revolutionary regime, which left the Baghdad Pact and began to cooperate closely with the Soviet Union. The stage was set for a long period of uncertainty and suspicion between Turkey and the new Iraqi regime. What was remarkable, however, about bilateral relations was that although the two were now in opposing camps, they soon began to restore good relations. In fact, the subsequent level of cooperation exceeded that characterizing their previous relations.

The secret to this seemingly surprising feature of Turkish-Iraqi relations lies in the two countries' common interests. Two main factors were involved. One is the presence of a large Kurdish population on both sides of their mutual, 200-mile-long border. The Kurds, who number 7 to 8 million (about 15% of the population) in Turkey and 2.5 to 3 million (15-20%) in Iraq, have constituted a troublesome minority in both countries and have on occasion staged bloody rebellions against the central authority.[2] Thus, both Turkey and Iraq were interested in cooperating to quell Kurdish uprisings and to stop ideas of autonomy or independence from spreading in either direction across the border.

By the time the Gulf crisis erupted, Iraq had largely succeeded in restoring order in its Kurdish areas; but in Turkey, Kurdish underground guerrilla groups, particularly in the southeast region of the country, were very active. One indication of the level of cooperation between Turkey and Iraq on the Kurdish issue was the agreement, in force from 1984 to 1989, giving the Turks the right of hot pursuit into Iraqi territory.

Economic interests, specifically oil, became the second major factor determining Turkish-Iraqi relations. Iraq's rich oilfields in the Mosul region, close to the Turkish border, are a natural, relatively cheap source of oil for Turkey. Particularly since the 1973-1974 oil crisis, Turkey has come to depend more and more on Iraqi oil, with imports from Iraq reaching 65% of Turkey's total oil imports on the eve of Iraq's invasion of Kuwait.[3]

Iraq, for its part, has found Turkish territory a convenient route by which to transport oil to Mediterranean ports. It had the advantage of bypassing hostile Syria, which often shut down Iraqi pipelines crossing Syrian territory (and closed them completely since 1982) as well as avoiding the risk of Iranian attacks on Iraqi tankers sailing the Persian Gulf. This mutual dependency led to the construction of two pipelines, each about 800 miles long, running from Iraq's northern oil field of Kirkuk to the Turkish Mediterranean coast at Dortyol and Yumurtalik.

The first line, completed in 1977, was later expanded to carry close to 1 million barrels per day (about 45 to 50 million tons annually); the second pipeline was completed in 1987 and has about half that capacity. On the eve of the Gulf crisis, Iraq transported some 50% of its oil exports through these Turkish pipelines.[4] Turkey also derived certain benefits from these pipelines. Apart from receiving oil itself on preferential terms, Turkey also earned handsome royalties, amounting to some $250 to 300 million annually, from the actual transportation of oil across Turkish territory.[5] Significant revenues were also earned from the services provided to the Iraqis along the pipelines and at the terminals.

Furthermore, Iraq proved to be an important market for Turkish industrial products, and Turkey became Iraq's second supplier after Germany. On the eve of the war, Turkish exports amounted to more than $1 billion annually. At the same time, Turkish contractors, technicians, and laborers took part in Iraqi development projects, with contracts estimated at $3.5 billion.[6] Iraq also moved much of its exports and imports by train or truck through Turkish territory. During the Iran-Iraq war (in which Turkey maintained neutrality), trade across the Turkish-Iraqi border flourished, benefiting businessmen in both countries.

Despite all these examples of cooperation, relations between Turkey and Iraq have been beset by problems that, at times, caused considerable tension. These ranged from border incidents to cases of mistreatment of the small Turkish minority in Iraq (numbering 100,000 to 200,000 people). From time to time, Turkey also accused Iraq of ignoring Kurdish guerrilla activities across the border. In 1989, Iraq refused to renew the hot-pursuit agreement, probably seeking some concession in exchange. In the years leading up to the Gulf War, Iraq's financial troubles brought growing debts to Turkish companies and exporters and damaged trade. Nonetheless, all these problems were usually not permitted to cast too long a shadow over bilateral relations.

A considerably chillier atmosphere did, however, mark relations between the two countries closer to the outbreak of the Gulf crisis. More and more, relations were clouded by the long-standing question on the distribution of the Euphrates' waters, a bone of contention between Turkey and Syria as well. The Euphrates, which originates in Turkey's eastern highlands, flows into Syria, and then enters Iraq, where it eventually joins the Tigris and empties (as the Shatt al-Arab) into the Persian Gulf. The river, crossing largely arid lands, has been used in development projects in all three countries, but the water was not exploited to its full potential. In the 1980s, Turkey embarked on a large-scale development plan in southeastern Anatolia (the Guney Dogu Anadolu Projesi, or GAP) to use the waters of the Euphrates to open vast new areas for cultivation and produce electricity. This planned diversion of additional water from the Euphrates was viewed with great suspicion by both Syria and Iraq despite of assurances from the Turkish side.

In a temporary agreement with its neighbors, Turkey allowed 500 cubic meters per second to flow down the river as long as the project was not complete. That amount, however, was regarded as insufficient by both Syria and Iraq. Numerous attempts were made by the three countries to settle their differences and establish proper water-distribution criteria but all failed.[7]

Iraq, somewhat passive on the water issue during the Iraq-Iran war, intensified pressure against Turkey following the end of hostilities in 1988, using much harsher language and outright threats. Sensitive to accusations that it might use water as a political weapon, Turkey repeatedly denied any such intentions and, in turn, accused Iraq of blocking the development of the Anatolian project.[8] Tension considerably increased in January 1990 when Turkey stopped the flow of water in the river for a full month in order to fill one of its reservoirs.

The feeling in Turkey was that the water issue might, in time, cause a major conflagration. There was ample proof of Saddam Husayn's aggressiveness and ruthlessness; but what caused Turkey particular concern was the enormous buildup of Iraq's military capabilities. Saddam's war machine became a source of worry, especially after it became evident that the Iraqi ruler was seeking to develop an arsenal of unconventional weapons.

Turkey gained vivid evidence of Iraq's new methods of warfare late in 1988, when tens of thousands of terror-stricken Iraqi Kurds, threatened by chemical weapons, fled across the border to find temporary refuge in eastern Anatolia. Then, in April 1990, Turkish customs officials in Istanbul and Edirne uncovered and confiscated Iraq-bound shipments of pipes that seemed to be parts of the planned Iraqi "supergun." The Turkish army, already concerned about its lack of modern weapons, was alarmed at Iraq's buildup. By the time the Gulf crisis erupted in August 1990, Turkey had already come to accept that it might be a target of Saddam's aggressiveness and military capability and, therefore, had to be on the alert to face any eventuality.[9]

Iraq's invasion of Kuwait put Turkey in a delicate situation. It was clear from the outset that Turkey was reluctant to make any move that might involve it in a military campaign against Iraq, even under the pretext of defending Saudi Arabia. Indeed, even after the UN resolutions were passed and as the coalition was being formed, Turkey chose not to send troops. Instead, it repeatedly announced that it would strike at Iraq only if attacked.[10]

This position, which did not change even after military operations began, stemmed from a combination of reasons. First, war with Iraq was considered a costly and potentially destructive affair. It is probably no accident that considerable objection to the idea of Turkish involvement in the coalition came from the army, which was alarmed by the Iraqi "war machine" and felt unprepared to undertake a serious military campaign.[11]

War could inflict considerable destruction and casualties on Turkey. Furthermore, there was no telling whether it would not end in some political disadvantage to the Turks. Ataturk's famous guideline "Peace at Home, Peace in the World"—resting on a feeling that wars and armed conflicts somehow always breed negative results for Turkey—could no doubt be applied in this case, too.

The good relations that Turkey had established with the Arab world, based on noninterference in inter-Arab squabbles, also dictated caution and adherence to peace. It is true that most of the Arab countries took the side of the anti-Iraqi coalition, but they were not unanimous, and there was strong opposition voiced in many Arab circles toward any attack on a "brotherly" Arab country. Long-term relations with Iraq itself had to be considered, too, since Turkey's interest in Iraq's friendship was so well rooted. It is significant that in pronouncements made by Turkish officials during the crisis, friendship with the Iraqi people—though not the regime—was always stressed and extolled. As President Ozal stated, "We have taken our place besides the allies, but we have also taken care not to hurt the other side too much."[12]

Last, but not least, of the factors explaining Turkey's reluctance to involve itself in a conflict, President Ozal and his government could hardly ignore the feelings of many Turkish citizens who not only feared war but also felt some solidarity with Iraq, out of religious sentiments or leftist "progressive" attitudes. The parliamentary opposition was, in fact, vociferous all along in cautioning the government not to overact in the crisis and not to involve the country in an undesired war. If some of this opposition stemmed from simple partisan interests, it still reflected the widespread antiwar mood of the country. This attitude was also common in the press.

There was some speculation that Turkey might be interested in "restoring" to itself the oil-rich Mosul region, which had "slipped out" of Turkish hands during the settlements following world War I.[13] Turkish spokesmen, however, were adamant in denying such speculations, and it seems that they were sincere.

Other than a tiny minority of ultra-nationalists, no one in Turkey thought the idea feasible or desirable. The addition of a largely Kurdish population could only enhance the problems Turkey already had with the Kurds. It might even, in the long run, bring about the realization of the old idea of establishing an independent Kurdistan, a development that Turkish statesmen greatly feared. An invasion of Iraq could also whet the appetite of Turkey's other neighbors—Syria and Iran— and Turkey had no real interest in starting a conflict with either one.

Any change in the region's map bred further conflict in Turkish eyes, and Ankara was determined not to encourage such an eventuality. This is not to say that Turkey would not have thought of annexing Iraqi Kurdistan if the Iraqi state dissolved. Ozal did, in fact, warn during the war that Turkey would intervene in two cases—if there were an attempt to establish an independent Kurdistan or if Iran or Syria occupied parts of Iraq.[14]

Yet, if Turkey was perhaps hesitant about "going all the way" in the Gulf crisis and unhappy with the prospects of war in general, it most definitely proved itself committed to the interests of the international community and Western allies. The government resolutely denounced Iraq's invasion of Kuwait and joined other UN members in enforcing sanctions against its southern neighbor. As much as Turkey was reluctant to involve itself in war, there was no question of it remaining neutral as it had during the Iraq-Iran war.

Portraying itself as a strict observer of international law and order, Turkey could not condone an arbitrary, unlawful act like the one committed by Iraq. Furthermore, concerned as Ankara was with preserving stability and peace in the area, it abhorred the idea of a dictator brutally overrunning a neighboring state. In its eyes, granting of legitimacy to the use of force could one day backfire, since there were enough potential enemies around who might do the same to Turkey. In fact, when it looked at Iraq's aggressive behavior and interest in the water issue, Turkey felt that it could well be the victim in the next round. In the words of Ozal, "Doesn't anyone think that such an aggressive country will, in the future, constitute a problem for us, as well?"[15]

Clearly a show of resolve and determination was needed, and Saddam Husayn must be taught a lesson. In the Turkish view, the international community's unity in the face of such overt aggression was in itself important to show Saddam the limits of what he could do and to demonstrate that aggression would not pay. By joining the international community, Turkey would strengthen it and enhance the hope of a favorable settlement of the crisis. This alone, it was argued, should convince Saddam of the futility of his actions, force him to evacuate Kuwait, and avoid an all-out war.

If war did erupt after all, the Turks reasoned, Iraq and its army might suffer a massive blow that would remove their threat to Turkey for many years. Perhaps a war might even end the hostile, aggressive regime in Baghdad. Although Turkey wanted to avoid direct involvement in the war, there was no reason why it should not delight in the prospect of Saddam's downfall. If Turkey could stay out of the war while helping to ensure a quick, decisive victory by the allies, it would reap great benefits.

Furthermore, if and when Iraq's destiny would be decided—whether in a peaceful solution or war—Turkey did not want to be left out of the negotiations. For example, if Iraq's territorial integrity disintegrated and Iraqi Kurds gained some measure of independence, Turkey wanted its interests to be taken into consideration. This goal could best be assured, of course, only if Turkey stood resolutely behind the coalition.[16]

Turkey's overall relations with the West were another important factor shaping its policy during the crisis. To be sure, it was important for Turkey that any steps against Iraq should be taken under the UN's umbrella, untainted by Western or U.S. unilateralism. Government spokesmen accordingly alluded repeatedly to the UN resolutions and the need to abide by them. The government's actions were thus given proper international legitimacy, warding off any internal criticism that Turkey was serving foreign interests. As during the Korean War in 1950, Turkey sought to enhance its position by contributing to an international, UN-led operation.

In practice, however, the West was uppermost in the Turkish mind. Turkey's relations with the West were embedded in orientations and traditions dating back to the late Ottoman period, when Western political and sometimes military support was essential for the state's survival. They were further reinforced by the progress of Westernization in Turkey, culminating in Mustafa Kemal Ataturk's reforms. On both political and cultural levels the process was at times painful and tortuous due to conflicting interests as well as the historical, cultural, and religious differences separating Turks and Europeans. Turkish leaders of Westernization movements often had to contend not only with opposition at home but also with strong anti-Turkish biases and positions prevailing in the West.

There is little doubt, though, about the direction of Turkey's political and cultural development. Belonging to the Western family of nations became the goal for most enlightened Turks. A corollary to this development has been the Turks great sensitivity toward foreign criticism, their eagerness to attain respectability and honor in the world's eyes, and the great care Turks took to conduct themselves—and their state—according to Western norms and values. This state of mind has been very significant in shaping Turkey's foreign relations as well.

Perhaps even more important in explaining Turkey's joining with the West were the Cold War and the emergence of Soviet expansionism following World War II. Stalin voiced a demand in 1945 for the "joint defense" of the Turkish Straits, which meant, in effect, establishing a Soviet base on Turkish soil. The Soviets also demanded territorial concessions in eastern Anatolia, reawakening traditional Turkish fears of Russian aims and pushing Turkey into Western arms. Following the Truman Doctrine of 1947, initiated to support Turkey (and Greece) against new Soviet pressures, massive aid, particularly American, was extended to Turkey under a number of programs.

Turkey participated in the establishment of the Organization of European Economic Cooperation and qualified for help under the Marshall Plan. In 1950, it was admitted to the Council of Europe. Turkey also became, in 1952, a full-fledged member of the North Atlantic Treaty Organization (NATO) and took an active part in forming two regional security pacts, the Balkan Pact in 1954 and the Baghdad Pact in 1955.

Relations with the United States developed in an unprecedented way during the 1950s and culminated in the bilateral defense accord signed in 1959. Although relations with the United States and other Western countries were destined to undergo a number of ups and downs in the years that followed, Turkey's basic commitment to the Western alliance has remained a solid pillar of Turkish foreign policy to the present day.

Notwithstanding the enormous changes taking place in recent years in Europe and the world at large—and perhaps because of them—Turkey's interest in belonging to the Western family of nations has even grown. One important element has been Ankara's interest in joining the European Community, resting on the conviction that Turkey's economic future lies with these states. The bulk of Turkey's foreign trade is with Western Europe, and millions of Turkish workers find work there. Turkey signed its first association agreement with the Common Market in 1963, and has since passed through several stages along the road to full membership.

Ankara submitted a formal application for membership in 1987 and was put off because of European fears of being flooded by cheap Turkish products and labor; Greek objections; and the prospect of setting a precedent by which East European countries would have to be admitted, too. Nevertheless, Turkey has not given up. Thus, continuing to stand at Europe's doorstep, Turkey could not ignore Europe's disdain and fear toward Saddam Husayn's actions in Kuwait. Nor could it disregard Europe's readiness to participate in the effort to force Iraq's retreat. As in other matters, the Turks wanted to act in concert with the wishes of the European countries it wanted to emulate and join.

Even more significant, in this respect, has been the importance Turkey continues to place on relations with its chief ally, the United States. In addition to being an important trade partner and its chief arms supplier, Turkey continues to see in the United States, which maintains a number of bases on Turkish soil, its chief protector in case of need. Yet, given developments in the Soviet Union and the Cold War's end, serious concern has arisen in Turkey regarding its future status in NATO and the strength of its alliance with America. Among Turkish policymakers and the military, the suspicion has grown that their country may have lost its value in the eyes of the United States and of the West in general.

Consequently, in order to gain Western support, Turkey has felt the need to find a substitute for its traditional role as barrier to Soviet expansion southward.[17] Many Turks concluded the answer would be in terms of a regional role. In the conflict-ridden Middle East, Turkey could play the role of stabilizer, even "peacemaker." This would be an important benefit to Turkey both directly, by reducing threats to its own security, and indirectly, by proving Turkey's strategic value to the West and United States. In this way, Turkey could receive more aid, help in modernizing its armed forces, and guarantee a continued commitment to its security. Other benefits could be better trade quotas for Turkish products, support for Turkey on the Cyprus issue, and more understanding on the Armenian question.

It is no wonder that after operation Desert Storm began and more and more talk was heard of a new security framework for the region after the settlement of the crisis, Turkey repeatedly expressed willingness to assume a leading role in establishing these arrangements, to foster cooperation among Middle East countries, and even to host a peace conference to bring an end to the Arab-Israeli conflict.[18]

Thus, the Gulf crisis and ensuing war played right into Turkey's hands.[19] If Turkey wanted to be accepted as a civilized country, a European state, and a staunch ally of the United States and the West generally, what better way to do so than to abide strictly by the UN resolutions and commit itself to the allied cause? President Ozal was quick to grasp the opportunity and, overcoming opposition at home (some of it from his own Motherland party and the army) including accusations of warmongering, he carried through his policies. Turkey was among the first to enforce the trade embargo and at considerable financial cost shut down the oil pipelines and froze Iraqi and Kuwaiti assets.[20]

Next, in September, Ozal obtained a parliamentary resolution authorizing the government to send Turkish troops to foreign countries and allowing foreign troops to be stationed in Turkey. Although Turkey chose not to send troops to the Gulf, it did deploy over 100,000 men along the border with Iraq and moved aircraft to forward bases. By so doing it pinned down nine Iraqi divisions in the north and kept Saddam Husayn guessing as to its intentions. This deployment also showed Iraq that Turkey would deal strongly with any attack on its territory. Ankara, nevertheless, was not overly happy with the idea of a war erupting south of its border and throughout the initial crisis kept hoping that international pressure would finally affect Iraq. As time went on and the embargo was proving futile, the Turks resigned themselves to the likelihood of war and made the necessary preparations. As the January 15 deadline drew closer, Turkish forces in southeast Anatolia were reinforced by war planes sent from Germany, Italy, and Belgium in the framework of NATO's Allied Mobile Force. Other reinforcements arrived from the United States. Their arrival was considered as adding to Turkey's deterrent force, as well as a test of NATO's obligation to support Turkey if attacked.[21]

Once operations began in January 1991, the Turkish parliament authorized the use of the Turkish army and foreign forces deployed in Turkey to go into battle. Turkish spokesmen, though, still insisted that their country would enter the war only if attacked. Shortly afterward, the Turkish cabinet decided to give more support to countries participating in the Gulf operations by allowing "a more comprehensive" use of military bases in the country. The decision was explained as emanating from the UN resolution and the desire to ensure a speedy end to the war with the minimal casualties.[22]

Moreover, in a move that at the crisis's outset many doubted could happen and whose possibility official spokesmen had downplayed, Turkey now permitted U.S. warplanes to use the American air base in Incirlik near Adana to launch their sorties over northern and western Iraq. Turkey continued to point to the fact that it did not participate in the bombing and thus did not attack Iraq. The permission, however, did represent a major step toward actual involvement in hostilities, and Turkish spokesmen noted this valuable contribution to the allied effort.[23]

Turkey calculated that the coalition had the upper hand and that Saddam Husayn was in no position to retaliate against Turkish territory. The possibility of Iraqi retaliation and of a second front on the Turkish-Iraqi border remained remote throughout the war, given Iraqi preoccupation on the main front, the presence of NATO forces on Turkish soil, and the respect with which Iraq usually viewed Turkey's military capabilities. As things turned out, Turkey's gamble proved sound.

In steering a course through the Gulf crisis, Turkey once again demonstrated some of the characteristic features of its foreign policy: a commitment to peace and stability, a strong eagerness to join the West, and a concern with its international image. More novel, perhaps, was Turkey's willingness to side against a country that was a member of the Islamic Arab world, which Turkey had long courted, and a country with which it traditionally had good relations.

Ozal's policy drew much criticism within Turkey during the crisis, revolving around the danger of its being drawn into a war, Turkey's economic losses, and the apparent lack of enthusiasm among some of Turkey's partners to help it financially.[24] Critics also pointed to the futility of Turkey's efforts to be accepted by the West and to Ozal's single-handed "unconstitutional" conduct of Turkish foreign policy.

The defeat of Saddam Husayn's war machine did realize an important Turkish goal, however, by, at least for the time being, removing a serious threat to Turkey's security. Through arm shipments and military reinforcements it received during the crisis, Turkey obtained proof of NATO's commitment to defend it. The Turks also received significant expressions of appreciation and gratitude from allies for their role in ensuring the coalition's victory. This moved Turkey closer to its cherished goal of being recognized as a bastion of regional stability and a valuable Western ally.

Most significant, perhaps, was the fact that all this was achieved without the loss of a single Turkish soldier or a single Scud missile being fired on Turkish territory. If Ozal wished, as he stated it on the eve of the war, "to steer our country out of this crisis without having incurred any serious damages," he succeeded.[25] When the political benefits that may accrue to Turkey in the long run are considered, the country may be said to have done even better than that.

NOTES

1. No proper research has yet been published on Turkish-Iraqi relations although the subject has been treated in books covering the foreign relations of Turkey as a whole. See, for example, Altemur Kilic, *Turkey and the World* (Washington, D.C., 1959); Ferenc A. Vali, *Bridge Across the Bosporus: The Foreign Relations of Turkey,* (Baltimore, 1971); Kemal H. Karpat, *Turkey's Foreign Policy in Transition, 1950-1974* (Leiden, 1975).

2. These are estimates based on many sources. No exact statistics are available.

3. *Economist Intelligence Unit (EIU)-Country Report, Turkey,* no. 3 (1990), p. 15.

4. Ibid., p. 7.

5. Ibid., no. 4 (1990), p. 17.

6. *Milliyet,* August 16, 1990.

7. Turkey has called for a system of distribution using more advanced, efficient methods for irrigation and taking into consideration the waters of other rivers shared among the countries concerned. Syria and Iraq have argued for greater quantities to be allowed them and for a system of distribution based on the three countries' self-declared needs. The Turkish "regional" approach to the problem was also expressed in its proposals for a comprehensive irrigation system for the Middle East (the so-called Water for Peace Project), in which Turkey would play a leading part.

8. Prime Minister Akbulut, *Milliyet,* September 4, 1990.

9. Ozal seemed to have a personal grudge against Saddam, partly because he refused to stop Iraq's missile attacks on Tehran during Ozal's 1988 visit there See Ozal in interview on TRT Television, January 7, 1991, *Foreign Broadcast Information Service (FBIS),* West Europe, January 8, 1991; *Newspot* (Ankara), January 10, 1991. The Turkish president would also point to Saddam Husayn's aggressiveness, his raising of the water issue, and his ingratitude after so much Turkish help had been given during the war with Iran. *Sabah,* December 27, 1990.

10. Ozal himself hinted that if it were his decision alone, he might have decided to send troops to the Gulf. TRT Television, January 18, 1991, in *FBIS,* West Europe, January 23, 1991. With regard to Turkey's entry into the war, Ozal did say that Turkey might invade Iraq if there were certain developments that affected Turkish interests, whether or not Iraq attacked first. See note 13.

11. A sign of the military's objection to Turkey's joining in a war with Iraq was Chief of Staff General Necip Torumtay's resignation early in December. See *EIU-Country Report, Turkey,* no. 1 (1990), p. 10.

12. Radio Anatolia, February 3, 1991, in *FBIS,* West Europe, February 4, 1991.

13. At the crisis's start, Ozal enhanced speculation about Turkey's intentions when he spoke of the possibility of a change in the region's geography. He later clarified his statement and voiced interest in Iraq's territorial integrity. *Hurriyet,* November 1, 1990.

14. *Cumhuriyet,* January 12, 23, 1991; Radio Anatolia, February 17, 1991, in *FBIS,* West Europe, February 19, 1991.

15. TRT, January 18, 1991, in *FBIS,* West Europe, January 23, 1991.

16. Ozal to TRT, January 7, 1991, in *FBIS,* West Europe, January 8, 1991.

17. Ozal to Radio Madrid, September 12, 1990, in *FBIS,* West Europe, September 13, 1990.

18. *Cumhuriyet,* January 23, 1991; Ozal quoted in *Newspot* (Ankara), February 7, 1991.

19. *Sabah,* February 7, 1991; Foreign Minister Alptemocin, Ankara Radio, February 25, 1991, in *FBIS,* West Europe, February 25, 1991.

20. Ozal and other Turkish officials repeatedly emphasized Turkey's quick decision to enforce the embargo, describing it as a matter of principle. *Newspot* (Ankara), January 17, 1991.

21. Ozal to TRT Television, January 7, 1991, in *FBIS,* West Europe, January 8, 1991.

22. Ankara TRT, January 18, 1991, in *FBIS,* West Europe, January 22, 1991.

23. Ozal in an interview to *Washington Post,* quoted by *Newspot* (Ankara), January 22, 1991.

24. Estimates of Turkey's economic losses have gone as high as $10 billion, but around $4 billion is a more realistic figure. Costs were mostly from lost exports and higher oil prices. Some losses were covered by Turkey's allies. *EIU-Country Report, Turkey,* no. 2 (1991), p. 19. Ozal and other Turkish spokesmen highlighted aid from allies and the latter's help in modernizing the armed forces.

25. Ozal to TRT, January 7, 1991, in *FBIS,* Daily Report, West Europe, January 8, 1991.

14

Iran: War Ended, Hostility Continued

Shaul Bakhash

On August 14, 1990, 12 days after he had invaded Kuwait, Saddam Husayn addressed a letter to President 'Ali-Akbar Hashemi-Rafsanjani of Iran in which he appeared to meet all of Iran's conditions for a peace treaty formally ending the Iran-Iraq war. He offered to begin an unconditional withdrawal of Iraqi troops from Iran's territory within three days, start exchanging prisoners of war at the same time—an event pending ever since the ceasefire between the two countries took effect in August 1988—and negotiate their frontier in the Shatt al-Arab River on the basis of the 1975 Algiers accord.[1]

This final point was the critical issue. Under the Algiers treaty Iraq had agreed to Iran's demand that the *thalweg* line constitute their mutual border, in effect conceding to Iran joint sovereignty over the Shatt al-Arab. Saddam Husayn had launched the Iran-Iraq war in 1980 by going on television to denounce and tear up the 1975 treaty and to reassert full Iraqi sovereignty over the Shatt. Post-ceasefire negotiations between the two countries has stalled primarily over Iraq's demand regarding this issue. But now Iraq appeared to have changed course. "Oh President 'Ali-Akhbar Hashemi," Saddam Husayn said in his August 14 letter, "with our decision, everything has become clear, and everything you wanted and on which you have been concentrating has been achieved."

Saddam's dramatic offer to Iran was clearly related to the invasion of Kuwait. He wished to secure his eastern flank, to ensure Iran would not join in any military offensive again Iraq, and to free his troops for redeployment on the Kuwait-Saudi border. The Iraqi president conceded as much in his letter to Rafsanjani. He was making his offer, he said, "so as not to keep any of Iraq's potentials disrupted outside the field of the great battle, and to mobilize these potentials in the direction of the objectives whose correctness honest Muslims and Arabs are unanimous."

By holding out to Iran the offer of a peace treaty on Iranian terms, Saddam Husayn may have also hoped to induce Iran to break the trade sanctions that had already been put in place against Iraq. He thus looked to the establishment of "normal relations" between Iran and Iraq; to "cooperation" between the two countries to keep the Persian Gulf secure and free from "foreign fleets and foreign forces"; and also to cooperation "in other walks of life."

The offer itself came after two years of intermittent, largely fruitless negotiations between the two countries that had followed the August 1988 ceasefire. The ceasefire was based on UN Security Council Resolution 598 of July 20, 1987. The resolution demanded an immediate ceasefire and withdrawal to international borders, to be followed by a prisoner exchange. It urged negotiations between the two countries toward a comprehensive peace agreement.

Paragraph six requested the UN secretary-general to explore, in consultation with Iran and Iraq, the establishment of an impartial commission to inquire into responsibility for the initiation of the conflict. Paragraph seven asked the secretary-general to examine the feasibility of establishing a fund to assist the two countries in reconstruction. The secretary-general was also asked to report back to the Security Council on his progress in implementing the resolution. Paragraph ten hinted at Security Council sanctions against the party that refused to comply with the resolution's primary demand regarding an immediate ceasefire.

Paragraph six was adopted at Iran's insistence. The Islamic Republic had always made it a condition for peace that the world community recognize Iraq as the aggressor. Paragraph seven, regarding the assessment of war damage and the possible establishment of a reconstruction fund for the two countries, was a compromise, designed to avoid the Iranian demand for substantial reparations from Iraq.

But the rest of the resolution was largely tailored to Iraq's interests. At the time the resolution was adopted, it was Iran that held substantial Iraqi territory. Moreover, the resolution was so worded as to require withdrawal of forces to be accomplished simultaneously with the ceasefire. Iran was thus being asked to give up the one bargaining chip it held against Iraq. Tehran, not surprisingly, resisted the proposal. Before the adoption of Resolution 598, five of the permanent members of the Security Council agreed to a proposal to reword the resolution so that troop withdrawal would follow a ceasefire. But the initiative failed after an Iraqi intervention in Washington and U.S. objections.

In September 1987, UN Secretary-General Javier Perez de Cuellar reported to the Security Council he had discussed with the two parties a nine-point plan for the resolution's implementation. It envisaged a ceasefire to be accompanied by the establishment of a commission of inquiry to determine responsibility for the initiation of hostilities. Withdrawal of military forces to international frontiers was to begin within a specific date after the ceasefire went into effect.

The secretary-general's proposal was therefore much closer to the Iranian than to the Iraqi position. Furthermore, although Iran was ready to accept an informal ceasefire as a first step in this process, it continued to insist that the ceasefire would become "formal" only after the party responsible for starting the war had been identified. Iraq, on the other hand, insisted on a sequential implementation of the resolution. Perez de Cuellar reported to the Security Council that "Iraq believes that the various provisions of the resolution should be implemented in the order of their sequence in the resolution itself . . . under no circumstances would Iraq accept an undeclared ceasefire."

In the end, however, the stalemate between Iran and Iraq was resolved not at the negotiating table but on the battlefield. In a series of offensives between April and July, Iraq succeeded in expelling Iran from virtually all occupied Iraqi territory. It took back the Faw Peninsula in April, the area around Basra and Fish Lake in May, and the Majnoon Islands in June. Iraqi forces went on to occupy large slices of Iranian territory as well. By mid-summer Iranian resistance appeared to have collapsed. On July 18, Iran's foreign minister informed the UN Secretary-General that Iran would accept Resolution 598 and was ready for an immediate ceasefire. On July 21, Ayatollah Khomeini himself endorsed the decision, describing it as "more lethal to me than poison."

Iraq, however, continued its mopping-up operations and its push into Iranian territory. It finally accepted Resolution 598 on August 6, on condition that the ceasefire be followed immediately by direct talks. The ceasefire went into effect on August 20 and negotiations began in Geneva on August 25 under the aegis of the UN secretary-general. The discussions, however, were not direct. Iran refused to talk directly to Iraq. Instead, the talks were "triangular." Ostensibly Iranian and Iraqi officials were negotiating only through the secretary-general or his representative.

These talks got nowhere. With Iraqi troops in occupation of Iranian territory, Iraq's interpretation of Resolution 598 had changed. Iraq now rejected the view it had held in 1987 that troop withdrawal must accompany or directly follow the ceasefire, that the resolution must be implemented sequentially, and that withdrawal must precede negotiations on a comprehensive peace settlement. Iraq now insisted that the resolution was an integral whole and that the troop withdrawal could take place only as part of a comprehensive settlement. It was Iran that fell back on the concept of sequential implementation.

There was no international pressure on Iraq to withdraw from Iranian territory. Moreover, the two sides could not agree on the disposition of the Shatt al-Arab issue. Iran demanded a return to the 1975 Algiers agreement under which the frontier between the two countries was set at the *thalweg* line. Iraq demanded recognition by Iran of Iraq's complete sovereignty over the Shatt. With the two sides deadlocked, the UN-sponsored negotiations bogged down and were eventually abandoned.

A new phase in these negotiations were initiated on April 21, 1990, when Saddam Husayn addressed a letter directly to the leader of Iran, 'Ali Khamene'i, and the president, Hashemi-Rafsanjani, proposing direct talks between the leaders toward a settlement. This proposal led to an exchange between Rafsanjani and Saddam Husayn involving, in all, six letters from Iraq's president to his Iranian counterpart and four from Rafsanjani to Saddam Husayn. It was this exchange, and the renewed negotiations to which it eventually led, that culminated on August 14 in Saddam Husayn's dramatic offer to Rafsanjani.

The Saddam Husayn-Rafsanjani correspondence reflects the dual aspect of the Iraq-Iran conflict, involving both issues of state interest and of ideology. In their exchange of letters, Rafsanjani and Saddam Husayn were primarily concerned—as might be expected—with concrete issues of state interest: borders, sovereignty, prisoner exchange, war responsibility, reparations.

But both also sought to maintain and press ideological claims—to the leadership of the Arab or Islamic cause, the struggle against U.S. imperialism, and against Israel. They both sought to dress their positions in the mantle of Islam, tossing Qur'anic quotations at one another. Both urged that their exchanges concentrate on substance yet both continued until the very last exchange of letters to advance claims relating more to revolutionary or Islamic superiority than to land and borders.

Saddam sought to equate Iraq's cause with the cause of Arabism and to depict the conflict not as one only between Iran and Iraq but also a conflict between Iran and the Arabs. Iraq, he suggested in his first letter to Rafsanjani, was at that very moment the target of Zionist and imperialist plots because it was a barrier and threat to the spread of Zionism. In weakening Iraq, its enemies intended "to give Zionism a free hand to . . . bulldoze whoever . . . thwarts its vicious designs in the region and works to remove its occupation of Arab Palestine and

Jerusalem." These forces wanted to ignite renewed conflict "between Iran on the one hand and Iraq and the Arab nation on the other." Iraq, he suggested, was supported by the region's progressive elements.

Rafsanjani did not allow these claims to go unchallenged. "Of course," he responded, "we have no problem with the Arab nation and have benefitted of the sincere cooperation of some Arab governments." Iran, not Iraq, he suggested, was the true champion of Islam and the Palestinian cause: "Everyone knows," he wrote on May 2, "that from the beginning and always the Islamic revolution has adopted as its goals...the glory and dignity of Islam and Muslims, struggle against the usurping government of Israel, and the liberation of Palestine." He returned to this theme in his June 18 letter to Saddam, in response to the latter's invitation to join in the struggle in the region against imperialism and Zionism: "We were invited by you—claiming to be the defender of Palestinians, Palestinian affairs, and resistance forces—to confront the imperialist invasion. . . . [But] the authors of the letter are aware that the Islamic Republic of Iran pioneers in confronting imperialism. . . . The first target of the invasion of the arrogant will be the Islamic Republic of Iran."

If all Arab governments had cooperated with the Iranian revolution [as, clearly, Iraq had not done], Rafsanjani wrote, the balance of power in the Middle East would have shifted to Islam and Muslims. Moreover, the progressive forces in the region supported Iran; by Saddam's own admission, Iraq was supported by "kings, sheikhs and leaders who were not members of the Arab umma."

In his August 3 letter to Rafsanjani, Saddam Husayn treated the Iranian criticism of the Iraqi annexation of Kuwait as an attack on Arabism. "It is surprising," Rafsanjani replied in his letter of August 8, "that Arabism was resorted to criticize our just stand on the Iraqi Army's occupation of Kuwaiti territory, when one of the surest ways of paving the way for the extensive presence of foreign forces in the region is to destroy the tranquility of and create problems for the Muslim people . . . to neglect international commitments."

On the substance of the negotiations—issues to be discussed, territorial claims, war responsibility, reparations, even the venue and level of the discussions—there were from the start considerable differences between the two parties. This disparity was narrowed somewhat in the ensuing weeks, but on the basic issue of sovereignty over the Shatt al-Arab the two countries were still far from agreement when Saddam Husayn invaded Kuwait on August 2.

Iran's willingness to enter into direct negotiations without UN mediation, a framework it had resisted in the past, requires explanation. Iran had resisted direct talks outside the UN framework because, like the Arab side in the Arab-Israeli dispute, it felt itself to be the weaker party. Moreover, in keeping with its interpretation of Resolution 598, it did not wish to negotiate while Iraqi troops remained in occupation of Iranian territory.

Rafsanjani, however, perhaps saw something sufficiently promising in Saddam Husayn's initial April 21 proposal—or oral explanations that may have accompanied it—to wish to explore further Iraq's ideas regarding a settlement. Moreover, despite its advantage in size and population, Iran felt militarily vulnerable following the ceasefire.

Iraq ended the war with a far superior military arsenal, which it was able to expand through purchases on the international market in the two years after the ceasefire. Despite the end of hostilities, however, that market remained closed to Iran. Moreover, Rafsanjani knew he could not hope to attract significant foreign investment to Iran as long as the war remained unsettled. He was also anxious to free Iranian territory from Iraqi occupation and could not do so by force of arms.

But the Saddam Husayn-Rafsanjani correspondence suggests that the Iraqi president remained the one more eager to push ahead with negotiations and to seal an agreement. It may well be that Saddam Husayn had already decided to invade Kuwait when he first wrote to Rafsanjani in April. He may have hoped to have his differences with Iran settled and the Iran border secured by the time his troops moved south.

Initially, Saddam Husayn envisaged a summit involving, on the Iraqi side, himself and his second-in-command, vice-chairman of the Revolutionary Command Council 'Izzat Ibrahim, and, on the Iranian side, the two top Iranian officials, Khamene'i and Rafsanjani. At such a level, he may have reasoned, the negotiators would have the authority to conclude an agreement rapidly and efficiently. In fact, he proposed the talks begin on April 28, or just seven days after his first letter was handed to the Iranians. Saddam may also have placed much faith in his own persuasive power, believing that once he sat face to face with Iran's leaders, he could bring matters to a rapid, successful conclusion.

But Saddam also seemed to think the Iranian leadership was factionalized and thus wanted an agreement to be endorsed by the top figures in Tehran. He reverted to the idea of a summit comprising "all basic decision makers in the two countries" in his second letter to Rafsanjani of May 19, 1990. The participation of these officials in negotiating an agreement, he told Rafsanjani, would bind them "psychologically and ethically, to implementing and abiding by it" and would prevent subsequent "excuses that might block the peace process after agreement has been reached."

Rafsanjani, however, was unenthusiastic regarding a summit and proposed preliminary talks be held first on an ambassadorial plane. Meetings at a higher level, he said, "will be acceptable when . . . we have achieved specific results, which will be the basis for the next stages." At Rafsanjani's suggestion, Iran's permanent representative to the UN offices in Geneva, Cyrus Naseri, and his Iraqi counterpart, Barzan Ibrahim al-Takriti, opened talks in May and continued to meet off and on until August. The lack of progress in these discussions seemed to vindicate Rafsanjani's skepticism regarding an early summit. With these talks making little headway, Saddam on July 16 proposed that Rafsanjani receive his personal representatives, Foreign Minister Tariq 'Aziz and Barzan al-Takriti, for face-to-face talks. In his letter to Rafsanjani of July 30, he again proposed a summit between the "heads of state" to work out the terms for a comprehensive peace.

Saddam was also eager to regularize relations with Iran. His first letter to Rafsanjani proposed the resumption of diplomatic relations; he reverted to the idea of reopening embassies in his letter of July 30. In the meantime he had also proposed reestablishing telephone links and, as a compromise solution, exchanging diplomatic "representatives," presumably at a level below that of ambassadors.

In his replies to Saddam Husayn, Rafsanjani not only rejected the idea of an early summit, he also made clear Iran's supreme leader, "His Holiness Ali Khamene'i," would not participate in the talks at any level or at any time. He assured, however, the Iraqi president that Iran's representatives would be acting under Khamene'i's guidelines, and that if the Iranian president took part in the discussions "it will definitely be with full authority; and the decisions will certainly be implemented. You need not worry about the concerns you expressed in your letter."

In another of those symbolic gestures beloved of the Iraqi leadership, Saddam Husayn had proposed "noble Mecca" as the venue for the talks, apparently without having consulted King Fahd and secured his agreement to host the talks. Rafsanjani rejected Saudi Arabia as an unsuitable site given the parlous state of Iran-Saudi relations. Thus Geneva became the venue for meetings between the Iranian and Iraqi ambassadors. Rafsanjani also ignored Saddam's repeated proposals to resume diplomatic relations and his offer to send personal representatives to meet Iranian officials in Tehran. No high-ranking Iraqi official was received in Tehran until after Saddam's August 14 offer to Rafsanjani.

There were other differences. Saddam Husayn envisaged bilateral talks excluding the UN Secretary-General, charged by the Security Council with implementing Resolution 598 and designated as intermediary between the two sides. Iraq was not favorably inclined toward Perez de Cuellar, whom it regarded as pro-Iran. Iran continued to desire UN involvement. Rafsanjani took the position that the sides must keep the secretary-general informed of the course of the negotiations and seek his views and initiatives.

"We will refrain from limiting the path of peace to direct talks," Rafsanjani told Saddam on 18 June, "and we will not close other paths, including the main path [the UN] which already has been travelled." Iraq wished paragraph 6 of Resolution 598, on a commission of inquiry to establish responsibility for initiating the war, dropped. Iran insisted on retaining it. Some of the differences over procedural issues were narrowed. Rafsanjani initially cited the continued presence of Iraqi troops on Iranian soil as an obstruction to negotiations but dropped the issue after Saddam argued for negotiations without "preconditions."

The initial exchanges between Saddam Husayn and Rafsanjani were confined to generalities, procedural issues, and staking out ideological claims and very broad negotiating positions. Only on July 30 did Saddam Husayn for the first time made a detailed proposal. The invasion of Kuwait was but two days away. After four months of exchanges of letters and talks in Geneva, the two sides were no nearer an agreement. Rafsanjani later noted that the exchanges had consisted mainly of "editing letters and holding lengthy talks," with an emphasis on form rather than content. Other than "gaining greater familiarity with one another's views," he wrote, the Geneva talks had made no significant progress. Rafsanjani had not even answered Saddam's third letter of July 16 or his offer to send a personal representative to Tehran.

Saddam Husayn laid out his July 30 proposals in his fourth letter to Rafsanjani. He revived the proposal for a summit meeting, saying a peace agreement should cover all the issues outstanding between the two countries, laying down a principle that any agreement reached "be part of an indivisible whole and in the form of an integrated, interrelated package; the breach of any part of its articles will count as a breach of all of its articles."

He proposed that withdrawal of troops to international frontiers be completed within two months of the final ratification of a comprehensive peace agreement and that the prisoners-of-war exchange be completed within the same time period. Saddam addressed the critical issue of the Shatt al-Arab in paragraph six, saying discussions must be based on the following principles:

1) Iraq should have complete sovereignty as a legitimate historical right.
2) Iraq should have sovereignty over the Shatt al-Arab, and the thalweg line law should be applied regarding navigational rights between Iraq and Iran, including fishing rights, joint administration of navigation, and sharing of profits thereof.

The language of these paragraphs is convoluted, but it suggests, as Rafsanjani was subsequently to note, a softening of Iraq's position on the Shatt. Saddam was offering to recognize Iran's navigation and fishing rights and a form of joint administration (but not sovereignty) up to the thalweg line. Sovereignty, however, was still reserved for Iraq alone. Iraq, Saddam Husayn said, was willing to discuss the issue with Iran or even to submit it to mediation, on the basis of these principles and an understanding that "the first heading [sovereignty] is Iraq's right and the second heading [joint administration, navigation and fishing rights] represents Iran's wish."

Saddam also proposed an agreement on noninterference by the two parties in each other's internal affairs and a guarantee to Iraq of freedom of navigation in the Persian Gulf and through the Straits of Hormuz. On a more quixotic note, Saddam Husayn noted that while international aid for the purposes of war reconstruction was unlikely, any such assistance should be shared equally between the two countries.

Ironically for a regime that had shown contempt for international agreements and legal niceties, Saddam appeared eager to surround an agreement with Iran with legal protection. He proposed that implementation could begin only after all the requirements for treaty ratification under each country's constitution had been met, thus rendering the agreement "inviolable." (In Iran, this would require ratification by parliament. He proposed the two countries register their treaty with the UN secretary-general, even suggesting that an international authority such as the UN Security Council be invited to ensure implementation.

Rafsanjani never replied to Saddam Husayn's July 30 letter. Before he could do so, Iraq invaded Kuwait. A day after the invasion, on August 3, the Iraqi president addressed his fifth letter to the Iranian president. The letter was clearly motivated by concern that Iran might be tempted to side with Iraq's enemies. Saddam suggested that the invasion of Kuwait was an inter-Arab matter, not involving Iran. He warned Iran, in barely disguised terms, against involvement in the crisis. He had received reports, he said ominously, of Rafsanjani's "political" activities and his meetings with his military chiefs. He suggested that his July 30 offer might be rescinded as a basis for negotiation if Iran did not take it up or acted unwisely. Countries that suspend arms sales or break economic relations with Iraq, he said, could resume them. "But if Iran and Iraq deviate from their proper position, their nations will be deprived of an historic opportunity to achieve peace. . . . The damage will be very great, and I have no such wish for you or for myself."

Rafsanjani's response, on August 7, to this letter and to Saddam's detailed July 30 proposals is interesting because it lays down what was to become Iran's consistent position throughout the Kuwait crisis, at least until the Shiʿa uprising in the south in February-March 1991. On the one hand, Rafsanjani sought to keep the negotiations between Iran and Iraq alive. He acknowledged that Iraq's position on the Shatt had shifted somewhat but took the view that Saddam's proposal remained unacceptable to Iran: "Our specific proposal is to use the 1975 accord for the peace talks because without adherence to previous treaties, especially that treaty that bears your own signature, there can be no confidence in what is being said today."

But Rafsanjani reaffirmed Iran's interest in pursuing the peace talks and suggested shorter time frames for withdrawal of troops and prisoner exchange. On the other hand, he made clear that the invasion of Kuwait was unacceptable to Iran. He described it as "an unimaginable assault on a neighboring country." Iran had already called for Iraq's unconditional withdrawal, and, over the next six months, Iran's strategy remained the same: to try to nail down a peace treaty with Iraq on terms favorable to Iran—a goal that, with Saddam's August 14 letter, appeared within reach —even while working to force Iraq out of Kuwait.

Saddam Husayn's August 14 letter to Rafsanjani was widely interpreted as conceding to Iran the terms it had long demanded. This is certainly how Iran chose to interpret the letter, at least for domestic and international consumption. "The announcement of your renewed acceptance of the 1975 accord," Rafsanjani wrote Saddam the same day, "has paved the way for implementing Resolution 598, resolving the problems in that framework and transforming the existing ceasefire into a permanent and stable peace."

Moreover, Iraq rapidly completed the withdrawal of its troops from Iranian territory; and it moved quickly to exchange prisoners of war. Some differences subsequently developed about the number of prisoners of war held on each side, and about bits of territory claimed by Iran but still held by Iraq. But in the weeks following August 14, Iraq appeared to be moving with alacrity to carry out the measures promised by Saddam Husayn regarding troop withdrawal and prisoners-of-war exchange. In October, Rafsanjani agreed to resume diplomatic relations.

Between August 14 and the end of March, Iran played host to several high-powered Iraqi delegations. Tariq 'Aziz visited Tehran in early September, and the Iranian foreign minister, 'Ali Akbar Velayati, returned the visit in November. Early in January, Izzat Ibrahim, accompanied by the deputy prime minister, Sa'dun Hammadi, was in Tehran. Hammadi was back at the Iranian capital with a private message from Saddam Husayn for Rafsanjani at the end of January, and returned again in February. Tariq 'Aziz stopped in Tehran on his way both to and from Moscow in mid-February. On March 6, Hammadi arrived unannounced at the Iranian frontier. This trip occurred at the height of the Shi'a uprising in southern Iraq and apparently was aimed at persuading the Iranians not to intervene on the rebels' side. On each occasion, talks were held between Iraqi and Iranian officials at the highest level, including

Rafsanjani, Velayati, and the Iranian first deputy president (who served as an unacknowledged prime minister), Hasan Habibi.

No peace agreement resulted from all this coming and going and no such aim was mentioned in the brief communiqués, remarks by officials, or (with few exceptions) in the media on the occasion of these meetings. Two explanations come to mind.

First, it is likely that Saddam's offer to Iran of peace on highly favorable terms was from the beginning designed to wean Iran away from even tacit cooperation with the alliance of regional states that had joined the United States and Western European countries against Iraq. The Iraqis sought to induce Iran not to join in sanctions against Iraq. Alarmist reports that appeared in the *New York Times*, American television networks, and some of the European press around the time of Tariq 'Aziz's visit to Tehran (he was accompanied by his oil minister) may have been inspired by the Iraqis themselves. These reports claimed that Iran was about to break sanctions and to provide Iraq with food and other essential materials in exchange for massive deliveries of Iraqi oil.

But there was never even a slim chance that Iran would acquiesce—let alone actively conspire—in the successful annexation of Kuwait by Iraq. An Iraq strengthened by Kuwait's oil resources, wealth, and ports on the Persian Gulf would have posed a major threat to Iran's security. Iran did not waver in its demand for Iraq's unconditional withdrawal from Kuwait even as it chased the elusive comprehensive peace treaty with Iraq. It did not break sanctions and supported UN Security Council resolutions against Iraq. In practice, if not in rhetoric, it hewed to a line very close to that of the United States and its allies.

However, Iran was also sensitive to the concerns of a domestic constituency and a larger Islamic one abroad. At a rhetorical level, officials condemned the U.S. bombing of Iraqi cities and civilian centers. Limited humanitarian assistance, in the form of medicine, was extended to the Iraqi people. All this was also a way of keeping the Iran-Iraq peace negotiations on track. But on the crucial issue of sanctions and Iraq's withdrawal from Kuwait, Iran remained firm. The Iraqi officials who trooped to Tehran between September and March went home disappointed. Saddam had little reason to concede to Iran joint sovereignty in the Shatt if he was getting nothing in return.

A second reason why Saddam Husayn's August 14 offer was never translated into a peace treaty between the two countries may lie in the nature of the offer itself. A close reading of Saddam Husayn's August 14 letter to Rafsanjani suggests that it offered less than is apparent on the surface. The operative paragraph in which Saddam Husayn appeared to offer Iran a settlement in the Shatt on the basis of the 1975 Algiers treaty is the following: "We agree to your proposal as contained in your reply letter dated 8 August 1990 . . . stating the necessity of working on the basis of the 1975 accord, in conjunction with the content of [our] 30 July 1990 letter."

In treating Rafsanjani's August 8 proposal as if it were closely related to his own, Saddam Husayn was deliberately blurring the differences between the Iranian and Iraqi positions or at least reserving his position even while pretending fully to accept Rafsanjani's. Rafsanjani was proposing to return to a prewar situation in which the two countries shared sovereignty over the Shatt. Saddam Husayn was proposing a situation in which Iraq's "historical right" to sovereignty would be recognized and Iran's "wish" for navigation and administrative rights would be granted. At best, Saddam's letter could also be read as a readiness to discuss the two proposals side by side. Once discussions began at ministerial level following Saddam's August 14 initiative, the Iranians may have discovered that Saddam had not strayed far from his July 30 position.

The Shi'a rebellion in the south in February and March further exacerbated relations between the two countries. Iran did not instigate or direct the uprising, whose intensity and breadth showed that the propelling forces were indigenous. Until the uprising, it is Iranian restraint in regard to Iraq's Shi'a that is striking. Throughout the Kuwait crisis, and even after the extent of Saddam Husayn's military defeat became evident, Iran did not encourage Shi'a unrest in the south. It did not raise the issue, so prominent during Khomeini's lifetime, of a Shi'a government at Baghdad. It kept Ayatollah Muhammad Baqir al-Hakim, leader of the Supreme Assembly of the Islamic Revolution of Iraq, in exile in Iran, on a tight leash.

Once the uprising occurred, however, Rafsanjani could not afford to be seen sitting on his hands while Saddam Husayn massacred fellow Shi'a. Some of Hakim's "army" in Iran, recruited from among Iraqi Shi'a prisoners of war, was allowed to cross into Iraq. Iran no doubt provided financial and small arms assistance. Still, the scale of Iranian support remained small.

Nevertheless, this assistance, the brutal suppression of the uprising by Saddam Husayn, and the violation of shrines at Najaf and Karbala had predictable results. By the end of March 1991, relations between the two countries were once again badly strained, suspicions had been aroused on both sides, Iraq was accusing Iran of interfering in its internal affairs, and Iranian officials were calling on Saddam Husayn to step aside.

From the beginning there was perhaps less substance and promise in Saddam Husayn's August 14 offer to Rafsanjani than was generally assumed. Saddam was probably hinting at more on paper than he was willing to concede in reality. His offer in any case was tied to a wholly unrealistic expectation that Iran would turn a blind eye to Iraq's annexation of Kuwait and attach more importance to its desire for joint sovereignty over the Shatt than to the threat posed by Iraq's aggression. Finally, the very situation—the crisis resulting from Iraqi annexation of Kuwait—that produced Iraq's offer to Iran was full of pitfalls for an Iran-Iraq rapprochement. The Shi'a uprising in the south was only one of many events that underlined once again the deep, complex differences dividing the two countries.

NOTES

1. The exchange of letters between Iraqi president Saddam Husayn and Iranian president Ali-Akbar Hashemi-Rafsanjani in April and August 1990 was published in fragments in the Persian-language *Kayhan Hava'i,* September 29 and October 3, 1990. I have used the English translation that appeared in *Foreign Broadcast Information Service,* Near East and South Asia, November 1, 1990, pp. 39-50. Although the translation is somewhat awkward, I have not tampered with it except where necessary for the sake of clarity.

15

Israel Faces Iraq: The Politics of Confrontation

Avner Yaniv

Israeli analyses of threats normally divide the Arab world into two concentric geographic "circles": the inner circle of confrontation states and the outer ring of "other" adversaries.

The inner circle has never been perceived as a uniform whole. Lebanon and the Hashemite Kingdom of Jordan, for example, were for many years regarded as nonconfrontational neighbors and often even as tacit collaborators; Syria was always seen as an implacable foe; whereas since 1975 Egypt, previously Israel's principal opponent, has become regarded as much less of a threat.

Likewise the outer ring has also contained tacitly friendly or indifferent governments—Morocco, Tunis under Bourghiba, and occasionally Sudan—side by side with very hostile regimes such as Libya under Qadhafi and the People's Democratic Republic of Yemen. Nonetheless, despite this variety within both categories, there was always, in Israeli eyes, a *perceived*, invisible divide that underscored the validity of this method of categorization: Sheer geography made all confrontation states—including even the seemingly friendliest among them—potential participants in Arab-Israeli wars, whereas the same factor militated against the participation in such a war by states of the "outer" circle.

Iraq, however, has been the notable exception. Although geographically distant and lacking a common border with Israel, it has almost always featured in Israeli thinking as an active, formidable confrontation state. It sent significant expeditionary forces in the 1948, 1967, and 1973 wars. It took the lead in opposing Sadat's peace initiative and in the race for an Arab nuclear capability. Above all, on the eve of the Gulf war it deliberately fomented tensions with Israel and then—despite Israel's painstaking efforts to keep a "low profile"—attacked Israeli cities with SCUD missiles.

Israeli policymakers tended to attribute Iraq's attitude not to genuine devotion to the Arab cause—certainly not to any real concern for the Palestinians—but to the cynical ambitions of Iraqi leaders or, at most, to an abiding rhetorical commitment that Iraqi governments could defy only at their peril.

Successive Israeli governments faced a grave choice between two strategies: a *reactive,* low-profile posture or an anticipatory, *initiating,* high-profile posture. A low profile would have the advantage of allowing Iraq to go through the motions of hostility toward Israel without genuinely adding their weight on the side of the confrontation states. But it could also be construed by the rash, arrogant Iraqis, who were also running only a marginal risk, as a sign of Israeli weakness and thus encourage Iraqi participation in a war against Israel.

The high-profile alternative offered, of course, the reverse of the same logic: By posing a threat of punishment, it could conceivably deter Iraq from joining the fray. Yet this approach could also act as challenge that, rather than deterring Iraq, would spur it to increase its efforts against the Jewish state.

Given this dilemma, Israeli policy has swung back and forth between the two alternative courses of action toward Iraq. In the first decade of statehood there was a marked preference for a low profile. During the interval between Iraq's 1958 revolution and Iran's offensives of the mid-1980s, Israeli policy toward Iraq was closer to the high-profile end of the spectrum. Iraq's difficulties in the war with Iran led to a thaw and even to some Israeli attempt to enter into a dialogue with Saddam's regime.

This interlude came, however, to an abrupt end after the Iran-Iraq war and Saddam's return to an assertive policy. At first puzzled, then alarmed, Israel responded cautiously in order to deny Saddam the game of confrontation that he evidently sought and that Israel had every reason to avoid. The same policy continued when—after August 2, 1990—the United States, Syria, Saudi Arabia, Egypt, and Turkey assumed the leading role in containing Iraq.

THE 1948 WAR

Israeli attitudes toward Iraq's role in the 1948 war oscillated between concern and contempt. "The Iraqis are well armed and view this [coming] war a test for the Arab world," David Ben-Gurion wrote in his diary on February 9, 1948.[1] Yet just a month later, agents in Baghdad reassured him that for all the boldness of Iraqi official rhetoric and the Iraqi army's might on paper, Iraq's real strength was limited. The report read:

> Two thousand [volunteers] have so far signed up for the war in Palestine. More than fifty returned, their stories [work] in our favor. They were given antiquated weapons. Very poor personnel. There is a secret decision in the [Iraqi] Ministry of Defense to terminate the mobilization and the shipments. The money contributed by Iraq estimated at 200,000 Dinars. There are stories that most of it has been stolen. The press reports that three Iraqis died (in Palestine). Very difficult economic conditions. The people are tired and hungry. There are demonstrations, the political situation is unclear.[2]

All this was music to Ben-Gurion's ears. But he and his colleagues could not ignore the substantial Iraqi military presence that soon emerged right in Israel's center between Wadi Milech (southeast of Haifa) and Beit Naballa (east of Tel Aviv) as well as south of the Sea of Galilee near Kibbutz Gesher and the hydroelectric plant of Naharayim. It consisted of 16,000 combatants organized in 12 regular battalions, 4 battalions of "local" personnel (probably volunteers) and equipped with 100 armored personnel carriers, 50 artillery pieces, and 200 Fury fighter aircraft that were deployed in Transjordan's air base of Mafraq.[3]

Israel's army, with less than 50,000 soldiers, also had to deal with 45,000 Egyptian and Jordanian soldiers and lacked the heavy weapons possessed by Iraq. Small wonder, then, that halfway through the 1948 war the Iraqis were still regarded, according to Minister of Finance Eliezer Kaplan, as "a dangerous foe."[4]

The Israeli evaluation of the Iraqi threat changed, of course, as the 1948 war developed. When it became clear that a key issue was the Iraqi force's control of Wadi 'Ara, the Israeli General Staff was asked to evaluate the prospect for a quick military victory there. Major General Moshe Carmel's quick, confident reply was "Two brigades will take both sides of [the] Wadi 'Ara [valley] in 48 hours and will establish a new line north of the valley of Dotan. It is to be expected that an Iraqi counter-offensive will follow," Carmel hastened to add that "from our defensive positions we'll be able to wreak havoc" in the Iraqi force.[5]

The Iraqis probably had an equally low opinion of their ability to handle an Israeli offensive. Accordingly, with the negotiations deadlocked and signs that Israel might use force, Iraq's government announced on March 27, 1949, that its forces would withdraw without delay. Israel was naturally elated since as a result it eventually gained the Wadi 'Ara area without a fight at a time when politically (if not militarily) resuming hostilities would have been unwelcome. But Israel was also disappointed that Iraq chose to opt out of negotiations altogether, dashing all hope for a rapprochement between the two countries and, worse still, discouraging other Arab governments from reaching a ceasefire.

Paradoxically, Iraq's decisions to yield in Wadi 'Ara and not to join Egypt, Jordan, Syria, and Lebanon in the Rhodes Armistice talks stemmed from the same source. Iraq's regime was too weak to withstand the tidal wave of domestic unrest following the disappointing news from Palestine. Iraqi defense minister Shaqr al-Wadi told Lieutenant-General Riley of the UN ceasefire observation team in December 1948 that his government could not accept the ceasefire resolution because "it will cause severe riots."[6]

Yet despite the fact that Iraq announced the decision to withdraw its forces from Palestine _together_ with its decision _not_ to join the armistice talks, there were still riots in Baghdad, "the army stepped in," and no less than 150 people were wounded.[7]

BETWEEN WAR AND REVOLUTION, 1950-1958

The same ambiguity typifying Israel's relations with Iraq in 1948 also marked them in the decade thereafter, manifested with regard to the exodus of the Iraqi Jewish community and the issue of Iraq's involvement in the affairs of Jordan and Syria.

Following the anti-Jewish riots just after the collapse of the Rashid 'Ali al-Kaylani rebellion in 1941, the Jewish community of Iraq, with a great deal of help and guidance from the Haganah, established the _Shura_ (Hebrew for "line") or Babylonian Pioneer Movement, a self-defense organization. As of 1943, this network was engaged in the illegal migration of young Zionists to Palestine and, increasingly, in espionage on behalf of the Jewish Agency. By 1950 it had 16 branches throughout Iraq, a membership of 2,000 and a hard core of 300 militarily trained activists with relatively significant quantities of light firearms at their disposal.

Since a great deal of the group's work depended on bribery, its existence could hardly be described as a secret. The Iraqi authorities not only looked the other way but consented to the whisking away en masse from airfields inside

Iraq of more than 100,000 out of Iraq's 110,000 Jews. To allow Israel's reinforcement through this influx at a time when Arab diplomacy was still trying to undo that country's existence was, of course, incompatible with Iraq's professed devotion to the Arab cause. The motive was a combination of greed by scores of Iraqi officials and the thought that the Jewish community was a subversive element (the Iraqi Communist party, for example, was dominated by Jewish agitators) whose departure would enhance domestic stability.

In the spring of 1951 this tacit cooperation abruptly ended mainly—Israel's Foreign Ministry suspected—because, with the Jews mostly gone, the Iraqis wished to hide their collusion with Israel by acting tough. Accordingly, in May 1951 a major clampdown on the Israeli network was carried out. Most of the activists left in a hurry and 80 were arrested. This was followed by widely publicized spy trials in which two local agents were sentenced to death and numerous others, including Israelis such as Yehuda Tajer, were sentenced to long prison sentences at hard labor.[8]

Another contributing factor for this crisis was clearly related to the larger arena of Arab-Israeli relations. As a result of the 1948 war Iraq had lost the use of its oil pipeline to Haifa. Israel was quite willing to consider Iraq's resuming use of the pipeline *on condition that this be part of a larger understanding between Baghdad and Jerusalem*. But the Iraqis entertained grand ambitions for a united Fertile Crescent or at least some form of Arab leadership and evidently estimated that a public posture of implacable hostility—underscored by their refusal to terminate officially the state of war with Israel—served these ambitions.

Moreover, the same combination of guilt (for tacitly collaborating with Israel on the immigration issue) and ambition drove the Iraqis to act assertively with regard to Syria and Jordan. During 1950, at the peak of one of the most unstable eras in Syrian history, there was much talk about the possibility of merging Iraq and Syria into one state. Israel opposed it as creating a centralized power that would pose a greater threat than the divided Arab world. Officially, however, the Israeli diplomat Michael Comay explained to a ranking British official in September 1950, "An Iraqi-Syrian merger would . . . have the effect of bringing Iraq down to the northern Israel border." And since Iraq had not signed an armistice agreement, the "existing Armistice Agreement between the Israel and Syrian governments would become meaningless."[9]

When in 1951 Israel retaliated for the death of seven soldiers by bombing Syrian positions, Iraq quickly announced it was willing to stand by Syria and even deploy its warplanes there. After a 1954 coup in Syria there was again much talk about a Syria-Iraq merger. This led to a fierce debate in Israel's leadership. Chief of Staff Lieutenant-General Moshe Dayan argued that if Iraq moved into Syria, then Israel should seize demilitarized zones along the border and the Golan Heights overlooking them and make a deal with Lebanese Maronites to produce a more friendly government in that country.

Prime Minister Sharett and his aides vehemently opposed this and argued for indicating to Iraq that its merger with Syria would be resisted by Israel unless it was preceded by an Iraqi armistice agreement with Israel and by settling the water issue along the Israel-Syria border. But Sharett was not at all convinced that an Iraqi move was imminent and therefore avoided any announcements that could trigger a snowball effect.[10]

When David Ben-Gurion returned to power as Israel's prime minister in 1955 he faced a similar dilemma vis-à-vis Jordan. Whenever Jordan's regime seemed on the verge of imminent collapse—which was often in those years— Iraq would consider intervening. Israel believed that the real purpose of Iraqi intervention would not be to save King Husayn but rather to oust him and incorporate his kingdom into a Greater Iraq. The question was whether Israel should let this to happen and, if not, how could it stop Iraq.

What ultimately determined Israel's approach was Jordan's conduct. As long as Jordan was a quiescent neighbor, almost a tacit ally—as it had been ever since 1948—Israel had an interest in protecting it by issuing threats to deter Iraq from sending its troops across the border. But the removal of the Jordanian army's British advisers in 1956 effectively turned Jordan into a pro-Nasir confrontation state. Ben-Gurion was on the verge of completely reversing his attitude to Jordan.

Early in October 1956 he still wanted to prevent the entry of large Iraqi forces although both the British and U.S. governments favored such a move to help King Husayn.[11] Two weeks later, however, after Israel had lost 17 soldiers in a raid on Qalqilyeh, Ben-Gurion changed his position dramatically. "Jordan has no right to exist and ought to be partitioned," he told Dayan furiously. "The east bank should be annexed to Iraq, which will undertake to resettle in it the [Palestinian] refugees; the territories west of the Jordan [river]—to add as an autonomous region, to Israel."[12]

YEARS OF CONFRONTATION, 1958-1973

Ben-Gurion's disenchantment with Jordan and hence willingness to countenance partitioning it between Israel and Iraq was short-lived. Jordan, as far as Israel was concerned, behaved itself during the 1956 war. The long Israel-Jordan border was quiet while Israel pulverized Egypt's army in the Sinai. Given British and U.S. commitment to Jordan's existence, the proposition that it be partitioned *by an Israeli initiative* was not really serious.

Within two years Iraq itself was transformed by a bloody coup into a state with which Israel wanted no common border. Indeed, the advent of the revolutionary regime in Iraq caused a sea change in the Israeli perspective. From July 14, 1958, the prevailing view in Israel was that Iraq was a dangerous, radical power that might be contained by force but could not really be tamed, let alone qualify as a credible negotiating partner.

The immediate Israeli reaction to the Iraqi revolution was the launching of the Peripheral Alliance. The coup appeared to be yet another victory for Nasir. The Egyptian leader had pushed the British out of the Suez Canal area and the Sudan in 1954; made himself a world leader in the Bandung conference of the Non-Aligned Nations in 1955; turned a humiliating military defeat into a political victory in 1956; merged Egypt and Syria into the United Arab Republic in 1958 and now moved (as it seemed in the heat of the summer of 1958) to incorporate Iraq into this empire. Ben-Gurion had always been haunted by a fear lest the Arabs would be united by a latter day Salah al-Din. Nasir now seemed poised to play the part.[13]

The response lay, Ben-Gurion thought, in allying all the forces in the Middle East and beyond threatened by the tidal wave of Arab fervor allied with the Soviet Union. This mix included Sunni Muslim but non-Arab Turkey, Shi'a Iran, primarily Christian Ethiopia as well as the Christians of Lebanon, the Kurds in Iraq, and the non-Muslim population of Sudan. All these forces could be brought, Ben-Gurion and his disciples thought, into a framework with interests parallel to those of the United States. The latter could therefore be persuaded to help this alliance, which, in turn, would help consolidate it as a countervailing force against Nasir.

Israel stood to gain twice from such a policy: Acting as a linchpin of a new, pro-Western regional order would raise its value to the United States as well as to all these regional powers. At the same time, the alliance of all these different elements would underline the mosaiclike nature of the Middle East. Whereas in the Nasirist ethos, the region was mainly Arab and Sunni Muslim, and therefore had no place for a Jewish state, in Ben-Gurion's notion it was a zone of pluralism in which a Jewish state was not a peculiarity but very much part of the normal pattern of things.[14]

The idea of a peripheral alliance was not focused primarily on the Iraqi threat after its 1958 revolution, but there is little doubt that this event triggered the intellectual and diplomatic processes that led to Israel's attempt to put the alliance together. In the end, Iraq under Qasim was as much a rival of Egypt as it had been under the monarchy, and the Egyptian-Syrian union collapsed in enormous acrimony. Nasir did not lead the Arab world boldly toward unity but created enormous divisions.

As a result the raison d'être of the peripheral alliance was in doubt before long. Nonetheless, from Israel's standpoint Iraq was now a more hostile force and the alliance's premises suggested some ways to contain it. Israel could still rely on Tehran as a formidable force on Iraq's eastern flank, and the Tehran-Tel Aviv axis flourished in the 1960s, precisely at the time when the Iran-Iraq rivalry over the Gulf—soon to become a power vacuum as Britain withdrew—was fast becoming a very important feature of Middle East politics.[15]

An important element in Iran's strategy was to divert Iraq's attention from the Gulf to its far north and thus gain a free hand for Iran's own ambitions in the Gulf. For this purpose, Iran used the Kurdish minority. But since it had its own Kurdish minority to worry about and since it wished to avoid further antagonism toward itself in the Arab world, it offered Israel an opportunity to play a role. For Israel, the Kurdish plight evoked sympathy—which the Kurdish expatriate Jewish community in Jerusalem diligently amplified. But there was also a practical interest: If Iraq was busy with the Kurdish rebels, it could hardly spare forces for another Palestine war. Thus, Jerusalem was interested in using the Kurdish card.[16]

Judging by a number of published firsthand accounts, Israel's aid program to the anti-Iraq Kurdish guerrillas was modest—a few instructors, some light weapons, and medical equipment—but never any direct involvement in combat.[17] Iraq avoided publicizing it presumably to save themselves the embarrassment of admitting their difficulties with the Kurds and the presence on their sovereign territory of an Israeli military mission. But it can be assumed that the audacity of Israel's role in the Kurdish rebellion must have made Iraq frustrated and angry.

Such feelings were probably exacerbated by the so-called Operation 007. An Iraqi pilot named Munir Radfa, an Assyrian Christian, was noticeably alienated from his native land. The Mossad discovered this and used a female agent to seduce Radfa. He succumbed to her charms and she lured him to Israel via Paris. There he was given instructions for the operation. His family was whisked out of Iraq by Kurds and money was deposited under his name into a Swiss bank account. He flew his MiG-21 to an Israeli air force base on August 16, 1966. The prestige of Israel's intelligence community skyrocketed, Israel and the United States gained access to some of the most closely guarded secrets of Soviet weapon technology, and Iraq suffered a humiliating blow.[18]

Nor could Iraq find consolation in its experience in the 1967 war. The day after it began, a small number of Iraqi bombers tried to bomb Israel's city of Natanya and Ramat David air force base. They did very little damage and were shot down. In turn, Israel's air force attacked Iraq's air force base at H3. Flying with little preparation and barely sufficient maps, it caused some damage to Iraq's air force (which lost 23 planes in this war) but also lost four planes. The counterattack was more effective in hitting the Iraqi army's 18th armored brigade, leading a reinforced mechanized division through Jordan toward the Beit Sean valley. The division's advance was halted and it never reached the battlefield.[19]

By contrast, an Iraqi armored division did succeed in reaching the battlefield in the 1973 war. Iraq, not advised of the Syrian-Egyptian war plans ahead of time, was caught by surprise when the war broke out. As soon as the news reached Baghdad, Iraq's army was ordered to put together a special task force called the Saladdin Force, consisting of the 3rd Armored Division, the 6th Armored Division, the 20th infantry brigade, the 5th mountaineer brigade, and a brigade of special forces. Its objective was to take part in the Syrian effort to capture the Golan. But during the week it took this force to arrive at the front, Syria had already lost all its initial gains on Israel's side of the ceasefire lines and was fighting desperately to contain the offensive of three Israeli mechanized divisions under Major General Dan Lanner, Major General Moshe Peled, and Brigadier General Rafael Eitan. Thus, when the Iraqi forces arrived, their main contribution was to the Syrian defense in the Nasaj-Tal 'Antar-Tal Kharra sector inside Syria about 25 miles from Damascus and not, as initially intended, to the Syrian offensive in the Israeli-held Golan.

In the ensuing battles the Iraqi force demonstrated neither imagination nor particular valor. Its casualties were substantial—about 80 Centurion tanks lost—mostly captured in working order—with very little damage and virtually no casualties to the Israeli forces fighting them. Nonetheless, the Saladdin Task Force did have a significant impact. Israeli intelligence failed to detect it before it was actually spotted by an advance reconnaissance paratroop unit from Lanner's division. Israel quickly ordered the bulk of the division all the way back to the vicinity of Tal Sha'r for fear the Iraqis would otherwise encircle it.

Lanner's division then prepared a superb trap and, in a battle that lasted about 12 hours beginning on the night of October 12, destroyed substantial parts of the Iraqi 3rd Armored Division and force it to back off. The net strategic result of all this was that the Israeli attempt to drive a wedge between the 9th and the 3rd Syrian Armored divisions to reach a point from which Damascus could be threatened never materialized.[20] While not a catastrophe, this left a certain sense of unease in Israel, a feeling that was to grow very rapidly in the coming decade.

THE ROAD TO OSIRAQ, 1974-1981

During the 1970s, three major developments shaped Israel's attitude toward Iraq: the Algiers agreement ending the Kurdish rebellion; Iraq's leadership of the anti-Egypt campaign; and Iraq's drive for a nuclear capability.

The Algiers agreement boiled down to a U.S.-inspired Iranian sellout of the Kurds. Having established their supremacy in the Gulf area, Iran had no further use for the Kurdish decoy. The stability and consolidation they needed presupposed a relaxation of tensions with Baghdad. The Kurds paid the price. In comparison to this tragedy, Israel's loss from this about-face was marginal. But the potential strategic implication was serious.

Since 1971 Iraq had rapidly emerged as a major regional power. Enjoying the benefit of oil revenues second only to those of Saudi Arabia, Iraq could rapidly equip itself with as much armament as it wanted. Small wonder, then, that Israeli military estimates of another Arab-Israeli war increasingly anticipated an Iraqi role far bigger than its relatively small contribution to previous rounds.

Such forebodings were confirmed by Iraq's actions after Sadat's 1977 visit to Jerusalem. Egypt's decision to seek peace with Israel destroyed its leading role in the Arab world; Syria was compromised by its involvement in Lebanon. Iraq now had a golden opportunity to thrust itself forward but, to do so, it would eventually have to play the Arab-Israeli card.

Thus, as in 1948, an ambitious Iraqi regime that felt secure from Israel's military prowess because of distance invoked the rhetoric of confrontation to advance its status as a leader of the Arab world. With this in mind, the Iraqi government convened two special Arab summit meetings in November 1978 and April 1979 to rally the Arab world against the Egypt-Israel peace process. The conferences did not stop Sadat but hardened attitudes on both sides and deepened Israelis' concern about the direction of Iraqi policy.

What added a special sense of urgency to these growing concerns was Iraq's drive, with French help since 1974, for an independent nuclear capacity. By the time of the two conferences just mentioned, Israel had already been engaged for more than two years in a major diplomatic effort to stop the Iraqi program before it was too late. These efforts were doubled during 1979 and 1980, with diplomacy backed up by sabotage and threats.

Then, in September, Iraq invaded Iran in what seemed at the time a successful Blitzkrieg. In Menachem Begin's mind it must have seemed a Middle Eastern repeat of Hitler's swift conquest of the Low Lands, Norway, and France in the spring of 1940. Under these circumstances, to let Saddam complete his nuclear designs would be tantamount to Israel acquiescing to a fate worse than Poland's (which Begin had experienced firsthand). The implication was clear: Israel had to destroy the reactor by force.[21]

Beyond Begin's Holocaust memories there was also a more contemporary strategic calculation. If Iraq developed something like a second strike capability, there would be a nuclear standoff. Israel would lose its own undeclared nuclear monopoly. The purpose of this undeclared monopoly was neither status (as in

France's case) nor the imposition of a nuclear *pax Israeliana* on the Arabs (as the CIA suspected in the 1960s[22] and Saddam claimed to justify his own efforts to acquire the bomb[23]). Rather, the purpose was as an *insurance policy*. If all other means failed, if Israel's conventional power proved insufficient and if the United States did not stop an Arab military drive menacing Israel's survival, then, and only then, would Israel resort to nuclear threats.

Israel thus found it essential to prevent a nuclear stalemate. For the demise of Israel's tacit monopoly was an unacceptable situation in which the only usable weapons were conventional ones, arms the Arabs had in incomparably greater and ever-growing quantity. Underlying this logic was, of course, the very essence of the Arab-Israeli military dilemma: the absence of any form of mutually acceptable military equilibrium.

Before Iraq had embarked on a nuclear program, this problem had showed itself time and again in the conventional Arab-Israeli arms race. From Israel's viewpoint, the minimal requirement had been a military force able to achieve a quick victory over all Arab armies working in coordination and with complete surprise. Yet this meant that in a sense Israel always had a decisive edge over any *one* Arab army and that it always had a logical incentive for preemption.

But from the Arab standpoint this created a totally unacceptable situation. Thus, Egypt and subsequently Syria and Iraq struggled hard to evolve what the Syrians later called "strategic equilibrium" with the Jewish state. Translated into a nascent nuclear arms race, the lack of any point of conceivable equilibrium meant that the minimal requirement to make Israel feel secure created a sense of insecurity in the Arab world, whereas the minimal requirement to make the Arabs—in this case Iraq—secure was sufficient to make the Israelis feel that they were headed to a second holocaust in the same century.[24] This is how Begin's cabinet argued in its meetings of October 14 and 28, 1980, when it took the decision to attack Iraq's nuclear reactor at Osiraq.

THE ROAD TO WAR, 1981-1991

The destruction of Osiraq on June 7, 1981, took place at a time when Iraq's offensive in Khuzistan, whose initial success had been a critical factor in Israel's October 28 decision, had already bogged down. Nonetheless, the attack was launched out of fear that the reactor would soon go into operation.

Another incentive was the weakness of Iraq's position as an aggressor engaged in an expansionist war. Thus, Israel expected the reactions to its raid would be quite tolerable. Ultimately, the estimate was correct. Although there was a chorus of criticism on the raid—even the United States supported the UN condemnation of Israel—virtually everybody except the Iraqis was delighted to see the Iraqi nuclear program in ruins.

The Iraqis themselves, badly shaken, were determined to defy Israel, pick up the pieces, and proceed with their program to develop a whole panoply of unconventional weapons. Meanwhile, however, Baghdad had more pressing problems. The war was rapidly turning from a victory to a near calamity. Increasingly, the Iranians penetrated into Iraq's territory attempting to cut off Iraq completely from the Gulf and reach the Kuwait border. Under these circumstances, Iraq desperately needed Egyptian, Saudi, Kuwait, Jordanian, and, above all, U.S. support. The upshot was not only Iraqi rapprochement with Egypt but even indications of a changing attitude toward Israel.

This was the background to one of the most bizarre twists in Israel's encounter with Iraq. By silencing its criticism of Egypt's peace with Israel (in exchange for Cairo helping its war effort), Iraq seemingly rehabilitated itself in the U.S. government's eyes. Still reeling from the Iran crisis, the Americans were very receptive to the notion—peddled vigorously by Egypt—that Iraq was changing. In late 1984 this led to the resumption of full diplomatic relations between Washington and Baghdad.

The imaginative, indefatigable Nizar Hamdoun was sent to Washington as Iraq's ambassador. Hamdoun was fully aware of the fact that a number of high-powered Jewish Americans had worked hard in the process leading to the resumption of diplomatic relations. Their motives were irreproachable: A U.S. rapprochement with Iraq could conceivably be a starting point for a dialogue between Iraq and Israel and—who knows—perhaps even to Iraq joining Egypt in signing a peace treaty with the Jewish state.[25]

Yet for Hamdoun the implications were not quite identical. What he understood was not that Iraq had to go all the way to make peace with Israel, but rather that to gain U.S. backing for Iraq's war effort required signals of a changed Iraqi position on the Arab-Israeli conflict.

During 1987 this strategy gathered momentum. Leading Jewish personalities were increasingly invited to lavish receptions and dinners at the Iraqi ambassador's residence. Jewish and pro-Israeli academics were invited to Iraq, and those who went were given the red carpet treatment. Some of them then proceeded to write articles in influential publications such as the *New York Times*, the *New Republic*, the *New Yorker* and the *Middle East Journal* presenting Iraq in a new light. Gone were the charges of brutality and tyranny. If Iraq was not yet presented as a civilized pluralist democracy, the thrust of these reports was that a "new" Iraq was emerging that had learned its lesson the hard way in the war with the Iranian hordes.[26]

All this not only changed the climate of opinion in Washington but also had an impact in Israel. These were the days of the National Unity Government. Shimon Peres was prime minister and his diligent team of young disciples exuded boundless optimism about opportunities for a breakthrough in Arab-Israeli relations. The key to their peace strategy was an Israel-Jordan dialogue, but since Jordan was so closely aligned with Iraq, it seemed to be common sense to bring the Iraqis into the picture too. The notion that the Iraqis were ready to join in was enthusiastically encouraged by Husni Mubarak and occasionally backed up by a few Iraq-watchers in and around official circles in Israel.

Israel's Iraqi-born minister of energy, Moshe Shahal, was actually invited by President Mubarak to join him in a visit to Baghdad. Major General Avraham Tamir, a gray eminence who played a major role in the Egypt-Israel peace process, was also lobbying for exploratory contacts with the Iraqis and apparently engaged in some.[27] There was talk about an Iraqi oil pipeline to 'Aqaba with Israeli approval. An enormous amount of the war supplies flowing to Iraq came through 'Aqaba without any Israeli attempt to interfere.

All this occasioned a debate in the upper reaches of the Israeli government. Those who wanted to believe that Iraq was changing argued that the precepts of the periphery doctrine had been overtaken by events. Khomeini and his followers in Iran and Lebanon were so rabidly anti-Israeli that it was ludicrous to consider Iran a potential ally. Iraq, on the other hand, was showing signs of willingness to change. If Israel reciprocated these Iraqi feelers, it could perhaps obtain Baghdad's endorsement of the Egyptian approach to peace. This in turn would strengthen Jordan while isolating Syria (Iran's ally) and the PLO.

The trouble, however, was that proponents of this view had only indications, not real proof, of their analysis on Iraq.[28] Moreover, skeptics such as Minister of Defense Yitzhak Rabin—not to speak of the Likud partners in the cabinet—insisted that even if Iraq was sincere Israel did not have to choose between Iran and Iraq. The best policy might be to try to benefit from the conflict by taking a position somewhere between the two Gulf powers.[29]

The debate was never resolved because nothing ever came from the Iraqis to force a clear choice. Iraq achieved what it wanted—active U.S. support—when the Reagan administration, still reeling from the arms-for-hostages scandal, decided to reflag Kuwait ships in the Gulf. Thereafter the Iraqis had no use for any further wooing either of Israel or of its friends in the United States. Indeed, as the immediate aftermath of the Iran-Iraq war would reveal, Iraq remained just as hostile as it had been before Nizar Hamdoun had initiated his clever game.

In late 1988, analysts in Israel as elsewhere wondered if Saddam would turn back to his bad old ways of the late 1970s or whether had he learned a lesson making him favor reconstruction at home and stability in the region. From Israel's viewpoint, Saddam's choice could make the difference between war and peace. A mellow Saddam could help the peace process, pushing Jordan and the PLO to work together to reach an understanding with Israel. But an aggressive Saddam could transform the Arab-Israeli military balance in a way most alarming to Israel.[30]

Until the end of 1988, signs were still mixed. Saddam used chemical weapons against the Kurds and began to meddle in Asad's backyard in Lebanon. These were bad omens suggesting that Saddam remained the bully he had been before the war with Iran. At the same time some of the signals that had come from Baghdad during the war continued. Thus, late in 1988 or early in 1989, Minister of Defense Yitzhak Rabin was approached through Israeli businessman Azriel Einav by an American businessman of Arab origins with a message from Saddam. "Saddam views Rabin as the most powerful member of the Israeli Cabinet, and said he would be willing to meet him in order to discuss the interests of their countries." Rabin expressed interest and tentative dates for such a meeting were discussed. Before long it turned out, however, that the Iraqis were either not serious or had changed their mind.[31]

Rabin may have been interested for two different but related reasons. First, he believed Israel should examine seriously any chance for peace. Second, negotiations could at least check one more slide down a slippery slope leading to confrontation. The fact that Iraq was no longer fighting Iran was alarming from Israel's viewpoint because Iraq's army had grown to a huge size, gained presumably valuable combat experience, and, above all, had a missile capability that Israel could not easily block.

Rabin, already preoccupied by this in 1987, urged the Reagan administration to help Israel launch its own ATBM (the Arrow) program. The Americans (still largely in an anti-Iranian, pro-Iraqi mindset and having just extricated themselves from Israel's Lavi fighter aircraft program) were slow to react. The only way to prevail upon their hesitations was to attach the antimissile program somehow to the U.S. Strategic Defense Initiative.

In the summer of 1988, after a year of U.S.-Israel talks and a few weeks before the Iran-Iraq war's end, Rabin signed the first Memorandum of Understanding on the Arrow. But he knew it would take at least seven years before this weapon was ready. Meanwhile Iraq had used its SCUD missiles with devastating effect in its war with Iran. Rabin had to assume that Iraq would not hesitate to use this weapon against Israeli cities in another Arab-Israeli war.[32]

By late 1989, Iraq was clearly headed toward confrontation, not conciliation. Perhaps Saddam was only fomenting tension with Israel in the spring and summer of 1990 as a way of preparing to invade Kuwait. But this was not clear at the time and could hardly allay Israelis' apprehension.[33] They had seen before how Arab rhetoric gets out of hand and leads to war, and Saddam had made major errors of judgment before. Israel could do little apart from being alert, except perform a balancing act between not responding with sufficient vigor to Saddam's provocative threats (and thus encouraging him to think that Israel was weak) and, on the other hand, engaging him in an escalating war of words. Shamir's government appears to have been aware of this and handled the challenge with a steady hand.[34] But it could not admit that, if Saddam were not deterred, retaliation would be the only way to handle him, with all the complications that would involve. In Rabin's words:

> When I took office as Minister of Defense it was clear to me, that in the next war Israel would face simultaneously attacks in the front and on the rear. I knew the war would be harder and more painful [than anything we experienced in the past] and [that we will sustain many] more casualties. It is for this reason that the first thing which I stressed was the cultivation of our deterrence. Accordingly we made clear, in overt and covert ways, that our response to [their] hit on [our] rear will be the destruction of Arab capitals.[35]

What neither Iraqis nor Israelis could predict was that Bush would react to Saddam's invasion of Kuwait the way he did. For Israel, this was an almost unqualified blessing. For it ensured that Israel would not have to handle Saddam alone and that the United States would maintain a hegemonic presence in the Middle East as long as the Iraqi threat persisted. These factors gave Israel the fruits of an alliance at a very low cost. It did not have to undertake any commitments in exchange, and no one could even say that the 500,000 U.S. servicemen in Saudi Arabia were there to defend the Jewish state even though the net effect of their presence also did that.

This was the frame of mind in which Israeli officials and academics approached the gathering Desert Storm. Small wonder, then, that such a sober player as Rabin was almost carried away when General Schwarzkopf's troops proceeded to pulverize Iraq's military might. Rabin said:

> If anyone were to come and tell me a year ago that the decimation of Iraq's military might and possibly even the deposition of Saddam's megalomaniac regime, would be done by a huge force, and Israel would not have to shed the blood of her soldiers, and we shall have an advance warning of five and a half months before the outbreak of war—everybody would think [this person] was daydreaming. With all the anguish and misery caused by the [SCUD] missile attacks, this is a deluxe war.[36]

CONCLUSIONS

Israel's relations with Iraq have ranged between direct and indirect confrontation. As far as Israelis were concerned, Iraq was distant and the continuous confrontation with it was, consequently, quite unnecessary. The trouble, however, was that it was precisely this distance that had made Iraqi policy so reckless. Egypt, Syria, certainly Jordan, could be tamed through making them experience the costs of their struggle against Israel. This led Egypt to seek peace and Israel's other immediate neighbors to settle for a more or less stable truce.

But because of the distance Israel had no such dissuasive capacity vis-à-vis Iraq. As a result, Iraq could time and again use Israel as a punching bag, a target of opportunity and expediency not for its own sake but rather as a means of advancing the Baghdad regime's ambition. It was this logic that brought 16,000 Iraqi troops to the outskirts of Natanya, Hadera, and Haifa in 1948, and that brought Iraqi SCUD missiles on Haifa and Tel Aviv in 1991.

The lesson, then, is as clear theoretically as it is elusive as a policy proposition: As long as Iraq does not come to terms with itself and continues to search restlessly for a role in inter-Arab politics, it is likely to remain a source of agony not only to its own people and immediate neighbors but also to Israel, with which it has no common border and with which it does not really have any concrete quarrel.

NOTES

1. David Ben-Gurion, *The War of Independence,* Gershon Rivlin and Elhanan Orren, eds. (Tel Aviv, 1982), p. 225.
2. Ibid., p. 298.
3. Ibid., p. 856.
4. Ibid., p. 819.
5. Ibid., p. 955.
6. Ibid., p. 945.
7. Ibid.
8. For details, see Ian Black and Benny Morris, *Israel's Secret Wars* (London, 1991), pp. 86-95.
9. Report: 130.13/2595/8, "Meeting M. Comay and J. Chadwick (September 15, 1950)," in State of Israel, *Documents of the Foreign Policy of Israel, 1951* (Jerusalem, 1988), p. 537.

10. See Moshe Sharett, *Yoman Ishi* (Tel Aviv, 1978), pp. 232, 274, 374, 712, 868, 948-49, 984, 996, and 1248.

11. Ibid., pp. 1765, 1772, 1768, 1801, and 1812.

12. Moshe Dayan, *Avnei Derekh* (Jerusalem, 1976), p. 255.

13. Compare Ben-Gurion, *War Diary,* p. 853; David Ben-Gurion, "Al Ma Lahamnu, Madua Pininu, Ma Hisagnu?" *Ma'arachot* 296 (December 1984), p. 3. The latter is the text of a speech made shortly after the Sinai campaign and published posthumously.

14. For a detailed discussion of the same theme, see this author's *Deterrence Without the Bomb: the Politics of Israeli Strategy* (Lexington, Mass., 1987), pp. 88-97.

15. On Iranian-Israeli relations during this period see Soharb Sobhani, *The Pragmatic Entente: Israeli-Iranian Relations, 1948-1988* (Westport, Conn., 1989), pp. 33-64.

16. See Ofra Banjo, *The Kurdish Revolution in Iraq* (Tel Aviv, 1989), pp. 83-87.

17. See Rafael Eitan, *Raful—A Soldier's Story* (Tel Aviv, 1985), pp. 117-24; Arie Lova Eliav, *Rings of Faith* (Tel Aviv, 1983), pp. 156-64.

18. For details, see Yossi Melman and Dan Raviv, *The Imperfect Spies* (London, 1989), pp. 161-63; Eliezer Cohen (Cheeta) and Zvi Lavi, *The Sky Is Not the Limit,* (Tel Aviv, 1990), pp. 254-60 (Hebrew).

19. For more details, see Zvi Offer, *The Iraqi Army in the Yom Kippur War,* (Tel Aviv, 1986), p. 16 (Hebrew); and Cohen and Lavi, *The Sky Is Not the Limit,* pp. 317-20.

20. This author was a member of the advance party of paratroopers which was first to spot the Iraqi force. See also Brigadier General Moshe Bar-Kochba ("Bril"), "The Armored Campaign Against the Iraqis in the Yom Kippur War." *Ma'arachot,* (October-November 1977) pp. 258-59 (Hebrew). "Bril" was deputy commander of Lanner's armored division and handled personally the encounter with the Iraqi 3rd Armored Division.

21. For an abundance of details about the genesis of Israel's decision to attack the nuclear reactor, see Shlomo Nakdimon, *Tammuz in Flames* (Jerusalem, 1986). For an analysis of the impact of the holocaust on Begin's thinking, see Sasson Sofer, *Begin: An Anatomy of Leadership* (Oxford, 1988), especially Part 2.

22. See "secret" memorandum for the director of the CIA from Sherman Kent, chairman of the Board of National Estimates, in *Carrolton Press—Declassified Documents Recording System,* 1979/35B as quoted by Stephen Green, *Taking Sides* (New York, 1984), pp. 164-65.

23. Amatzia Baram graciously provided me with an excellent example of the use of this logic by Iraq in order to justify its effort to acquire nuclear weapons. In a June 23, 1981, speech Saddam Husayn said, "Irrespective of Iraq's

intentions and of its present or future capabilities, I believe that anyone or any state in the world which really wants peace and security and which really respects peoples and does not want them to be subjugated to foreign forces should help the Arabs in one way or another to acquire atomic bombs to confront the actual Israeli atomic bombs, not to champion the Arabs and not to fuel war, but to safeguard and achieve peace. Irrespective of the Arabs' intentions and capabilities and even if the Arabs do not want them and are unable to use them, I believe that any state in the world that is internationally and positively responsible to humanity and peace must tell the Arabs: Here, take these weapons in order to face the Zionist threat with atomic bombs and prevent the Zionist entity from using atomic bombs against the Arabs, thus saving the world from the danger of using atomic bombs in wars." See BBC Monitoring Service, June 24, 1981. This emphasis in Iraqi thinking was picked up by observers such as Gary Milhollin, head of the Wisconsin Project on Nuclear Arms Control, to argue that the key to the prevention of nuclear proliferation lay in some control over the Israeli nuclear program. As he put it in a recent testimony to Congress, "if you listen to what the Libyans or the Iraqis are saying on nuclear weapons, they explain that they are merely struggling to catch up with Israeli efforts in this field. The United States and the West have overlooked Israel's nuclear program for a long time, and now we see that the matter does not stay within the boundaries of Israel, but provokes reactions elsewhere. This is a chain reaction." Quoted by Ori Nir in "Peruz Garinin Mesukan" ("A Dangerous Nuclear Demilitarization"), Ha'aretz, December 20, 1990.

24. This analysis of the Israeli rationale draws primarily on this author's *Politika Ve-strategia BeIsrael* (Tel Aviv, forthcoming).

25. Private information.

26. Leading the charge were Daniel Pipes, Milton Viorst, and Laurie Mylroie. Compare the latter's article, "After the Guns Fell Silent: Iraq in the Middle East," *Middle East Journal* 43, no. 1 (Winter 1989), pp. 51-67.

27. On Maj. Gen. Avraham Tamir's role in the Egyptian-Israeli peace process, see his *A Soldier in Search of Peace* (New York, 1988), Part 1, as well as Ezer Weizman, *The Battle for Peace* (Jerusalem, 1981), pp. 127-28.

28. For example, a statement made by Iraqi Foreign Minister Tariq 'Aziz in an interview to Eric Rouleau published in *Le Monde* on January 8, 1983.

29. Private information, as well as Mylroie, "When the Guns Fell Silent."

30. See for example my own unpublished paper, "No Way Back: The Middle East in the Aftermath of the Iran-Iraq War," Washington, D.C., The Washington Institute for Near East Policy, 1988, mimeo.

31. *Ha'aretz*, November 5, 1990.

32. On Rabin's concerns with regard to Iraq's missiles, see his interview in *Ma'ariv*, February 22, 1991.

33. For obvious reasons there were few announcements about this but tension was already building. See, for example, this author's article, "The Iraqi Threat is Not an Israeli Invention," *Ha'aretz*, April 6, 1989. Also my article, "The Rifles Will Remain in the Depots," *Ha'aretz*, May 29, 1990.

34. See my article "Timren Heitev" ("Maneuvered Well"), *Ha'aretz*, November 28, 1990, commending Shamir's handling of Saddam's threats.

35. *Ma'ariv*, February 22, 1991. Also my, "The Rifles Will Remain in the Depots."

36. *Ma'ariv*, February 22, 1991. I anticipated by this in "The US Will Stay in the Picture," *Ha'aretz*, August 28, 1990, and in "Saddam's Aid to Israel," *Jerusalem Report*, November 15, 1990, and in "The New Strategic Landscape," *Ha'aretz*, March 5, 1991.

The World and Iraq

16

The United States and Iraq: From Appeasement to War

Barry Rubin

Within two years, from 1988 to 1990, Iraq went from being a virtual U.S. ally to becoming the first Arab state to fight a war with the United States. The development of this rocky relationship is one of the most interesting chapters in the history of U.S. policy toward the Middle East.[1]

At the start of the 1980s, U.S.-Iraq relations were extremely hostile. The new era ushered in by their common interests during the Iran-Iraq war could be described as somewhere between estrangement and alliance; if not an arm's length relationship, at least an elbow-length one. In September 1984, diplomatic relations were restored. The U.S. government developed some illusions about Iraq's intentions, especially between 1988 and 1990. But when Baghdad grabbed Kuwait in the latter year, the United States reacted strongly and defeated Iraq in the January-February 1991 Gulf war. Thus, while short-range interests had created a temporary harmony, this could not overcome the remaining differences.

Two essential factors have dominated U.S.-Iraq relations. First, the essence of Gulf politics was a strategic triangle between two stronger powers—Iran and Iraq—and the weaker Gulf Arab monarchies. This last group sought U.S. help to deter their mightier, aggressive neighbors. Toward this end, in the 1970s, the United States supported Iran against Iraq and, in the 1980s, it backed Iraq against Iran. In the 1990s, with both Tehran and Baghdad hostile, Washington had to intervene directly to save Saudi Arabia and Kuwait. In the long run, Iraq's goal was to dominate these states and the Gulf while the U.S. objective was to support regional stability and defend the monarchies.

Second, fundamental differences between the two states' systems made a clash inevitable. This point, so obvious between 1958 and 1978, became obscured after Iran's revolution. Thus, according to President Carter's national security adviser Zbigniew Brzezinski, America and Iraq wanted the same thing, "a secure Persian Gulf." The *Wall Street Journal* was equally starry-eyed: "The rhetoric shouldn't obscure the fact that Iraq, probably more than any other Mideast nation except Israel, is embracing Western values and technology." It was becoming an advanced secular society, "with a car in every garage, a television set in every living room, universal education, and chic French fashions for emancipated Iraqi women. Such a society should eventually become congenial to the West."[2]

Assistant Secretary of Defense Richard Perl took a more skeptical and ultimately accurate view: "It is foolish to think that a pro-Marxist, pro-Soviet Ba'th regime, the leader of Arab radicalism and rejectionism, is about to become an American ally or even a tacit partner without exacting an enormous price." It was dangerous to encourage Iraq's "imperial ambitions."[3]

The view that Iraq was being transformed into a moderate state was encouraged by U.S. commercial interests after Iraq's oil income zoomed upward in the mid-1970s. American business magazines ran headlines such as, "The Dramatic Turnaround in U.S.-Iraq Trade," "Iraq Starts to Thaw," and "New Scramble for $8 billion in Contracts." In May 1977 Carter sent a senior State Department official to Baghdad offering conciliation as part of a plan to "aggressively challenge" Moscow for influence in radical states. Carter and the Commerce Department were eager to let General Electric sell Iraq's navy engines for four Italian-built frigates until Congress blocked delivery as "contrary to common sense." Brzezinski announced in April 1980, "We see no fundamental incompatibility of interests between the United States and Iraq." Whatever their intention, such statements were taken by Baghdad as encouragement to attack Iran.[4]

This new attitude was in large part due to events in Iran, which became the common enemy of the United States and Iraq after the 1979 revolution in Tehran and seizure of U.S. diplomats as hostages, as well as Iraq's 1980 invasion of Iran. Now the United States wanted to rebuild relations with Iraq, a country that had long been second to none in anti-American vitriol and sponsoring terrorism, while Iraq needed help from the United States, a nation it had long portrayed as the headquarters of imperialism and Zionism.

The U.S. motive was a mere by-product of its effort to defend the Gulf monarchies; Iraq's incentive was to obtain help for its war against Iran. At first, though, Iraq was quite suspicious, charging that President Reagan was "malicious and hatred-filled" toward it, fearing that once the hostages in Iran were freed, the United States would return to its old alliance with that country.

When U.S.-Iran relations remained cold after 1981, however, Iraq and the United States began courting each other, with Baghdad's campaign assisted by Kuwait and Saudi Arabia. The Reagan administration sent a diplomat to Baghdad in April 1981 to test the waters. Secretary of State Alexander Haig claimed the Iraqis showed "a greater sense of concern about the behavior of Soviet imperialism in the Middle Eastern area." Trade increased and the U.S. government cleared the sale of five Boeing transport planes and International Harvester dump trucks. The number of Iraqi students in America tripled to 2,500. Vice President George Bush condemned Israel's 1981 destruction of Iraq's nuclear reactor as "not in keeping with international standards"—something he never said about Iraq's behavior—and endorsed a UN resolution against it. For expelling the Palestinian terrorist Abu Nidal, though his colleagues continued to operate from Baghdad, Iraq was dropped from the State Department's list of countries sponsoring terrorism.

Iraq also became a large market for U.S. agricultural exports, which supplied around 30% of its needs, a fact that endeared Baghdad to farm state legislators. Virtually all these sales were under U.S. government credit and subsidy programs that eventually totaled $1 billion a year. Iraq was the second largest export loan recipient and seventh largest subsidy recipient, receiving about $4 billion in the 1980s.[5]

More quietly, the United States gave Iraq satellite photographs of Iran's military positions and operations. While initiating Operation Staunch to block arms sales to Iran in 1983, the United States encouraged allies to sell weapons to Iraq. In many respects Iraq was treated as an ally. There was never any criticism for its being the aggressor or starting the tanker war. And in 1984, full diplomatic relations were restored.[6]

In contrast, though, Saddam's regime made few concessions to America. It did ignore a previous pledge never to restore relations as long as Washington supported Israel, and it accepted U.S. warships in the Gulf to convoy Kuwaiti tankers. Yet while Washington began idealizing Iraq, Iraq did not return the sentiment. Indeed, since Saddam believed Washington could end the war whenever it chose, its failure to do so implied a U.S. conspiracy to weaken Iraq. The secret U.S. arms dealings with Iran in 1985-1986 reinforced this mistrust.[7]

One of the most intriguing aspects of Iraq's charm offensive was the role of Nizar Hamdoun, the articulate, Westernized son of an Iraqi general. Fluent in

English, Hamdoun was the first Arab ambassador in Washington really to understand the American system: the importance not merely of contacts with U.S. diplomats, but also of influencing Congress, the media, and public opinion. As Iraq's representative until relations were reestablished and its ambassador thereafter until 1987, he befriended a wide range of opinionmakers and policymakers, even in the Jewish community, to convince them that Iraq was now moderate and deserved U.S. support.

One of his most striking innovations was to send a map, purportedly obtained from captured Iranian soldiers in 1985, showing their ultimate target to be Jerusalem. Hamdoun quoted Khomeini as saying, "Israel must be vanished from the face of the earth." The deliberate, but carefully unstated, implication was that Iraq was even fighting to protect Israel, as well as the Gulf monarchies.

Up to that point, the Reagan administration had followed a consistent position on the war. By being ostensibly neutral, it avoided entanglement in the fighting or pushing Tehran to ally with the Soviet Union, which had a long border with Iran and 100,000 troops in neighboring Afghanistan. The United States also sold arms to the Gulf monarchies to defend themselves.

At the same time, by tilting toward Iraq, Washington also helped block an Iranian victory that might turn the whole Gulf into an anti-American inferno of radical fundamentalism. Thus, the United States gave Iraq trade credits and intelligence. It did not discourage allies from selling Baghdad arms while embargoing weapons to Iran. Some U.S. friends—including Egypt, France, Jordan, and Saudi Arabia—aided Iraq; others—notably Israel, Pakistan, and Turkey—kept channels to Iran open through overt or covert trade and diplomacy.

With the Iran-Iraq war deadlocked by 1985, Baghdad and Tehran each sought a new route to victory. The two radical, anti-American states both saw the United States as the key to success. By secretly negotiating with the Reagan administration for arms and support, Iranian leaders tried to regain the use of an American card. By attacking Iran's tankers and oil facilities, Iraq tried to escalate the war to bring U.S. intercession. The Kuwaitis and Saudis acted the same way, disregarding the Palestinian issue and previous anti-interventionist demands to seek U.S. protection. Anti-American, Arab nationalist, and Islamic rhetoric all proved meaningless: Everyone wanted the favor of the superpower that held the balance of power.

The U.S. secret arms deals with Iran in 1985-1986 would become a source of Iraqi suspicion thereafter. But it should also be noted that Iran's initiative failed, while Iraq's strategy for gaining even more U.S. support worked. In 1985, Iraq began attacking Iran's tankers in an attempt to escalate the war. Only if the export of Gulf oil was endangered, Baghdad reasoned, would the great powers have to step in to end the war.

Iran hit back against the ships of Iraq's allies, especially Kuwait, and lashed out by sponsoring terrorism. As a result, Kuwait asked for U.S. naval forces to convoy its tankers, reflagged as American ships. The United States complied in 1987 and sporadically fought Iranian forces. As Iraq had hoped, this show of strength was matched by U.S. diplomatic efforts to push Iran into agreeing to a ceasefire. On July 20, 1987, the UN Security Council passed Resolution 598, demanding that the war come to an end.

Thus, Iran was steadily pushed on the defensive by three factors in 1987 and 1988. First, the United States assembled a multinational coalition for convoying tankers—including Britain, France, and Italy—to block Iranian attacks on them. Second, U.S. forces were willing to fight Iranian interference with shipping, while Iraq was free to continue attacking Iran's tankers. Third, Iraq launched successful attacks on land.

The turning point for Tehran came when a U.S warship shot down an Iranian airliner on July 3, 1988—mistaking it as an attacking plane—and killing 290 passengers. While labeling this incident a "barbaric massacre," Iran interpreted it as signaling an open U.S.-Iraq military alliance. Khomeini decided to end the war and announced a ceasefire on July 20, 1988. The United States had played a large part in winning the war for Saddam.

But from Iraq's point of view, rapprochement with the United States had been a temporary measure. After all, Iraq's ambition and aggression had been the direct cause of the war itself and the escalation into the tanker war. Defeating Iran gave Iraq its turn to try seizing the region. Having saved Iran's intended victims, Saddam set out to make them his own. The United States came to understand what was happening only when Saddam had already gone beyond the point where he could be deterred.

"Barring unforeseen circumstances," wrote the pro-Iraq journalist Fuad Mattar in 1989, "1990 and 1991 should be the year of Saddam Husayn in the United States." But he was expecting this would mean something far different from a crisis or war. On the contrary, he predicted, "Americans would love to see him on the television screen." They would find Saddam "as handsome as any star on the 'Dynasty' television series and like the hero of the famous 'Bonanza' television program who is always depicted as a brave man preserving his land and abiding by the law." Indeed, Americans might even ask "Why should Saddam Husayn not be the region's policeman, given the real vacuum?"[8]

Such expectations were laughably off the mark. Yet it is easy to understand why an Arab writer saw U.S.-Iraq relations as being so good at the time. The suave Iraqi ambassador Hamdoun masterfully courted and persuaded U.S. officials and opinionmakers during his time in Washington between 1982 and 1987. Some of his conquests seemed valuable. A former high-ranking State

Department official heading the U.S.-Iraq Chamber of Commerce wrote the *Washington Post* denouncing sanctions against Iraq as counterproductive.[9] A man of similar background, a paid lobbyist for Iraq, forced a foreign policy study group to revise its report so as to be more in line with Baghdad's interests. Young "experts," one of whom later held a high government job monitoring proliferation of unconventional weapons to Iraq, were flown to audiences with Saddam and their books were subsidized or circulated by Iraq's government.

The message was that Iraq was now a moderate state and the United States should support it. Yet if Hamdoun had been pushing at a locked door, he would have gotten nowhere. The fact was that U.S. and Iraqi interests did overlap during the Iran-Iraq war. Equally important was how American political culture dealt with such a situation. The United States wanted Iraq to like it rather than insisting Baghdad act in a manner worthy of America's esteem. The implication was that since Iraq could not be expected to back down, the United States must do so.

The word for this approach is appeasement. No U.S. official condemned Iraq's outspoken anti-Americanism or repression. Why go looking for trouble? The merchants of ignorance preached that any criticism of Iraq would bring a united Arab world to Baghdad's defense, just as their arguments implied that Arab states were doing America a favor by letting it help them.

The whole purpose of U.S. support for Iraq had been to stop Iran's expansionism. Nonetheless, when the war ended in August 1988, U.S. policy did not change. Most U.S. officials and experts expected Iraq to concentrate on development and reduce military spending. They did not really understand that Saddam put a priority on maintaining his power and realizing his ambition rather than putting the emphasis on reconstruction. After all, they reasoned, what country would be more likely to follow a pacific course than one that had just barely survived a terrible eight-year war?

But this only showed the cultural and intellectual gap between those accustomed to democracy and the behavior pattern of a radical dictatorship. Iraq had always spent much of its money on the military or prestige projects that strengthened the state without yielding much profit. Now it preferred to keep a huge army and expensive, top-priority programs to build superweapons.

Iraq's leaders, then, were armed, desperate, and dangerous. They drew confidence from their total control at home, victory over Iran, and huge military machine. While Saddam was playing rugby, America was playing croquet. He had never trusted the United States, even though the Reagan and Bush administrations largely trusted him. On the regional level, Saddam wanted to make it impossible for any Arab state to seek U.S. help against him. In bilateral relations, he shafted America at every opportunity and the United States exacted no price from him for this behavior.

For example, the White House had allowed the sale of 45 Bell transport helicopters to Iraq in 1985 on condition that it not use them for military purposes. Baghdad violated this promise, but no official criticism was voiced and the U.S. government permitted 60 more Hughes helicopters to be sold.[10]

Iraq even used U.S. credits to defraud American banks and illegally buy weapons. An astounding 2,500 letters of credit for a total of $3 billion were railroaded through the Atlanta branch of the Banco Nazionale del Lavoro between February 1988 and July 1989. Two-thirds of these loans eventually proved uncollectible. As evidence came to light, the State Department cautioned the Justice Department not to be too tough on the bank in its investigation and prosecution.[11]

An Egyptian-born U.S. citizen working at Aerojet General in California was jailed for trying to smuggle a restricted material for making missile nosecones in 1988 for joint Egypt-Iraq projects. Iraq's Ministry of Industry and Minerals filed fictitious export applications. State's own human rights report called Iraq's record "abysmal" and "unacceptable" but there was no U.S. government move to reduce credits then totaling $1 billion annually.[12]

The Reagan and Bush administrations also resisted any pressure to put sanctions on Iraq for its murderous treatment of the Kurds. Immediately after the Iran-Iraq war, Saddam forcibly moved about 500,000 Kurds to camps and razed 700 villages to create a security zone along that border. Amnesty International reported the imprisonment, torture, and murder of hundreds of children. American doctors examining Kurdish refugees discovered injuries caused by chemical weapons. The U.S. State Department found that Iraq had used such arms on Kurdish towns, killing about 8,000 people.[13]

Despite Iraq's crimes against U.S. laws and human rights, the White House did nothing, calling sanctions, "terribly premature and counterproductive, [endangering] billions of dollars" of business for U.S. companies. Senator John Heinz said the sanctions plan would only hurt U.S. business while Iraq bought arms and technology elsewhere. "Getting tough on the use of chemical weapons by Iraq," was just being "tough on certain U.S. exporters." In September 1988, the House of Representatives voted 388 to 16 in favor of economic sanctions against Iraq, but the White House succeeded in having the Senate water down the proposal. In exchange for Export-Import Bank credits, Iraq merely had to promise not to use chemical weapons again, with agricultural credits exempted from even this limited requirement.[14]

Thus, in response to Saddam's continued verbal attacks on the United States, Washington sent signals of weakness to Baghdad. Saddam interpreted such behavior as proof that the United States feared confrontation. Each act of appeasement increased Iraq's boldness without ever convincing it the United

States wanted friendship. The Americans "are out to hurt Iraq," one of its top leaders claimed. The problem was not that U.S. actions alienated Iraq but that the nature of Iraq's regime inevitably made it antagonistic to the United States.[15] But Iraq's massive military buildup became a self-fulfilling prophecy, increasing the very U.S. and Israeli antagonism that Iraq claimed to fear. Saddam's belligerent rhetoric and Baghdad's own publicity about new super-weapons, to impress its populace and other Arabs, sparked more Western news coverage and export controls. Once others began publicizing and criticizing Iraq's missile, chemical, bacteriological, and nuclear programs, Baghdad changed its tune. Now Iraq protested its innocence, claiming these reports were just a U.S.-Israel propaganda campaign to discredit Iraq and justify a military attack against it.[16]

While the U.S. government ignored much of this data by claiming it came from Israel or pro-Israel sources, U.S. intelligence estimated that Baghdad was only a few years away from building an atomic bomb. When it succeeded, said U.S. military expert Anthony Cordesman, will be known only "when one sees a mushroom cloud above northern Iraq."[17]

The United States did step up efforts to block Iraqi smuggling of materials and equipment useful in making unconventional weapons, but these nonproliferation efforts were often circumvented. The Commerce Department favored loose controls on technology exports to promote business and was quite willing, for example, to sell Iraq a high-temperature furnace useful in its nuclear program, which claimed was for medical purposes.[18]

With more patience, Saddam might have waited to invade Kuwait until he had an array of weapons—paid for by his intended victims and sold him by democratic states—sufficient to protect him from any outside interference. But Iraq's economic woes, Arab politics, America's apparent weakness, and his own ambitions moved Saddam forward throughout 1989 and 1990.[19]

Similarly, the United States also had policy options. Given Iraq's financial weakness, a U.S. cut in subsidies and credits would have undermined the regime's stability, giving it a big incentive to moderate its policies. But instead of pushing Saddam toward more caution, U.S. aid underwrote his military expansion and built up his confidence.

The U.S. refusal to define Iraq as a regional threat also made it complacent. During 1989 congressional hearings, Deputy Assistant Secretary of State Richard Clarke justified a $3 billion tank sale to Saudi Arabia by saying "Saudi Arabia lives in a bad neighborhood. . . . The principal military threat in the region is Iraq."

Representative Mel Levine then asked, "Do you believe that Saudi Arabia could repulse an Iraqi invasion?"

If the Saudis had a strong force, Clarke replied, it might deter Baghdad or "slow that attack down until the United States and other friendly forces were able to do something." But then Deputy Assistant Secretary Edward Gnehm, soon to be U.S. ambassador to Kuwait, leaped in. "I don't think it is appropriate to focus on Iraq as the principal threat because, in truth, at the present time, Saudi-Iraqi relations are good."[20]

By evincing no strong reaction to Iraq's use of chemical weapons on the Kurds, threats against Israel, outspoken anti-Americanism, or ultimatum to Kuwait, the United States had helped convince Saddam that he could get away with occupying and annexing his neighbor. By seeking to avoid any friction with Iraq, U.S. policy had helped precipitate a much bigger crisis.[21]

Having protected the Gulf Arab states from Iran in the 1980s, the United States now had to help defend Saudi Arabia and save Kuwait from Iraq. Otherwise, Saddam would be master of 20% of OPEC's production, able to dictate oil prices and production levels, use his income to build more horrible weapons, invade other countries, intimidate any opposition, and drive U.S. interests from the Gulf.

A post-Cold War era provided an opportunity for U.S. leadership to reduce international conflict. Yet failure to act strongly against Iraq's August 1990 invasion of Kuwait would make that event the first in a series of international depredations and crises.

In line with these considerations, Bush condemned Iraq's assault on Kuwait, demanded a quick withdrawal, froze the two countries' assets in the United States, and imposed sanctions on Iraq. He was backed by the European Common Market, the Soviet Union, and the Arab League. A U.S. mission led by Deputy National Security Advisor Robert Gates brought Saudi leaders satellite photos showing that Iraq was reinforcing its army for a possible attack on Saudi Arabia. In a total reversal of all previous Saudi policy, King Fahd invited U.S. troops in to protect his kingdom. The majority of the Arab League supported him.

Bush immediately responded to Fahd's invitation by ordering a massive U.S. military airlift to Saudi Arabia. A U.S.-led multinational force and an international coalition to embargo Iraq economically and isolate it politically were organized to make Iraq withdraw, without violence if possible, with force if necessary. Bush called Saudi Arabia's defense a vital U.S. interest and named the principles guiding U.S. policy: protection of Saudi Arabia and the Gulf; protection of U.S. citizens; the complete, immediate, unconditional withdrawal of Iraqi troops; and restoration of Kuwait's government. On August 30, Bush commented that he would not be disappointed if the Iraqi people overthrew Saddam but that this was not a U.S. objective.[22]

The Bush administration put Iraq on the list of countries supporting terrorism, reduced by two-thirds the Iraqi embassy's staff in Washington (after Baghdad closed the U.S. embassy in Kuwait), and canceled almost $7 billion in Egypt's debts. In a speech broadcast on Iraqi television, Bush explained to Iraq's people, "The pain you are now suffering from is a direct result of the course of action chosen by your leadership." He assured them, "It is impossible for Iraq to succeed."[23]

Unfortunately, after so much appeasement Bush was now unable to convince Saddam that he would back warnings with force. "If you fight us," said Saddam, "it will be a greater tragedy for you than Vietnam. . . . The United States would no longer be number-one in the world. . . . God is on our side and Satan is on the side of America. Can Satan win over God?" An Iraqi newspaper extended the analogy, "The U.S. military establishment lost in Vietnam thousands of victims and the army's military reputation against local forces who were less in power and ability." Americans could not bear the desert climate or accept heavy losses from Iraqi forces better armed and more experienced than the Vietnamese. Iraqi newspapers cited American publications, *Time* magazine for example, to show how their country was so powerful and how much the West feared it.[24]

The situation after August 2, 1990 was rich in irony. To avoid war and secure Iraq's withdrawal, the United States had to convince Iraq of its readiness to attack. To keep Kuwait, Iraq had to convince America of its fearlessness and the futility of fighting. This conflict was a recipe for confrontation. Nonetheless, many Americans—and an even higher proportion of Middle East experts—believed Saddam would withdraw. Instead, Iraq thought threatening war was its best weapon to make the Americans back down as they had done before.

Having committed his prestige and army to force Iraq out of Kuwait, Bush knew a failure to do so would be a devastating blow. It was tempting to believe that the anti-Iraq coalition could be maintained for the many months or years necessary to wear down Baghdad. Yet this seemed unlikely. If Saudi Arabia decided that the United States was bluffing, it would make its own peace with Baghdad and ask the expeditionary force to leave.

Nor would the domestic U.S. scene remain silent. Complaints about high spending, lack of clear purpose, and absence of loved ones would inspire public, media, and congressional criticism. As Saddam concluded that his aggression had succeeded, he would become more arrogant; as other Arabs thought him victor, they would rally against the West, Israel, and anti-Iraq regimes. Inaction would solve nothing and might actually destabilize the Middle East.

Negotiation was a more complex alternative. If Iraq was compelled to withdraw from Kuwait without gaining any advantage, it would be a defeat for Saddam. But if U.S. inducements were added to make his pullback attractive—

money, border changes, Iraqi control over Kuwait's new regime—the adventure would seem a triumph. Iraq might also wait until the last moment, then spin out endless talks to wear down the coalition. As long as serious exchanges were being held, there would be tremendous pressure on the United States not to take military action.

Despite the U.S. threats and military buildup in Saudi Arabia, Iraq had some reason to assume the coalition would not dare attack. Bush faced three problems in escalating to a confrontation. First, he had to unite his administration for a military option. Second, he needed to win public and congressional backing. Third, he had to hold together an international coalition whose members had disparate interests and policies.

But by refusing to offer an attractive compromise that might have split the U.S. government, public, or coalition, Saddam's own behavior made Bush's tasks easier. He also failed to see that Bush did pass these obstacles during the last three months of 1990.

While a U.S. president leads his own government he must muster support throughout its ranks to ensure his policy is implemented. At the start of the Kuwait crisis, Bush's lieutenants were split over whether the United States should refuse major concessions and go to war if Iraq did not withdraw. Defense Secretary Richard Cheney was Bush's closest ally in urging a tough policy. The other three top officials working on the issue—Secretary of State James Baker, National Security Advisor Scowcroft, and Chairman of the Joint Chiefs of Staff Colin Powell—were far more doubtful.

Baker was an old associate of the president but lacked foreign policy experience and worried about European and Arab reluctance to be steadfast. He preferred a compromise even if it meant making concessions to Baghdad on the Gulf or Arab-Israeli conflict. Scowcroft, a West Point graduate and air force pilot who had worked with in the Reagan and Ford administrations, had a similar view. He had been a major architect of the pro-Iraq policy before the invasion. His Middle East staffer, Richard Haass, had opposed efforts to pressure Baghdad all along, ridiculing the idea that Saddam might invade Kuwait.

Powell, the 53-year-old son of Caribbean immigrants, was the first black, first nonservice academy man, and youngest officer ever to be chairman of the Joint Chiefs of Staff. He had run the National Security Council and served two tours of duty in Vietnam. To him, however, the Vietnam syndrome was a warning for caution, not a bar on using force altogether. Powell's doubts were related to the military's concern that it have the forces and public support necessary to achieve victory. Otherwise, it might be caught in a new Vietnam-type dilemma in which its performance was criticized and reputation tarnished. No one expressed the effects of the Vietnam factor better than General Norman

Schwarzkopf: "I *hate* what Vietnam has done to our country! I *hate* what Vietnam has done to our Army! The government sends you off to fight its war. It's not *your* war, it's the government's war. . . . And suddenly, a decision is made, 'Well, look, you guys were all wrong.'"[25]

After spending almost two decades rebuilding their reputation, no one in the U.S. military wanted this to happen again. Already they were on the defensive, facing significant pressure to cut military spending because of the Cold War's end. Preparations were being made to shut down M-1 tank production, put battleships in mothballs, and withdraw many of the U.S. troops in Europe. For Powell and the Pentagon, Bush's commitment to give them the tools, freedom of action, and forces they deemed necessary consolidated their support. Of particular importance was Bush's agreement in early November to commit over 400,000 U.S. troops to the coming battle. Knowing they had political support and a clear mission, the military enthusiastically took up its usual professional attitude of getting the job done.

Several factors pulled together this government team by the end of October. Bush's subordinates, of course, fell into line to his command, but events were also showing them that the president was right. Saddam's behavior indicated no willingness to compromise; intelligence reports predicted the embargo could not succeed by itself. News of atrocities in Kuwait had a tremendous psychological effect increasing support for a tough policy.

Bush had more difficulty winning popular and congressional support at home than in mobilizing his own forces. The president was his own worst enemy in this regard, given his poor speaking ability and weakness at formulating a political vision. He never quite succeeded in explaining what the crisis was all about. The best presentations were made by Baker, chiefly in his October 29 speech to the Los Angeles World Affairs Council. America was acting on "hard and terrible experience," he explained. Iraq's aggression threatened to shatter chances for a better world at "one of those rare transforming moments in history." Appeasement was self-defeating because Iraq would grow stronger by building biological, chemical, and nuclear weapons. As a proven aggressor—Baker's citing Iraq's attack on Iran was ironic given the U.S. policy of tilting toward Baghdad during the war—Saddam would not stop until he was stopped. "If his way of doing business prevails, there will be no hope for peace in this area"; by seizing control of so much oil he could plunge the world into deep recession.[26]

The administration was "exhausting every diplomatic avenue to achieve a solution without further bloodshed," continued Baker, and the coalition was winning. "Every day as the sun sets, Iraq gets weaker. Every day as the sun rises, the international community remains firmly committed to implementation of the Security Council resolutions." But force must be used if necessary to ensure

Iraq reaped no reward for its aggression. "Let no nation think it can devour another nation and that the United States will somehow turn a blind eye. Let no dictator believe that we are deaf to the tolling of the bell as our fundamental principles are attacked. And let no one believe that because the Cold War is over, the United States is somehow going to abdicate its international leadership."[27]

As for public and congressional backing, a president set on war has a great deal of political capital through the loyalty inspired by patriotism and party, an ability to reward or punish legislators, and control over the events and images reported by the news media. There was a great deal of genuine outrage at the events unfolding in the Gulf, while the broad international support for U.S. actions was heartening. Before the end of 1990, Bush had won support from most of the American public.

He had a harder time, as sympathetic Democratic chairman of the House Armed Services Committee Representative Les Aspin put it, gaining "a political mandate for a military attack."[28] Members of Congress defended their prerogatives. After many foreign policy battles over Vietnam, Central America, and covert operations, Democrats were suspicious about the White House bypassing them. They argued that Bush had no legal authority to commit U.S. troops to war. Even Senator Sam Nunn, a hard-liner on defense matters, preferred waiting for sanctions to work.

Second, no politician wanted to be held responsible for a long, bloody, or disastrous war. The Republicans were nervous about the potential for a political catastrophe if the policy went wrong; the Democrats were eager to gain some partisan advantage from Bush's mistakes. Faced with an almost hopeless task of getting back into the White House, the opposition seized on the crisis as another case of Republican warmongering.

But it was hard for leftist demonstrators or liberal politicians to portray the issue as a new Vietnam or Nicaragua. Iraq was a ruthless aggressor; Kuwait, an undemocratic but real victim. The strategic stakes were undeniably high. The United States could not be said to be acting unilaterally—a favorite Democratic argument—given its broad supporting coalition and lavish use of the United Nations. In what passes for ideology in American politics, most Democrats were nervous about the use of force, which they identified with immorality. But in this case, force and morality, American leadership and multilateralism, were closely linked. The Democrats themselves were split. Ironically, each antiwar speech or demonstration fed Saddam's belief that Americans would not fight and, hence, made war far more likely.

Although a number of groups were organized to support the administration, there were still criticisms—particularly over using force—from both the left and right ends of the political spectrum. The antiwar movement never got over its inherently problematic contradiction of refusing to oppose the unprovoked aggression by a dictator who so viciously violated human rights. More appealing was the wishful thinking that a long siege strategy would work. The embargo and boycott, wrote the *New York Times* columnist Tom Wicker, were "squeezing Iraq" into a resolution, whereas war "would shatter the anti-Iraq coalition" since it was uncertain that Arab states could "lead their populations into full-scale war against a brother Arab nation."[29]

The Bush administration correctly rejected linkage. Not only was strengthening Iraq's position against U.S. interests, but Saddam gave no indication that it would work. Bush tried to address Iraq's arguments in an October UN speech by saying he would address the Arab-Israeli conflict and remove troops from the Gulf as soon as possible after the crisis ended. Trying to reverse the linkage issue, Bush suggested it was Saddam's fault that no progress was being made on the Arab-Israel issue.

Unfortunately, these statements had the exact opposite effect on U.S. public opinion and Iraq from what Bush intended. Listeners heard Bush hint that Iraq's withdrawal from Kuwait would bring more U.S. concessions and disclose an impatience to bring the troops home. The media took Bush's comments to mean that he was accepting linkage; the French and Soviets launched initiatives that would give Iraq rewards for eventually leaving Kuwait. From Iraq's standpoint, the anti-Saddam coalition was weakening.

Paradoxically, the more eager the United States appeared to reach a peaceful solution, the less chance for successful negotiations with Iraq. Bush's behavior confirmed Baghdad's thinking that the Americans, fearing a fight, could be outwaited and outwitted. Once again, U.S. policy suffered because it was acting from an illusory position of weakness rather than asserting its power and determination.

While the administration wanted to exhaust all peaceful means to resolve the dispute, it concluded that time was limited. By the end of October, U.S. officials thought sanctions would take too long to work by themselves. Intelligence reports warned that Iraq was dismantling Kuwait and nearing a point of no return after which it could not be rebuilt. U.S. officials worried that the Saudis would not indefinitely host so many foreign forces and that domestic, European, and Arab support would diminish. The war must start before March 1991, explained an Egyptian magazine, because if Iraq could stall until the holy month of Ramadan, the pilgrimage to Mecca, and the hot summer, it would stay in Kuwait for over a year and hence, perhaps, forever.

Baghdad could have used diplomacy for this purpose, assuming that U.S. public opinion and allies would not permit war to start while there was still hope of a peaceful solution. Or it could offer to pull out of part of Kuwait, excluding some oilfields and strategic islands, for financial remuneration. That might have divided the anti-Iraq alliance and thrown U.S. policy into confusion. But Iraq did neither. Saddam made a strategic error, just as he did in 1980 when he thought Iran would sue for peace or collapse.

Iraq was not bargaining toughly; it was simply not bargaining at all. Contrary to Baker, Saddam also believed that every day as the sun rose his position was stronger. America could not fight and lacked the stamina to continue the confrontation for very long. The fact that the United States had more airplanes than Iraq was irrelevant. For him, the real question was whether America would use them. Thus, he played for time, reasoning that Bush was losing the battle to hold together his international alliance and to hold off domestic criticism.[30]

Aside from continued hope in total success, Saddam and his regime had another incentive to avoid withdrawal from Kuwait: The regime's legitimacy rested on intimidating its own citizens and neighbors. The Iraqi public's awe toward the ruling elite—a necessary component in the regime's survival—could be shattered if Saddam appeared cowardly. Thus, Iraq never showed an interest in accepting border changes or islands even though a partial victory would allow Saddam the increased prestige that would make him an Arab hero and prompt Saudi Arabia and its neighbors toward future appeasement. Surrounded by yes men and profoundly ignorant of the outside world—characteristics shared by many other dictators—he was walking into a trap of his own devising.[31]

Since the United States held firm against Iraq, Arab states in the coalition did not buckle either. But acknowledging the partial accuracy of Saddam's analysis, the United States knew it did not have unlimited time. The Bush administration pushed for the deadline set in UN Security Council Resolution 678 of November 29, decreeing that Iraq must withdraw or face war by January 15, 1991. Iraq rejected the deadline, but Bush made a final offer to invite Tariq 'Aziz to Washington and send Baker to Baghdad to try to avert war. Iraq proposed December 17 for the first visit and January 12 for the second, a schedule the United States saw as a stalling tactic. The United States responded by suggesting 15 dates between December 20 and January 3, 1991, all rejected by Iraq.

As a last-ditch effort to avoid war, Bush offered high-level talks before the deadline. When it was announced that Baker would meet Tariq 'Aziz on January 7, 1991, Iraq claimed victory, since the United States had previously rejected negotiations until Iraq left Kuwait. High Iraqi officials had been telling visiting journalists of secret meetings in Europe. A deal, they hinted, was in the making. American officials thought Iraq was weakening. Iraq thought that the United States was so concerned about the costs of war that it was looking for an excuse to back down.

Thus, at the seven-hour meeting at the Intercontinental Hotel in Geneva, a delighted 'Aziz exuded confidence though no progress was made. He told Baker they could resolve everything. "If the American administration changes its position and works with us," Iraq "would love to be partners" in the new world order. Baker's assessment was different. He was there not to negotiate but to communicate a warning. Obviously, Baker did not communicate very persuasively. According to intelligence sources, Saddam's relative and trusted personal watchdog in Geneva, Barzun Tikriti, reported that the United States would not go to war. Misunderstanding reached an all-time high.

From Iraq's standpoint, public opposition was rising. Every demonstration and critical speech shown on Cable News Network (CNN) was seen at Iraq's Foreign Ministry, Information Ministry, and Presidential Palace. For Iraqis, living in a society where no dissent was permitted and democracy was poorly understood, Bush seemed to face something approaching an internal revolt. Iraqi propaganda held the United States to be a soft, flabby democracy. According to Saddam, America had retreated from Vietnam and Lebanon and deserted the Shah. Saddam, Iraqi officials told visiting journalists and diplomats, was ready to sacrifice tens of thousands of lives. Smiling Iraqi officials asked, "Do you really believe that Bush is ready to do the same?" They shook their heads. "No, this is unlikely."

But if this was propaganda, it is not unusual for Middle Eastern dictators to believe their own claims. How serious could Bush be if he called Saddam a Hitler and rejected negotiations until after an Iraqi withdrawal, then agreed to talks? Americans never understood how Iraq and other Arab states saw their acts before, during, or after the crisis. The techniques that served Saddam so well in the past—intimidate your enemy, force him to surrender by refusing to concede, make clear the high price he would pay—were used yet again.

Five days after Baker and 'Aziz met in Geneva on January 7, 1991, Congress passed a joint resolution after a sharp debate—in the Senate, 52 to 47; in the House, 250 to 183—authorizing Bush to use force. The deadline came on January 15. With no Iraqi pullback, the United States and the coalition implemented the UN ultimatum and attacked at dawn on January 16, 1991.

Once again in its dealings with Iraq, the United States had exaggerated the inevitability of moderation prevailing. In 1980, Saddam expected an easy victory over Iran. A decade later, he believed that the United States would do nothing if he took over Kuwait and greatly overestimated Arab support for Iraq.

In relations with Iraq, U.S. policy in the 1980s had helped strengthen Baghdad and lay a basis for the Kuwait crisis. The need to counter Iran made this partly necessary, but its extension into the postwar era further fed Saddam's misunderstanding of U.S. behavior. During the Kuwait crisis, the Bush administration took a better measure of Iraq's ambitions and countered them. Yet even then it did not undermine Saddam's confidence that Bush really sought a face-saving way out.

In the January-February 1991 war, the U.S.-led coalition totally defeated Iraq militarily. Diplomatically, however, the old patterns of bilateral relations partly reasserted themselves. The U.S. government's refusal to overturn Saddam or help antiregime rebels after the war allowed the dictatorship and its arrogance to survive. The United States tried to continue sanctions and pressures against Iraq's unconventional weapons programs. U.S.-Iraq relations had come full circle to the hostility of the 1960s and 1970s, but the impact of the historic lessons experienced in the interim had been blunted.

NOTES

1. The subject is explored further in the authors *Cauldron of Turmoil: America in the Middle East* (New York, 1992).

2. *Washington Post,* June 12, 1977; See various publications cited in Amos Perlmutter, "The Courtship of Iraq," *New Republic,* May 3, 1980; *Wall Street Journal,* April 29, 1981.

3. *Wall Street Journal,* April 29, 1981; Amatzia Baram, "Saddam Hussein: A Political Profile," *Jerusalem Quarterly* 17 (Fall 1980).

4. *Business Week,* August 4, 1975, and June 6, 1977; *Newsweek,* July 4, 1977; "MacNeil/Lehrer Report," April 19, 1980, transcript, pp. 19-22.

5. Susan Epstein, "The World Embargo on Food Exports to Iraq," Congressional Research Service, September 25, 1990; *Washington Post,* August 8 and 13, September 16, 17, 1990; *Los Angeles Times,* August 7, 1990. See also Paul Gigot, "A Great American Screw-Up," *The National Interest* (Winter 1990-1991).

6. *Washington Post,* April 11, 1981.

7. Ibid.; Amatzia Baram, "Saddam Hussein: A Political Profile," *Jerusalem Quarterly* 17 (Fall 1980).

8. Fuad Mattar, *al-Tadamun* (London), July 10, 1989, in *Foreign Broadcast Information Service (FBIS),* July 26, 1989, pp. 19-23.

9. Letter from Marshall Wiley, *Washington Post,* October 20, 1988.

10. *Washington Post,* October 6, 1988.

11. *The Economist,* October 27, 1990.

12. *New York Times,* May 23, 1990.

13. *Los Angeles Times,* July 12, 1989; *Washington Times,* August 16, 1989; *New York Times* and *Washington Post,* March 1, 1989; February 8, 1989, briefing transcript; *Le Monde,* November 10, 1988.

14. *Washington Times,* October 17, 1988; *Washington Post,* October 12, 1988; letter from Marshall Wiley, *Washington Post,* October 20, 1988.

15. *Washington Post,* October 4, 6, and 12, 1988; Taha Yasin Ramadan, *al-'Anba,* October 8, 1988 in *FBIS,* October 12, 1988, pp. 27-30).

16. See, for example, *New York Times,* January 17, 18, 29, and 31, 1989; *Washington Post,* January 14 and 19, 1989; *Washington Times,* January 19, 1989. Publicity about a new Libyan factory for making chemical weapons heightened attention on the issue. *Washington Times,* March 8, 1989. Iraqis began seeking chemical production facilities in the 1970s and, by the early 1980s, established plants able to produce up to 1,000 tons of such poison material a year.

17. *Washington Times,* December 14, 1989. For a tour of an Iraqi nuclear facility, *Alif Ba,* July 26, 1989, in *FBIS,* August 7, 1989, pp. 18-20.

18. Not all American politicians understood the importance of nonproliferation. Former president Jimmy Carter announced, "It may be that the very knowledge that there are chemical, biological and nuclear weapons in the Middle East will cause these leaders to be cautious in what they do."

19. *Washington Post,* September 13, 1990.

20. House Foreign Affairs Committee hearings, November 7, 1989, Federal Transcripts; *Middle East Mirror,* November 15, 1989, p. 25.

21. Interviews with U.S. officials; *Washington Post,* February 9, 1990.

22. *New York Times,* August 29, 1990; Baker testimony to Senate, September 5, 1990.

23. *New York Times,* September 12, 1990; speech of September 16 (*FBIS,* September 17, 1990). See also Baker's testimony to the Senate Foreign Relations Committee, September 4, 1990.

24. See, for example, *al-Thawra,* October 1, 1990. Other Iraqi propaganda themes—as in *al-Thawra,* October 10, and *al-Qadisayya,* October 16—included the spread of corruption in Saudi Arabia by Western troops and Iraq's use of disinformation to fool the enemy. Baghdad Radio, November 7, 1990, in *FBIS,* November 8, 1990.

25. C. D. B. Bryan, "Operation Desert Norm," *New Republic,* March 11, 1991.

26. Transcript of speech.

27. Ibid.

28. *New York Times,* August 28, 1990.

29. On pro-administration groups, see the Committee for Peace and Security in the Gulf press release, December 12, 1990 and "The Stakes in the Gulf," *New Republic,* January 7-14, 1991. The critical remarks are from Tom Wicker, "The Wrong Strategy," *New York Times,* November 14, 1990.

30. *Al-Sharq al-Awsat,* December 2, 1990, in *FBIS,* December 5, 1990; *al-Masa,* November 25, 1990.

31. My thanks to Dr. Amatzia Baram for suggesting some of these points.

17

Western Europe and Iraq: The Cases of France and West Germany

Helmut Hubel

When the Gulf War ended on February 28, 1991, the world could feel relieved that Saddam Husayn had neither used his French-made sophisticated fighter aircraft nor fired his chemical warheads or improved SCUD-B missiles that German and other Western companies helped him produce against Israel, Saudi Arabia, or coalition soldiers. If that had happened, the war's outcome might have been different and Germany would have probably faced its worst international crisis since World War II.

France and Germany were not the only Europeans that had dealt with Iraq. British, Italian, and many other West European companies had profited from selling almost everything industrialized countries could offer. In most instances, these transactions were primarily commercial, not political. Only for France did political considerations play a principle role, part of the strategy to bolster its "grandeur."

To this day, Western Europe has never behaved as a homogeneous political actor. Despite the Common Market countries' efforts to unify their foreign policies, they did not pursue a common approach toward the Gulf in general or Iraq in particular. The Iraq-Kuwait crisis confirmed this experience. This does not mean that there has been no common policy at all. Regarding issues of "low politics"—such as common declarations, peace diplomacy, or development aid—one can indeed find a West European position. Yet in issues of "high politics"—particularly in security matters or arms exports—one still has to speak about different national approaches.

Therefore it does not make sense to speak about a single or coherent West European policy toward a Middle Eastern country such as Iraq. There are only a few basic attitudes most West Europeans shared toward that country. Since its 1958 revolution Iraq was an "outsider" in the Gulf, refusing close ties with the British or Americans and quarreling with the region's monarchies. When the Soviet Union began cooperating with the Baghdad regime, West Europeans predominantly understood this relationship as part of the global East-West conflict. In the 1970s some West Europeans legitimized their dealing with Iraq by arguing that it would "weaken Soviet influence in the Gulf." Developing ties with Iraq—they explained—would be politically beneficial also to the United States, since Washington did not have formal relations with Baghdad after June 1967.

Second, and more important, was a common economic interest for the energy-dependent Europeans, especially after the 1973-1974 oil price increases. Since the Iraqi regime engaged in an ambitious development program, many Europeans saw their chance to "recycle petrodollars" by selling industrial goods and services in exchange for oil.

The third principal interest arose after Khomeini's Islamic revolution in Iran. The West European governments—similar to many Arab states, the United States, and the Soviet Union—feared that the spread of Khomeini's revolution would damage their economic and political interests in the Middle East. Neglecting the fact that Iraq started the war against Iran, most West Europeans regarded Saddam Husayn's regime as the bulwark against the Islamic fundamentalist tide.

These three factors may characterize a general West European attitude. Yet they are insufficient to explain the considerable differences between these countries' behavior. The cases of France and the Federal Republic of Germany do not fully represent Western Europe. Rather, they represent extreme positions on the spectrum.

France, more than any other West European or Western country, had a distinct policy toward Iraq. After the 1973-1974 oil crisis the French pursued a policy of forging "privileged relationships" with key Third World countries, including Iraq. From France's perspective, close relations should serve both political and economic purposes. West Germany, on the other hand, focused mostly on European affairs and had no political ambitions toward Baghdad. German interests were primarily economic: to secure export markets.

FRANCE AND IRAQ: THE "PRIVILEGED RELATIONSHIP"[1]

Since 1967, when President Charles de Gaulle stopped French military supplies to Israel, France pursued a distinctive approach toward the Arab world. After France ended its Algerian entanglement in 1962, it felt free to reestablish a prominent role in the Middle East. Having broken with NATO in 1966, France did not want to leave the Middle East either to the United States or the Soviet Union. This quest for political "grandeur" as a "third force" was supported by a strong economic interest. Depending heavily on oil and gas imports, France was determined to establish privileged political relations to secure its energy needs.

The test of this approach came in 1973-1974, after the first oil crisis. When the United States and the other West Europeans established a "countercartel" against OPEC—the International Energy Agency—France did not join. Instead, Paris took the opposite approach of establishing "privileged relations" with oil-and gas-producing countries such as Algeria, Iraq, Libya, Nigeria, and Saudi Arabia. Iraq, then aiming at lessening its dependence on the Soviet Union, responded quickly. To pay for oil imports, France wanted to increase its exports: industrial goods and services, nuclear power plants, and weapons. Saddam Husayn realized the opportunity the French were offering to him, and he decided to gain a West European foothold.[2]

In exporting fighter aircraft, helicopters, tanks, missiles, and the like, France was also aiming at securing its independent arms procurement. Developing and producing arms only for the French army would not have been feasible without exports. Thus, the customers of French weapons, such as Iraq, Libya, and many others, served to "guarantee" French military and political independence.[3] This threefold approach—political "grandeur," economic advantage, and maintenance of an independent arms industry—explains the scope and intensity of French-Iraqi relations.

In dealing with Iraq, France acted like the Soviet Union. Whereas Iran under the rule of the Shah and the monarchies on the Arabian peninsula were more or less an Anglo-American sphere of influence, Moscow and later Paris decided to take care of the "outsider." France offered special advantages to an Iraqi regime that wanted to avoid excessive dependence on the Soviet Union and to obtain superior Western technology at affordable prices.

French-Iraqi economic cooperation started in the 1960s. After Iraq nationalized its oilfields in 1972, energy cooperation intensified. France was Iraq's third most important trading partner and second most important customer of oil. In 1974, responding to the first "oil shock," French Gaullist leaders initiated an even closer relationship, inaugurated by visits of Foreign Minister Michel Jobert and Prime Minister Jacques Chirac in Baghdad. On November 18, 1975, Chirac signed the first agreement on nuclear cooperation with Saddam Husayn.

This contract and the following agreements were part of the French strategy to deal with the repercussions of the oil crisis by establishing special relations between industrialized and developing countries. France concluded similar nuclear agreements with Iran, South Africa, Pakistan, and South Korea. Seeking a great-power role in nuclear energy, the Gaullists had an "essentially fatalistic" approach toward the problem of proliferation: "In a world of inequality and violence the spread of nuclear weapons was regarded as 'natural' and consequently as unavoidable."[4] A French investigative journalist quoted a French "high official" as saying that the decision to build the Osiraq reactor was aimed to balance forces in the region as a counter to Israel's nuclear capacity.[5]

After Chirac left office in August 1976, President Valéry Giscard d'Estaing canceled some nuclear agreements. The agreement with Iraq, however, remained valid. Since the second half of the 1970s French business invested heavily in Iraq's oil and construction industry and in telecommunications. Weapons sales increased. The biggest project was the sale of 60 Mirage F-1 fighter aircraft, concluded in 1977. Other major items were AMX-30 tanks, helicopters, and missiles.[6] From 1977 to 1985 French arms' sales to Iraq reached 55,8 billions francs (almost \$12 billion).[7]

When Saddam Husayn attacked Iran in September 1980, France remained his staunchest ally. After Iran's Islamic revolution, French hope of building close ties with the new regime were quickly disappointed. Although Giscard d'Estaing had given Khomeini asylum and had tolerated his political activities on French soil (including speeches calling for the Shah's overthrow), Khomeini showed no gratitude. The spread of an Iran-inspired Islamic revolt to the Arab world would have severely threatened French political and economic interests, while supporting the Arabs against Khomeini would enhance France's regional interests. Thus, France's continuing military support of Iraq was a strategic decision.

Compare French reactions in 1980 with President Charles de Gaulle's policy during and after the 1967 war of punishing the "aggressor" Israel by stopping French military supplies. During the 1980s French presidents Giscard d'Estaing and François Mitterrand continued large-scale supplies to the aggressor Iraq.

In March 1980, shortly after the Soviet intervention in Afghanistan, President Giscard d'Estaing visited the Gulf monarchies. His major interest was to secure Saudi-Arabian energy supplies and credits to deal with the consequences of the second oil crisis. To achieve this goal, Giscard d'Estaing also modified the French position toward the Palestinian problem by stressing now that the "Palestinian people" had the "right of self-determination." In France some observers criticized this gesture, arguing that the president was now "exchanging Palestine for Petrol."[8]

The Israeli attack against the French-Iraqi nuclear reactor in June 1981[9] confronted the newly elected President François Mitterrand with his first

Middle East challenge. During his election campaign Mitterrand had criticized his predecessor's decision to sell highly enriched uranium to Iraq. Further, he had called for improving French-Israeli relations and reviewing French arms sales policy. Therefore, the new French government reacted cautiously. Mitterrand confirmed that France would not allow nuclear technology to be used militarily. After several years of intense negotiations, Iraq's government agreed that France would deliver lower-enriched fuel (*Caramel*) and French technicians would oversee the rebuilding of the reactor.

Despite Iranian protests, Paris continued to deliver sophisticated weapons to Iraq. French support became even more important after 1982, when Iran's forces gained the initiative and threatened to break through the front. Iraq was no longer able to export large quantities of oil. In response, Baghdad decided to widen the war by declaring the northern Gulf as "war zone." At this time Iraq's debts to France had risen enormously. A military defeat of Saddam Husayn also would have resulted in grave French financial losses.

It seems no coincidence that the major financial agreement in May 1983, in which Iraqi debts were rescheduled and Saudi Arabia provided additional oil deliveries, was followed by new French arms deliveries to Iraq. It was the "Saudi connection" that alleviated French financial concerns. France had managed to develop the relationship with Iraq and the Gulf Cooperation Council (GCC) countries simultaneously and to establish a kind of triangular relationship: Paris would support Iraq with sophisticated weapons, and Saudi Arabia and its GCC partners would pay the growing Iraqi debts in cash, credits, or oil.

In lending five Super-Etendard fighter aircraft to Iraq (carrying the Exocet missile), Paris enabled Saddam Husayn to pursue his economic warfare against Iran. The Super-Etendards managed to hit Iranian tankers but did not destroy the crucial oil terminals on Kharg island. It was only in August 1985 that Mirage F-1 and other fighter aircraft managed to damage these Iranian oil facilities severely. (There have been rumors that French pilots helped to do the job.) Finally, French, Soviet, and other countries' military support of Iraq was insufficient to end the war. U.S. military intervention in 1987-1988, defending Kuwaiti oil tankers against Iranian attacks, was probably the crucial factor that exhausted Iranian fervor and led to the ceasefire. After the Iraq-Iran war French foreign minister Roland Dumas tried for a more balanced policy between Baghdad and Tehran.

Traditional French policy toward the Arab states could work only as long as Iraq and the GCC countries were united against the "Iranian threat." When Saddam Husayn and conservative Gulf rulers started quarreling about territory, oil production, and prizes, the French approach could no longer be sustained. After Iraq's intervention in Kuwait, France became a victim of the crisis.

Pursuing high-level contacts with Baghdad, Paris was only able to manage the release of French hostages in Iraq and Kuwait a few weeks earlier than others. As the confrontation quickly turned into an Iraqi-American one, France (like the Soviet Union) could no longer use its "special relationship" with Baghdad for a distinct political role. Also, Iraq's aggression divided the Arab world and finally forced France to take sides. Already in May 1991 Paris had stopped arms' deliveries to Iraq due to Baghdad's nonpayment.

One week after Iraq invaded Kuwait France sent additional ships and helicopters to the Gulf. On August 21 President Mitterrand ordered some armed forces to Saudi Arabia and the United Arab Emirates. It was after Iraq had ignored warnings from Paris and occupied the French embassy in Kuwait only on September 14 that France substantially increased its military engagement. Already in August French-U.S. secret talks on Iraqi arms delivered by France had started.[10] Mitterrand regarded close cooperation with Washington essential not only because of the Middle East challenge. At a time of fundamental change in Europe, he wanted to keep the Americans in Europe to "balance the Soviet Union militarily and Germany politically."[11]

Nevertheless, Mitterrand's peace plan of September 25, 1990, and last-minute initiative before January 15, 1991, when the UN deadline ran out, offered Saddam Husayn a face-saving way out because they linked the Iraqi troop withdrawal and the restoration of Kuwait's sovereignty with international efforts to deal with other Middle Eastern crises.

President Bush was determined not only to force Iraq out of Kuwait, but to disarm Saddam Husayn as well. France's mediating approach—Mitterrand's emissaries were said to have kept contact with Iraqi officials throughout the crisis—would have left Iraq's arsenal intact. When Bush began the air war, France's policy toward Iraq fell into shambles. Some members of the French "political class" did not want to accept this fact, such as Defense Minister Jean-Pierre Chevènement, who resigned on January 30, 1991. Yet Mitterrand again proved himself a brilliant tactician and—with some hesitation—joined allied attacks against Iraqi military installations also on Iraqi territory. Ironically, rather old French Jaguar fighters attacked Iraq's modern arsenal, 20% of which came from France. Finally, French Foreign Legion units took the lead in encircling the Iraqi forces fleeing from Kuwait.

In a balancing act of great virtuosity Mitterrand managed to stay on the right side and to preserve "France's role and rank."[12] However, Foreign Minister Dumas soon had to concede that France's "politique arabe," the traditional policy toward the Arabs, was now a "myth."[13] France's government and taxpayers were also left with an Iraqi debt of about 24 billion francs.[14] Finally, the French armament industry lost its biggest customer.

THE FEDERAL REPUBLIC OF GERMANY AND IRAQ: THE PRIMACY OF ECONOMICS

While France and Britain, the two former European colonial powers in the Middle East, wanted to play a special political role in the Gulf, West Germany had no such ambition. Its preoccupation with domestic and European affairs was intensified by the East European revolutions in 1989 and the painful process of German social and economic unification in 1990. The Iraq-Kuwait crisis could not have happened at a worse time for a Germany preoccupied with the final negotiations on unification.[15] It was a shock for most Germans that the "peace diplomacy" that had worked brilliantly in Europe now failed miserably in the Gulf.

To understand German attitudes and behavior during the Kuwait war, some basic points should be made. There is no coherent German Middle East policy but rather a set of principles guiding reactions to events in that area. One factor is the special German-Jewish history, German responsibility for the Holocaust, and a general desire to support Israel. This attitude is widely shared among leading politicians of all major parties and the general public.

On the other hand, there has never been any German-Arab armed hostility. In 1965 Arab governments broke diplomatic relations with West Germany because it established diplomatic relations with Israel. At the same time West Germany stopped delivering weapons to Israel, something it had done secretly since 1957. When West German-Arab relations were resumed after 1969, the former's problem in dealing with Arab governments was that they often expected more political and military support than Bonn wanted to deliver.

Absorbed by the East-West conflict and Germany's division, the West German government did not want to engage in high-risk Middle East endeavors. Close links with Israel were sought not only for historical reasons; they also fit well with the U.S.-Israel and the U.S.-West German special relationships. It was after the impact of the 1973-1974 oil crisis, (and after the government had tolerated East Germany as a "second state in Germany") that Bonn sought to develop a "more balanced approach" toward the Middle East. Following the lead of France and Great Britain, the Federal Republic joined the declared European consensus proposal of a "territory for peace" solution for the Arab-Israeli conflict and recognizing the PLO as the Palestinians' representative.[16]

Characteristically, Bonn did not seek an independent Middle East policy but used the West European framework to gain more freedom of maneuver. Toward oil-rich Arab/Islamic countries, this interest was motivated primarily by economic considerations. After the first oil crisis, Bonn regarded improved political relations as necessary to secure oil imports and export markets. Also, after the Shah's fall, Saudi Arabia and other conservative Gulf states helped to overcome the financial setbacks of the second oil crisis and thus eased West Germany's economic and social problems.

Interestingly, West Germany—unlike France—did not sell major weapons to countries such as Saudi Arabia, whose leadership regarded the sale of Leopard-2 tanks as a "test of friendship." Because of internal opposition, mostly from the Social Democrats and some Liberals, and with respect to Israel, neither Chancellor Helmut Schmidt nor his successor Helmut Kohl tried to push the sale through parliament. Despite some pressure from the business community, Bonn did not essentially change its official arms export policy that German arms sales "outside the NATO" area should not "increase tensions," as the official guidelines of 1982 stressed. However, Bonn did not object to the export of major multinationally produced weapons in which German companies had a considerable share, such as the Tornado fighter aircraft to Saudi Arabia or the Roland air-defense missile to Iraq.

West Germany's relations with Iraq followed the general pattern just outlined. There was never any German ambition to play a major political role, while statistics prove that after the second oil crisis German imports of Iraqi oil became minor—like German energy imports from the whole Gulf region. But Iraq was an attractive market for all kinds of enterprises—construction, road building, factories, and other services. The West German government, with its liberal trade policy, supported these activities. Therefore, Bonn favored West German-Iraqi relations because of export interests, not energy dependence.

During the Iran-Iraq war, West Germany pursued a neutral policy that tried to keep links open with both warring countries. Contrary to France and Britain, there was no major crisis in West German-Iranian relations. Foreign Minister Hans-Dietrich Genscher was the only West European foreign minister to visit Tehran during the war, in 1984. Without explicitly stating it, there was a "division of labor" between Paris and Bonn. While the French actively helped Iraq, the West Germans tried to keep links open to Iran. In 1987-1988 Bonn, contributing to the wording of UN Resolution 578, worked hard to induce the Iranian government to agree to the ceasefire. It was in this context that in July 1987 Foreign Minister Genscher explicitly called Iraq the "aggressor."[17]

One major German dilemma during the Iraq-Kuwait crisis was a consequence of Bonn's liberal trade policy.[18] Since the early 1960s the government had not given any official export license for arms exports to Iraq. Yet, as the scandal of the Libyan "fertilizer plant" and other reports indicated, small German companies and experts worked in several sensitive Third World arms programs. Already in 1984, when Iraq had used poison gas, there were allegations that the German Karl Kolb company had delivered some of the necessary chemicals to Iraq.

Until February 1991, when allegations of German involvement in Iraqi chemical weapons and missile programs forced Bonn to tighten export controls drastically, German authorities were insufficiently equipped to deal with the modern "merchants of death." Despite repeated US warnings and consultations on the highest levels in Washington and Bonn, the Rabta affair in 1989 (the construction of a poison gas factory for Libya by the German Imhausen company) did not lead to a decisive toughening of West German export controls.

West German law prohibited the export of items to develop nuclear or chemical weapons. Missing was the political will and the ability to enforce the law. The export control agency was in the Economics Ministry. The bureaucracy dealing with export controls was too small and unequipped to handle the caseloads.

In January-February 1991 the German government indeed believed that German experts were involved in Iraq's unconventional weapons programs.[19] Responding to Iraqi attacks, Foreign Minister Genscher visited Israel on January 24-25 to confirm solidarity and "shame" about German involvement in Iraq's weapons programs. At this time, he and others feared that Iraq's SCUD-B missiles falling on Tel Aviv, Haifa, and Riyadh contained German technology and know-how. Later it became known that Israeli authorities had not found any Western components in the debris.[20]

The SCUD-B's are one example demonstrating the difficulty of proving suspicions and accusations in court, helping to explain why German authorities sometimes hesitated to pursue certain cases. On the other hand, the German government's readiness to tighten export controls in February 1991 confirms that there were indeed grave deficiencies. The problem of illegal arms transfers, of course, was not only a German one. For example, British and Italian companies were involved in the Iraqi "supergun" project directed by the Canadian Gerald Bull.[21]

Whereas France finally fought to destroy some of the weapons it had delivered, West Germany did not dispatch soldiers to the Gulf. The government stressed the argument that the *Grundgesetz* (Basic Law) did not allow German armed forces to act outside the "NATO area." But several German legal experts did not share this interpretation, and the problem was clearly political. On November 3, 1982, Foreign Minister Genscher of the Liberal party ensured that this reading of the constitution was adopted by the Federal Security Council chaired by Chancellor Helmut Schmidt. Schmidt's successor, Helmut

Kohl, knew that the Social Democratic opposition and probably a majority of the population shared this view and did not challenge it for several years.

It was only during the Iraq-Kuwait crisis, when the U.S. government asked Bonn to contribute more to the international effort against Iraq, that Kohl indicated he would prefer a more active German role. Nevertheless, he agreed with his Liberal coalition partner and the Social Democratic party's leaders that parliament should clarify the Basic Law after the first all-German election of December 1990. Since changing the constitution requires a two-thirds majority vote, such an amendment seemed unlikely.

To be sure, in autumn 1990 nobody expected German soldiers on the front. Yet the government could have sent minesweepers not only to the Mediterranean but to the Gulf—which it did in March 1991, before a formal ceasefire was proclaimed. In April 1991, German armed forces engaged in what was called a "humanitarian mission"—to avoid provoking a renewed legal debate about the "out-of-area issue"—to relieve the misery of Iraqi Kurdish refugees in Turkey and Iran. Nevertheless, it was significant that, with the consent of the Social Democratic opposition at home and the Tehran government abroad, army units now even operated on Iranian soil.

Absorbed by the unification process and constrained by their own restrictions, Germans seemed to confirm Western critics who denounced their "cowardice" during the crisis. However, despite the impression of hesitancy, Germany fully abided by the UN embargo and Security Council resolutions. Moreover, German authorities gave allies prompt, comprehensive logistical support of their military preparations. Hundreds of trains ensured that the 7th U.S. Corps and other units with their equipment were transported to the Gulf. Without this support the U.S. armed forces would not have been able to reach the Gulf so quickly.[22] Finally, a major part of the U.S. command, control, and communications network ran through Germany.

Given this support, Germany was technically and legally participating in the war against Saddam Husayn. However, the government, expecting public criticism, preferred to downplay its involvement. In order to demonstrate solidarity with its Western allies, Bonn increased its financial contribution, which finally reached the sum of almost 18 billion marks.[23]

It was obvious that money had to compensate for a quandary the German "political class" and the government felt they could not otherwise escape. Given Germany's growing financial burdens, resulting from unification and agreements with the Soviet Union and East European countries, it was obvious that such a "checkbook diplomacy" would soon reach a dead end. For Germany, the Iraq-Kuwait crisis came much too early and it revealed the necessity of redefining Germany's future international role also beyond Europe.

WESTERN EUROPE AND THE SECOND GULF WAR

As General de Gaulle used to say, wars are the moment of truth. Europe, united again in democracy, was not prepared for this war. The European Community, despite serious efforts to forge a unified stance, did not act as a political entity. Great Britain, from the very beginning of the crisis, decided to cooperate closely with the United States. Prime Minister Margaret Thatcher took the chance to revitalize a special relationship she had feared already lost to the Germans. France tried to use its special relationship with Baghdad to find a nonviolent solution but failed. At the end, West Europeans had no choice but to follow U.S. leadership. All of them (more or less) followed the sanctions imposed by the UN Security Council. The West and East Europeans supported the international military alliance. Most of them provided transit rights and some also comprehensive logistical support.

Despite all this proven solidarity, some West European countries received critical marks. Spain and Germany played a major role in supporting the allied forces. However, sensing public uneasiness about this support, the governments of both countries did not dare to say in a loud, detailed way what they were doing and why they did it. In Germany this restraint left the streets to a minority of peace demonstrators. Some of them not only failed to identify the aggressor but forgot to condemn the Iraqi missile attacks when they criticized the allied air raids.

The Kuwait crisis spurred West Europeans in discussing closer foreign and defense cooperation, highlighting deficiencies in these areas. It remains to be seen whether this experience was strong enough to overcome traditional impediments to stronger integration.

NOTES

1. This chapter draws on my study *Frankreich's Rolle im Nahen Osten* (France's Role in the Middle East) (Bonn, 1985), pp. 62 ff.

2. See Saddam Husayn's speech to Iraqi ambassadors in Western Europe and Japan on June 12, 1975, Saddam Husayn, *On Social & Foreign Affairs in Iraq* (London, 1979), pp. 63-84.

3. See Edward A. Kolodziej, *Making and Marketing Arms. The French Experience and Its Implications for the International System* (Princeton, N.J., 1987).

4. Pierre Lellouche, "Frankreich im internationalen Disput über die Kernenergie" (France in the international debate on nuclear energy), *Europa-Archiv* 18 (1978), pp. 541 ff; 544 (translation by H.H.).

5. Pierre Péan, *Les deux bombes. Comment la France a donné la bombe à Israël et à l'Iraq,* (Paris, 1982), p. 174 (translation by H.H.). On French-Israeli nuclear cooperation in the 1950s see Péan, pp. 21 ff., and Sylvie Crosbie, *A Tacit Alliance. France and Israel from Suez to the Six Day War* (Princeton, N.J., 1974), pp. 114 ff.

6. For details see SIPRI Yearbooks, *World Armament and Disarmament;* IISS, *Military Balance;* and JCSS, *Middle East Military Balance.*

7. See Kenneth Timmerman, "Un nouvel Iraq?" *Politique Internationale* (Winter 1985/86), pp. 163 ff; 173.

8. Karl Jetter, "Tausche Palästina gegen Erdöl," *Frankfurter Allgemeine Zeitung,* March 10, 1980.

9. For a detailed analysis see Shai Feldman, "The Bombing of Osiraq Revisited," *International Security* (Fall 1982), pp. 114 ff.

10. See *International Herald Tribune,* August 14, 1990.

11. Dominique Moïsi, "The Gulf Crisis. A Roundtable Discussion," *France Magazine* (Spring 1991), pp. 10 ff.

12. See the president's declaration after the cessation of hostilities, *Le Monde,* March 3, 1991.

13. *Le Monde,* March 12, 1991. For an assessment of the new approach see Olivier Roy, "Sur la 'politique arabe de la France,'" *Monde Arabe. Maghreb-Machrek* no. 132, (April-June 1991), pp. 15-20.

14. Approximately 15 billion francs are said to be guaranteed by the French state. *Frankfurter Allgemeine Zeitung,* April 12, 1991.

15. See Karl Kaiser, "Germany's Unification," *Foreign Affairs* 1990/91 (America and the World), pp. 179-205.

16. See Friedemann Büttner and Peter Hünseler, "Die politischen Beziehungen zwischen der Bundesrepublik Deutschland und den arabischen Staaten" (Political Relations between the Federal Republic of Germany and the Arab States), Karl Kaiser and Udo Steinbach, eds., *Deutsch-arabische Beziehungen* (German-Arab Relations), (Munich/Vienna, 1981), pp. 109-52 . For an analysis from an Israeli point of view, see Susan Hattis Rolef, *The Middle East Policy of the Federal Republic of Germany,* (Jerusalem, The Hebrew University, The Leonard Davis Institute for International Relations, Jerusalem Papers on Peace Problems, no. 39, 1985).

17. See Keesing's *Archiv der Gegenwart,* 1987, pp. 31476 ff.

18. The following section draws on my study *Der zweite Golfkrieg in der internationalen Politik* (The Second Gulf War in International Politics), (Bonn, Forschungsinstitut der Deutschen Gesellschaft für Auswärtige Politik, Arbeitspapiere zur internationalen Politik, 62, 1991), pp. 52 ff.

19. The minister of the chancellor's office, Lutz G. Stavenhagen, responsible for the German secret service, made such statements. (See *International Herald Tribune*, January 25, 1991, and Presse-und Informationsamt der Bundesregierung, *Bulletin* 8 (1991), p. 45.

20. See the statement of Jürgen Möllemann, minister of economics, *Die Welt*, March 21, 1991. For the contrary allegation, see Michael Ledeen, "Iraq's German Connection," *Commentary*, (April 1991), pp. 27-30.

21. The UN team, authorized to inspect and destroy Iraqi nonconventional weapons factories by UN Security Council Resolution 687 on April 3, 1991, reported in July 1991 that companies from 13 countries had supplied components. Among them, German companies were said to rank "prominently." *Frankfurter Allgemeine Zeitung*, August 7, 1991.

22. See the statement of General John Galvin, Supreme Commander of NATO, before the U.S. Senate, in United States Information Service (Bonn), *U.S. Foreign Policy and Texts*, no. 39, (1991), pp. 23-35; pp. 28 ff. and 35.

23. The United States received 8,73 billion marks ($5.5 billion), Britain 800 million marks, and France 300 million marks financial support. In autumn 1990 Germany gave additional aid to Egypt, Turkey, and Jordan to compensate for their losses from the boycott against Iraq. See *Frankfurter Allgemeine Zeitung*, March 27, 1991, and *Süddeutsche Zeitung*, March 30/April 1, 1991.

18

The Gulf Crisis in Historical Perspective

P. J. Vatikiotis

The 1990-1991 crisis over Iraq's invasion of Kuwait can teach much about the Middle East and, more broadly, the era in world politics and international relations lasting from 1945 to 1990.

Most obviously, the Gulf crisis reminded everyone of how irredentism created disputes and conflict over frontiers among Middle East states. It reiterated a link between tyranny and unprovoked aggression as a threat not only to the stability and security of regional states and governments but also to the strategic and commercial interests of the industrialized countries of Europe, the United States and Japan, and the international community of nations as a whole.

The Gulf crisis exposed the weakness of Arab regional institutions—chief among them the Arab League—and their inability to manage or resolve disputes among Arab states. Also highlighted was the individual Arab states' inability to defend themselves against external threats to their territorial integrity and independence. In the Iraq-generated Gulf crisis those states feeling an immediate threat to their security and territorial integrity had no choice but to seek the assistance and protection of a foreign power, of infidels.

What impact this may have on notions of Arab unity and Islamic solidarity in the Middle East is a matter of the greatest importance, as is the effect on inter-Arab solidarity, collective or regional defense (as opposed to bilateral defense arrangements with foreign powers), and the impact of all these issues on the Arab-Israeli conflict.

Since 1945, the Middle East's political direction was affected by the Axis force's defeat in World War II, the ensuing Third World decolonization process, and the Cold War between rival superpowers creating a bipolar world. Among the new social forces were peasant revolution, socialism and centrally planned state economies, radical nationalism, and movements of national liberation from Western imperialism and colonialism.

On a regional level, the search by external powers for more permanent regional security arrangements as an extension of the ongoing Cold War led to the extension of bipolarity in the Middle East. The two superpowers often carried out their Cold War competition through client states that were given large-scale economic aid, weapons, and technical assistance. The local states took advantage of such aid in pursuit of their respective national policies and objectives.

The core of each side in the Cold War comprised a group of culturally and politically akin states. The newly emerging Third World states locked into this bipolar world were forced to observe the rules made by the two rivals. Yet more traditional domestic and regional conflicts caused by the indigenous political culture erupted periodically within and between these states that, by the end of the 1950s, were clients of one or the other superpower patron. Thus, while the superpowers used the Third World states, the Third World states also used the superpowers.

Now this era was over, or at least dramatically altered. Third World states, especially in the Middle East, had to adapt and orient themselves to new conditions created by communism's collapse in Eastern Europe; the Soviet Union's disintegration; the Cold War's end in what essentially amounted to a U.S. victory; and Europe's integration into a powerful, relatively harmonious trading bloc.

The Gulf crisis and war fit into these events. The employment of awesome military force by the United States to counter Iraqi aggression in the Gulf is considered by some as the extension of "the Western triumph in Europe." But at any rate, Middle East states can no longer seek security and advantage the way they did in the Cold War era. Can it be sought in regional or local collective schemes, or must it be sought primarily in bilateral agreements with foreign powers?

Another problem is the solidity of the individual states themselves. The revolt by Iraqi Kurds and Shi'a reflected a problem of sectarianism that may prove as intractable and difficult to manage or resolve as the Arab-Israeli conflict. Although the state has been consistently acquiring strength throughout the Middle East, the *nation* has yet to take firm hold in most of that world, including the Middle East. Consequently, civil wars have proliferated. The Gulf crisis helped highlight the problem of minorities—as did the Lebanese civil war—despite claims of Arab homogeneity and unity.

In light of such developments and problems, most people refer to a new economic-political map, a "New Regional Order" for the Middle East. Some assumed that, given its military success in the Gulf, the United States is the one superpower to devise and impose a new arrangement for the region, including the resolution of outstanding problems and conflicts. The question though is: Can a new arrangement for the Middle East be brokered and/or imposed from the outside, or must it be devised by local states—even if assisted by external powers—if it is to have a chance of securing the consensus of the states and thus of surviving?

We can approach this matter by asking if the Gulf in 1990-1991 was like the Fertile Crescent and Levant of 1918-1920. The short answer is no. Was it like the Muhammad Ali Syrian Ottoman crisis of 1839-1840? The short answer is not quite.

After World War I, the victorious Entente Powers promoted or used local nationalism in the Middle East in an effort to defeat their enemy, the Ottoman Empire, and as a basis of a quasi-imperial regional order they controlled and supervised. Thus France and Britain especially feared a German-Turkish and/or Russian challenge of their imperial positions [India and the Suez Canal for Britain].

Thus, an Ottoman imperial order was succeeded by a quasi-imperial order controlled by Britain and France—and Italy. Much of the Middle East's history and political evolution during and after the period between the two world wars consisted of relations between local nationalist movements, under the tutelage of European powers, struggling for self-determination or complete independence and such related issues as the Arab-Jewish contest over the possession of Palestine and the treatment of minorities still protected by European power.

The retreat of European power from the Middle East after World War II left the region open to the Cold War rivalry and global confrontation between the two rival superpowers. The Western search for formal regional security arrangements was unsuccessful but so was the Soviet search for alliances and military advantage in the region. The West was defied and challenged by local radical nationalist leaders, mainly military despots, over the Suez Canal, Jordan, South Arabia, and the Gulf, areas vital to the West's access to the strategic commodity oil, to transport, and to fleet deployment.

Despite the collapse of communism in Eastern Europe and the end of the Cold War, the threat to Western strategic and commercial interests in the Gulf and the Middle East by local regional despots—that is, the threat to the status quo in the region— remains. Israel, for its part, had to fight three wars against a coalition of hostile Arab states.

There is a new kind of conflict that is not quite controlled by foreign powers: It is outside NATO; it is not East-West, but it relates to the actions of new regional powers in a potentially North-South contest or dichotomy. It is complicated by the cultural rejection of religious militancy, the unresolved Israeli-Palestinian and corollary Arab-Israeli conflict. It is further complicated by the aggressive irredentism of Iraq in the Gulf, Syria in Lebanon and the Levant, inter-Arab rivalries in the Arabian Peninsula, historic rivalry between the Nile Valley and Mesopotamia, as well as the status and fate of minorities. These factors offer a lingering specter of civil wars throughout the region.

One might say generally that the empire of Alexander and his successors hellenized the elites in the Middle East; the Roman Empire romanized them; but the modern European quasi-empire in this century merely confused the Middle East elites. Despite the Gulf crisis and its consequences, there is a residue of continuity: The Gulf area remains a source of wealth for future Arab regional development. How will these states use it?

Clearly, there is a trend toward reducing the role of Arab nationalism and the importance of Pan-Arab schemes in favor of the stronger role for individual states. This in turn may force a more rapid pace of regime change, regional economic cooperation and development. It may accelerate the adoption of market economies in preference to centrally planned state economies and thus create a challenge to more traditional—including militant religious—schemes or movements in the struggle for power, thus improving the chances of more secular pluralist regimes in the region.

The real question is who will devise a system for the peaceful resolution of regional conflict, and is this possible without the involvement of the non-Arab states in the region, Turkey, Iran, and Israel, as well as foreign powers? And is regional economic development based on sovereign independent states a catalyst for peace that ought to include all the states in the region? To what extent are limits and controls on arms, including the banning of weapons of mass destruction, a precondition of a new order in the Middle East? And will it be an order of consensus or domination?

Should we seek a regional order based on a balance of power guaranteed by an external great power or an international order within which the Middle East fits? Do these frameworks imply new alliances and alignments, or an evolution toward more democratic regimes in the area? What would be the relative role for states such as Egypt, a more moderate regime, in contrast to the sectarian fortress regime of Asad's Syria, traditional/tribal Saudi Arabia, and sectarian, quasi-fascist Iraq? How can the latter be brought back into the regional system of states, and does this require the replacement of Saddam Husayn as head of state, as part of the reform of the Iraqi political system to accommodate minority representation?

For a brief period, many Arabs were tempted to believe that the tide was turning in their favor in a battle with the West waged since the eighteenth century. The underlying factor in this conflict today seems to be the challenge of Western culture and civilization, whose allure for Arabs and Muslims makes them seem all the more threatening. They hoped, however, that oil wealth and the possession of modern weapons of mass destruction would permit them a comeback after so many retreats.

In the end, though, Saddam's failure was the most significant fact about his bid for hegemony. His inability to unify the Arabs by force, to control the world's most strategic commodity, to expel Western—and especially U.S.—influence from the area, or to destroy Israel forced Arabs and Muslims to do some serious rethinking on all these issues. The outcome of their reevaluation and readjustment will set the framework for the next era of Middle East history.

On a regional level, what is most significant about Saddam's bid for hegemony was its failure. He had launched a major effort to unify the Arab world by force, control the world's most strategic commodity. expel Western—and especially U.S.—influence from the region, and destroy Israel. His inability to fulfill any of these goals forced a serious rethinking on each of these points.

For a brief period, lasting only a few months, many Arabs were tempted to believe that Middle East history had reached a watershed, and that the tide would turn in a battle with the West waged since the eighteenth century. In their view this constituted an Arab-Muslim comeback in a resistance long marked by retreat. Iraq raised—only to dash—their confidence that access to oil wealth and modern weapons of mass destruction would let them move onto the offensive.

Whatever the factors articulated to explain this conflict, the real reason seems to be the challenge of Western culture and civilization. Its allure for Arabs and Muslims makes the problem all the greater. And Saddam's defeat only strengthens its appeal. Rather than a defeat for all the forces enumerated above, the crisis turned into a victory. But if Arab states and social forces are able to adjust to this situation, they, too can benefit from these historic events.

CONTRIBUTORS

AMATZIA BARAM is a senior lecturer at the Department of Middle East History at the University of Haifa and deputy director of the Jewish-Arab Center and of the Gustav Heinemann Center for Middle Eastern Studies. He is author of *Culture, History and Ideology in the Formation of Ba'thist Iraq* (Oxford, 1991).

BARRY RUBIN is a fellow at the Johns Hopkins University Foreign Policy Institute and author of 12 books on the Middle East and international affairs, most recently *Cauldron of Turmoil: America in the Middle East* (New York, 1992), *Modern Dictators* (New York, 1988) and *Secrets of State: The State Department and the Struggle Over U.S. Foreign Policy* (New York, 1985).

SHAUL BAKHASH is a professor at the Center for Middle East Studies of George Mason University and author of *The Region of the Ayatollahs* (New York, 1984, 1986).

OFRA BENGIO is a research associate at Tel Aviv University's Moshe Dayan Center for Middle East Studies and teaches in the Department of Middle East History. She is author of *Saddam Hussein Speaks* (Syracuse, N.Y., 1992) and *The Kurdish Revolt in Iraq* (Hebrew), (Tel Aviv, 1989).

PATRICK CLAWSON is editor of *Orbis* magazine. He was desk officer at the International Monetary Fund for Iraq and Kuwait in the mid-1980s. His chapter draws on his "How Vulnerable is Iraq's Economy?" Policy Focus no. 14 of the Washington Institute for Near East Policy (October 1990).

MICHAEL EPPEL is a lecturer in the Department of Middle East History at the University of Haifa. He is the author of *Iraq and Palestine, 1930-1948* (London, 1994).

JACOB GOLDBERG was a senior research fellow at the Moshe Dayan Center of Tel Aviv University and author of *The Foreign Policy of Saudi Arabia: The Formative Years* (Cambridge, Mass., 1986).

MARK A. HELLER is a senior research associate at the Jaffee Center for Strategic Studies, Tel Aviv University. His recent publications include *The Dynamics of Soviet Policy in the Middle East: Between Old Thinking and New*, JCSS Study no. 18 (1991), and "Middle East Security and Arms Control," in Steven Spiegel, ed., *The Arab-Israeli Search for Peace* (Boulder, Colo., 1992).

HELMET HUBEL is a senior research fellow at the Research Institute of the Deutsche Gesellschaft fur Auswartige Politik in Bonn, Germany, and a lecturer at the University of Bonn. He is the author of *Frankreich's Rolle Im Nahen Osten* (Bonn, 1985).

JOSEPH KOSTINER is a senior lecturer at Tel Aviv University and a Senior Researcher at the Moshe Dayan Center of Tel Aviv University. He is a co-editor of *Tribes and State Formation in the Middle East* (London, 1991).

DAVID KUSHNER is an associate professor in the Department of Middle East History at the University of Haifa and dean of the Faculty of Humanities. He is the author of *The Rise of Turkish Nationalism* (London, 1977).

ROBERT LIEBER is a professor and chairman of the Department of Government at Georgetown University. Most recently he edited and contributed to *Eagle in a New World: American Grand Strategy in the Post-Cold War Era* (New York, 1992).

YORAM MEITAL is a tutor in the Department of Middle East History at the University of Haifa.

JOSEPH NEVO is a senior lecturer at the University of Haifa and author of *Jordan in the Middle East: The Making of a Pivotal State* (London, 1992) and *Abdallah and the Arabs of Palestine* (Hebrew).

ILAN PAPPE is a senior lecturer in the Department of Middle East History at the University of Haifa. He is the author of *The Making of the Arab-Israeli Conflict, 1947-51* (London, 1992).

P. J. VATIKIOTIS is a professor at London University. His most recent book is *Among the Arabs and the Jews* (London, 1991).

AVNER YANIV was vice president and professor of political science at the University of Haifa. He is author of *Dilemmas of Security: Politics, Strategy, and the Israeli Experience in Lebanon* (New York, 1987) and *Deterrence Without the Bomb* (Lexington, Mass., 1987).

INDEX